PRINCIPLES OF MARKETING
for a Digital Age

Sara Miller McCune founded SAGE Publishing in 1965 to support the dissemination of usable knowledge and educate a global community. SAGE publishes more than 1000 journals and over 800 new books each year, spanning a wide range of subject areas. Our growing selection of library products includes archives, data, case studies and video. SAGE remains majority owned by our founder and after her lifetime will become owned by a charitable trust that secures the company's continued independence.

Los Angeles | London | New Delhi | Singapore | Washington DC | Melbourne

PRINCIPLES OF MARKETING
for a Digital Age

Tracy L. Tuten

$SAGE

Los Angeles | London | New Delhi
Singapore | Washington DC | Melbourne

Los Angeles | London | New Delhi
Singapore | Washington DC | Melbourne

SAGE Publications Ltd
1 Oliver's Yard
55 City Road
London EC1Y 1SP

SAGE Publications Inc.
2455 Teller Road
Thousand Oaks, California 91320

SAGE Publications India Pvt Ltd
B 1/I 1 Mohan Cooperative Industrial Area
Mathura Road
New Delhi 110 044

SAGE Publications Asia-Pacific Pte Ltd
3 Church Street
#10-04 Samsung Hub
Singapore 049483

Editor: Matthew Waters
Development editor: Nina Smith
Assistant editor: Jasleen Kaur
Assistant editor, digital: Sunita Patel
Production editor: Nicola Carrier
Copyeditor: Gemma Marren
Proofreader: Leigh C. Smithson
Indexer: Gary Kirby
Marketing manager: Lucia Sweet
Cover and interior design: Francis Kenney
Typeset by: C&M Digitals (P) Ltd, Chennai, India
Printed in the UK by Bell and Bain Ltd, Glasgow

Library of Congress Control Number: 2019938922

British Library Cataloguing in Publication data

A catalogue record for this book is available from the British Library

ISBN 978-1-5264-2333-7
ISBN 978-1-5264-2334-4 (pbk)

At SAGE we take sustainability seriously. Most of our products are printed in the UK using responsibly sourced papers and boards. When we print overseas we ensure sustainable papers are used as measured by the PREPS grading system. We undertake an annual audit to monitor our sustainability.

BRIEF CONTENTS

CONTENTS

PART 1: The Marketing Environment

1

UNDERSTANDING MARKETING

2

UNDERSTANDING BUYERS

PART 2: The Marketing Toolbox

3

SEGMENTATION, TARGETING, AND POSITIONING

4

MARKETING RESEARCH AND ANALYSIS

5

MARKETING STRATEGY

PART 3:
The Marketing Mix

6

CREATING VALUE: PRODUCTS AND SERVICES

7

OFFERING VALUE: PRICE

8

DISTRIBUTING VALUE: PLACE

9

COMMUNICATING VALUE: PROMOTION

PART 4: The Marketing Long Game

10

EXTENDING VALUE: PEOPLE, PROCESS, AND PRESENCE IN THE CUSTOMER EXPERIENCE

11

MAINTAINING VALUE: BRANDING AND BRAND MANAGEMENT

12

MANAGING VALUE: ANALYTICS AND MARKETING VALUE MANAGEMENT SYSTEMS

INSTRUCTORS

The textbook is supported by a comprehensive set of online resources, including PowerPoint slides, an instructor's manual, and a testbank of multiple choice questions to help support your teaching in the classroom or via your online learning platform.

Visit **https://study.sagepub.com/tuten** to set yourself up or use your existing SAGE instructor login to access.

LIST OF FIGURES AND TABLES

FIGURES

TABLES

Just bought the book. Have you checked it out? ✓✓

Arshad:
Yes! I plan to use the case studies 🔍 at the start and end of each chapter to link theory and practice in our assignment

Lin:
Yeah! So many cool global companies Nutella 😋, Birchbox, 📊 and Netflix 🎥

I'm planning on writing an assignment on sustainability. Anything on that? ✓✓

Arshad:
Yes – check out the UN PRME boxes ⅄

Lin:
The multiple choice questions ❓ and key words 👌 will be so useful when I come to study

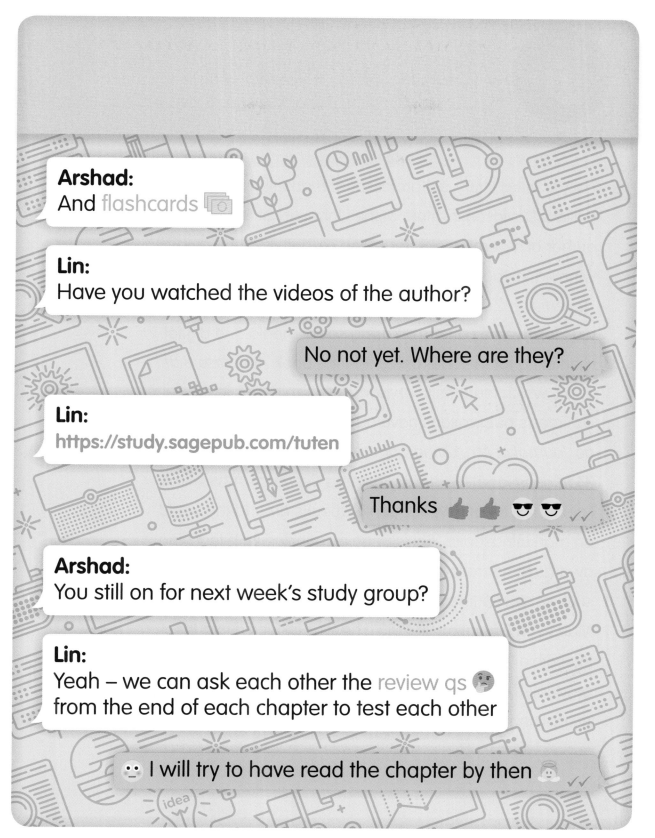

Arshad:
And flashcards 🎴

Lin:
Have you watched the videos of the author?

No not yet. Where are they? ✓✓

Lin:
https://study.sagepub.com/tuten

Thanks 👍 👍 😎 😎 ✓✓

Arshad:
You still on for next week's study group?

Lin:
Yeah – we can ask each other the review qs 🤢 from the end of each chapter to test each other

😶 I will try to have read the chapter by then 🧕 ✓✓

ABOUT THE AUTHOR

Tracy L. Tuten, Ph.D., is a professor of marketing with the William Davidson Institute at the University of Michigan and author of several books, including co-author of the award-winning textbook *Social Media Marketing*. Her first book, *Advertising 2.0: Social Media Marketing in a Web 2.0 World*, was followed by others on using social media and digital marketing for the enterprise, and the book *Advertisers at Work*, which features interviews with luminaries in the field. Dr. Tuten's publications have appeared in such journals as *Journal of Marketing Communications*, *Psychology & Marketing*, and *Journal of Business Research*. A two-time Fulbright Scholar, she frequently speaks around the world on marketing topics. She's been recognized with teaching awards at her respective institutions and with national awards, such as the O'Hara Leadership Award in Direct & Interactive Marketing Education. In 2013, she was inducted into the Incredible Women of ECU series, which highlights female graduates of East Carolina University who have reached exceptional levels of achievement in their respective careers.

FOREWORD

The practitioner's view

The digital revolution is opening the door to new marketing principles that are guiding the way companies create products and services that customers want. In *Principles of Marketing for a Digital Age*, Tracy Tuten explores how the digital revolution is impacting every aspect of marketing and demonstrates how digital technology is being deployed not only to help companies achieve business growth, but to also help agencies, such as the United Nations, achieve broader, global goals.

Tracy introduces the fundamentals of 'jobs-to-be-done theory – the notion that people buy products and services to get a 'job' done – and how this theory is being used to clarify what it takes to advance marketing in the digital age. At a high level, the digital revolution is simply the application of new technology to help people get the jobs they are already trying to get done.

When looking at marketing through a jobs-to-be-done lens, the convergence of the digital revolution with marketing has been noted in Strategyn's client engagements for years. We have discovered that in nearly every market there exists some set of unmet customer needs that are well suited to be addressed with a digital solution. They are generally unmet needs (desired outcomes) that can only be addressed effectively if the right information is available at the right time to get the job done. Getting this information to the customer at the right time is what an effective digital strategy is trying to deliver.

About ten years ago we worked with a major agriculture company to study the job of growers who are responsible for growing crops. Growers of over a dozen different crops were studied. At the time, our client offered growers a variety of products including seed, pesticides, and herbicides. They also offered a variety of consultative services. But they did not offer any digital solutions. In fact, the company did not have a digital strategy. Nor did it believe that one was necessary. Our study changed their worldview.

The job of 'growing a crop' includes everything from preparing the soil, to planting, growing and harvesting a crop. As part of our study, we conducted over thirty interviews with growers and uncovered 150 desired outcome statements. A desired outcome is a specially constructed need statement that has a unique set of characteristics: desired outcomes are devoid of solutions, stable over time, measurable, controllable, structured for reliable prioritization in a quantitative customer survey, and are tied to the job the customer is trying to get done.

The statements were then incorporated into a survey and presented to several hundred growers for quantification. The goal of the survey was to learn which outcomes were important, but not satisfied by current solutions, i.e., which outcomes were unmet.

What we found was fascinating. Nearly all the unmet needs, which totaled 60 or so in number, were information related – they were associated with not having the right information at the right time. In other words, the biggest opportunities in the market were not addressable by adding features to existing products. Instead, it pointed out the need for an information-based, digital solution that would tie together all the loose ends.

This insight led us to recommend the creation of a digital faming solution – which was revolutionary at the time. The platform as envisioned would inform all aspects of the farming job. Digital farming has since become a major trend in the agriculture industry as digital farming solutions have advanced over the years. While our client was skeptical at first, watching its competitors advance digital farming solutions convinced them that it was the wave of the future. This company, Bayer CropScience, is now at the forefront of the digital revolution in agriculture.

The lessons we learned in agriculture were applicable in many other industries. In fact, over the past ten years we have discovered similar information-related opportunities in dozens of other markets. And this is why Tracy's work and this book are so important. It turns out that digital opportunities exist in nearly every market and that digital considerations should be part of every market strategy.

In *Principles of Marketing for a Digital Age*, Tracy elevates the importance of the digital revolution not only to product and service creation, but to all aspects of product consumption - sometimes referred to as the customer journey or the user experience. When looking at product consumption through a jobs-to-be-done lens, we talk about consumption chain jobs. These jobs include product evaluation and purchase, installation, set up, learning how to use it, interfacing with it, storing, cleaning and transporting it, and maintaining, repairing, upgrading and product disposal.

While the application of digital solutions for lead generation and other pure marketing activities is obvious, the benefits of applying digital solutions to other aspects of product consumption have escaped many companies. While people buy products to get a job done, they do not buy products to get consumption jobs done. In fact, eliminating the need to install, set up, interface with, and maintain, repair and dispose of a product creates significant customer value, as product use is greatly simplified. Such advancements also create significant company value, as they eliminate costs associated with having to execute the consumption chain jobs. Digitizing the way a customer learns how to use a product or learns how to resolve a problem with the company helps the company execute consumption chain jobs better and more cheaply.

Looking at the digital revolution through a jobs-to-be-done lens helps companies engage in that revolution in a way that will result in the creation of significant new customer value. It ensures digital technology is used to help customers get their core and consumption chain jobs done better and more cheaply. Applying technology for technology's sake is a futile effort. A digital strategy can be a complete waste of time if it is not targeted at satisfying unmet customer needs. Following Tracy's advice throughout this book will help ensure your digital strategy pays off.

Tony Ulwick, Founder and CEO, Strategyn

ACKNOWLEDGEMENTS

A project of this magnitude is the result of a team effort. Here, I recognize and thank those who have contributed. I thank Matthew Waters, the commissioning editor at SAGE. He recognized the value of a book that integrated digital elements of marketing in a unified way. I am grateful for his vision, commitment, and belief in me. Nina Smith worked tirelessly to keep the project on track, provide support, and contribute recommendations. The entire Sage team have been phenomenal in their availability, responsiveness, and attention. It's been a joy to work with them. I am indebted to Ashby Brame, Alex Burnett-Hayes, Mike Doherty, and Christian Lohner for their assistance throughout the project. ✓✓

The author and SAGE would like to thank all the lecturers and students who reviewed this book's content, design and online resources to ensure it is as useful as possible. ✓✓

Lecturers

Riccardo Benzo, Birkbeck, University of London
John Branch, University of Michigan
Ethel Claffey, Waterford Institute of Technology
Mary Conran, Fox School of Business at Temple University
Deborah L. Cowles, Virginia Commonwealth University
Scott Cowley, Western Michigan University
Joe Liddiatt, University of the West of England
Charlotte Lystor, University of Winchester
Christopher Pich, Nottingham Trent University
Declan Scully, University of Roehampton
Ann M. Torres, National University of Ireland Galway
Nadine Waehning, York St John University
Donna Wertalik, Virginia Tech

Students

Chiara Bimbatti
Sophia Göppinger
Monique Gordon
Gaia Guadagnini
Olivia Metzger
Alexiane Lavisse
Lucrezia Leone
Niklas Vater

ABBREVIATIONS

AGV	autonomous guided vehicles
AI	artificial intelligence
AIDA	attention, interest, desire, action
AMA	American Marketing Association
APM	alternative payment method
AR	augmented reality
ATF	above-the-fold
B2B	business-to-business
B2C	business-to-consumer
BCG	Boston Consulting Group
BOP	base of the pyramid
C2B	consumer-to-business
C2C	consumer-to-consumer
CGI	customer growth indicator
CIM	Chartered Institute of Marketing
CLV	customer lifetime value
CPG	consumer-packaged goods
CRM	customer relationship management
CSR	corporate social responsibility
CVM	comprehensive value management
CX	customer experience
DMO	destination marketing organization
DTV	design-to-value
EDLP	every day low pricing
EEG	electroencephalography

EMSS	enterprise marketing software suites
FFS	Farmer Field Schools
FMOT	First Moment of Truth
fMRI	functional magnetic resonance imaging
FNOL	first notice of loss
GDPR	General Data Protection Regulation
HOE	hierarchy of effects
IMC	integrated marketing communications
IoD	Internet of Data
IoE	Internet of Everything
IoP	Internet of People
IoT	Internet of Things
IPA	intelligent process automation
IRI	Information Resources Inc.
JTBD	Jobs-To-Be-Done
KPI	key performance indicator
MARCOM	marketing communications
MDSS	marketing decision support system
MIS	marketing information system
ML	machine learning
MMM	marketing mix modeling
MMO	marketing mix optimization
MoT	moment of truth
MR	mixed reality
MVMS	marketing value management systems

NGO	non-government organization
NLP	natural language processing
ODI	Outcome-Driven Innovation
P2P	peer-to-peer
PAYG	pay as you go
PODs	points of differentiation
POPs	points of parity
POP	point of purchase
PPC	pay per click
PR	public relations
PRME	Principles for Responsible Management Education
PWYW	pay what you want
ROI	return on investment
ROMI	return on marketing investment
SaaS	software as a service
SBA	Small Business Association
SBU	strategic business unit
SD	service dominant
SDG	sustainable development goal
SEO	search engine optimization
SMOT	Second Moment of Truth
SST	steady state topography
TMOT	Third Moment of Truth
VR	virtual reality
ZMOT	Zero Moment of Truth

ENDORSEMENTS

'At last, marketing educators will have a marketing principles textbook that truly integrates digital implications affecting marketing activities, the offers brought to market, and buyer behavior. Students will delight in the emphasis on cutting-edge technologies woven seamlessly alongside the foundations of marketing. Every chapter features a plethora of examples and cases within a variety of settings from powerhouse to niche brands from around the world. Plus instructors will love the "flipped classroom" lesson plans in the Instructor's Manual – ready and easy to use.'

Jikyeong Kang, President, Dean and MVP Professor of Marketing at the Asian Institute of Management, Honorary Professor of Marketing at Manchester Business School, and International Board Member for AACSB International

'This much needed textbook comes at a vital time for marketing educators who are struggling to find pedagogical content that matches today's marketing environment. Packed with examples and cases, it is also succinct and clearly written to engage students. A must have for instructors and their classes.'

Svend Hollensen, Associate Professor of International Marketing at the University of Southern Denmark, Author of bestselling textbook Global Marketing, *8th edition, 2010, Pearson*

PART I

The Marketing Environment

Chapter 1

UNDERSTANDING MARKETING

In this chapter, we'll learn the answers to the following questions:

1 What has been the evolution of marketing over time? In what ways has marketing shifted in response to consumer demands?

2 What is marketing? What are the core concepts of marketing?

3 What are the elements of the marketing mix? What can be marketed?

4 How are the technologies of Industry 4.0 revolutionizing marketing and the customer experience?

5 What is MarTech and how does it support marketing in the age of convergence?

INTRODUCTION

Marketing is a part of daily life for people and organizations everywhere, perhaps more so than any other business discipline. We turn to markets to find, evaluate, select, and buy solutions to meet our needs. Sellers bring their offers to market to reach prospective buyers. In fact, this view of marketing as facilitating exchanges among buyers and sellers goes back to ancient times. As a discipline, marketing is relatively young. It developed with the first industrial revolution, grew in recognition and relevance with the second, and experienced substantial changes during the third. Figure 1.1 illustrates these stages. The fourth industrial revolution, Industry 4.0, is at hand and with it has come a new era of marketing. In this chapter, we'll explore the foundations of marketing and the digital revolution driving the era of marketing convergence.

OPENING VIGNETTE

TESCO'S MARKETING EVOLUTION

Tesco is one of the leading grocery retailers in the UK. Whether online or via its more than 6,000 stores in 10 countries, the grocery brand fulfills about 80 million shopping trips every week! The Tesco website describes the company's commitment to its customers in its mission – "to be the champion for customers, helping them to enjoy a better quality of life and an easier way of living".[1] To fulfill that mission, Tesco promises to provide great products at great value delivered to customers with ease. Tesco's marketing strategies and tactics are key to its success. And successful it is. A recent study estimated the value of the Tesco brand at more than $9 billion making it the 7th most valuable brand in the UK! (Bloomfield, 2018).

Tesco's recent advertising campaign, Food Love Stories, reinforced the brand's value. It was as popular with critics as it was with the public, winning Grand Prix awards for creativity and excellence in media planning at the 2018 Cannes Lions Festival. The campaign was personalized for consumers using data targeting and shared via paid digital media, email, out-of-home and radio. It garnered a 53% improvement over previous quality scores, making Food Love Stories Tesco's most effective campaign on record (Mediatel Newsline, 2018).

Tesco positions itself as the source for the best quality products at the best price. Discount grocery brands, Aldi and Lidl, represent a major threat, but Tesco is confident that customers will ultimately prefer its superior assortment, quantity of products, and shopping experience at a comparable price to the bare bones discount brands. Tesco

---

[1] www.tescoplc.com/about-us/our-businesses/ (accessed 23 May 2019).

boasts that its stores stock thousands of products, but a major part of its product strategy is its own private-label brands. Private-label brands are manufactured by a third party but labeled under the retailer's brand. Tesco features 15 private-label product lines, some of which have names and packaging designed to emulate British premium brands, like Eastman's Deli Foods and Bay Fishmongers (Uttley, 2018). Tesco's Finest line includes nearly 1,500 products that are competitive with the premium brand in each category but offered at a lower price. This product strategy is one way that Tesco keeps customers' overall shopping costs close to those of Aldi or Lidl. The move is paying off – more than 50% of food sales at Tesco are now its own label, up from just 35% a few years ago.

Grocery shoppers tend to be price sensitive and this is reflected in Tesco's commitment to value pricing. The company regularly makes price comparisons with its competitors by purchasing the same 30 items at Tesco and at competitors' stores. This helps Tesco stay abreast of how the average cost of a shopping trip at its store compares to the competition and helps it gauge whether its pricing decisions are effective. In a recent test, the Tesco basket cost £30.58, compared to £32.41 and £32.68 for two of its competitors. To further defend against Aldi and Lidl, Tesco also created a new discount grocery chain, called Jack's (Patchett and Gwynn, 2018). Jack's is named for Tesco's founder and serves as a branding theme throughout Jack's stores, signage, and product packaging. The stores are relatively small with only 10% of the products stocked at a full-service Tesco. Most of those are the Jack's private-label brand. Although the Jack's brand name fits company history, using a different name helps to ensure that the discount image won't negatively affect the valuable Tesco brand.

Jack's isn't just part of Tesco's pricing strategy. The stores are distribution channels that connect customers to the products they want. Tesco's distribution channel includes eight store brands – Tesco, Jack's, Tesco Express, Tesco Extra, Tesco Metro, Tesco Compact, Tesco Homeplus and Tesco Superstore. Each of the store brands targets a different market. They vary by location, size, speed of checkout, product assortment, price, level of personal service offered, signage and atmosphere. Jack's targets the most price-sensitive shopper, but people who are in a hurry but want a few convenience items are better served by Tesco Express.

Retail distribution isn't the only concern for marketers. Stores interface with end customers, but a major cost of business for Tesco is tied to how it manages the selection of products and product quantity, sourcing, procurement, inventory, and transportation necessary to get products to its stores. Brands may rely on other companies for supplies and services. There's a balancing act for retailers like Tesco in that they need to buy what customers want and enough of what they want, but at a cost low enough to earn a profit. Uncontrollable forces may make this challenge even more difficult. Tesco faces just such a challenge now. Because of Brexit, Tesco will pay a customs tax on food it sources from the European Union, resulting in

(Continued)

higher costs. This might not sound serious, but more than 30% of the food purchased in the UK is imported from the EU (Davey, 2019). The company warned that it may eliminate thousands of jobs to cut costs.

Does it surprise you to learn that Tesco's supply chain team of employees is made up primarily of data scientists, programmers, and engineering graduates (Information Age, 2013)? Analytical skills and statistical programs are critical to Tesco's ability to forecast demand for products, understand customer behavior affecting sales and store traffic, and keep costs down. For instance, the team matched historical weather data to the location, day, and time of sales records from 3,000 of its stores. With the data, they were able to determine how shopping patterns varied based on specific types of weather. Then, the team built an algorithm that automatically monitors the weather forecast by store location and issues alerts for weather events that are likely to affect demand. If bad weather means customers will delay shopping, Tesco can reduce the inventory in stores to avoid spoilage and waste. If an impending snow storm threatens to send customers to stores in droves to stock up, Tesco can be certain sufficient inventory is in stock.

Tesco's Clubcard is a loyalty program that offers cardholders special benefits like member-only discounts. Member use of the card makes it possible for the analysts to glean more detailed insights like which discounts are popular or not, how purchase patterns vary by demographic or geographic characteristics, and so on (Bhasin, 2018). With this insight, they are able to sell more products and better meet the needs of their customers in a competitive retail environment. Today, data is among the most valuable marketing assets, but the vast amounts of data generated and collected mean that companies need a powerful system to store and manage data that may represent billions of data points. Tesco partners with Hadoop, which provides cloud storage and cutting-edge data-processing technology. With Hadoop, Tesco marketing managers at any of its stores around the world have real-time access to the reports they need (Rossi, 2017).

Tesco has embraced many digital technologies and applications, both to improve operational efficiencies on the back-end and deliver valuable innovations to customers on the front-end (Davis, 2018). Customers today expect to shop for anything, anywhere and they want the experience personalized and effortless. They may want to choose products at Tesco's website using their smartphone and have the groceries delivered to their homes. Or they might go to a store but check their phone for coupons while choosing products from the shelves. Customers can even order using a Google Home voice assistant or Alexa using an Amazon Echo (Davis, 2018). Tesco uses web platform IFTTT (If This Then That) to automate some online shopping tasks. Customers can choose certain shopping-related actions to happen when their designated triggers occur (TescoLabs, 2017). Want to be sure you don't miss this week's sale on your dog's favorite brand of food? Not to worry. You can simply set a trigger to order the food when the sale starts or before it ends. Tesco even offers home delivery by robot! The device uses cameras and Global Positioning System (GPS) technology to make deliveries within three miles of a store or warehouse, while the customer tracks delivery using Tesco's mobile app (Farley, 2018). In Tesco Express stores, customers can use Tesco's Scan Pay Go app to scan their items and pay with their smartphone (Wood, 2018). Self-checkout kiosks are equipped with facial recognition that scans a customer's face to estimate age when customers are purchasing age-restricted items like cigarettes and alcohol (Archer, 2018). Many of these ideas were first developed and tested at Tesco Labs, where researchers determine which new technologies will help the grocery giant fight competitors like Amazon (Rossi, 2017). In fact, a study that measured digital maturity ranked Tesco in the top five companies in the UK! (Bearing Point, 2019).

EVERYTHING MATTERS: THE EVOLUTION OF MARKETING

As a discipline, marketing has evolved over time, responding to environmental shifts. Figure 1.1 highlights these evolutions in marketing, and the relationship between marketing eras and the stages of the industrial revolution.

Each marketing era's orientation mirrors the stage of the industrial revolution it follows. Industry 1.0 introduced mechanization and factories powered by steam capable of efficiencies in production. Demand outstripped supply in many product categories. Marketing's production era followed a production orientation that emphasized functional benefits and offered little in the way of alternatives. The moving assembly lines of Industry 2.0 increased supply and resulted in more competition. The selling era was marked by marketers' adoption of a selling orientation, which valued persuasion as a way to push products and convince prospective buyers.

Industry 3.0 saw the development of computers and robotics and marked an age of information. The marketing concept era began (Keith, 1960). The marketing concept is a philosophical orientation focused on achieving organizational goals by identifying and meeting the needs of target markets, and doing so better than competitors. Mottos of the marketing concept include "Find a need and fill it!" and "The customer is king". Peter Drucker captured the shift from the selling orientation to the marketing concept when he said "The aim of marketing is to make selling superfluous. The aim of marketing is to know and understand the customer so well that the product or service fits her and sells itself" (Drucker, 1973/1993: 64–65).

We still embrace the importance of identifying and serving customer needs. But in the 1970s, demand for services increased and thought leaders recognized society as a marketing stakeholder. The result was the societal marketing concept and several related marketing approaches, including social marketing, cause marketing, cause-related marketing, corporate philanthropy, and corporate social responsibility (CSR) (Kotler and Lee, 2005). Marketing guru Phillip Kotler advocated for a shift to the societal marketing concept, stating "the organization's task is to determine the needs, wants, and interests of target markets and to deliver the

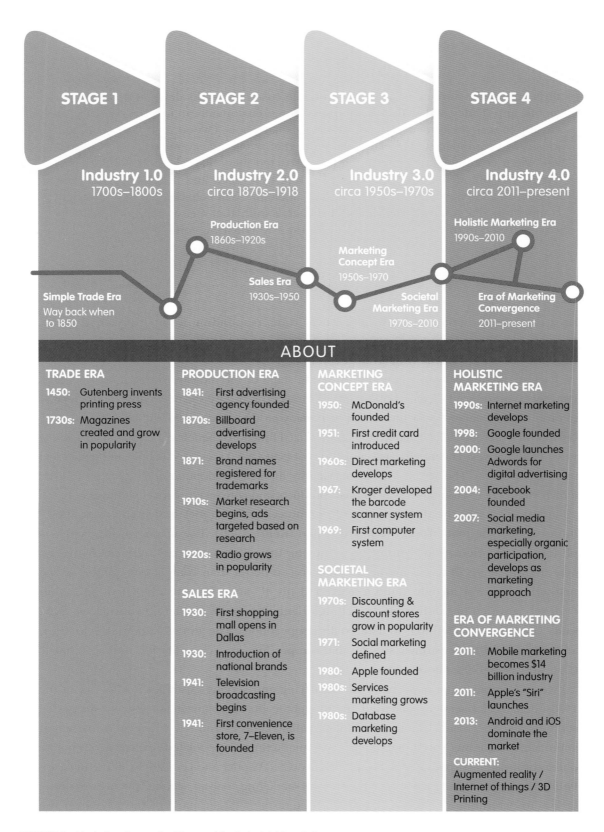

FIGURE 1.1 Marketing Across the Stages of the Industrial Revolution

desired satisfactions more effectively and efficiently than competitors in a way that preserves or enhances the consumer's and society's well-being" (Kotler, 1994: 29). In an effort to better capture marketing's competing priorities, Kotler and Keller later proposed the holistic marketing concept, which includes four marketing dimensions: 1) relationship marketing, 2) integrated marketing, 3) internal marketing, and 4) performance marketing (Kotler and Keller, 2015). Table 1.1 features definitions of these and other types of marketing that have since developed.

TABLE 1.1   Understanding Marketing Orientations

Concept	Definition
Social marketing	Use of marketing to drive social change in behaviors that benefit individuals and society (Kotler, 1977).
Cause marketing	Promoting the corporate sponsorship of causes and charities (Selfish Giving, 2015).
Cause-related marketing	Company support of a cause tied to customer response to campaign; American Express donated one cent to the Statue of Liberty's restoration every time someone used its charge card. The campaign increased new cardholders by 45% and card usage by 28% (Lellahom, 2017).
Ecological/green marketing	Promoting organizational business practices that preserve, protect, and conserve the physical environment (Goyal, Kazmi, Kumar and Rahman, 2012).
Sustainability marketing	Organization promotes business activities that preserve, protect, and provide ecological, social, and/or economic benefits (Belz and Peattie, 2012).
Corporate social responsibility (CSR)	Organization supports social causes and adopts business practices with societal benefits (Balmer and Greyser, 2006); organization adopts "purpose-driven engagement" (Lellahom, 2017). "It goes beyond philanthropy and compliance and addresses how companies manage their economic, social, and environmental impacts, as well as their relationships in all key spheres of influence: the workplace, the marketplace, the supply chain, the community, and the public policy realm" (Whaley, 2013).
Relationship marketing/customer relationship management (CRM)	Organization utilizes data capture, data-mining, and data modeling to analyze, plan, and implement marketing activities focused on building long-term relationships with stakeholders, customer retention, customer lifetime value (CLV), and loyalty (Peppers and Rogers, 1993).
Holistic marketing concept	Development, design, and implementation of marketing that recognizes interdependent priorities; motto is "everything matters" (Kotler and Keller, 2015).
Integrated marketing	Organization designs and implements marketing activities that are coordinated, aligned, and create synergy.
Internal marketing	Organization recognizes employees as stakeholders and creates marketing programs designed to meet employee needs.
Performance marketing	Organization recognizes the importance of measuring return (financial and non-financial) on marketing activities; emphasis on marketing metrics.

Today, marketers face change, complexity, and challenges unlike any era prior. We have entered the era of marketing convergence. Convergence is when two or more things come together to form a new whole. Bullmastiffs, for example, were created by converging the Bulldog and Mastiff dog breeds. IBM fused machine-learning and Internet of Things (IoT) technology to create the artificial intelligence platform for its Watson innovation (Ray, 2017). Technological convergence is a major driver for the advanced innovations of Industry 4.0. Tesco's delivery robot, Amazon's drones, self-driving cars, virtual reality headsets – all these and more were created by fusing (converging) individual technologies. What's more, innovation is a process. An innovation born of technological convergence may converge with another technology, device, or context producing yet another innovation, and so on. It was through this cycle of ongoing convergence and innovation that Industry 4.0 came to influence marketing as technological convergence generated new products, and product convergence led to industry-level innovations (Mantena and Sundaraarajan, 2002).

Smartphones are a great example of convergence. The innovation resulted from converging mobile phones, the Internet connectivity of laptops, digital cameras, and mp3 players. As apps have evolved, smartphones gained the functionality of maps, Internet search, social media, and more. Prospective customers can see ads on websites, by text, in apps, in casual games, and in their social media feeds – all using the smartphone device. The ads are response-enabled, yet another innovation of marketing convergence. Not only can we communicate with consumers, the consumers can also make purchases by responding directly to the ads. This is just one series of innovations developing from convergence.

With the advent of Industry 4.0, marketing is revolutionized by technological innovations and social responsibility initiatives. The Body Shop is a prime example. Long known for its commitment to social responsibility and purpose-driven engagement, The Body Shop's "Forever Against Animal Testing" campaign uses mobile devices and smart payment technology to engage customers. Participants sign the campaign's online petition and add the campaign wallet pass app to their smartphones. The app provides updates and branded rewards to participants including special offers they can share with friends (Hobbs, 2017). With technological advances, marketing is better equipped to do good and do well.

MARKETING: DEFINITIONS AND CORE CONCEPTS
WHAT IS MARKETING?

At its core, marketing is about creating and providing value in a market such that value is also produced for the marketer. The American Marketing Association (AMA) formally defines marketing as the activity, set of institutions, and processes for creating, communicating, delivering, and exchanging offerings that have value for customers, clients, partners, and society at large (American Marketing Association, 2013).

The UK Chartered Institute of Marketing (CIM) defines marketing as "the management process responsible for identifying, anticipating and satisfying customer requirements profitably" (CIM, 2015: 2). But the simple definition published in the *Oxford English Dictionary* in 1922 rings true today: Marketing means "to bring to market" and "to produce [an offer] to be sold in the market" (Business Balls, n.d.). Thus, marketing encompasses all the decisions and activities related to bringing an offer to a market of prospective buyers and successfully selling the offer to customers.

WHAT ARE THE CORE CONCEPTS RELATED TO MARKETING?

MARKET

A market is the aggregate of all prospects and customers with an unmet need and the ability to buy. As such, markets can be identified by type of buyer, type of seller, product category, industry, geographic region, and so on. One typology of market is based on the type of seller and the type of buyer targeted, as shown in Table 1.2.

TABLE 1.2 Market Typology

Offer targeted to Offer sold by	Consumers	Businesses
Consumers	C2C Consumer-to-Consumer	C2B Consumer-to-Business
Businesses	B2C Business-to-Consumer	B2B Business-to-Business

- C2C markets are sometimes called P2P, peer-to-peer. Mobile pay apps like Apple Pay and Venmo are especially beneficial for C2C markets.

- C2B markets include freelancers and independent contractors who provide services to business clients (Pryhodko, 2017).

- B2C markets target individuals and households and products for personal use. B2C markets utilize traditional shopping venues like shopping malls, grocery stores, and department stores as well as e-commerce via online stores and marketplaces.

- B2B markets focus on products needed for business and professional use. Government organizations may be grouped in this market or considered as a separate type of target market. Vertical markets refer to one specific industry segment such as healthcare or education. Horizontal markets refer to products that are valued across a range of different industries such as information technology and office equipment.

Platforms are a more recent type of market that resulted from technological and marketing convergence. Broadly defined, platforms make resources and participants more accessible to each other on an as-needed basis. By definition, platforms are two-sided or multi-sided markets, but they have grown in popularity in large part because they facilitate C2C transactions. Online marketplaces like Etsy and sharing platforms like BlaBlaCar and Couchsurfing are examples. BlaBlaCar helps to match drivers with space for passengers with riders willing to share fuel costs. Both participants benefit by saving money. Couchsurfing matches travelers with hosts. The participants benefit from the social experience.

EXCHANGE

Marketing is critical to the success of any business. In fact, Peter Drucker said "The purpose of a business is to create a customer" (Drucker, 1954: 39–40). Customers are created when they choose to exchange something of value for the organization's offer. Exchange is a *transfer of value* between buyer and seller (Solomon, Marshall and Stuart, 2009). Why do customers engage in exchanges with marketing organizations? They do so to fulfill their needs and wants.

NEEDS

A need is something that is wanted or required to bridge a gap between an actual state and a desired state. The most famous framework for understanding need states is that of Maslow's Hierarchy of Needs (shown in Figure 1.2). According to Maslow, physiological needs (e.g., hunger, thirst) are first, followed by security needs, social needs (affiliation), self-esteem needs (purpose-driven achievement), cognitive needs to know and understand, aesthetic needs, and finally self-actualization needs (Maslow, 1970). The need hierarchy can also be applied to organizations (Ginsburg, 2014). A key principle is that *unmet needs motivate behavior* to resolve the gap between actual and desired state. For this reason, understanding the needs and motives of prospective buyers in the market is a marketing core competency.

UTILITY

Basically, motives are "means-end beliefs" that buying a certain product will provide the necessary utility to meet a need. Utility is the state of being beneficial (*Cambridge English Dictionary*). Benefits are advantages or desirable outcomes. In the context of marketing, products benefit customers by providing utilities that meet customer needs. From the customer's perspective, utility could relate to any need state – functional, physical, emotional, social, and so on. Marketers consider utility in terms of providing the right product (form utility) at the right time (time utility), in the right place (place utility), at the right price (possession utility), and communicating this offer to the market (information utility).

INDIVIDUAL NEED HIERARCHY

Self-actualization – fulfillment
Aesthetic – knowledge through beauty, form, design
Cognitive – knowledge, curiousity
Esteem – achievement, recognition
Social – relationships, love, friendship
Safety – protection, security
Physiological – hunger, thirst, rest

ORGANIZATIONAL NEED HIERARCHY

Organizational-actualization – vision achievement, purpose-driven engagement, corporate social responsibility
Aesthetic – construction and acquisition of knowledge via design
Cognitive – thought leadership, training, R&D
Esteem – achievement, reputation, brand equity
Social – culture, teamwork, CRM
Safety – security, risk management, compliance
Operational – business model, operations, systems functionality

FIGURE 1.2   Maslow's Hierarchy of Needs

- Form utility: value created by producing a product useful for meeting market needs.

- Time utility: value of making a product available when it is needed.

- Place utility: value of making a product available for purchase via a channel where customers can buy it.

- Possession utility: the exchange of money for a product, the possession of which provides value by meeting a need.

- Information utility: value provided by communicating with prospects and customers.

THE OFFER AND THE MARKETING MIX
WHAT ARE THE ELEMENTS OF THE MARKETING MIX? WHAT CAN BE MARKETED?

Organizations design offers made up of components of the marketing mix, depicted in Figure 1.3. The classic marketing mix includes the 4 Ps: product, price, place, and promotion. The mix expanded to accommodate services with three additional Ps: people, process, and presence (traditionally referred to as physical environment). We'll examine each of these in detail later in the book, but let's briefly review each P in the marketing mix. Figure 1.3 highlights some of the marketing decisions associated with each P in the marketing mix.

PRODUCT

A product is an entity offered for sale. Its form makes manifest a core benefit or utility of value. Products may be tangible or intangible (Levitt, 1981). In essence, anything of value could be marketed as a product for sale including goods, services, experiences, events, ideas, locations, organizations, people, and property (e.g., intellectual, financial, and real property) (Kotler and Keller, 2015). Theodore Levitt pointed out that whether a product is tangible or intangible, customers are essentially asked to buy promises – promises that the needs motivating the purchase will be satisfied (Levitt, 1981). Product decisions in the marketing mix also encompass product design, features, packaging, and branding. We cover product further in Chapter 6.

PRICE

Price is the assignment of value required for an exchange to occur (Solomon et al., 2009). When customers evaluate a product for possible purchase, they consider its perceived value against the asking price (Almquist, Senior and Bloch, 2016). Pricing decisions incorporate elasticity of demand, perceived value, price comparisons, mental accounting, costs, price strategy (e.g., skimming, penetration), discounts, allowances, and financing options. We cover price further in Chapter 7.

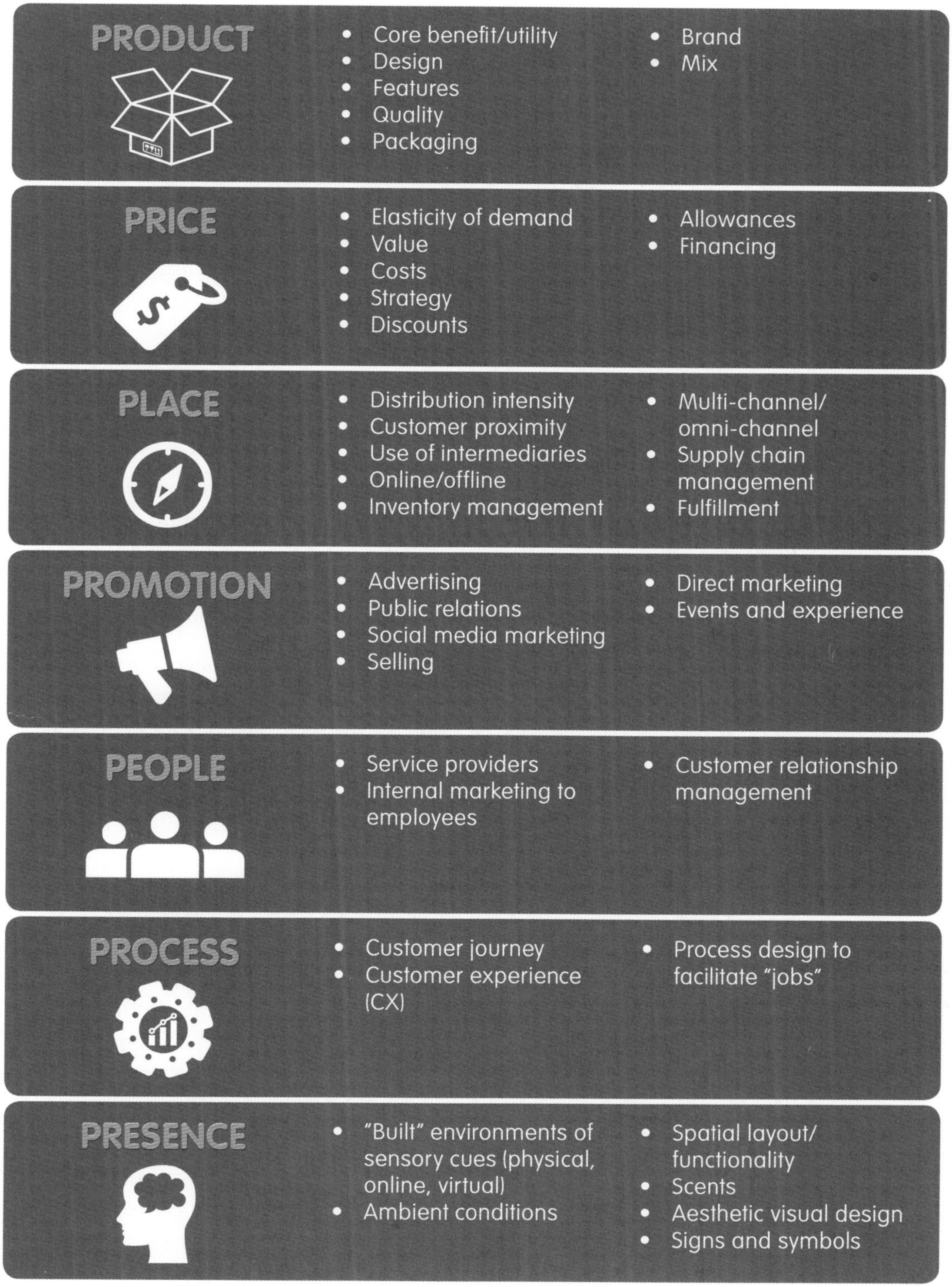

PRODUCT
- Core benefit/utility
- Design
- Features
- Quality
- Packaging
- Brand
- Mix

PRICE
- Elasticity of demand
- Value
- Costs
- Strategy
- Discounts
- Allowances
- Financing

PLACE
- Distribution intensity
- Customer proximity
- Use of intermediaries
- Online/offline
- Inventory management
- Multi-channel/omni-channel
- Supply chain management
- Fulfillment

PROMOTION
- Advertising
- Public relations
- Social media marketing
- Selling
- Direct marketing
- Events and experience

PEOPLE
- Service providers
- Internal marketing to employees
- Customer relationship management

PROCESS
- Customer journey
- Customer experience (CX)
- Process design to facilitate "jobs"

PRESENCE
- "Built" environments of sensory cues (physical, online, virtual)
- Ambient conditions
- Spatial layout/functionality
- Scents
- Aesthetic visual design
- Signs and symbols

FIGURE 1.3   The 7 Ps in the Marketing Mix

PLACE

Place refers to the channel of distribution used to make the product available for purchase at a time and location chosen by the prospective customer. Place decisions encompass supply chain management, decisions regarding distribution intensity, directness of channels and use of intermediaries (e.g., wholesalers, retailers), retail settings, geographic proximity to the customer, online/offline, multi-channel/omnichannel, inventory management, and fulfillment. We cover place in depth in Chapter 8.

PROMOTION

The promotional mix includes all the activities and communication channels marketers may use to communicate with prospects and customers. It includes advertising, public relations, social media marketing, selling, direct marketing, events and experiences, and can utilize many forms of media. It is sometimes called integrated marketing communications (IMC) and MARCOM (marketing communications). We learn more about promotion in Chapter 9.

PEOPLE

The people P was added to the marketing mix to address the influence of service providers on customer experiences and outcomes when buying services. The relevance of people in the marketing mix has grown as marketers embrace internal marketing (marketing within the organization, especially to employees) and the value of customer relationship management. We cover people in Chapter 10.

PROCESS

Like people, process joined the marketing mix because of the unique nature of services. In traditional service settings, the consumption of a service cannot be separated from the manufacture of the service. Because customers experience the manufacturing process, process design can influence the customer experience and satisfaction with the outcomes. Service marketers "blueprint" the service process to identify possible improvements. Research into customer journeys (discussed further in Chapter 2) shows that process is also relevant to other customer experiences. For instance, the processes of finding product information, placing an order, returning a product, and asking for customer service help may affect customer perceptions and outcomes. We talk further about the design of process in Chapter 10.

PRESENCE

Presence includes the characteristics that influence perceptions of the marketing environment. Initially called physical environment, it was added to the marketing mix to provide for tangible evidence in the form of sensory cues to support the underlying promises when marketing services. Chapter 10 features more coverage on how marketers use presence as part of the marketing mix. Digital marketing is limited to sight and sound, so marketers use design elements to suggest sensory perceptions in virtual environments. The term presence captures the state or perception of being somewhere (International Society for Presence Research, 2000), whether that somewhere is a physical or virtual location. In either case, marketers "build" environments of sensory cues (auditory, visual, kinesthetic, olfactory, and gustatory) by designing ambient conditions, spatial layout/functionality, sounds (e.g., music selections), scents, aesthetics, and signs and symbols.

INDUSTRY 4.0 AND THE ERA OF MARKETING CONVERGENCE
HOW ARE THE TECHNOLOGIES OF INDUSTRY 4.0 REVOLUTIONIZING MARKETING AND THE CUSTOMER EXPERIENCE?

In this section of the chapter, we explore the technologies of Industry 4.0 and the era of marketing convergence. Industry 4.0 applies physical and digital technologies, including the Internet of Things, advanced analytics, robotics, high-performance computing, artificial intelligence and cognitive technologies, virtual and augmented reality, and multi-source data to manufacturing (Cotteleer and Sniderman, 2017). Digitization affects the entire **value chain** and makes new business models possible. These technologies make the digitization of products, distribution channels, media and promotions, and pricing approaches possible. As customers interact with brands online and offline, data is produced and, when captured, stored, and used in advanced analytics, represents an asset. The resulting big data drives powerful insights into buyer behavior. An article from Deloitte explains, "The Fourth Industrial Revolution is important to understand because it doesn't just touch 'manufacturers' – it can touch all of us" (Cotteleer and Sniderman, 2017).

What are the digital elements of Industry 4.0 driving the era of marketing convergence?

- Internet of Everything (IoE).
- Digital reality (e.g., augmented and virtual reality).
- Cognitive technologies (i.e., artificial intelligence, bots).
- Blockchain.
- Additive manufacturing (e.g., 3D printing, digital twins).
- Big data analytics and algorithms.

Let's take a look.

THE TECHNOLOGIES
INTERNET OF EVERYTHING (IOE)

The Internet of Everything (IoE) is defined as "the networked connection of things, people, process, and data" (Cisco, 2013). We most often hear about the Internet of Things (IoT) component of IoE, but over time understanding all four components of the IoE will be increasingly relevant. The IoT refers to physical objects capable of connecting to the Internet and capturing, communicating, and analyzing data and communication (Deloitte, 2018b). Sensors like radio-frequency identification (RFID) tags, GPS, and accelerometers and IoT gateways can be attached to any object, making the object "smart" (Treadway, 2016). You probably already have a smartphone, but anything can be made smart – smart homes, smart cars, smart bike locks, smart assistants (Nield, 2017). For example, Waymo is a self-driving smart car (check it out at https://waymo.com/). Tile is a Bluetooth sensor you can attach to your wallet, keys, and other easily misplaced items to make them smart and trackable. Even light bulbs like Philips HUE can be smart!

Internet of People (IoP) means that people connect (P2P) through networked devices (i.e., IoT) as well as through social networks, like Instagram and Facebook. Internet of Data (IoD) refers to the data produced, captured, analyzed, and processed where and when it is needed to inform decisions. The data may be generated by things or people, declared (data voluntarily reported by a user) or inferred (system assigned using predictive analytics) (Dolan, 2016).

The final component of IoE is process, which refers to the management, analysis, communication, and application of data. Cloud computing, defined as storing and accessing data over the Internet, is a process, as is edge computing, defined as processing data close to the source (Markman, 2018). Cisco created the Internet of Everything Value Index to measure the realized value of IoE technologies in the world's largest economies (Bradley, Laucks, Macaulay and Noronhan, 2013).

DIGITAL REALITY

Digital reality, a term coined by Deloitte Consulting, encompasses technologies that enable immersive experiences and simulations of reality including augmented reality (AR), virtual reality (VR), mixed reality (MR), and 360-degree video (Deloitte, 2018a). Digital reality utilizes data from sensors and cameras to create presentations including visual and auditory elements with which users can interact using gestures and voice commands.

- AR overlays digital content on an actual, real environment.
- VR immerses users in an artificial, digital environment.

- MR generates new environments with digital and physical objects and their data can coexist and interact with each other.

- 360-degree video captures and presents video imagery such that viewers can look in every direction.

How are marketers using AR? IKEA uses AR technology to enable customers to visualize furniture in their own home. Smashbox is featured in Modiface's Makeup app allowing consumers to sample Smashbox products and colors virtually with the AR app (Gilliland, 2018). Lowe's home improvement stores use Microsoft's HoloLens augmented reality app to facilitate customer choices like which paint color to buy.

COGNITIVE TECHNOLOGIES

Cognitive technologies perform tasks, inform decisions, and accomplish objectives that traditionally required human intelligence including reasoning and learning. There are several types including artificial intelligence (AI) and machine learning, robotics and automation, and language processing including voice/speech, image, video, text, and sentiment. Machine learning is a set of statistical techniques that automate analytical model-building using algorithms that iteratively learn from data without the need for explicit programming. Robotic automation combines artificial intelligence and automation to process data and automate processes. Language processing refers to statistical techniques that enable the analysis, understanding, and generation of human languages. Marketing organizations can use cognitive technologies to predict consumer purchases, recognize fraudulent credit card activity, and automate personalized targeting of digital ads. Chatbots are an example of artificial intelligence consumers can use to aid in decision-making, perform tasks like placing an order, and even provide customer service. According to Gartner (n.d.), by 2020 chatbots will handle 85% of all customer service interactions.

Alexa, the artificial intelligence in the Echo device, utilizes cognitive technologies. The digital assistant processes and interprets voice commands in multiple languages and uses artificial intelligence and automation to perform search queries and select and share relevant information. She also performs many thousands of skills like keeping grocery lists, guiding meditations, playing trivia, and providing news and weather (Kuefler, 2017).

BLOCKCHAIN

A blockchain is essentially a digital ledger, or database, of transactions and records replicated in real-time across a network of computers or nodes (Deloitte, 2016). Because the records are copied to all of the computers in a participating network, it is sometimes called a distributed ledger. Fixed structures called blocks store data. A blockchain database links to all previous blocks and consequently maintains a complete history of all assets and instructions executed since the very first one. This makes blockchain data secure, verifiable, and independently auditable. These characteristics make blockchain especially valuable for financial exchanges, regulatory compliance, security applications, and execution of smart contracts. There is no need for a central authority to approve the transaction, which makes it useful in C2C transactions common in the sharing economy.

Perhaps the most well-known marketing application of blockchain thus far is the use of cryptocurrencies like Bitcoin for payment. Overstock, a popular online retailer selling in more than 100 countries, accepts all major digital currencies (e.g., Bitcoin, Litecoin, Ethereum, Dash) as payment from customers (Roberts, 2017). Overstock customers spend about $50,000 a week in Bitcoin. Fortune has launched an online video program covering news and developments in blockchain, fintech, and cryptocurrencies, called Balancing the Ledger.[2]

ADDITIVE MANUFACTURING

Additive manufacturing refers to a process by which digital 3D design data is used to build up a component in layers by depositing material (EOS, n.d.). Though most relevant in manufacturing settings, 3D printing has marketing applications in product design, prototyping, research and development, quality testing, small-batch customized production, as well as post-sale service and maintenance. For example, clothing retailer Ministry of Supply installed a 3D printer in stores to enable in-store production of customized clothing in under 90 minutes. Additive manufacturing embraces the use of digital twins to simulate the physical world, using the digital twin like a sandbox. In other words, just as you might have played in a sandbox as a child, digital twins make it possible to experiment, test, and play with design decisions without the risk of damaging the physical object.

A digital twin is defined as a digital model of a physical process, object, or environment built on historical data and with data sensors and cognitive technologies capable of learning and evolving. The living, learning model facilitates research and development, quality testing, "what-if" scenarios, and more, helping businesses to improve time to market for new product innovations, anticipate maintenance needs, and reduce costs (Kevan, 2017). Object twins could document ingredients, provenance, shipping history, and so on. For example, a wine lover in London could check the provenance of a bottle of fine French wine, confirm the vintage, and track its movement through the channel of distribution (*The Economist*, 2017). Because of the ability to twin and test processes, experts predict digital twin technology to be valuable for improving customer experiences and protecting against fraud and other security concerns.

---

[2]Balancing the Ledger can be seen by visiting the website http://fortune.com/tag/balancing-the-ledger/ (accessed 27 May 2019).

What can be twinned? Almost anything – processes (like manufacturing, repairs, installation, and maintenance), objects (including the tangible objects in an environment like a retail store and physical products), and even people. By combining detailed transactional data with insights from social media and consumption/usage data from IoT-enabled devices (smartphones, connected home lighting, appliances, home entertainment systems, heating and cooling, and cars, for example), it is now becoming possible to create "digital twins" of consumers. Digital twins of people have massive potential to advance medical research like effectiveness and outcomes of pharmaceutical treatments for disease. The insurance industry used digital twin technology to model individual policyholders (using more than 4,000 variables including demographics, past behaviors, and health factors) and possible loss scenarios (Rao, 2017). The Innovation Hub calls the application of digital twins in the consumer realm object marketing (Innovation Hub, n.d.). It can model a product and its interactions with the customer through the entire life cycle from purchase to disposal.

BIG DATA ANALYTICS

By now, you've likely recognized that everything happening in the era of marketing convergence is data-driven. Technology produces, captures, and utilizes data at every step of every process. The *Oxford English Dictionary* defines big data as "data of a very large size, typically to the extent that its manipulation and management present significant logistical challenges". Alternately, big data has been defined by its properties – the 3 Vs: 1) volume, 2) variety, and 3) velocity. Volume refers to the amount of data, variety refers to the number of types of data, and velocity refers to the speed of data processing. A more meaningful definition for marketers is "the ability of society to harness information in novel ways to produce useful insights or goods and services of significant value" (Press, 2014).

The Big Data Life Cycle includes four phases (Federal Trade Commission, 2016):

- Phase 1 – Collection: little bits of data are collected about individuals from a variety of sources, such as online shopping, cross-device tracking, online cookies or the Internet of Things (i.e., connected products or services).

- Phase 2 – Compilation and Consolidation: the "little" data is compiled and consolidated into "big" data, often by data brokers who build profiles about individual consumers. This phase also includes the "acquisition" of data as data sets from a multitude of sources can be acquired by organizations and merged with other data sets.

- Phase 3 – Data Mining and Analytics: the "big" data is analyzed to uncover patterns of past consumer behavior or predict future consumer behavior.

- Phase 4 – Use: organizations use the resulting analysis to drive insights, develop new products, target prospective buyers with personalized offers, automate marketing tasks, and so on (Walker, 2015).

Much of the time we are the delighted users of technology that can result in data records about us. We welcome GPS, cell tower, and even WiFi location tracking of our cell phones so that we can make calls more easily and use location services to get directions, "check-in", and find special offers nearby. We willingly share information to feed big data algorithms so dating sites can find us compatible mates, career sites can help us more quickly find jobs, online bookstores can recommend books for us to read, and social networking sites can connect us with new friends.

Big data can include data sets made up of data collected from 1) human behavior and human data submissions such as social media data, 2) traditional data sourced from the organizational records of public agencies and businesses, and 3) machine data, which is data that is recorded and collected as a by-product of the use of machines (Vale, 2013).

TABLE 1.3   The Make-Up of Big Data

Human-Sourced Information (Active Data)	Business Process Data	Machine Data
Internet searches	Consumer purchases	Security surveillance
Queries to "smart" appliances like Amazon's Echo	Medical records	Mobile tracking sensors like traffic sensors
Digital user-generated content (e.g., pictures shared online, videos, blog posts, tweets, comments)	Financial records, stock records	GPS data from mobile phones, cars, etc.
Mobile data content (i.e., text messages)	Credit card transactions	Satellite images
Wearables entries (e.g., Fitbit)	Customer service inquiries	Log files

Human-sourced data, also known as active data, is generated when the user chooses to submit information. Users don't submit passive data. It's recorded automatically or from the active data of another user. Your activity online, known as digital exhaust or as a digital footprint, is an example. Digital footprints include both active and passive data related to several variables such as IP address, date and time of activity, location, and more. So much data is available from online behaviors, but keep in mind that machine data can be collected from other types of machines as well. Your DVR, for instance, stores information about your frequency and recency of use and what programs you chose to record, whether you watched them, and if so, when you watched them. As you browse the Internet, cookies record your behaviors and movement from site to site. Are you curious which sites are tracking you and storing your digital exhaust? An app called Collusion (or its competitor, Ghostery) can be added to your Internet browser. It identifies the sites that are tracking your activities and illustrates the relationships among the companies that are collecting the information.

Big data may also include elements of metadata, which is basically data about data. Examples include the date and time you called somebody or the location from which you last accessed your email. The data collected generally does not contain personal or content-specific details, but rather transactional information about the user, the device, and activities taking place. In some cases, you can limit the information that is collected – by turning off location services on your cell phone for instance – but many times you cannot. It may also include inferred data.

One of the most powerful sources of information is your mobile device, which creates a rough approximation of your whereabouts by checking in with nearby cell towers or a more precise pinpoint when the GPS function is enabled. Automated Teller Machines (ATMs) record our financial transactions, and surveillance cameras and smart card readers can identify when and where you used public transportation. This is just the tip of the iceberg. Smart televisions, DVRs, smart appliances like the Amazon Echo, and smart houses all record residual data. With the IoT, any object could become a connected device. The documentary *The House That Data Built* (http://lifeedited.com/the-house-that-data-built/) traces the story of Aleks Krotoski as she lives in a futuristic home that monitors her every move.

However, there are risks involved as well. We must ensure human rights are safeguarded (United Nations, n.d.). Much new data is collected passively – from the digital footprints people leave behind and from sensor-enabled objects – or is inferred via algorithms. Combining multiple data sets may lead to the re-identification of individuals or groups of individuals, subjecting them to potential harms.

Should you be concerned about the data and how it can be used? For most of us, the level of comfort is tied to the organization collecting the information. For instance, most consumers reported being comfortable with data about their grocery purchases being collected and used, but a much smaller percentage felt okay about data recorded by Facebook and their mobile phone provider. We can't always anticipate how data might be used. Target, a mass merchandise retailer in the US, developed a "pregnancy prediction score" which was then used to identify Target shoppers with a high likelihood of being pregnant (Duhigg, 2012). Target's strategy was to communicate special offers to pregnant shoppers early in their pregnancy, a stage of life in which new mothers are more likely to change old shopping habits and create new ones. Target collects customer data including purchases, demographic data, credit card information, and mail and email address. Target's analysts ran predictive models to identify several products that were correlated with shoppers registered with Target's Baby Registry. Then, the analysts used those same product purchases as indicators of a "pregnancy prediction score", which was then used to target specific shoppers with pregnancy-related product offers and coupons. Since you are in a marketing class, you are probably thinking this sounds like a great example of how marketers can strategically and effectively use big data! But as a person, how do you feel about Target's research? You might feel your privacy was invaded, especially if direct mail from Target announced your pregnancy to your parents or roommates. That's exactly what happened to one pregnant teenager who hadn't yet broken the news to her parents! This is just one example of possible risks individuals face. To help prevent the misuse or mishandling of personal data, the European Union developed the General Data Protection Regulation (GDPR) to specify proper data protection measures and rules organizations must follow.[3]

MARKETING APPLICATIONS OF INDUSTRY 4.0 TECHNOLOGIES: MARTECH

Though we can categorize and define the digital technologies affecting marketing, you may have noticed that many marketing applications incorporate hardware, software, and data in ways that cross categories. For instance, GSK, one of the world's largest consumer healthcare companies, created its "Shopper Science Lab" to study the way consumers shop. The lab is a physical model, not a digital twin, but it is equipped with IoT sensors including geospatial and accelerator monitors to capture how consumers move through the store and at what speeds, and eye-tracking technology to gauge what packaging and signage are noticed. The data captured can be merged (big data) and used for advanced analytics including segmentation analysis, predictive modeling, and so on.

Blockchain and IoT technologies are increasingly important in our food chains. In 2013 UK supermarket chains discovered that products labeled as beef were actually horsemeat. In the future, this kind of scandal will be preventable (Fitter, Perez, Raftery, Thalbauer and Wellers, 2018). IoT sensors will track the provenance and identity of every animal from stall to store along with unalterable but auditable blockchain data.

Cognitive technologies and additive manufacturing can be combined to create personalized products and other offer innovations. For example, Nutella used an algorithm to design labels for 7 million "one-of-a-kind" jars. The algorithm pulled from dozens of patterns and thousands of colors to create millions of unique and aesthetically pleasing label graphics, all in a matter of seconds. The jars sold out in moments of reaching store shelves (Holmes, 2017).

Consumers are increasingly comfortable with chatbots and many brands are incorporating conversational artificial intelligence in mobile apps. This kind of cognitive technology can also be implemented in other smart objects. Charly, the Smart Mirror, is an

---

[3]General Data Protection Regulation (GDPR) (n.d.) available at Intersoft Consulting, https://gdpr-info. eu/ (accessed 27 May 2019).

example. Like a scene from the Disney classic *Snow White and the Seven Dwarfs*, Charly will evaluate what you try on and suggest which choices suit you best. Charly can also act like a digital salesperson, suggesting shoes to go with your outfit (De Brujin, 2018). Burberry went even further in its flagship store in London. The store is equipped with full-length screens that project immersive video and live streams of models. Shoppers can interact with the digital reality on the screens using their mobile phones. That's not all. The clothes are equipped with IoT sensors that trigger the display of information like video of the design process or fabric origins on mirrors in the dressing rooms. Salespeople are equipped with connected devices to help customers answer questions. In fact, Burberry's store experience is a great example of why we call this the era of marketing convergence. It's an offline, physical shopping experience converged with the best of online shopping (*Digitalist Magazine*, 2016).

These technologies can also address logistical challenges companies face. For instance, getting products shipped to customers quickly, known as last-mile delivery, is a major challenge for online retailers. Organizations are turning to Uber-like apps to employ non-professional drivers to deliver packages (crowdsourced distribution networks – Dutzler, Hochrainer, Nitschke, Schmaus and Schrauf, 2016), self-driving delivery robots, and even drones to drop packages from the sky onto customers' front porches (Berttram and Schrauf, 2016).

Customer care is also changing. Brands can use so-called living services to predict and support customer needs for service, repair, and maintenance. Living services use IoE, cognitive technologies, and digital realities to predict and react to individual customer needs in real-time (Think With Google, 2015). For instance, products may be programmed with AI-powered technical product manuals that can provide "smart documentation" to instruct customers in how to troubleshoot problems and make product repairs. Customers can simply ask the product, "Hey, how do I ___?" (Marr, 2018). Ultimately, these technologies can influence all aspects of marketing from understanding buyer behavior and performing segmentation and targeting to planning strategy and offer design across the 7 Ps of the marketing mix to measurement and control.

The combination of digital technology and marketing is known as MarTech. Companies may develop capabilities in-house and/or work with partners to develop the set of digital technologies it will use to conduct and improve its marketing activities. The field of MarTech applications and vendor partners has grown rapidly in recent years. Table 1.4 lists the most popular areas of MarTech, specific applications in each area, and exemplar vendors (Riemersma, 2018). Some companies offer enterprise marketing software suites (EMSS) which incorporate many marketing system capabilities from a single provider. EMSS providers include Adobe, IBM Watson Marketing, Oracle, Salesforce, SAP Hybris, SAS, and Marketo (Stanhope, 2018). Visit Chiefmartech.com (https://chiefmartec.com/2018/04/marketing-technology-landscape-supergraphic-2018/) to see a graphic depicting MarTech categories and its many vendors.

TABLE 1.4   An Overview of the MarTech Landscape

MarTech Category	Applications	Vendors
Advertising/Promotion	Display advertising, PPC (pay per click), search engine optimization (SEO), retargeting, email marketing, programmatic advertising, mobile advertising	Google Ad, Moz, Adroll, DoubleClick, Constant Contact
Content delivery	Content creation, lead generation, inbound marketing, content automation, content promotion, optimization	Hubspot, Marketo
Social media management	Calendar scheduling, campaign management, workflows, engagement automation, monitoring and listening, native social advertising	Hootsuite, SproutSocial, Facebook
Collaboration/Management	Team workflows, collaboration, coordination, production and scheduling	Slack, Trello, Basecamp
Commerce/Sales/CRM	CRM, social commerce, e-commerce, conversion	Salesforce Pardot, Shopify, Magento, Amazon
Data management and analytics	Activity metrics, performance metrics, system integration	Tableau, Adobe Analytics, SAS, SAP Hybris, Google Analytics 360

Companies create a marketing technology stack, the set of technology tools used to support and operate marketing activities. The Chiefmartech.com website includes a visual library of MarTech stacks from a range of brands (Brinker, 2017).

CASE STUDY

RED WING SHOES

Red Wing Shoes is the leading brand of occupational safety boots used by workers in construction and industrial settings. The brand began in response to an unmet need in the marketplace – workers needed safety boots that were durable and comfortable. It became the "go to" brand for oil-field workers with the introduction of a handmade but durable boot designed specifically for the harsh conditions common to the oil industry – the Oil King Boot. Today, Red Wing is sold in more than 100 countries worldwide. The brand is more than 100 years old but you wouldn't guess that from its innovative adoption of digital technology.

The company uses marketing technology for a wide range of marketing activities. MarTech is used to operate its e-commerce website and to promote the brand and manage customer relationships, whether to end consumers, businesses who purchase the brand for their employees, or franchisees for its retail stores. Not surprisingly, the company uses big data and analytics in a variety of ways. For example, Red Wing worked with IBM Watson Advertising to build brand awareness and drive store traffic. By analyzing the weather conditions coinciding with customer purchase patterns in its retail stores, they identified weather conditions that were likely to trigger a spike in work boot sales. This intelligence was then used to develop an algorithm to guide the delivery of mobile advertising targeted by location, weather, and workplace setting in real-time. In other words, people who worked outdoors at places like construction sites experiencing weather trigger events, and who were likely to be in need of work boots, saw mobile ads displaying the closest Red Wing store. The investment in digital paid off, resulting in a 41.4% lift in store visits! (IBM Watson Advertising, 2018). Dynamic marketing automation was used to optimize email marketing too. Rather than deploying a one-size-fits-all email message, customers received messages tailored to their past behavior such as store location, favorite

FIGURE 1.4   Red Wing Shoes

Source: ©Pixabay ericksonlori

(Continued)

footwear, and hobbies and interests. Most of these emails were opened on a mobile device, so they used a responsive layout that automatically conformed to mobile screen size.

In stores, customers benefit from digital scans of their feet, which results in personalized recommendations based on foot size, arch, and pressure points. One day the digital scans may be used to create digital twins of customer feet that will be used to manufacture custom boots on-demand in the retail store using 3D printing. Customers can even take a virtual reality tour through the factory!

That's not all. Big data and analytics are also used for market intelligence like demand forecasting for inventory management (Dosdall, 2018). Red Wing even created a custom digital platform, called RWfb (Red Wing for business) for its business-to-business customers (Retail Supply Chain Insights, 2018). The company incorporates blockchain and additive manufacturing technologies like 3D printing in product design and manufacturing as well, resulting in innovative new products. Red Wing Shoes illustrates how the digitization of marketing builds competitive advantage across the marketing mix.

PRME

INDUSTRY 4.0 DIGITAL TECHNOLOGIES, SUSTAINABLE DEVELOPMENT, AND MARKETING

In 2015, the member states of the United Nations committed to pursue an ambitious plan to solve the world's greatest challenges, known as the 2030 Agenda for Sustainable Development. The heart of the plan is a set of 17 goals (shown in Figure 1.5), each tied to a critical issue, known as the sustainable development goals (SDGs) or Global Goals (DSDG, n.d.).

Importantly, the UN recognized that companies can be powerful partners and their use of marketing technologies, including those introduced in this chapter, can facilitate the accomplishment of the sustainable development goals. Table 1.5 lists the 17 SDGs and the roles digital technology can play (United Nations, n.d.).

Antonio Guterres, the United Nations Secretary-General, said, "Never has this task been more important. Bold leadership and innovative thinking are needed to achieve the Sustainable Development Goals" (PRME, n.d.). Recognizing that today's university business students are the business leaders of tomorrow, the United Nations created the Principles for Responsible Management Education (PRME) initiative as a platform to bring awareness of the sustainability issues facing the world to the attention of business students and to educate students as to how businesses can contribute, thereby ensuring the students have the skills needed to balance the economic goals of business with the sustainability goals of the world. To reach and educate business students, PRME appealed to business professors and university programs to incorporate the SDGs in our teaching and research.

FIGURE 1.5   The United Nations' Sustainable Development Goals

Source: https://www.un.org/sustainabledevelopment/

With this noble mission in mind, each chapter in the book includes a PRME case. Each case explains how a brand applied the marketing lessons featured in the chapter to contribute to accomplishing the SDGs. In this way, we have the opportunity to reinforce how the marketing concepts can be applied while also highlighting the valuable role businesses play in making the world a better place. You can learn more about the initiative by visiting the UN SDG website and viewing videos at www.un.org/sustainabledevelopment/development-agenda/.

TABLE 1.5   Sustainable Development Goals and Technology Solutions

SDG Category	Relevant Digital Technologies
No poverty	Blockchain and cryptocurrency may provide financial services for people at the "**bottom of the pyramid**", the poorest two-thirds of the world's population. This group eschews formal banking institutions but cryptocurrency eliminates the need for a banking institution or central authority, solves exchange rate issues, tracks transaction records, and prevents fraud.

(Continued)

TABLE 1.5   (Continued)

SDG Category	Relevant Digital Technologies
Zero hunger	IoT sensors and blockchain can track food supplies, monitor safety standards and freshness dates, and facilitate accurate and timely delivery to crisis populations.
Good health and well-being	Big data analytics can facilitate early prediction of infectious diseases, monitor spread of diseases, and determine relative impact of treatment options. Digital twins can facilitate medical research. Connected devices can capture environmental data on pollution and other health-related variables.
Quality education	Digital reality and artificial intelligence can be used to create engaging, shareable, accessible education and training. Analytics can identify threats to continuing education.
Gender equality	Data and analytics can provide insights into the drivers of female empowerment. IoP can enable coaching and mentoring.
Clean water and sanitation	Sensors can monitor water supplies and provide alerts as to water safety.
Affordable and clean energy	Smart devices can control energy use, and provide suggestions for efficient energy use.
Decent work and economic growth	Technology creates new areas of focus for knowledge workers. Blockchain technology facilitates accounting and financial records, fraud protection, and smart contracts.
Industry, innovation, and infrastructure	Industry 4.0 technologies facilitate manufacturing efficiencies and address challenges along the supply chain.
Reduced inequalities	Fintech (financial technology) can aid in resolving income inequality in part due to the benefits of cryptocurrency, but there may be more threats to this SDG than benefits. Robotic automation and AI replace unskilled jobs, displacing low-income workers. P2P (IoP) networks in the sharing (i.e., gig) economy like Fiverr and Uber also displace workers.
Sustainable cities and communities	Smart cities use IoT sensors and big data analytics to manage assets like public parking, transportation systems, wastewater and sanitation systems, and roads. Alerts and AI recommendations can be routed to individual mobile devices and connected cars to minimize traffic jams, alert people to possible danger, and improve asset utilization.
Responsible consumption and production	Online search and e-commerce provides increased access to green product choices. Digital twin technology facilitates research and development tests of different ingredients, package design, and disposal options.
Climate action	Geospatial data and sensor data can monitor climate changes. 3D printing can alleviate some manufacturing and supply chain-related emissions. AI can plan more efficient transportation routes. Smart grids will make energy consumption and production more efficient.

SDG Category	Relevant Digital Technologies
Life below water	IoT sensors on drones, fishing nets, and boats can monitor the ocean's environmental health and provide real-time reporting for dynamic fishing management.
Life on land	IoT sensors and analytics can monitor variables related to deforestation, movement of animal populations, effects of drought and other natural disasters. Digital reality applications like the EarthTime animation tool can illustrate planet-scale changes. The minerals used in hardware protection and mining processes are a threat.
Peace, justice, and strong institutions	Blockchain technology can protect against identity fraud, document citizens, ensure that promises and contract agreements are honored throughout the digital chain, and facilitate value exchange among groups.
Goal partnerships	Shared data and technology resources among partnering brands can facilitate all SDG goals. SAP Hybris, an EMSS provider, is an SDG partner.

As you can see, technology not only makes marketing more successful, it can also help solve the world's greatest problems. Let's take a look at a brand that has committed to contributing to the full slate of SDGs in the United Nations' 2030 Agenda for Sustainable Development – Ford Motor Company. Each year, Ford's Sustainability Report (see sustainability.ford.com) explains its priorities and accomplishments for sustainable development. This report details Ford's contributions in all 17 areas, but six goals are prioritized. Ford's mission for sustainable development is to drive human progress through mobility. In so doing, Ford creates positive change for society. Table 1.6 highlights Ford's work toward these six SDGs (Ford, 2017).

TABLE 1.6   Ford's Contribution to Sustainable Development Goals

Goal	Description	Ford Contribution	Example
Good health and well-being	Ensure healthy lives and promote well-being for all at all ages	Develop driver assist technologies to improve vehicle safety	Ford Reality Check is a virtual reality (VR) app that simulates distracted driving scenarios
Clean water and sanitation	Ensure availability and sustainable management of water and sanitation for all	Reduce use of drinkable water, use more saltwater/wastewater	Ford's global waste reduction plan is how Ford minimizes waste sent to landfills

(Continued)

TABLE 1.6   (Continued)

Goal	Description	Ford Contribution	Example
Industry, innovation and infrastructure	Build resilient infrastructure, promote inclusive and sustainable industrialization and foster innovation	Develop alternative fuels and powertrain technology with improved fuel economy and lower emissions, including significant investments in electrified vehicle and autonomous vehicle technology	On track to deliver 40 hybrid or fully electric models by 2022
Sustainable cities and communities	Make cities and human settlements inclusive, safe, resilient and sustainable	Research self-driving vehicles and technology needed for smart cities	Cellular vehicle-to-everything (C–V2X) enables various technologies and applications in a city to communicate
Responsible consumption and production	Ensure sustainable consumption and production patterns	Use recycled, renewable, and sustainable materials	Soybean-based foam used to make seat cushions. Other renewable materials used include wheat, rice, castor, jute, and coconut
Climate action	Take urgent action to combat climate change and its impacts	Execute climate change strategy to reduce vehicle emissions and reduce energy consumption and emissions at our facilities	Use of renewable materials reduced C02 emissions by 228 million pounds

 Visit **https://study.sagepub.com/tuten** for free additional resources related to this chapter.

CHAPTER SUMMARY

The chapter reviews three definitions of marketing. The American Marketing Association formally defines marketing as the activity, set of institutions, and processes for creating, communicating, delivering, and exchanging offerings that have value for customers, clients, partners, and society at large (American Marketing Association, 2013). The UK Chartered Institute of Marketing (CIM) defines marketing as "the management process responsible for identifying, anticipating and satisfying customer requirements profitably' (CIM, 2015: 2). But the simple definition published in the *Oxford English Dictionary* in 1922 rings true today: Marketing means "to bring to market" and "to produce [an offer] to be sold in the market" (Business Balls, n.d.). The chapter also defined several core concepts including market, needs, exchange, and utility. A market is the aggregate of all prospects and customers with an unmet need and the ability to buy. As such, markets can be identified by type of buyer, type of seller, product category, industry, geographic region, and so on. Customers are created when they choose to exchange something of value for the organization's offer. Exchange is a *transfer of value* between buyer and seller (Solomon et al., 2009). Customers engage in exchanges with marketing organizations to fulfill their needs and wants.

A need is something that is wanted or required to bridge a gap between an actual state and a desired state. The most famous framework for understanding need states is that of Maslow's Hierarchy of Needs. According to Maslow, physiological needs (e.g., hunger, thirst) are first, followed by security needs, social needs (affiliation), self-esteem needs (purpose-driven achievement), cognitive needs to know and understand, aesthetic needs, and finally self-actualization needs (Maslow, 1970). The need hierarchy can also be applied to organizations (Ginsburg, 2014). A key principle is that *unmet needs motivate behavior* to resolve the gap between actual and desire state.

Motives are "means-end beliefs" that buying a certain product will provide the necessary utility to meet a need. Utility is the state of being beneficial. Benefits are advantages or desirable outcomes. In the context of marketing, products benefit customers by providing utilities that meet customer needs. From the customer's perspective, utility could relate to any need state – functional, physical, emotional, social, and so on. Marketers consider utility in terms of providing the right product (form utility) at the right time (time utility), in the right place (place utility), at the right price (possession utility), and communicating this offer to the market (information utility).

The marketing mix, also known as an offer, includes 7 Ps. Product, price, place, and promotion were the original 4 Ps. The additional three were developed to better plan offers for services: people, process, and physical environment. We use presence in lieu of physical environment to better express environmental cues across virtual and physical settings.

Industry 4.0 is the fourth industrial revolution. It includes several types of technology applied to manufacturing, including the Internet of Everything (which encompasses the Internet of Things, Internet of People, Internet of Data, and Process), digital reality (i.e., augmented reality, virtual reality, mixed reality), cognitive intelligence (e.g., artificial intelligence, machine learning), additive manufacturing (i.e., 3D printing), and big data analytics. Like early industrial revolutions, Industry 4.0 technologies have triggered a new era of marketing – the era of marketing convergence.

MarTech is short for marketing technology and it refers to the range of software solutions and technologies an organization uses to facilitate its marketing activities and processes. The set of marketing technology a company uses is called a MarTech stack.

REVIEW QUESTIONS

1. What are the four stages of industrial revolution? How did each stage influence the marketing orientation that prevailed during and after?

2. What are the eras of marketing? How are societal marketing and the era of marketing convergence different from the eras that preceded the marketing concept?

3. How do you define marketing?

4. Why is utility relevant in the study of marketing?

5. How can Maslow's hierarchy of needs be applied to organizational needs?

6. What are the 7 Ps? What kinds of marketing decisions are associated with each one?

7. What are the primary forms of technology used in Industry 4.0 and influencing MarTech stacks?

KEY TERMS

1. **Additive manufacturing** – refers to a process by which digital 3D design data is used to build up a component in layers by depositing material.

2. **Artificial intelligence (AI)** – machine learning, robotics and automation, and language processing including voice/speech, image, video, text, and sentiment.

3. Benefits – advantages or desirable outcomes.

4. Big data – data of a very large size, typically to the extent that its manipulation and management present significant logistical challenges.

5. Big Data Life Cycle – a four-phase process outlining how data is collected, manipulated, and used by organizations to make decisions.

6. Blockchain – a digital ledger, or database, of transactions and records replicated in real-time across a network of computers or nodes.

7. Bottom of the pyramid – the poorest two-thirds of the world's population.

8. Cloud computing – storing and accessing data over the Internet.

9. Cognitive technologies – perform tasks, inform decisions, and accomplish objectives that traditionally required human intelligence including reasoning and learning.

10. Data brokers – third-party providers of big data that purchase data from multiple sources to compile and build comprehensive profiles of consumers.

11. Declared – data voluntarily reported by a user.

12. Digital reality – technologies that enable immersive experiences and simulations of reality including augmented reality (AR), virtual reality (VR), mixed reality (MR), and 360-degree video.

13. Digital twin – a digital model of a physical process, object, or environment built on historical data and with data sensors and cognitive technologies capable of learning and evolving.

14. Edge computing – processing data close to the source.

15. Exchange – a transfer of value between buyer and seller.

16. General Data Protection Regulation (GDPR) – sets out strict rules for protecting individual data within the European Union.

17. **Holistic marketing concept** – features four marketing dimensions: 1) relationship marketing, 2) integrated marketing, 3) internal marketing, and 4) performance marketing.

18. **Horizontal markets** – refer to products that are valued across a range of different industries such as information technology and office equipment.

19. **Industry 1.0** – introduced mechanization and factories powered by steam capable of efficiencies in production.

20. **Industry 2.0** – increased supply by introducing moving assembly lines and resulted in more competition.

21. **Industry 3.0** – the development of computers and robotics and marked an age of information.

22. **Industry 4.0** – physical and digital technologies, including the Internet of Things (IoT), advanced analytics, robotics, high-performance computing, artificial intelligence and cognitive technologies, virtual and augmented reality, and multi-source data to manufacturing.

23. **Inferred** – system assigned using predictive analytics.

24. **Internet of Data (IoD)** – refers to the data produced, captured, analyzed, and processed where and when it is needed to inform decisions.

25. **Internet of Everything (IoE)** – the intelligent connection of things, people, process, and data, refers to physical objects capable of connecting to the Internet and capturing, communicating, and analyzing data and communication.

26. **Internet of Everything Value Index** – measures the realized value of IoE technologies in the world's largest economies.

27. **Internet of People (IoP)** – when people connect through networked devices as well as through social networks.

28. **Internet of Things (IoT)** – refers to physical objects capable of connecting to the Internet and capturing, communicating, and analyzing data and communication.

29. **IoT gateways** – are attached to any object, making the object "smart", including sensors like RFID tags, GPS, and accelerometers.

30. **Language processing** – refers to statistical techniques that enable the analysis, understanding, and generation of human languages.

31. **Living services** – use IoE, cognitive technologies, and digital realities to predict and react to individual customer needs in real-time.

32. **Machine learning** – a set of statistical techniques that automate analytical model-building using algorithms that iteratively learn from data without the need for explicit programming.

33. **Market** – the aggregate of all prospects and customers with an unmet need and the ability to buy.

34. **Marketing** – the activity, set of institutions, and processes for creating, communicating, delivering, and exchanging offerings that have value for customers, clients, partners, and society at large.

35. **Marketing concept era** – a philosophical orientation focused on achieving organizational goals by identifying and meeting the needs of target markets, and doing so better than competitors.

36. **Marketing convergence** – marketing is revolutionized by technological innovations but continues to embrace social responsibility.

37. **Marketing mix** – includes the 4 Ps: product, price, place, and promotion. The mix expanded to accommodate services with three additional Ps: people, process, and presence.

38. **Marketing technology stack** – set of technology solutions used to support and operate marketing activities.

39. **MarTech** – a combination of digital technology and marketing.

40. **Metadata** – basically data about data that generally does not contain personal or content-specific details, but rather transactional information about a user, the device, and activities taking place.

41. Need – something that is wanted or required to bridge a gap between an actual state and a desired state.

42. Object marketing – this application models a product and its interactions with the customer through the entire life cycle from purchase to disposal.

43. People – added to the marketing mix to address the influence of service providers on customer experiences and outcomes when buying services.

44. Place – refers to the channel of distribution used to make the product available for purchase at a time and location chosen by the prospective customer.

45. Platforms – two-sided or multi-sided markets, which make resources and participants more accessible to each other on an as-needed basis.

46. Presence – the characteristics that influence perceptions of the marketing environment.

47. Price – the assignment of value required for an exchange to occur.

48. Process – the consumption of a service cannot be separated from the manufacture of the service, therefore process design can influence the customer experience and satisfaction with the outcomes.

49. Product – an entity offered for sale.

50. Production era – followed a production orientation that emphasized functional benefits and offered little in the way of alternatives.

51. Promotional mix – includes all the activities and communication channels marketers may use to communicate with prospects and customers.

52. Robotic automation – combines artificial intelligence and automation to process data and automate processes.

53. Selling era – marked by marketers' adoption of a selling orientation, which valued persuasion as a way to push products and convince prospective buyers.

54. **Societal marketing concept** – to determine the needs, wants, and interests of target markets and to deliver the desired satisfaction more effectively and efficiently than competitors in a way that preserves or enhances the consumer's and society's well-being.

55. **Utility** – the state of being beneficial.

56. **Value chain** – the processes needed to deliver the value proposition are part of a system of interdependent organizational functions.

57. **Vertical markets** – refer to one specific industry segment such as healthcare or education.

Chapter 2

UNDERSTANDING BUYERS

In this chapter, we study the buying decision-making process and the factors that influence it. Along the way, we'll explore the impact of digital technologies on buyer behavior and what this means for marketers. We'll learn the answers to the following questions:

1 What is buyer behavior and why do marketers seek to understand it?

2 How are purchase decisions made? What factors and characteristics influence these behaviors?

3 Why are customer journey maps used to describe consumer decision processes?

4 What are moments of truth and micro-moments? How do they relate to the growing importance of customer experience management?

5 What do we know about organizational buyer behaviors and the factors and characteristics that influence them?

INTRODUCTION

Understanding buyer behavior benefits marketers' ability to make decisions, ranging from targeting to offer design to assessment. It is perhaps the most influential source of information across marketing decision-making. While digital advances have forced marketing to evolve, they have also forever changed the context, roles, and process of buying. Ultimately, today's digitally savvy buyers use and are influenced by a vast array of digitally enabled devices, channels, applications, and experiences. That alone is a game changer for marketers. But the story doesn't stop with buyer empowerment. Marketers also use digital innovations to reach, influence, and do business with buyers on the front-end and back-end.

Many of these changes are linked to the introduction and adoption of the Internet. Connectivity provides people with access to more information, more alternatives, and more power. More than half the world's population has Internet access and in North America and Europe, penetration is near 90% (Internet World Stats, 2019). Of those, 86% access the Internet daily. Google's Consumer Barometer Study 2017 (Think With Google, 2017a) reported that 73% of the world's population uses a smartphone daily. Mobile ubiquity consistently correlates to increased online activity including search engine usage, online entertainment, and shopping.

The use of Internet and mobile smart devices makes it easy for people to engage in a wide variety of activities like video viewing, telecommuting, shopping, socializing, and banking without geographical and physical constraints. The digital influence on buyer behavior isn't only tied to the Internet. Customer experiences today may benefit from artificial intelligence (AI), virtual reality (VR), mobile apps, and digital payment systems. Technology has become so pervasive that life without digital activities and the power, control, and experience they provide seems almost inconceivable. For this reason, we don't think of ourselves as "digital customers" or about our "digital customer experiences". We are customers and we care about experiences. But make no mistake – the digital age has disrupted traditional consumer behavior patterns. As marketers, the pressure is on to deeply understand this brave new world. In this chapter, we explore the realm of digital buyer behavior.

OPENING VIGNETTE

AI TOOL, JETLORE, HELPS SECRET ESCAPES PERSONALIZE TRAVEL OFFERS (FLUCKINGER, 2018)

Millions of people search, plan, and buy travel-related services online. Since the early days of e-commerce, travel has been a sweet spot for consumers and industry alike. Competition abounds with deal sites, travel communities, travel planning apps, and more. When you are ready to plan your next holiday, where do you begin?

Secret Escapes is a members-only travel club which offers luxury travel deals to its more than 20 million members scattered across the world. Secret Escapes offers hundreds of flash sales and deals at luxury locations every week, communicating the offers to members via its website, email marketing, and its mobile app. The challenge is how to match the best offers for its members, ensuring members see the most relevant options and aren't overwhelmed with too many marketing messages.

The solution? Secret Escapes partnered with Jetlore, which uses artificial intelligence (AI) to map consumer behavior into predictive attributes. By analyzing billions of customer-centric data points such as vacation offers ignored, viewed, and purchased, Jetlore can predict the best offers to deliver to each individual member. The offer recommendations are delivered via marketing automation that pipes the personalized information into digital dynamic templates for a webpage, email, or mobile app.

With so many customers, so many unique offers, and so much data, this might seem like an impossible task. But the bottom line is that Secret Escapes can figure out, for instance, that a female millennial with a passion for cycling has an affinity for last-minute deals on travel for recreational bike race events, while a fashionista

FIGURE 2.1   Jetlore

Source: Shutterstock

(Continued)

prefers deals to the fashion capitals of the world. The personalized offers increase the likelihood that an offer will capture the attention of the target member and spark the purchase process. Likewise, members are more prone to evaluate the offers positively because the offers are already optimized to member needs and preferences.

Did it work? Yes! Secret Escapes provided personalized content for shoppers that resulted in increased sales conversions and overall revenue. Its success came from understanding the behavior of its digitally savvy prospects and leveraging innovative back-end systems to deliver on those insights.

THE RELEVANCE OF BUYER BEHAVIOR

BUYER BEHAVIOR DEFINED

Marketers must understand the needs and wants of the market they wish to serve as well as the market's buying behavior; that is, how prospective customers evaluate, select, buy, use, and dispose of products. Buying behavior encompasses the decision processes and acts of people involved in buying and using products. Acknowledging that buying behavior is influenced by individual characteristics, socio-cultural influences, and environmental factors, the American Marketing Association defined consumer behavior as "the dynamic interaction of affect and cognition, behavior, and the environment by which human beings conduct the exchange aspects of their lives" (cited in Stephens, 2016: 6). Affect refers to the emotional aspects of attitude. Cognition captures beliefs and memory structures. Behavior includes choices and behavioral patterns such as searching for product information online, paying with credit card or mobile payment system, or watching streaming video. We capture these elements by focusing on what and why buyers think, feel, and do. Environment may include the situation and shopping context (such as a website's mobile interface), micro-environmental factors (such as competitive offers), and macro-environmental factors (like the state of the economic environment).

In addition to referring to these interactions tied to specific behaviors, buyer behavior and related terms are also often used to describe this field of scientific study. Other terms used include consumer psychology, consumerology, and buyology.

WHY STUDY BUYER BEHAVIOR?

Why do marketers study buyer behavior? In short, understanding the thoughts, feelings, and actions of our target audiences helps marketers make better decisions. This understanding could lead to ideas for new products and product improvements, changes to service procedures, messages used in marketing communications, pricing decisions, and more. What kinds of buyer behavior questions might marketers study? Some possibilities include:

- how consumers feel and think about a set of alternative brands, products, or retailers
- how culture influences decisions and behaviors
- how family members and influential others affect buyer decisions
- how motives, lifestyle, personality, and knowledge influence decisions and behaviors
- how people evaluate a purchase decision
- how people dispose of products.

TYPES OF BUYERS AND COMMERCIAL MARKETS

Who are the buyers? They may be individuals, groups (including families), or organizations. B2C (business-to-consumer) marketers study the behavior of end consumers. B2B (business-to-business) marketers study the behavior of organizational buyers. Expect to see expansion in the number of buyer types that marketers study. For instance, online shopping platforms like eBay and Etsy led to the growth of peer-to-peer marketplaces that support C2C (consumer-to-consumer) transactions.

When commercial transactions occur online, it is called e-commerce. Are you tempted to believe that modern buyers have wholly embraced e-commerce and physical retail markets are doomed to a "retail apocalypse"? Despite the digital disruptions affecting marketers and buyers alike, nothing could be farther from the truth. Rather, e-commerce (and its variations including mobile commerce and social commerce) and physical retailing represent an example of the era of marketing convergence introduced in Chapter 1.

Connected buyers toggle between online and offline channels to research, evaluate, and buy products and to get customer service assistance, share experiences with others, and engage with brands and other shoppers. Global e-commerce sales account for only about 10% of all retail sales worldwide (Statista, 2019). But make no mistake – digital marketing plays a major role in buyer behavior. A study by Deloitte found that digital experiences influenced 56 cents of every dollar spent in physical stores (Rouse, 2018).

The result is omnichannel commerce, a recognition that purchases and other buyer–brand interactions in today's digital age may involve many (even all) available commercial channels. The prefix omni-, from the Latin omnis, literally means all or every. Acknowledging that buyers may fluidly shift from channel to channel, mobile to stationary, physical to digital as they shop, marketers strive to provide a seamless shopping experience in every context. This may mean offering products in online and offline distribution channels, providing customer care and order options by phone, text, messaging apps and chatbots, webchat, social media ads and storefronts, e-commerce websites, and yes, in physical locations.

We'll discuss omnichannel commerce further in our coverage of place in the marketing mix (distribution channel decisions) in Chapter 8. Place decisions seek to offer products to prospective buyers in the marketplace such that buyers can purchase what they want, where they want, when they want, and how they want. Omnichannel is absolutely a digital trend affecting place, but it's important to note that use of omnichannel commerce extends beyond that of a buyer's chosen purchase location. Digital consumers take an omnichannel approach to each and every typical buyer behavior.

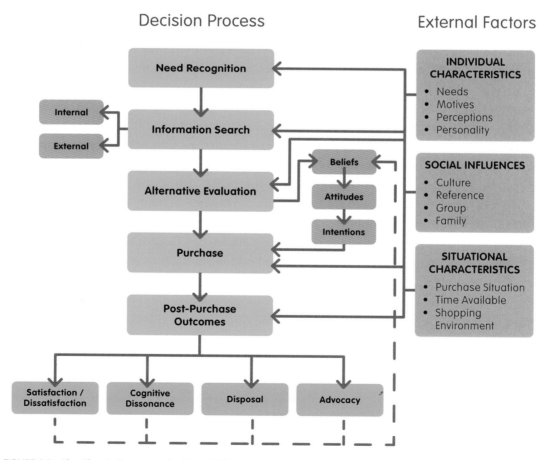

FIGURE 2.2   The Classic Consumer Decision-Making Process

THE CONSUMER DECISION-MAKING PROCESS

Traditionally, the consumer decision-making model was depicted as five stages of activities a person experiences when making a purchase. Shown in Figure 2.2, the stages include 1) need recognition, 2) information search, 3) evaluation of alternatives, 4) purchase, and 5) post-purchase outcomes. Each stage may be influenced by a person's individual characteristics such as personality and lifestyle, social influences including culture and family, friends, and reference groups, and situational factors like the time available to make a decision and the degree of risk perceived. Let's begin with a brief review of each stage and then we'll consider how the process has evolved in the digital age.

NEED RECOGNITION

Much of the time consumers are *passive*, rather than active, participants in commerce. The average person goes about daily life until some stimulus triggers the need recognition stage, as shown in Figure 2.3. Recall that we introduced the concept of unmet needs as motives that drive exchange between organizations and their customers. Consumer and business needs alike can be categorized as basic survival, security, social, esteem, cognitive, or self-actualization needs following Maslow's hierarchy of needs. A stimulus (or trigger) draws attention to a gap between the person's actual state and desired state of being, shifting the buyer from passive to active. Internal stimuli are those *from within* the individual, such as hunger, thirst, or desire. External stimuli are those *from outside* the person, such as advertising, the smell of food from a nearby restaurant, and a friend's recommendation. Needs may be recognized on impulse or anticipated and planned.

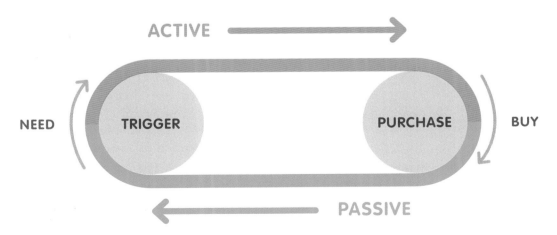

FIGURE 2.3   Passive Versus Active Consumption Stages

Source: Worrell (2017)

JOBS-TO-BE-DONE (JTBD) FRAMEWORK

From the customers' point of view, need recognition is simple. They need to get things done. They basically hire products to do the job. This is the foundation of the Jobs-To-Be-Done theory. The job-to-be-done represents a functional need. Consider a few jobs you might need doing below and fill in the blank with the brand you'd first consider hiring to do them.

You need a ride to campus: _____

You need to answer a question: _____

You need to relax after mid-term exams: _____

You need to purchase books in the 10 minutes between classes: _____

In each instance, you don't need the brand you named or even the product category in which the brand competes. You need the job done. Theodore Levitt, one of the most influential marketing professors of all time, used this example: "People don't want to buy a quarter-inch drill. They want a quarter-inch hole!" These people may have purchased a drill, but the job to be done was to acquire a hole (Christensen, Cook and Hall, 2005).

Job is essentially shorthand for what the customer seeks to accomplish in a given circumstance. To identify customer needs using the JTBD framework, marketers use a process called job mapping. Job mapping deconstructs the steps customers complete as they seek to get the job done. A job map does not detail what the customer is doing (a solutions view), rather it details what they are trying to accomplish (a needs view) (Bettencourt and Ulwick, 2008). The resulting job map captures all of the customers' needs including experiential, social, and emotional dimensions. For example, consumers report that most of their time and effort expended to make purchases is spent learning about and evaluating choices. For items priced above $50, 25% report spending the most effort on product research and 20% do so on comparison shopping (Spenner and Freeman, 2012). Job mapping would reveal a need for a more efficient selection process – one that is simple and fast, assuming the primary job would still be performed effectively.

Why does accurate need identification matter to marketers? In a nutshell, if marketers can understand the job, they can design an offer that will perform the job to the customer's specifications. Clay Christensen put it this way: "The marketer's task is therefore to understand what jobs periodically arise in customers' lives for which they might hire products the company could make" (Christensen et al., 2005). Without this process, marketers may miss the mark. Peter Drucker explained why, saying, "The customer rarely buys what the company thinks it's selling" (Drucker, 1964/2016: 113).

Let's consider sales of smart thermostats like Nest and Ecobee. The product category is growing, with sales of $2 billion and about 12 million smart thermostats sold in 2018 and expectations to reach $8 billion in sales and 22 million units sold annually by 2021 (Charara, 2018). What job might homeowners want done? Research on the needs of prospective buyers of smart home thermostats found that 75% sought enhanced home comfort, 68% wanted more efficient energy usage, and 56% said the most important feature in choosing a brand was access to a trustworthy consultant (Claveria, 2019). Home comfort and energy efficiency aligns with the features promoted on Nest's website: 1) Nest learns what temperature you like and builds a schedule around yours; 2) Nest has saved billions of kWh of energy in millions of homes worldwide; 3) on average, people save 10–12% on heating bills and 15% on cooling bills, resulting in a product that pays for itself in less than two years of use. Nest believes that customers need an easy way to keep their homes at a comfortable temperature, while saving energy and justifying the cost over other possible solutions. Jobs-to-be-done might discover other needs.

Job mapping may discover that homeowners who travel a lot are frustrated that they may arrive home only to suffer for the first few hours while they wait for the space to warm up or cool down. The core issue is still comfortable temperature, but the situational context and pain point highlights the value of using a smart thermostat to do the job. As we explore further, we might learn that our homeowner makes a common mistake – distracted by the stress of pending travel, he tends to forget to adjust the thermostat before leaving for extended trips. The pain point? The utility bill is artificially high for a home that was vacant for much of the time. Our customer needs to be able to check the temperature setting and make adjustments from a distance if needed. The energy saving isn't the core need. Rather, a solution to the practical problem of forgetting to adjust the thermostat, relief of the guilt felt, and resource savings by minimizing waste and unnecessary expense are more accurate representations of the homeowner's needs. Lastly, the job of choosing a brand represented by a trusted consultant points to additional needs, possibly decision simplicity and confidence, based on expert recommendations, despite a lack of personal knowledge of smart thermostat systems.

INFORMATION SEARCH

The second stage is information search. During this stage, consumers identify possible alternatives to satisfy the need and gather information about the alternatives. The person may already be knowledgeable about possible options and rely on recalling information stored in memory. This is an internal source. External information sources are outside sources of information such as search engine results, catalogs, online product reviews, buying guides, and salespeople. This stage should produce a set of options, called the evoked set or consideration set.

EVALUATION OF ALTERNATIVES

In the third stage the decision-maker compares the alternatives in the consideration set using evaluative criteria. The criteria include important characteristics for meeting the need in question given the situation. Multi-attribute models capture the relative importance of the chosen criteria, the evaluation of each brand alternative on those criteria, and resulting scores. They allow many pieces of information to be included in the evaluation of possible choices. The consumer arrives at an evaluation toward various choices by evaluating each option on a set of attributes such as perceived quality, value, ability to perform the job, and so on. Perceived attitudes and beliefs of others (such as friends) may also be considered.

PURCHASE

In the fourth stage, a choice is made. To make a decision, people may rely upon heuristics (i.e., rules of thumb) such as choosing a brand based on loyalty, lowest price, or highest rated. Risky decisions may be approached with more systematic approaches including compensatory and non-compensatory decision rules. A compensatory decision rule is used when a person selects the brand with the best score based on weighting and evaluating a set of criteria. A non-compensatory decision rule eliminates options that fail to meet a minimum requirement on any of the evaluative attributes. In other words, good performance on an attribute cannot compensate for poor performance on another.

Does this sound as though purchase decisions are rational? It does, but that is not always the case. People frequently make decisions based on emotion and intuition – even when the decision may seem decidedly irrational! The tenets of behavioral economics, which incorporates psychology and economics, help us to understand these patterns in buyer decision-making. For example, people tend to use heuristics, also called thinslicing, when they are under time pressure or are experiencing mental fatigue from making several decisions (even if the decisions were not related to the purchase). In such a situation, they may use an availability heuristic and choose an option that is quick and easy, or a representativeness heuristic and choose an option that has been shown as the most popular choice by others. Most purchase decisions use one or more heuristics so understanding these patterns helps marketers to structure effective offers. Framing, the way choices and related information are presented to prospective buyers, is an example. When Amazon presents shoppers with a list of products that match their search and places one of the options in the "buy box", it is framing the choice based on the availability heuristic. Amazon's success rate with this tactic is evidence of the importance of behavioral economics in marketing – 82% of Amazon shoppers purchase the product from the buy box, even though some of the other choices in the search list may be less expensive and/ or more highly rated!

POST-PURCHASE OUTCOMES

The final stage captures the evaluations and behaviors following the purchase decision. The buyer experiences the product and evaluates whether his or her expectations have been met. Customer satisfaction occurs if expectations are met or exceeded; customer dissatisfaction occurs if expectations are not met. Cognitive dissonance may occur if there is a gap between the buyer's attitudes and the outcomes. This stage may also include word-of-mouth communication (such as sharing online reviews and rating the product) and disposal of the product and/or product packaging.

Disposal may be triggered by a new purchase. This is common in the electronics industry as consumers are encouraged to have the latest and greatest product on the market. The tactic is called planned obsolescence. Companies take steps to make their products obsolete and unusable after a period of time to encourage sales of new products and reduce the time between purchases. For example, the average smartphone owner gets a new smartphone every 21 months, even though the phones being replaced are still functioning.

FACTORS INFLUENCING THE PROCESS

The stages in the decision-making model can be influenced by a person's individual characteristics, social influences, and situational factors. Individual characteristics include unmet needs, wants, and motives, attitudes and perceptions, personality characteristics such as need for variety, and lifestyle and demographic characteristics. Social influences may include the attitudes and beliefs of important others like family and friends, family characteristics such as family life cycle stage, reference groups and influencers, culture and social class characteristics. Situational factors may include temporal influences such as lack of time, purchase task such as selecting a gift, dispositional variables like mood or fear, and the characteristics of the shopping location.

Purchases can vary from low involvement to high involvement and this will affect the effort invested in the process. High-involvement decisions may be more complex than low-involvement decisions and carry more risk if a mistake is made in the purchase decision (such as paying a high price for a dissatisfying decision). For these reasons, high-involvement decisions typically involve extended decision-making, while low-involvement decisions may rely more on heuristics and impulse.

If you take a course dedicated to consumer behavior, you'll study these influences in depth. While we will focus on shifts in our understanding of consumer decision-making rather than these internal and external influences, remember they are just as relevant as ever in dissecting the reasons why people do what they do.

DECISION-MAKING AND THE MARKETING FUNNEL

The classic model captures the basic stages people experience when making a purchase decision. Inherent in this illustration is marketing's objective to encourage prospects to activate the purchase process and move successfully through each stage of the process. Marketers can trigger and interrupt stages of the process with push communications such as advertising and special offers. A television commercial might serve as a stimulus to trigger a prospect's need recognition stage. A company website or brochure can provide information. A competitive comparison chart or video demonstration could influence how alternatives are evaluated. A special discount offer could incentivize purchase. These are simple examples, but the point is that marketing efforts are designed to trigger movement into and through the process. The relationship between the classic decision-making process, marketing objectives, and marketing actions is illustrated as a funnel (sometimes called the marketing funnel, sales funnel, or conversion funnel), as shown in Figure 2.4.

While it is still worthwhile to consider key decision stages and the factors that influence them, the "path to purchase" has experienced several changes in the digital age.

DIGITAL DISRUPTION

Digital disruption affects all aspects of buyer behavior, including influence factors and buyer attitudes and behavior in the stages of the decision-making process. Digital buyers live in a world of "always on" and pervasive connectivity, conveniences afforded by voice recognition and artificial intelligence, and hyper-personalized and interactive experiences. Let's take a look at some of the changes we see in buyer behavior due to the digital age.

- Consumers discover products and research purchases online. Search, the use of search engines to discover information to guide purchase decisions, is now considered a ubiquitous part of the wired consumer's purchase process. Think With Google reports that 75% of smartphone owners use the smartphone to search for purchase information on the go, at home, and in real-time at that "point of sale". 76% of those who search for a retailer near them visit that retailer on the same day. Mobile searches for "same day shipping" have more than doubled in the last two years (Gevelber, 2017).

- Consumers may see a benefit in researching all kinds of products, even convenience goods like toothpaste and bottled water. Online information search is so easy and accessible that people are just as likely to search for reviews of the "best" in product class before purchasing a low-involvement product like toothpaste as they are for high-involvement products like a car.

- Search isn't limited to search engines. A study of consumers in the UK, US, France and Germany found that 85% of people use Google and 76% use Amazon, and 36% use brand websites to research purchase information (Sterling, 2017). More than 55% of people said their first step in online research begins with Amazon. Of the 56% of online

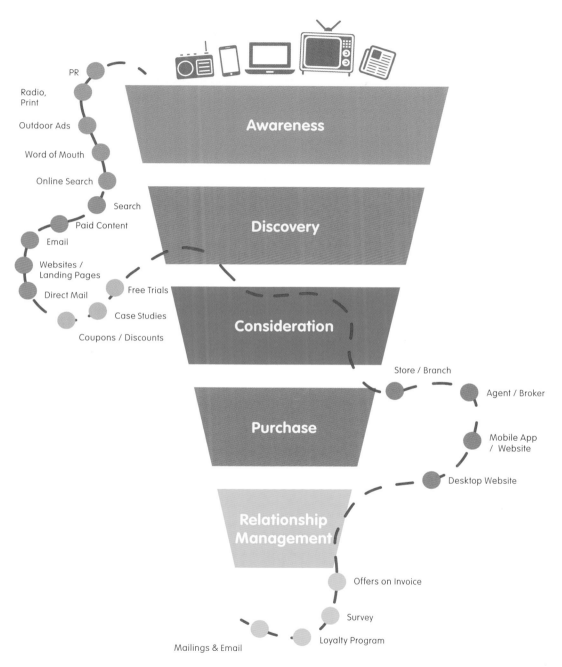

FIGURE 2.4   The Marketing Funnel

shoppers who say they begin the search for information with Amazon, 22% of them say they don't look any further if Amazon has a suitable product available (Sterling, 2017).

- Connected consumers could be influenced by many sources. Today, you are just as likely to be influenced by the online reviews of people you'll never even meet, social media influencers on Instagram, or the recommendations of a chatbot. Videos with the word "review" in the title had more than 50,000 hours of viewing time on smartphones alone (Think With Google, n.d.)! At the same time, we also have more control. A study commissioned by Salsify found that 77% of people use smartphones to check price and product availability while shopping in-store to avoid speaking to a salesperson (Salsify, 2017).

- Consumers are multi-channel optimizers, switching channels depending on their needs. People may also move fluidly between online and offline channels, showrooming to evaluate a product in an offline store but shifting online to purchase, and webrooming to evaluate information online but purchase in-store (Charoensuksai and Wolny, 2014). "When asked about their shopping behaviors prior to making a purchase in a physical retail store, 39% of digital consumers visited a brand's website, 36% read customer reviews, 33% attempted to price match the product online, with 32% finding the brand on Amazon" (Wallace, 2019).

- Consumers use digital technologies to examine the truth behind brand promises. Generally, people lack trust in brands, with just 53% reporting that they "trust business to do what is right". Digital technology has enabled an age of transparency, making it possible for people to check the facts for themselves before making a purchase (Deloitte, 2017a). Consumers can scan QR codes to learn about materials, sourcing practices, and labor practices. For example, Anvil Knitwear's customers can track products through its entire supply chain using the Track My T app. Free2Work and Slavery Footprint are smartphone apps that grade companies on a forced labor risk factor and reveal the extent to which slave or child labor may be used. As brands promote initiatives such as their commitment to the United Nations' Sustainable Development Goals, consumers may increasingly rely upon artificial intelligence to validate brand claims. Don't think slave labor is an issue in the brands you buy? Think again. If you use cosmetics such as blush, foundation, and lip gloss, you may be supporting a brand connected to child labor. As many as 20,000 children work in mica mines which supply 25% of the mineral used by beauty brands including L'Oréal and Estée Lauder (Bengtsen and Paddison, 2016).

- Automated shopping enabled by innovations like Amazon Dash buttons, apps, and even subscription services represents a whole new subset of e-commerce called A-commerce. For instance, Plum (http://withplum.com) is an auto-saving app that moves small amounts of money to a savings account. Based in the UK, thousands of users have saved millions without thought or action after the initial setup! After a user's initial choice to use the app, subsequent decisions are automated. Marketers have long sought to become a customer's habitual choice, but A-commerce skips the development of habit by automating choice.

- Consumer adoption of voice search using digital assistants like Siri and Alexa could lead to consideration sets dominated by commodity products and generic brands. In less than two years, experts expect that half of all online information searches for product information will be made by voice using digital assistants like Alexa. One in three voice shoppers will use the device to complete the purchase transaction. The market leaders in voice search will be able to push their preferred products, including their own private-label brands. This is already happening. Amazon's private-label brand has grown 90% and now incorporates more than 80 brands including Amazon's Basics product line (Creswell, 2018).

- Digital shopping applications can change the decision context consumers experience by shifting social and situational factors. Shopping atmospherics and product demonstrations can benefit from virtual reality. Star ratings and number of online reviews provide indicators of social proof and the implied approval of others. Blockchain technologies may enhance perceptions of safety and security and reduce fear and perceptions of risk. Virtual companions, AI chatbots capable of modeling human conversations and relationship interactions, could be the new age equivalent of "purchase pals". For example, Replika is an AI chatbot designed to mirror the personality of its human user. The bot learns its user's values and communication patterns and integrates them into its own personality.

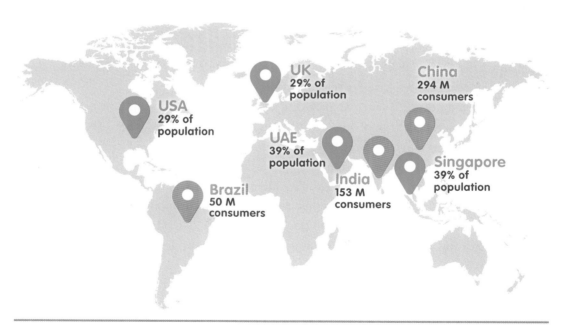

 Top countries by percentage of the total population ready for hyper-personalized services

 Top countries in actual numbers of people ready for hyper-personalized services

Sample: Total population

FIGURE 2.5   Top Countries on Accenture's Engage Me Index

This is just a brief list of digital innovations that influence marketers and buyers alike. Of course, connectivity and digital adoption can vary in different parts of the world. Accenture's Engage Me Index is a valuable indicator for global marketers. It measures the degree of digital readiness in countries around the world. Based on the results of the Digital Consumer Survey of 26,000 people in 26 countries (Accenture, 2017), the index suggests a steadily increasing readiness among digital consumers around the world, especially in the UK, India, China, Brazil, US, and Singapore. Consumers, especially teenagers, are adopting AI features like digital voice assistants and interacting with brands using live chat and mobile messaging apps supported by AI-driven chatbots. In fact, 50% of those surveyed use an AI-driven app at least monthly and prefer AI-service apps because of their ease, convenience, and effectiveness.

THE DIGITAL CUSTOMER JOURNEY

Clearly, today's reality is better captured by describing consumer decision processes in the context of a digital ecosystem, which recognizes a variety of influence sources, channels, behaviors, decision points, and experiences. We call this expanded view a customer journey. Companies engage in the research activity of customer journey mapping to capture the details of consumer decision-making, and the resulting customer journey maps are then used along with other target audience insights to guide marketing decision-making.

Just as we might describe a trip exploring the beaches along the Gulf Coast as a journey, customer journeys reflect how people travel through decision stages, where decision points occur, and what the experience is like. Two common applications of customer journey mapping include 1) taking a brand-agnostic approach to understand how consumers receive information, what information sources are influential, and what specific behaviors they engage in when making purchase decisions, as well as 2) capturing the series of interactions and touchpoints a customer has with a specific brand to accomplish typical tasks such as ordering, returning a product, or requesting a repair. Journeys depict consumer movement along a series of touchpoints (Court, Elzinga, Mulder and Vetvik, 2009). Touchpoints are the individual interactions people have with brands before, during, and after purchase. Marketers care about touchpoints because they represent opportunities for customers and prospects to learn, have a positive brand experience, and form attitudes and associations about the brand that could lead to future purchases, brand loyalty, and positive word-of-mouth communication.

Prima facie, a basic customer journey may appear very similar to the classic customer decision-making model. When passive, consumers are not actively considering a purchase but may still be exposed to brand-related messages that build brand awareness, brand perceptions, and attitudes. Once a trigger draws attention to an unmet need or want, people shift to active evaluation in pursuit of a decision that will fulfil the need. Once a decision is made (whether to buy or which brand to choose) and the purchase is evaluated, the journey ends and the consumer returns to a passive state. When fully mapped, however, a customer journey can reveal a wealth of insight into the factors influencing the journey, the specific actions customers take along the journey, the devices and tools they use, the channels and sources of information, the emotions felt, and more. They can also provide detailed snapshots of the experiences customers may have when conducting common tasks like ordering, requesting customer service, or making a return. Figure 2.6 illustrates one journey template.

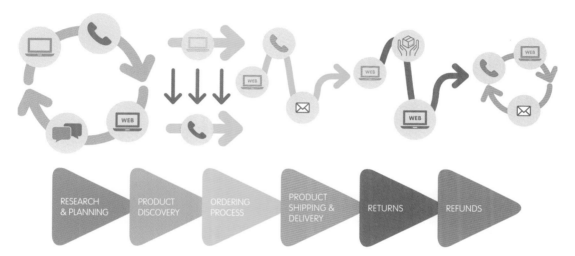

FIGURE 2.6   An Exemplar Customer Journey

THE RATIONALE FOR THE SHIFT TO CUSTOMER JOURNEYS

First conceived by McKinsey & Company in 2009, the customer journey concept sought to more realistically reflect the digital path to purchase used by connected consumers. The ability for consumers to research relevant information and contribute product reviews and recommendations (user-generated content) online sparked a paradigm shift in how consumers gather information, what information sources they seek out and trust, how many touchpoints and channels they use, and what they share with others. Journey maps could illustrate the multi-device, multi-channel, multi-source, multi-purpose components of digital customer purchase experiences.

McKinsey's research discovered that during active evaluation (the journey stage that encompasses the information search and alternative evaluation stages from the classic model) most of the influence sources are consumer-initiated rather than marketing-initiated!

As consumers used their computing devices to search the web for brand information, reviews, and ratings, they were able to pull relevant information from a variety of sources. With the ease of online research, marketing-initiated communications declined in its share of influence.

McKinsey concluded that marketing efforts would be more effective if focused on 1) building brand awareness *prior* to the decision trigger to ensure the brand is included in the initial consideration set, and 2) maximizing customer satisfaction with the experience *after purchase* to encourage customer retention, brand loyalty, and online brand advocacy. In other words, because consumers controlled information and evaluation during the active stage, marketers could be most influential during the passive periods before (when brand awareness, brand associations, and memory structures are formed) and after (when loyalty can be developed).

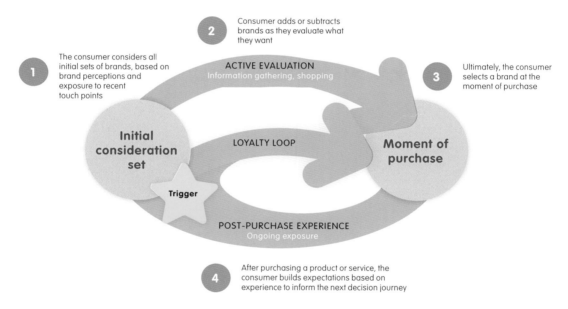

FIGURE 2.7   McKinsey's Original Consumer Decision Journey Model

Importantly, the conceptual model depicted a "loyalty loop" by which customers who were satisfied post-purchase developed brand loyalty, leading to future brand purchases which bypass the evaluation stage. Advances in marketing technologies including marketing automation make it possible for subsequent purchase journeys to accelerate, speeding up the sales cycle, improving customer retention, and strengthening the customer relationship (Edelman and Singer, 2015). We can see this loyalty loop coming to fruition in the A-commerce applications.

MOMENTS OF TRUTH, CUSTOMER EXPERIENCE, AND THE EVOLUTION OF CUSTOMER JOURNEYS

McKinsey's original conceptualization of the customer journey remains the foundation for our current understanding of customer journeys. In fact, it foreshadowed the rise of two critical developments in our understanding of what customers experience during and after a journey. These are 1) moments of truth and 2) customer experience management.

What are moments of truth (MoT)? A moment of truth is a moment in the customer journey at which the relationship between the consumer and the brand is at stake (Normann, 1991). They are the critical moments of a customer journey; moments that determine whether a brand wins the customer's business and whether the customer will be satisfied. Along the customer journey, four major moments of truth as well as micro-moments occur during which buyers' needs, attitudes, and perceptions guide their subsequent behavior. A study of buyer behavior would be incomplete without considering these moments. They are the 1) First Moment of Truth (FMOT), 2) Second Moment of Truth (SMOT), 3) Third Moment of Truth (TMOT), 4) Zero Moment of Truth (ZMOT), and 5) micro-moments.

They can be thought of as forks in the road the customer follows along his or her journey. The MoT concept is not new. First applied to services marketing, it entered the broader marketing lexicon when A.G. Lafley, then CEO of Proctor & Gamble, used the term to explain two decision points consumers face and what brands must do to win in those moments. Lafley wrote:

> ... when consumers stand in front of a store shelf ... and decide whether to buy a P&G brand, or a competing product. A lot happens in that moment ... consumers assess the performance, quality and value P&G brands offer relative to other products on the shelf. When we strike the right balance between brand promise and store price, we win that first moment of truth.

> ... Soon after, P&G brands face a second moment of truth ... consumers decide whether P&G brands live up to their promises. When we get this right ... then we begin to earn the trust on which great brands are built. (Lafley, 2002: 1)

The First Moment of Truth (FMOT) occurs when the customer is considering a product at the point of purchase (POP) and their decision is influenced by product characteristics, shelf-placement and display attributes, and the mix of alternatives available (Huang, Hui, Inman and Suher, 2013). In the modern digital environment, the FMOT is not restricted to viewing products on shelves. It could occur in a variety of instances. Consider these examples of the FMOT for a prospective vacationer considering hotels for an upcoming trip to Seoul:

- deals of the day on the Secret Escapes website
- search engine results to the query "where should I stay when I visit Seoul?"
- list of area hotels by room availability and price on Expedia
- hotel ratings and reviews on TripAdvisor.

Emphasizing this point, Antonio Sciuto, CMO for Nestlé Waters, explained that online search must be treated like shelf space. "It's where people now turn to make decisions. We need to think about search with the same obsession that we think about our store shelving. Our share of search must be higher than our share of market. In a physical store, if you aren't on the shelf, you don't have a chance. It's exactly the same for search" (Sciuto, 2017).

The Second Moment of Truth (SMOT) occurs post-purchase as the customer uses the product and evaluates whether the product delivered as expected. It is the SMOT that largely determines whether customers feel satisfaction or dissatisfaction, validation or cognitive dissonance, and disgust or delight. This moment precedes and contributes to post-purchase behaviors including product returns, complaints, and repeat business. Historically, consumer response to the SMOT has been tied to the needs that motivated the purchase and the consumer's expectations that the anticipated benefits of product use would meet those needs.

Research on how digital innovations can influence the customer journey revealed two insights relevant for winning the SMOT. First, the SMOT is cumulative as customers evaluate their experiences with brands throughout their purchase journey (McKinsey, 2017). Brands can use digital innovations to improve these experiences end-to-end. Second, consumers don't evaluate all experiences and journey outcomes equally. Consequently, studying consumer values and preferences helps to ensure that the most impactful elements are targeted for innovation. Third, the SMOT evaluation can be poor even when touchpoints along the journey perform well, particularly when the journey is subject to situational factors beyond the brand's control (McKinsey, 2017). For instance, a delivery could be late or result in a damaged product due to the shipping company at no fault of the chosen brand. The customer may still feel disgust at the SMOT.

Gaps between what the consumer wanted to experience and the actual experience, particularly if the gap represented a possible barrier to completing the journey, is called friction (Leach, 2017). Friction creates feelings of discomfort and can result in moments of truth throughout the customer journey. For this reason, marketers have focused on using digital advances to reduce customer situations prone to friction. Starbucks' mobile ordering service is an example. Starbucks knows that waiting in line to order is a source of friction for its customers. The mobile ordering app minimizes that source of friction in its customers' coffee-buying journey and should ultimately result in a more positive evaluation at the SMOT.

The Third Moment of Truth (TMOT) captures the moment of customer feedback. Pete Blackwell, also of P&G, coined the term emphasizing, "The third moment is that powerful inflection point where the product experience catalyzes an emotion, curiosity, passion, or even anger to talk about the brand. By opening up that pipeline, we not only absorb insight and deeper consumer understanding but also nurture empowerment and advocacy" (Blackshaw, 2006). Since its introduction, the TMOT has risen in importance as people take to sites like Yelp to leave reviews and ratings, and Twitter to share brand complaints (and sometimes compliments). In recent years, some have come to call this moment the Ultimate Moment of Truth. Using social listening and customer relationship management systems as part of the company's MarTech stack ensures companies can respond to customer feedback and possibly recover by addressing the concerns (Karr, 2017). Recovery occurs when brands successfully respond to a customer complaint in such a way that the relationship is strengthened rather than harmed. Without the TMOT, recovery is not possible. Complaints provide valuable feedback that brands can use for improvements. The reviews and ratings shared online provide information other buyers may use during the information search and evaluation stage of their own customer journeys. In this way, the TMOT becomes an input for the Zero Moment of Truth (ZMOT).

In 2011, Google proposed another MoT – the Zero Moment of Truth. Consistent with McKinsey's discovery that online search patterns of empowered, wired consumers had shifted the balance of power from marketing-directed to consumer-initiated information, Google explained that the online search for and discovery of information represented a critical moment *prior* to the FMOT. Google dubbed this the Zero Moment of Truth (Lecinski, 2011). Drawing upon research data, Google demonstrated the sizable increase in consumers researching products online prior to purchase using search engine queries and in the average number of information sources used prior to the purchase decision.

Now, Google has declared this the era of the research-obsessed consumer (Think With Google, 2017b). With smartphones, people can get the information they want to guide purchase decisions anytime and anywhere. We see this in the increase in mobile searches using the keywords "best" and "reviews". What's more, the ZMOT changes typical consumer behavior for small-ticket purchases just as much as big-ticket items. Traditional thinking assumed that consumers would spend more time gathering information and evaluating alternatives for purchases that were high-involvement, expensive, and/or risky than for low-involvement purchases. Mobile search patterns show that digital consumers are searching for ZMOT information on consumer-packaged goods (CPG) too. For instance, mobile searches for best water bottles and best salt have increased 165% and 375% respectively (Think With Google, 2017b). The ZMOT was truly a paradigm shift in how marketers view buyer behavior from the classic consumer decision-making model to customer journeys. Figure 2.8 illustrates where the ZMOT fits in the moments of truth model.

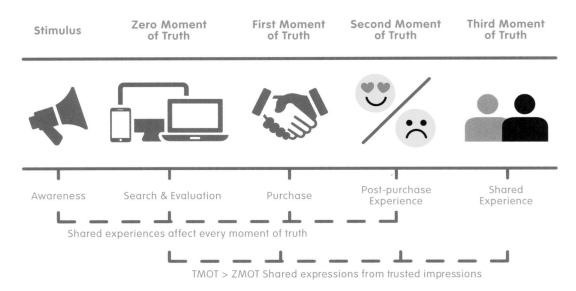

FIGURE 2.8   ZMOT in the Moments of Truth

Source: Adapted from Think With Google

MICRO-MOMENTS

Along with the major moments of truth, Google research also identified the presence of micro-moments in the customer journey. Micro-moments are "intent-driven moments of decision-making and preference-shaping that occur throughout the entire consumer journey" (Ramaswamy, 2015). They focus on the different motives and desires customers may experience on the path to purchase. During these need states, consumers spend short bursts of time discovering relevant information online, primarily using smartphones. Four essential micro-moments capture how motives shift throughout a journey and influence the process. These are want-to-know moments, want-to-go moments, want-to-do and want-to-buy moments.

Let's return to our travel planning example: 40% of US travel website visits are from mobile devices. The average length of site visit has shrunk by 5%. Yet conversion rates in the travel industry are up nearly 10%. Micro-moments explain these trends. Travelers turn to mobile devices in short spurts to make informed decisions quickly. These moments may occur in any downtime that occurs in daily life. You may search for activities you want to do during an upcoming holiday while waiting in line to pick up a cup of coffee, riding the subway, or even while walking to class. The development of voice search makes micro-moments even more popular among consumers. Of leisure travelers who are smartphone users, 69% search for travel ideas during spare moments, 91% look up information on their smartphones while in the middle of a task, and 82% consult their phones while they're standing in a store deciding which product to buy (Ramaswamy, 2015). These micro-moments feed the moments of truth. Micro-moments produce the information sources used in the ZMOT. Because one in 10 consumers report buying a different product than they originally planned, we also know that the FMOT is influenced as well.

CUSTOMER EXPERIENCE (CX) MANAGEMENT

Though the moments of truth can be thought of as an independent model, there is value in viewing consumer behavior as an integrated model. The ZMOT occurs during a journey's active evaluation. During this period, consumers may use micro-moments to perform tasks related to the purchase journey. The FMOT occurs at the point of sale. The SMOT occurs at the point of experience evaluation and influences the TMOT. The TMOT serves to encourage feedback and brand advocacy, inform future journeys, and guide customers through the loyalty loop. Customer experience management empowers companies to match marketing strategies and tactics to improving the buyer journey experience. We'll cover customer experience management in depth in Chapter 10.

B2B BUYER BEHAVIOR
DIFFERENCES BETWEEN B2B AND B2C BUYERS

End consumers get a lot of attention from marketers, but we also must consider B2B buyer behaviors and the factors that influence their journeys. B2B buyers differ from B2C buyers because of the characteristics of the organization and the nature of the purchase task and situation. Some of the typical differences include the characteristics of the decision unit, the relevance of hard and soft costs, partner buying relationships, and mutual dependence. In B2B buying, decisions may be made by individuals such as purchase managers but are often made by buying centers. Buying centers are committees tasked with purchase decisions and made up of employees with technical, economic, and performance-based expertise relevant to the purchase. The purchase process will be guided by organizational rules, policies, and procedures, which can influence the time required, the information required for evaluation and the number of alternatives considered. Hard costs include the monetary price of the products being considered and associated purchase costs like shipping, installation, training, and maintenance agreements. Organizations also consider soft costs, which are costs incurred due to related expenses absorbed by the company, such as human resource hours required, potential opportunity costs, or downtime. Though businesses may make independent purchase decisions, they oftentimes develop partnership relationships with suppliers. These relationships have value in terms of trust, synergy, and pricing discounts tied to volume and contract period. You could think of B2B buyers being influenced by internal factors (organizational motives, characteristics, perceptions, knowledge) and external factors (relationship influences such as partnerships, associations as reference groups, and situational factors such as decision urgency, risk, and relevance).

THE B2B BUYER DECISION-MAKING MODEL

The decision-making model for organizational buyers includes the following stages:

1. Problem recognition.
2. Specifications necessary to meet organizational needs, possibly resulting in an RFP or request for proposal.
3. Search for possible suppliers and related information.
4. Solicitation of bids or proposals.
5. Evaluation of alternative proposals.
6. Supplier selection and order.
7. Post-purchase evaluation.

Note the similarities to the consumer decision-making model. Both require recognition of a need, information search, alternative evaluation, purchase, and post-purchase evaluation.

THE SHIFT TO BUYER JOURNEYS

Like in B2C industries, B2B buyer behavior can be viewed as a buyer journey to better understand buyer needs, the process as an end-to-end experience, the channels used, influence sources, friction points, moments of truth, and possible outcomes. But just as consumers have taken control of their journey using technology, so have industry buyers. More so than ever before, suppliers must ensure that relevant brand information is findable during the online information search stage. One survey of B2B buyers found that more than half of their buying journeys were completed with online search and evaluation before they ever contacted the supplier company (Mull, 2013). In other words, B2B buyers are also using ZMOT sources of information to add and eliminate alternatives. In fact, 94% of business buyers say they use online search at some point in the active research and evaluation stage of the journey, and for 62%, web search is one of the first three resources they use to learn about a solution (Hines, 2017).

If a competitor doesn't show up in a search, they lose the opportunity to compete for the business. On the other hand, this also represents an opportunity for suppliers. This is because 71% of buyers say they begin with a general online search to discover solutions and suppliers rather than beginning with an initial consideration set of suppliers. B2B buyers conduct 12 online search sessions on average before engaging with a specific brand's site. Social media are among the influence sources consulted! Of B2B buyers, 53% report turning to LinkedIn to get expert opinions and recommendations. Further, the supplier choice is no longer a simple matter of bid price. Supplier brands can leverage marketing innovations that better meet industry buyer needs, influencing the FMOT and facilitating ongoing partnership (loyalty loop). For example, Monsanto created an online brand community for its buyers to provide complementary advice on product selection and business optimization strategies. In so doing, Monsanto has positioned itself as a valuable partner and expert resource rather than one of many commodity suppliers (Maechler, Poenaru, Rüdt von Collenberg and Schulze, 2017).

FRICTION IN THE B2B BUYER JOURNEY

Industry buyers are affected by friction and they want a better journey experience. In a survey of 1,000 B2B decision-makers, lack of speed in interactions with their suppliers was the number-one "pain point", mentioned twice as often as price (Maechler et al., 2017). These executives want automated digital solutions that can make routine tasks in the journey more efficient. 86% of respondents said they prefer using self-service tools for ordering, rather than talking to a sales representative.

There are key journey experiences that reflect the most critical need states for industry buyers. These represent areas where marketing innovations can add value to the customer experience and create competitive advantages.

1. *Identifying products and services that meet a need.* B2B customers often find it challenging to identify the right product or service to meet their needs, but they also prefer "self-service" journeys. Developing recommendation apps and automated solutions can meet this need.

2. *Selecting a supplier.* Innovations in marketing that increase the supplier brand presence early in the journey and in a meaningful way will ultimately influence supplier choice. Monsanto's online educational community is an example. A comparison engine that could provide information on energy requirements, installation costs, expected maintenance, lifetime ownership costs, and other evaluation criteria for major competitors would also facilitate the buyer journey, while highlighting the supplier brand as a valued partner in the experience.

3. *Dealing with unexpected events and getting service.* Coping with purchase-related problems, such as equipment breakdowns, is an industry SMOT. This is the moment when the customer is the most vulnerable. For example, the journey could be improved by providing digital self-help guides, a tracking system on problem resolution status, augmented reality repair guides for technicians, and a service-scheduling system to make appointments.

Marketing innovations can purposefully influence a buyer journey with digital self-service, digitally enabled human interactions, and personalized interactions by customers. Doing so can directly influence the SMOT. Experience management along the journey can result in more positive evaluations at the journey's end and result in stronger partnerships, loyalty, and advocacy.

CASE STUDY

SMARTPHONE CONSUMERS AND THE CASE OF SUSTAINABLE CONSUMPTION

Smartphones are among the most widely used consumer goods. More than 36% of the world's population use a smartphone. Smartphones have provided many benefits, including a reduced reliance on some other electronics like digital cameras, alarm clocks, and mp3 players. Unfortunately, most of us don't dispose of our phones properly. This results in e-waste which negatively affects the environment and leads to unnecessary mining of materials needed for production (Judl, Tilkanen, Riddlestone and Rubbens, 2018).

Certainly, businesses have a responsibility to address the growing concerns of e-waste, possibly by extending the lifespans of products, recycling e-waste to reuse component parts and recover raw materials for use in manufacturing, and offering a takeback program to collect e-waste from customers. As part of SDG 12 (responsible consumption and production), businesses do not bear this burden alone. Consumers need to take action too by embracing sustainable consumption. While sustainable development is development to meet the needs of the present without compromising future generations, sustainable consumption is the practice of consuming needed products in such a way as to use resources efficiently, minimize emissions and waste, share in the access to products, and contribute to environmental, social, and economic sustainability that will positively impact future generations. In other words, sustainable consumption is the consumer role in meeting sustainable development goals. Businesses bring products to market to meet consumer demand. Consequently, as consumers, we are complicit in the problems and solutions affecting the pursuit of sustainability.

The relationship between consumer behavior and the smartphone e-waste problem is clear (Ahmed, 2016). More than 1.5 billion smartphones are sold each year. In part, consumers are influenced by planned obsolescence. Smartphone marketers like Apple and Samsung develop better models and encourage consumers to upgrade. Many of those purchased are replacement phones, but most people do not recycle the old device. The collection rates for recycling smartphones is only around 15%. Instead, the devices are stored by the owner or end up in a landfill.

What are the reasons why most people don't recycle their old phones? Research suggests several possible reasons (Welfens, Nordmann and Seibt, 2016):

1. People may hold on to an old phone in case a family member needs a phone or they later need a back-up.

2. Despite the new phone, people may feel an emotional attachment to the old phone.

3. People may not know what options they have for recycling the phone, such as the collection agencies available.

4. Some people lack knowledge of the negative impact caused by phones that end up in landfills and/or the potential value of raw materials in their old phones.

5. People may not be willing to make the effort needed to recycle the phone.

6. Some people know of recycling options but mistrust that the devices would actually be recycled.

To increase consumer participation in reducing e-waste and increasing recycling of smartphones, we must find ways to overcome these barriers. Though the goal is to encourage sustainable consumption in the purchase and disposal of smartphones, brands can make consumer participation more likely. Keith Weed, Unilever's chief marketing and communication officer, said "It is a brand's role to help consumers be responsible citizens" (Weed, 2015). Manufacturers who don't already have a "take-back" program can develop one. Manufacturers could make it easy for customers to participate by providing clear instructions on return procedures (possibly even including a pre-paid return envelope) in the packaging of new phones. This recommendation would inform consumers of recycling options and lower the consumers' perceived effort by making proper disposal easy. They could also offer a financial incentive to customers who return their old device (e.g., turn your old device in and get $100 off your new phone).

Social marketing, the use of marketing to achieve social benefits, could address the education gap. Communications could inform people about what e-waste is and how it damages the environment (to address the lack of information), why they should care (to change the cost/benefit assessment), how they can help (to explain how their behavior can make a difference), and what others are already doing (to set new social norms to guide behavior).

Will these efforts work? In the short term, it's doubtful. A study on sustainability information and choice found that information about environmental impact did not influence behavior (O'Rourke and Ringer, 2015). Indeed, the study suggested that sustainability messages must be tied directly to health implications for the target audience in order to change behavior. Health was the only sustainability factor that influenced behavior in the study. Until social norms change, sustainability appeals will need to show the value of smartphone recycling, the instrumental role each consumer plays, and the ease of doing the right thing.

PRME

SAMSUNG COMMITS TO E-WASTE INITIATIVE

In September 2016, Samsung suspended sales of and recalled units for its Galaxy Note7 smartphone after discovering that a defect made the phones prone to fires and explosions. The recall resulted in the need to dispose of millions of discarded phones, bringing to light the ever-growing challenge of e-waste disposal and its environmental implications.

E-waste refers to electronic waste. It includes electrical and electronic equipment and their parts that have been discarded without the intent of reuse. It includes many types of products, including mobile phones. According to the Global E-Waste Monitor report, worldwide, we generate a staggering 44.7 million metric tonnes (Mt) of e-waste each year (Baldé, Forti, Gray, Kuehr, and Stegmann, 2017). To put this into perspective, this is akin to 4,500 Eiffel Towers! Only 20% of e-waste is recycled. The rest presumably ends up in landfills where the toxins common in e-waste can contaminate air, water, and soil. What's more, billions of dollars in valuable raw materials like gold and silver are lost each year, resulting in unnecessary mining for metals used in the production of smartphones. Thus, e-waste poses a substantial threat to achieving the UN's sustainable development goals. Samsung's responsibility in the wake of the Galaxy Note7 recall applies directly to SDG 12, responsible consumption and production. But, the effects of improper disposal cause harm related to several other SDGs, including life below water, life on land, clear water and sanitation, and good health and well-being.

A few short months after the recall, Greenpeace criticized Samsung for failing to produce a recycling plan for the approximately 4.3 million defective and recalled Galaxy Note7 smartphones. The pressure worked and Samsung took steps to address the immediate concern as well as adopt principles to contribute to the reduction of e-waste in the future (Waste 360, 2017). Samsung recycled raw materials from the defective phones and repurposed components like cameras for use in new models. The company also incorporated e-waste initiatives in its sustainability plan, including the adoption of a circular economy approach, introduction of a global e-waste take-back and recycling program (called Samsung Re+), and responsible disposal of e-waste deemed unsuitable for reuse or recycling. According to Samsung's Sustainability Report, the Samsung R+ program was responsible for collecting 2.64 million tons of e-waste last year. The company will have collected at least 3.8 million tons of cumulative electronic waste by 2020 (Samsung, 2017).

Of these initiatives, perhaps the one with the greatest potential impact on achieving the SDGs is that of the circular economy. The phrase refers to the recycling of e-waste to extract raw materials and component parts, and the redesign of products to facilitate the use of such materials. The circular economy approach is not unique to Samsung. It is advocated as a best practice in manufacturing because it can reduce the amount of resources used in manufacturing, minimize misuse of resources, and reduce the depletion of natural resources.

online resources

Visit **https://study.sagepub.com/tuten**
for free additional resources related to this chapter.

CHAPTER SUMMARY

As marketers it is critical that we address buyer behavior as more than a needs-based action. Consumers are guided not just by need but also by emotions, beliefs, and situations. Advances in technology have made it even easier for consumers to remove traditional media and advertising with a controlled narrative. This has caused a shift away from the classic consumer decision-making process toward a journey-based model full of micro-moments that brands can leverage into touchpoints. This means that brand awareness advertising and customer service initiatives must be priorities for marketers and these efforts must meet consumers where they are, which is increasingly digital and mobile. The rise of digital influencers and the trust consumers place in peer review continues to decrease the control companies have and instead demands that companies consider how customer experience management affects marketing efforts. In addition, markets must consider the differences in B2C buying behavior and B2B buying behavior. Shifting how marketers approach either type of buyer, from a process to a journey, means fundamentally rethinking the role of marketing in purchase decisions, embracing digital tactics and micro-moments as a way to enhance the consumer's journey instead of trying to control the process.

REVIEW QUESTIONS

1. What is meant by the term buyer behavior?

2. What are the variables included in our understanding of buyer behavior?

3. What are the stages in the classic consumer decision-making model?

4. How has the digital age affected the utility of the classic consumer decision-making model for marketers?

5. How has the base of power shifted between marketers and consumers with access to online tools and information?

6. What is a customer journey and how is it different from the classic decision-making model?

7. What are moments of truth and micro-moments? What is their relationship to customer experience management?

8. How are organizational buyers different from consumers and what characteristics influence their decision-making processes?

KEY TERMS

1. **A-commerce** – automated shopping enabled by innovations like buttons, apps, and even subscription services, which represents a whole new subset of e-commerce.

2. **Affect** – refers to the emotional aspects of attitude.

3. **Availability heuristic** – purchase decision made by choosing an option that is quick and easy.

4. **Behavior** – includes choices and behavioral patterns such as searching for product information online, paying with credit card or mobile payment system, or watching streaming video.

5. **Behavioral economics** – incorporates psychology and economics to understand patterns in buyer decision-making.

6. **B2B (business-to-business)** – marketers study the behavior of organizational buyers.

7. **B2C (business-to-consumer)** – marketers study the behavior of end consumers.

8. **Buying behavior** – how prospective customers evaluate, select, buy, use, and dispose of products.

9. **Buying centers** – committees tasked with purchase decisions and made up of employees with technical, economic, and performance-based expertise relevant to the purchase.

10. **Circular economy** – the recycling of e-waste to extract raw materials and component parts and the redesign of products to facilitate the use of such materials.

11. **Cognition** – captures beliefs and memory structures.

12. **Cognitive dissonance** – occurs if there is a gap between the buyer's attitudes and the outcomes.

13. **Compensatory decision rule** – used when a person selects the brand with the best score based on weighting and evaluating a set of criteria.

14. C2C (consumer-to-consumer) – peer-to-peer marketplaces.

15. Customer dissatisfaction – occurs if expectations are not met.

16. Customer experience management – the process of assessing and improving marketing elements that influence how customers perceive their interactions with the brand.

17. Customer journey – describes consumer decision processes in the context of a digital ecosystem, which recognizes a variety of influence sources, channels, behaviors, decision points, and experiences.

18. Customer journey mapping – used to capture the details of consumer decision-making, and the resulting customer journey maps are then used along with other target audience insights to guide marketing decision-making.

19. Customer satisfaction – occurs if expectations are met or exceeded.

20. E-commerce – using the Internet for commercial transactions.

21. Environment – may include the situation and shopping context, micro-environmental factors, and macro-environmental factors.

22. Evaluative criteria – the criteria include important characteristics for meeting the need in question given the situation; the decision-maker compares the alternatives in the consideration.

23. Evoked set (or consideration set) – a group of relevant brands that a prospective consumer is favorably familiar with when they are thinking about making a purchase.

24. External information sources – outside sources of information such as search engine results, catalogs, online product reviews, buying guides, and salespeople.

25. External stimuli – are those from outside the person such as advertising, the smell of food from a nearby restaurant, and a friend's recommendation.

26. First Moment of Truth (FMOT) – occurs when the customer is considering a product at the point of purchase (POP).

27. Framing – the way choices and related information are presented to prospective buyers.

28. Friction – gaps between what the consumer wanted to experience and the actual experience, particularly if the gap represented a possible barrier to completing the journey.

29. Hard costs – include the monetary price of the products being considered and associated purchase costs like shipping, installation, training, and maintenance agreements.

30. Heuristics (i.e., rules of thumb) – choosing a brand based on loyalty, lowest price, or highest rating.

31. Information search – during this stage, consumers identify possible alternatives to satisfy the need and gather information about the alternatives.

32. Internal source – a consumer may already be knowledgeable about possible options and rely on recalling information stored in memory.

33. Internal stimuli – are those from within the individual such as hunger, thirst, or desire.

34. Marketing funnel (sales funnel or conversion funnel) – the relationship between the classic decision-making process, marketing objectives, and marketing actions is illustrated as a funnel.

35. Micro-moments – intent-driven moments of decision-making and preference-shaping that occur throughout the entire consumer journey.

36. Moment of truth (MoT) – a moment in the customer journey at which the relationship between the consumer and the brand is at stake.

37. Non-compensatory decision rule – eliminates options that fail to meet a minimum requirement on any of the evaluative attributes.

38. Omnichannel commerce – purchases and other buyer-brand interactions in today's digital age may involve many available commercial channels.

39. Planned obsolescence – when companies take steps to make their products obsolete and unusable after a period of time to encourage sales of new products and reduce the time between purchases.

40. Recovery – occurs when brands successfully respond to a customer complaint in such a way that the relationship is strengthened rather than harmed.

41. Representativeness heuristic – purchase decision made by choosing an option that has been shown as the most popular choice by others.

42. Second Moment of Truth (SMOT) – occurs post-purchase as the customer uses the product and evaluates whether the product delivered as expected.

43. Showrooming – used to evaluate a product in an offline store but shifting online to purchase.

44. Soft costs – costs incurred due to related expenses absorbed by the company, such as human resource hours required, potential opportunity costs, and downtime.

45. Stimulus (or trigger) – draws attention to a gap between the person's actual state and desired state of being.

46. Sustainable consumption – the practice of consuming needed products in such a way as to use resources efficiently, minimize emissions and waste, share in the access to products, and contribute to environmental, social, and economic sustainability that will positively impact future generations.

47. Thinslicing – when consumers use heuristics during the purchase decision process when under time pressure or when experiencing mental fatigue from making several decisions.

48. Third Moment of Truth (TMOT) – captures the moment of customer feedback.

49. Touchpoints – the individual interactions people have with brands before, during, and after purchase

50. Voice search – speaking an Internet search request using a voice-assistant such as Amazon Echo's Alexa.

51. Webrooming – used to evaluate information online but purchase in-store.

52. Zero Moment of Truth (ZMOT) – the online search for and discovery of information, a critical moment prior to the FMOT.

PART II

The Marketing Toolbox

Chapter 3

SEGMENTATION, TARGETING, AND POSITIONING

In this chapter, we'll learn the answers to the following questions:

1   What is segmentation and why is it important?

2   What are bases used in segmentation?

3   What is the procedure for segmenting markets?

4   How do marketers choose which segments to target?

5   What role does strategic fit play in the market segments a company ultimately chooses to target?

6   How can companies establish an effective position in the market?

INTRODUCTION

Let's begin with a question: How similar are you to other consumers? Your answer may declare your individuality and uniqueness. Just like your fingerprint, you are unique in all the world. Or your answer may point out that you share some similarities and some differences depending upon the characteristics and others in question. Both answers would be correct and both shine a light on the challenges facing marketers as they seek to gain the attention, meet the needs, and satisfy the expectations of a large and heterogeneous population.

In this chapter, we'll review how marketers gain a competitive advantage by segmenting the market and targeting select groups with brand positioning designed to meet the needs, values, and characteristics of each target segment. The market may include people, groups, or organizations – which we can generically think of as *units* – with needs or wants and the ability and willingness to buy. The three steps marketers use are called the STP model, shown in Figure 3.1:

Step 1: Segment your market.

Step 2: Target the best segment(s).

Step 3: Position the offer.

The model is useful because it helps marketers organize a large, heterogeneous market into meaningful, homogeneous groups and optimize marketing decisions by targeted groups.

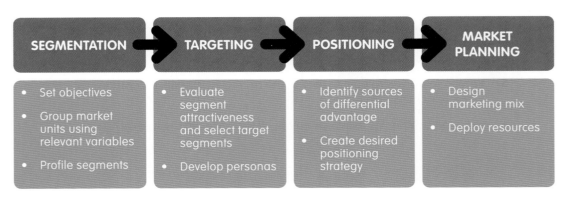

FIGURE 3.1   The STP Model

SEGMENTATION, TARGETING, AND POSITIONING IN THE BEAUTY AND COSMETICS INDUSTRY – HOUSE99

The global beauty and cosmetics market is worth more than $500 billion! Perhaps not surprisingly, most of the sales are attributed to women. Segmentation analyses are leading to shifts in the market including new brand entrants and new products, especially for men. Spending on male personal care products is projected to reach $60 billion by 2020! Despite this, there is a gap in product offerings. Of the more than 2 million skin care products available, just 2% target men. Perhaps it's not surprising then that mass market brands like Dove and luxury brands like Chanel have developed personal care product lines devoted to men.

When it comes to the men's grooming market, the most popular products are functional – deodorant, shampoo and soap, and facial hair care. The market for male skincare and beauty products seemed limited to metrosexuals. Yet in recent years, men report paying more attention to their personal appearance. The range of beauty and personal care products seen as socially acceptable for men has widened. A third of men report spending more than 30 minutes a day on grooming, making men a more attractive target market for beauty brands.

Men are different from women when it comes to personal care purchases. They tend to buy products less frequently (monthly rather than weekly) and spend more for perceived quality. Men also tend to be brand loyal; 67% of men say they buy the same brand for all of their personal care needs. Many men report hesitating to purchase anti-aging, sunscreen, and self-tanner products but their wives and girlfriends are encouraging them to embrace skincare products and habits.

Personal care patterns and purchases vary among men, by demographic, geographic, and psychographic characteristics. Key demographic variables include income level, age, and family life cycle stage. Among men aged 18–44 years in the US, 84% report using skin care products.

It turns out that more than one-third of dads say they care about preventing the signs of aging, compared to 23% of men without kids (Cheng, 2018).

Geographically, the global male grooming product market includes four major regions: US and Canada, Asia-Pacific, Europe, and the rest of the world (including South America, the Middle East, and Africa). Of these, Europe is the most valuable in terms of projected sales. For example, 33% of men in the UK use face creams and lotions. However, French and German men represent challenges. A high percentage of French men report using no grooming products at all and believe personal care products are inherently feminine. German men tend to be price sensitive, resulting in restricted purchases and a preference for inexpensive products sold in supermarkets.

(Continued)

Though Europe is the largest market now, the Asia-Pacific region is growing the fastest. This is likely due to rising incomes and changing gender stereotypes. Korea is leading the way, including sales of male cosmetics like foundation and nail polish. Korean men use an average of 13.3 beauty items per month (Coresight Research, 2017).

At the most basic level, men can be categorized as low or high maintenance from a psychographic standpoint. Low-maintenance men don't use many personal care products, see skincare as feminine, and prefer a simple routine when it comes to personal care. High-maintenance men are more open to a variety of products, especially as a form of self-care and self-expression. Some of the psychographic categories identified for male personal care users include image-conscious achiever, Marlboro man, the player, the road warrior, Joe boxer, and zen man (Inkwood Research, 2019). For instance, the Marlboro man believes personal care products are only for effeminate men. He's rustic, unsophisticated, stubborn, and egotistical. He prefers a barber shop to a salon and sticks to basic products like unscented deodorant and all-in-one hair care products. In the past, marketers assumed men were motivated to use personal care products to attract women. Recent research, though, suggests men are now more motivated by a sense of confidence and to achieve a competitive edge in their careers (Nielsen, 2017). The most common need reported is anti-aging (Mills, 2015). These men want personal care products that are easy to use, made for them (gender-neutral or designed for men – not women), and scent-free.

House99 is among the new brands designed for the male personal care market. Created by David Beckham, House99 segmented the male personal care market drawing upon demographics, geographics, psychographics, behavior, and benefits sought. The chosen target market includes men who want personal care products for their skin, hair, beard, and body. Men can purchase online and join the online brand community or purchase in retail stores like Ulta. First launched in the UK, House99 is now available in 20 countries around the world.

The brand speaks to the motives that are most important to these men – feeling comfortable, trying new things, evolving a personal sense of style and identity. Beckham's masculine and athletic persona is valuable for overcoming the sensitivity men in the target market may feel about embracing products that they might otherwise consider to be feminine. The brand positioning draws from Beckham's celebrity personality and iconic barbershop culture.

SEGMENTATION AND ITS MARKETING VALUE

All organizations exist to provide some kind of product to a target customer. At its core, every aspect of an organization's activity should focus on enabling the success of this essential activity. Without such a focus, organizations become inefficient and risk failure, at least in competitive markets. Segmentation facilitates the identification of new markets and the profiling of market segments. A survey of marketers on the topic of customer segmentation and its uses found that 97% of the companies represented use segmentation to inform decisions about marketing strategy (Forte Consultancy, 2010).

What is market segmentation? Market segmentation is the process of dividing the total market into a number of smaller, more homogeneous sub-markets, called market segments (Campbell, Marshall and Thoeni, 2016). Simply, the members of a market segment share something in common and differ from members of other segments. Segmentation enables marketers to achieve a trade-off between the efficiency of treating all customers the same and the effectiveness of addressing each customer's unique needs and characteristics. Henry Ford is renowned in part for his early and highly efficient one-color-fits-all approach to offering the Model T only in black. Personalized marketing to segments of one represents the epitome of effectiveness: each person or organization in the market has an offer designed perfectly for his or her needs. Segmentation allows the best of both. By grouping the market into similar clusters, each cluster can be targeted with an effective offer, while ensuring the cluster is large enough to achieve efficiency in economies of scale.

Jerry Thomas of Decision Analyst highlights the relationship between market segmentation's purpose and military strategy, explaining: "It's analogous to the military principle of 'concentration of force' to overwhelm an enemy. Concentration of marketing energy (or force) is the essence of all marketing strategy, and market segmentation is the conceptual tool to help achieve this focus" (Thomas, 2017). The basic principles of segmentation date back to the fourth century B.C., when Aristotle urged communicators to create messages that matched their audience's political orientations (Hine, Phillips, Driver and Morrison, 2017). The concept was introduced to marketers in the 1950s (Smith, 1956, cited in Hine et al., 2017). Initially, marketers based segmentation primarily on demographics such as age, gender, education level, and socio-economic status, but eventually other variables like values and preferences were added.

Does segmentation matter? You may have heard that most new products fail. Why? For many, the reason is failure to segment the market successfully. In fact, 85% of 30,000 new product launches fail because of poor market segmentation (Active Marketing, n.d.). Let's consider a world in which "customers" are treated as a single group with the same needs. If everyone was treated the same, marketers would take no account of the different needs of different groups of people. There would be no choices.

Segmentation enables strategic decision-making in terms of the identification of new opportunities, prioritization of those opportunities, development of relevant positioning, and product development. But it also supports tactical decisions across the marketing mix from communications, pricing, and channel decisions. Going beyond the initial use of segmentation for segment identification, re-analysis of segmentation data can answer many valuable questions for marketers (Decision Analyst, 2010).

Figure 3.2 illustrates the central role of segmentation to guiding marketing decisions. At the core, marketers seek to identify prospective customers and understand their needs. Having done so, marketers can anticipate an offer that can meet those needs and achieve a competitive advantage. Lastly, related decisions are made to enable implementation of the marketing strategy for chosen target segments (Wind and Bell, 2008).

Let's consider an example from the beauty and cosmetics industry. Segmentation was the key to BirchBox identifying the market of women who were "beauty indifferents". That was

FIGURE 3.2   The Role of Segmentation in Marketing Strategy

Source: Adapted from Wind and Bell (2008)

a new market opportunity and BirchBox responded with a box of beauty products delivered monthly by subscription. What else could be learned? That same data could be used to answer the following questions: What attitudes tend to drive purchases, cancellations, and renewals? Do customers value the element of surprise in each month's box or the product mix included more? What needs remain unmet that could serve as opportunities to up-sell or cross-sell to customers? What is the mix of cosmetic brands being used by BirchBox customers? Which competitors appeal most to the target segment? Do customers view the competitors in their mix as complements or alternatives? What media habits are prevalent among the target segment? These questions can likely be answered by further analyzing the existing segmentation data. You can see that marketers benefit from segmentation in many ways, as highlighted in Figure 3.3.

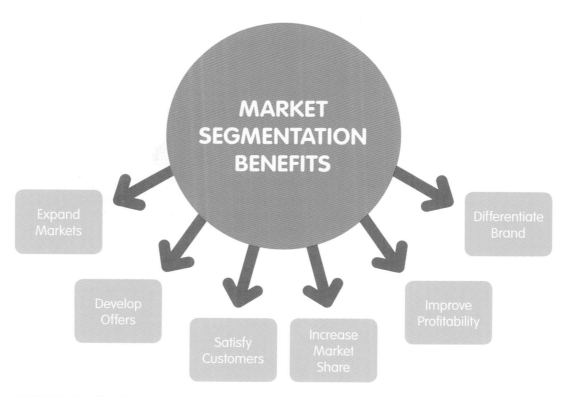

FIGURE 3.3   Benefits of Segmentation

THE BASES FOR SEGMENTATION

Determining the variables – the basis – to use for segmenting the market is a critical step in the process. Both B2C and B2B markets utilize essentially the same basic segmentation bases. Table 3.1 identifies the most common segmentation bases and their variables.

TABLE 3.1   Segmentation Bases and Variables by Market Type

Segmentation Base	Brief Description	Consumer Markets	Business Markets
Demographic/ Firmographic	Grouping market units by categorical, descriptive characteristics; answers "who" questions	• Age • Gender • Income • Occupation • Marital status • Family life cycle • Education • Socio-economic status	• Industry vertical • Size • Performance • Structure • Ownership • Years in business • Customer type • Technology
Geographic	Grouping units in the market using variables tied to location; answers "where" questions	• Region • Country • Geospatial data (e.g., geocode) • Market size • Population density • Climate • Environmental context (e.g., indoor or outdoor) • Language	• Region • Country • Density • Infrastructure • Regulations • Language
Psychographic	Grouping market units using psychological, sociological, and anthropological variables; answers "why" questions	• Motives • Personality traits (e.g., openness, need for variety, impression management) • Values • Attitudes • Interests	• Buyer motives • Organizational personality (i.e., organizational culture, decision style, risk tolerance) • Values (e.g., deal seeker, partner-focused) • Attitudes • Interests
Behavioral	Grouping market units based on past or predicted behavior; answers "how" questions	• Role (e.g., buyer, user, influencer) • Purchase occasions • Customer value (e.g., RFM – recency, frequency, monetary value of purchases) • Usage rate • Readiness stage • Shopping patterns (e.g., searching online, reading reviews, purchase preferences)	• Purchase approach/ decision procedures • Occasion • User status (e.g., RFM) • Usage rate • Readiness stage • Research patterns

Segmentation Base	Brief Description	Consumer Markets	Business Markets
		• Payment patterns • Media consumption (e.g., time spent on social media, magazine readership)	• Payment patterns • Industry engagement (e.g., trade show attendance)
Benefits sought	Grouping market units based on the underlying utility or need driving decisions; answers "what" questions	• Needs/Utility • Jobs-To-Be-Done	• Needs/Utility • Jobs-To-Be-Done

Segmentation analyses may draw from several of these bases depending upon the intended objectives and the data available. Eric Paquette of Copernicus Marketing Consulting & Research explained the impact, saying that "Fifty-nine percent of senior executives in large companies have done a segmentation study in the past 2 years, but only 14% of those senior executives involved in a segmentation study derived any value" (Pekala, 2010). The segmentation bases and variables utilized influence the usefulness of the resulting analysis.

DEMOGRAPHICS AND FIRMOGRAPHICS

Segmentation is valuable, but only if it is done well. In the past, marketers relied heavily on demographic data largely because it was easily accessible and inexpensive to acquire. The characteristics served as proxies for information on the benefits sought and the influences impacting the path to purchase. Reliance on demographic segmentation variables is still common in a priori market segmentation, which classifies the market using a basic understanding of the chosen segmentation variables but does not utilize primary data analysis.

But as the world becomes increasingly multi-cultural, it will be difficult to fit consumers into a single demographic bucket. Unlike decades past, when buying power was mostly concentrated in the hands of the Baby Boomers, there is no longer a "typical" consumer profile (Conroy, Narula and Finn, 2015). Consequently, predicting consumer habits solely by focusing on identifiers such as demographics is misguided. Beauty Boulevard experienced this first hand when it learned that older women were just as likely to buy Glitter Lips as younger women.

Understanding an individual's basic demographic profile doesn't yield the kind of robust insights that businesses need to design marketing strategies. Imagine a hipster couple each earning six figure salaries and living in a poverty-stricken neighborhood in an urban city. If we look at the geographic location, we might assume the couple is poor and not an attractive target. If we look at their income level, we might assume the couple is ripe for targeting by luxury brands. Only by considering multiple variables and gathering other information, such as views toward materialism and gentrification, can we really understand the couple. Forsyth, an executive with McKinsey, put it this way: "You have two people, we know they're the same age, we know they're British citizens, and we know they're of royal blood. One of them is Prince Charles. The other is Ozzy Osbourne, the Prince of Darkness. They're in the same demographic segment, but I can't imagine marketing to them the same way" (Gavett, 2014).

Firmographics, the business market equivalent to demographics, also have the advantage of accessible data and the disadvantage of providing limited insights into the underlying motives and needs driving market behavior. Organizational culture affects purchasing much as individual personality and lifestyles do, resulting in support for using psychographic, behavioral, and benefits sought as bases for segmenting business markets (Barry and Weinstein, 2009).

GEOGRAPHICS

Geographic segmentation variables are growing in relevance. Connected devices capture data including geospatial data, online search patterns like micro-moments, media consumption patterns, and more. When people refer to geospatial data, they are often describing address-related data (a specific address, point of interest, ZIP code, and so on) (Halper, 2013). This data can be matched to a specific latitude and longitude using a process known as geocoding. Rather than anticipating behavior, marketers can capture prospect behavior in real-time, including data on the environmental context. Location data is particularly valuable for marketing to prospects shopping offline. Mobile ads might be tailored and targeted for consumers who happen to be in a certain area or even in or within a small radius of a seller's store at a certain time. For example, prospective customers who are close to a competitor location can be offered a discount to reduce switching behavior. The value of this type of data for segmentation and targeting is evidenced in the growth of real-time location-based advertising expenditures, which is expected to hit $15 billion in 2018 or approximately 40% of total mobile advertising (Spann, Molitor and Daurer, 2016). Some of the marketing decisions that can benefit from location data include advertising in real-time (via mobile devices), advertising special offers to encourage switching behaviors from competitors, dynamic pricing, and store layouts including placement of product categories, point-of-purchase (POP) displays, and in-store advertising (Spann et al., 2016).

Despite the potential value, there are limitations. For instance, GPS data can provide accurate spatial and temporal information about selected people but cannot provide objective data on the activity or purpose of the location. Are the prospects in question at a specific location for personal reasons like shopping or for work? Researchers are studying methods for estimating context tied to geospatial data including heuristic rules, predictive analytics, and machine-learning (Gong, Morikawa and Yamamoto, 2016). What's more – geographic location can limit marketers' ability to use technology for segmentation and targeting. For instance, the EU's General Data Protection Regulation (GDPR) restricts what data marketers collect and how it is used.[1]

PSYCHOGRAPHICS

Psychographics encompasses personality traits, motives, attitudes, and interests. Because psychographic segmentation requires primary data, psychographic studies are oftentimes conducted as syndicated studies of megatrends, geographic regions, and industry verticals. One of the most famous psychographic segmentation schemes is VALS, which classifies consumers by primary motivation (ideals, achievement, or self-expression) and resources.

Forrester's Empowered Customer segmentation framework is a more recent classification model based on five key characteristics: 1) willingness to experiment, 2) self-efficacy, 3) digital/physical integration, 4) information savviness, and 5) device usage (Fleming, 2017).

- Willingness to experiment describes a person's use of emerging technologies and willingness to try new experiences.

- Self-efficacy refers to a person's confidence in his or her ability to effectively use digital services and access information.

- Digital/physical integration explains the extent to which people perceive digital experiences as separate from physical experiences.

- Information savviness captures one's skill at finding, navigating, evaluating, and discerning the value of information.

- Device usage measures the use of connected devices to accomplish everyday tasks.

These five variables explain shifts in consumer behavior and perceived customer empowerment. The most empowered consumers are willing to experiment, reliant on technology, inclined to integrate digital and physical experiences, able to handle large volumes of information, and determined to create the best experiences for themselves. Forrester surveyed thousands of people in Europe, Asia/Pacific, South America, and North America, finding that consumers can be categorized into one of five segments as described in Table 3.2. At one end of the spectrum are Progressive Pioneers, who rapidly evolve and feel most empowered. At the other end are Reserved Resisters, who are wary of change and innovation.

---

[1]General Data Protection Regulation (GDPR) (n.d.) available at Intersoft Consulting, https://gdpr-info. eu/ (accessed 27 May 2019).

TABLE 3.2   Forrester's Empowered Customer Segmentation Framework

Segment	Profile Characteristics
Progressive Pioneers	Heavy online shoppers, heavy reliance on technology, willing to try new technologies, expect seamless digital experiences, comprehensive information consumption skills, opportunity-seeking mindset, high spending power, cord-cutters streaming entertainment online.
Savvy Seekers	Information junkies, receptive to brand-driven and peer-generated online content, active social media users, comfortable with digital payment methods, high levels of digital media consumption.
Convenience Conformers	Willing to experiment, high need for technology, high expectations for seamless digital experiences but lack information savviness and self-efficacy. Prefer mainstream, simple digital services that enhance convenience but are not innovators or early adopters.
Settled Survivors	Average reliance on technology, unlikely to adopt emerging technologies, most use traditional retail stores and payment methods.
Reserved Resisters	Highly risk-averse, lowest interaction with digital information resources, rarely shop online, unlikely to use digital services experience innovation, tend to be older with lowest income.

Source: Lai (2016) *The Rise of the Empowered Customer.* Forrester.

JOBS-TO-BE-DONE FOR SEGMENTATION

The **Jobs-To-Be-Done** (JTBD) **theory**, introduced in Chapter 2 as a way to better understand customer needs, has gained popularity for segmentation analyses based on understanding benefits sought. Ulwick, the theory's creator, advised that "companies should stop focusing on the product and the customer and instead should understand the 'underlying process' (or job) the customer is trying to execute when they are using a product or service" (Ulwick, 2017c). The theory holds that in order to create a product or service that customers will want to buy, marketers must understand the outcomes prospective customers are seeking. For this reason, JTBD theory is closely tied to **Outcome-Driven Innovation (ODI)**, Ulwick's approach to marketing strategy.

The key takeaway behind using the JTBD framework for market segmentation is this: "A customer's unmet needs, need priorities, and preference for solutions often vary by context – but they are consistent within context when you segment around unmet needs" (Ulwick, 2017d). Clay Christensen explains that customers "hire" products because they need a specific job performed, not because they belong to a certain segment (Christensen, Hall, Dillon and Duncan, 2016).

To use JTBD as a segmentation variable, marketers must answer these questions:

1. What functional job is your customer trying to get done at each stage of the customer journey? (Ulwick, 2017b)

2. What does the customer need (desired outcomes) at each stage? (McAllister, 2017)

The first question is answered by creating a job map, which depicts the eight process stages people experience to complete a job. Table 3.3 lists the stages in a job map. The second question is answered by identifying the desired outcomes consumers may have at each stage. They will be expressed in need statements following this formula: verb + metric + object of control + contextual clarifier. For example, "minimize the time it takes to identify the most popular cosmetic products for my beauty routine" is a desired outcome associated with the core job of buying cosmetics. The unmet needs reflected in the desired outcomes are then applied as the segmentation variable used to group the market into segments (Ulwick, 2017a). A need is unmet when it is not satisfied with the products/services currently being used (Ulwick, 2017a).

TABLE 3.3   The Stages in a Job Map for the Jobs-To-Be-Done (JTBD) Theory

Stage
1. Define
2. Locate
3. Prepare
4. Confirm
5. Execute
6. Monitor
7. Modify
8. Conclude

Using JTBD results in a different view of the marketplace and a deeper understanding of the consumers in that market. For example, rather than viewing the cosmetics market as people who may purchase make-up and skincare, we would consider what job those people are trying to accomplish.

THE SEGMENTATION PROCEDURE

There are six main stages in the segmentation procedure, as shown in Figure 3.4.

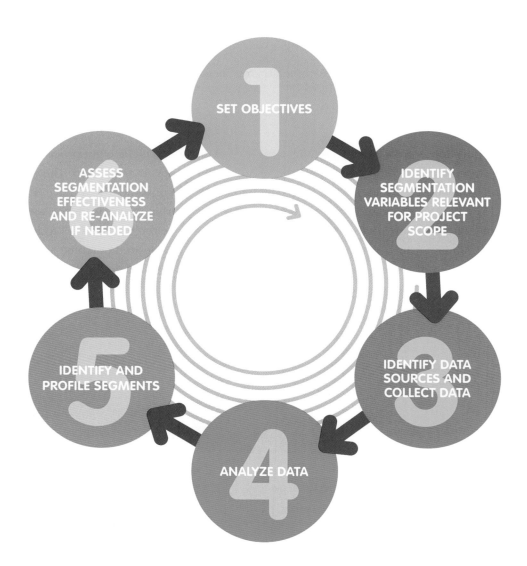

FIGURE 3.4   The Segmentation Procedure

STEP 1: SET OBJECTIVES

The first step is to identify the objectives guiding the segmentation analysis. Generally, segmentation objectives may be strategic, managerial, or operational (Thoeni, Marshall and Campbell, 2016). Strategic segmentation can inform an organization's mission and strategic focus by identifying fundamental needs in the market (Morgan and Piercy, 1993). Managerial segmentation guides resource allocation and marketing planning. Operational segmentation focuses on the execution of the marketing mix. For example, in our opening vignette, segmentation may initially have sought to identify opportunities in the personal care market.

STEP 2: IDENTIFY SEGMENTATION VARIABLES RELEVANT FOR PROJECT SCOPE

The bases and their variables tie back to the internal and external influences on buyer behavior we discussed in Chapter 2. Thinking about which of these bases and variables are influential in the customer journey is instrumental in choosing the right variables for segmentation. In this age of big data and marketing automation, segmentation can be based on potentially hundreds of variables or on a single behavioral indicator. Presumably, any variable could be used as a basis to segment a market, but the results will only add value if the variables are relevant to the marketing objectives. For example, if we seek to identify new product concepts, segmenting on needs and benefits sought will be relevant; for pricing decisions – price sensitivity, deal-seeking, and value perceptions; for advertising decisions – media usage, lifestyle, and benefits sought; for distribution decisions – online shopping behaviors and store preferences. The variables chosen should differentiate among segments based on their response to marketing variables (e.g., buyers vs. non-buyers, deal-seekers vs. brand loyalists, etc.). In addition, variables that describe key characteristics like demographics can be useful for profiling segments. Benefits sought and psychographics are valuable, but these variables are hard to observe (Chiang, 2017). Demographic/firmographic variables are easy to observe but have little meaning. The distinctions are illustrated in Figure 3.5.

STEP 3: IDENTIFY DATA SOURCES AND COLLECT DATA

Traditionally, three types of data exist. First-party data is captured over the course of a direct relationship with a customer, as part of a company's customer relationship management system.

Second-party data is obtained through a direct relationship with a non-competitive brand partner, such as Google or Facebook. This is essentially another company's first-party data shared in an aggregated and anonymized format. Third-party data, sometimes called compiled data, is off-the-shelf data that can be purchased from data aggregators such as credit agencies. Besides these traditional data types, deterministic data identifies a single user across a range of situations, devices (e.g., tablet, mobile phone, laptop), and environments (web browser, mobile app, social media website) (Giametta and Krakovsky, 2018). Primary data may also be collected using surveys specifically for use in segmentation analysis. Hybrid segmentation utilizes multiple data sources drawn from a combination of different types of consumer data to build a picture of the market (Ritson, 2017).

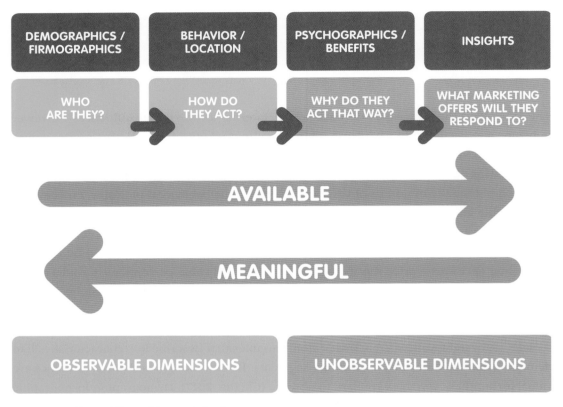

FIGURE 3.5   Observability and Segmentation Bases

STEP 4: ANALYZE DATA

The data is analyzed to produce segments that are homogeneous within each segment and heterogeneous between segments with respect to the chosen segmentation variables. The specific analytic techniques used will vary depending upon the segmentation objectives, variables, and data formats. Typical analytical techniques for segmentation include cluster analysis, factor analysis, and choice modeling (Horn and Huang, 2016).

STEP 5: IDENTIFY AND PROFILE SEGMENTS

The segments produced by the data analysis will be identified and profiled to provide information on the size of the segment, expected growth and profit potential, and other information that will be useful as the company evaluates the segments as possible target markets. The profiles provide the information necessary for selecting the segments to target.

STEP 6: ASSESS SEGMENTATION EFFECTIVENESS AND RE-ANALYZE IF NEEDED

The final step is to assess the effectiveness of the segmentation analysis. Even if the objectives were successfully met, there may be value in segmentation re-analysis to extract additional insights to guide marketing decisions.

TARGETING

In the next step in the STP model, we decide to target one or more segments. Organizations that pursue mass marketing do not differentiate offers by target segment. Instead, they try to cover the market with one offer. Organizations benefit from segmentation by using a multi-segment strategy of positioning differentiated offers for each targeted segment. Organizations can achieve synergy across multiple segments with product or market specialization. Firms can also follow a concentration strategy by choosing a niche, only one segment to target. Access to online behavioral data and marketing automation makes micro-segments and individualized segments of one viable target (Moran, 2016). The multi-segment strategy is most common, with approximately 75% of marketing organizations using this differentiated approach (Weinstein, 2014). Figure 3.6 illustrates how these targeting approaches vary in their underlying view of the market, from broad to narrow.

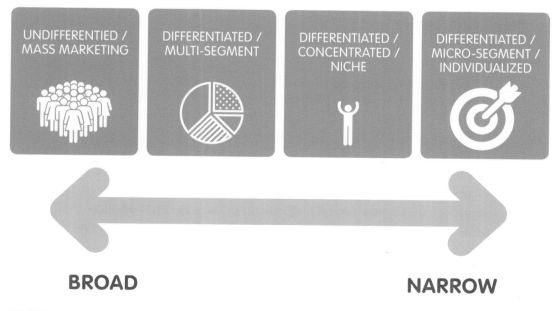

FIGURE 3.6   Targeting Approaches

TARGET MARKET SELECTION

How do marketers choose which segments to target? The choice is determined by segment attractiveness and strategic fit. The relative attractiveness of segments can be assessed using the following characteristics (Gavett, 2014):

1. Identifiable – Can we identify prospects with the segment's characteristics?

2. Substantial – Is the size of the segment large enough to be potentially profitable?

3. Accessible – Can the segment members be reached via media and distribution channels?

4. Durable – Will the segment be stable long enough for the company to market to it?

5. Differentiable – Are the prospects in the segment homogeneous within the segment, but different from those in other segments?

6. Actionable – Do the insights produced by the segmentation analysis clearly inform marketing strategy and tactics? Is the segment likely to be responsive to marketing tactics?

Organizations further assess strategic fit using the following questions (Wind, [1978] 2018):

- Which segments' needs are unmet? Which segments' needs can the organization best satisfy?

- What are the likely costs of effectively reaching the target segment? Does the organization have the necessary resources and competencies to effectively reach and serve the segment?

- Which segments will be the most profitable? Which are sufficiently valuable and/ or expected to grow?

- What is the competitive threat associated with each segment? Does the organization have a differential advantage to leverage against the competition?

Answering these questions about the different market segments defined during the segmentation analysis guides the selection of segments to target. Importantly, firms with a strong emphasis on competitive analysis as part of the target market selection process are more successful in target marketing. Assessing attractiveness and strategic fit can also help organizations avoid common targeting mistakes (Thomas, 2017), including targeting a segment that isn't substantial, targeting too many segments, or failing to identify universal characteristics across segments.

TARGET MARKET PROFILING

Once target segments are selected, customer journeys and buyer personas are developed for each target segment. A buyer persona is a snapshot of a prototypical customer in the target segment. It tells the buyer's story using the information you used for segmentation (i.e., demographic, geographic, psychographic, benefits sought, and behavior). This 'bio' provides a composite sketch of the desired target market. A template is shown in Figure 3.7. The segment profiles identified during the segmentation phase inform the journeys and personas, providing texture.

With personas, marketers are better able to identify, understand, acquire, engage, and retain the target audience. For example, Geckoboard, a company offering data visualization software for social media analytics, describes its buyer persona as a young to middle-aged founder or chief executive-level decision-maker, at an organization in a high-growth, digital business with 11–200 employees, located in the United States, Western Europe, Australia, or Canada (Tyson, 2016).

Creating journey maps for each persona highlights aspects of the customer experience that can be designed to perform better at the moments of truth (covered in Chapter 2). For example, research into the beauty customer journey emphasizes the relevance of online shopping (Lang and Zhu, 2017). About two-thirds of consumer beauty purchases were made at brick-and-mortar stores, but more than 70% of buyers used digital touchpoints such as viewing beauty brand posts on Instagram, reading online reviews, watching beauty how-to videos on YouTube, and searching for web coupons at some point in their journey. Social media are especially influential during the discovery phase of the journey. In fact, 46% of beauty buyers don't know which brands they may choose when they begin the purchase process. Beauty buyers who purchase online are more likely to choose premium brands and less likely to be brand loyal. Those who shop in a physical store want a personalized point-of-sale experience with well-designed product displays and knowledgeable salespeople. The 'Beauty Sleuth' persona is portrayed in Figure 3.8.

Digital analytics facilitate targeting micro-segments and even segments of one by applying predictive modeling to target profile data, ranking prospects by value and responsiveness, and selecting optimal targets (Saxena, 2018). It is this use of technology for targeting that makes personalization at the individual level possible. In fact, some industry experts believe individualization is the future of marketing (Parsons, 2017a).

Targeting choices and understanding the characteristics and preferences of the target segments is key to every subsequent decision that marketers make about the marketing mix. Whether product portfolio decisions, product design, service design, pricing, distribution, marketing communications, customer experience, branding, or customer relationship management, targeting informs marketing.

Ernst & Young's (EY) research into the future consumer (learn more at www.ey.com/en_gl/future-consumer-now) predicts an interesting dilemma facing marketers (Rogers and Cosgrove, 2018). AI bots already facilitate some purchases, and as these systems become more intelligent, they'll likely complete many of the purchases for us.

The technologies will evaluate what products we need, when we need them and where best to buy them, and find the right price, all while sourcing brands and suppliers that align with our values. In so doing, they will preempt conscious choice. People will trust these intermediary technologies to curate the right choices and purchases on our behalf. Already, 47% of consumers say they are open to the idea of buying products using chatbots.

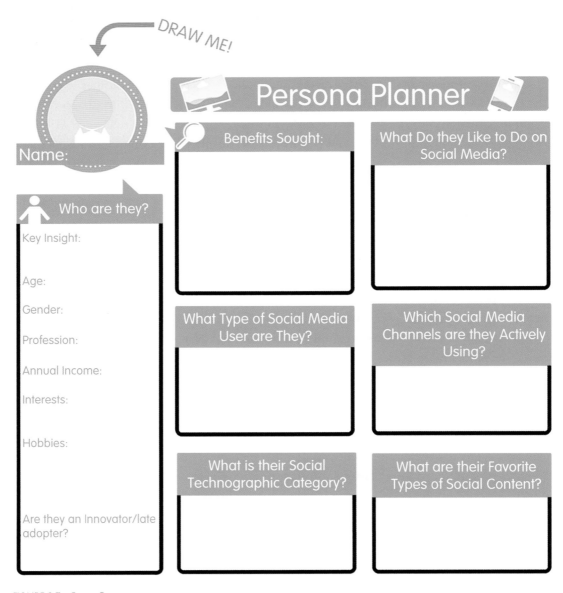

FIGURE 3.7   Buyer Persona

Meet The BEAUTY SLEUTH

A well-connected consumer who enjoys discovering & experimenting with products

Who is she?

Cora is a 34 year-old, married professional living in an urban area. As an advertising account manager, she works in a professional environment filled with people sporting the latest in fashion; her major interests now are fashion and beauty. She loves luxury brands like *Max Mara* and *MAC*. While she's known to splurge on special items, she counts on retailers like *H&M* and *ZARA*, as well as outlet malls, to maintain a wardrobe that is on trend. *Instagram* is her go-to social network where she follows several beauty brands and fashion influencers. When it comes to beauty products, **Cora** wants products that follow currents trends in color, texture, and style.

64% of millennials believe being active on social media is important

 12 magazine issues/month
vs. 10.2 for total women

 **60%** desire to stand out of the crowd

 22 hours online per week
vs. 19.5 for total women

63% are more likely to trust blogger and user reviews over a brand's claims

34 hours TV per week
vs. 32.8 for total women

 89% of millennials consider eating healthily important for wellness & beauty

 17 hours radio per week
vs. 32.8 for total women

FIGURE 3.8   The Beauty Sleuth Persona

Over time, people will become disengaged from most product purchases. If the prediction is correct, targeting may become a specialized skill reserved for the few brands that maintain engagement with the customer. Or marketers may be tasked with learning how to effectively target the bots.

POSITIONING

The final step in the STP model is positioning. Positioning is the process of designing a brand's offer and meaning to occupy a specific place relative to the competition in the mind of the target market. Just as the segmentation analysis informed selecting and profiling of the target segments, knowledge of the needs, preferences, and characteristics informs the positioning strategy. A positioning strategy should differentiate the brand from the competition and create and reinforce desirable brand associations. It answers the question, "What do we want the target segment to perceive about the brand, relative to the competing brands?".

IDENTIFYING THE POSITIONING STRATEGY

Specifying the positioning strategy requires identifying a competitive frame of reference and the brand's points of differentiation (PODs) relative to the desires of the target segment (Kotler and Keller, 2015). The competitive frame of reference is the set of brands offering substitutable products and competing for the target market's business. Brands typically have points of parity as well. Points of parity (POPs) are attributes that are similar across competitors and considered necessary to compete in the product category. Differentiation involves creating differences in the brand's offer that sets it apart from the competition. These differences make up the points of differentiation, the brand associations that are perceived as unique relative to the competition. They provide a differential advantage. When a POD is a tangible characteristic, it is called a unique selling proposition. For instance, Estée Lauder anti-aging products feature Moringa extract as an exclusive key ingredient (Trefis Team and Great Speculations, 2016). You can think of the place where the brand's point of differentiation meets the target market's desires as the positioning sweet spot. We see this in the four Ds used to select the brand attributes to feature as points of differentiation in a positioning strategy: 1) desirable to the target market, 2) deliverable by the brand, 3) different from competitors, and 4) durable (sustainable) over time (Kotler and Keller, 2015).

Much like the segmentation bases, there are several bases that may be used to identify points of differentiation for positioning. In principle, companies can position their brands on an almost infinite number of associations. For example, cosmetic brands can be positioned on function, benefits, price, quality, ingredients, values, stylishness, user, distribution, country-of-origin, customer experience, and brand personality. For example, Lush cosmetics emphasizes its values of fresh, organic ingredients, social good, and no animal testing (Lush, n.d.). Some of the available positioning bases are highlighted in Table 3.4.

TABLE 3.4   Positioning Bases

Positioning Base	Descriptive Options
Price/Quality	Cost leader/value, reasonable price, value for money, affordability, premium/exclusive, upper class, top of range, status, prestigious
Leadership	Proven market leader, success, size, innovation, heritage/history
User/Surrogate	Persona, lifestyle (current or aspirational), user values
Problem solution	Functional, rational reasons product solves problem
Excellence	Performance-focus – best, biggest, most
Transformational	Brand image and ideal self, symbolism
Usage moment	Occasion like everyday use, special events (e.g., vacation, wedding)
Emotion	Romance/love, happiness/joy, fear, confidence
Values	Social good, environmental sustainability, animal protection, natural/organic, well-being
Brand story	Brand narrative, brand journalism, cultural branding, brand archetype
Service/Concern for customer	Impressive service, personal attention, consider people as important, friendly
Country of origin	Patriotism, regions of excellence
Aesthetics/Design	Attractiveness, good aesthetics and product design, attractive, cool, modern/trendy, classic
Reliability	Reliable, durable, warranty, safety
Attribute/Features	Product features

Source: This list draws upon several sources including Aaker (2014); Blankson and Kalafatis (2004); Fuchs and Diamantopoulos (2010); Luth Research (2016); Lamb, Hair and McDaniel (2013)

The positioning strategy should be formalized in a positioning statement. Positioning statements communicate the strategy to internal audiences who make marketing decisions. The traditional positioning statement typically includes four elements: 1) the target market, 2) the product category (or competitive frame of reference), 3) the key benefit, and 4) reasons to believe the benefit claim. The template for positioning statements is as follows:

To [insert target definition/customer group], [brand name] is the brand of [competitive frame of reference] that provides [benefit]. That's because [reasons to believe].

Consider this example for Aveeno (Namaky, 2016):

To women who believe nature has the power to enhance beauty in a healthy way, Aveeno® is the affordable skincare brand that supports naturally healthy skin. Unlike conventional skincare brands, only Aveeno® contains ACTIVE NATURALS® ingredients selected from nature for their safe and effective skincare benefits, tested rigorously, and recommended by professionals.

The positioning strategy is related to the value proposition, an assertion of the reasons the target market should choose the brand's offer (Kotler and Keller, 2015). It articulates the brand's most enduring and valuable benefit (Phillips, 2012). The template for expressing a value proposition is:

For [insert target definition/customer group], [brand name's product] with [point of differentiation] provides [key benefit].

Aveeno's value proposition is stated as follows:

Aveeno® products harness the power of ACTIVE NATURALS® ingredients, sourced from nature and uniquely formulated, to deliver real benefits for your skin and hair.

The positioning strategy and value proposition are expressed to the target market in the form of a tagline or slogan, a short and memorable phrase that captures the essence of the brand promise. Aveeno's tagline is "naturally beautiful" (www.aveeno.com).

USING POSITIONING MAPS

Developing positioning maps is useful for identifying open positions in the competitive frame of reference and clarifying possible points of differentiation. The position map (also called a perceptual map) displays the competing brands based on their respective positions on two dimensions. Creating a positioning map requires three steps: 1) define the market (the competitive frame of reference) and relevant needs of the target market, 2) choose the two dimensions, and 3) plot the positions of each competing brand (D'Aveni, 2007). Figure 3.9 illustrates an example of a positioning map for the cosmetics industry based on price and the type of ingredients used.

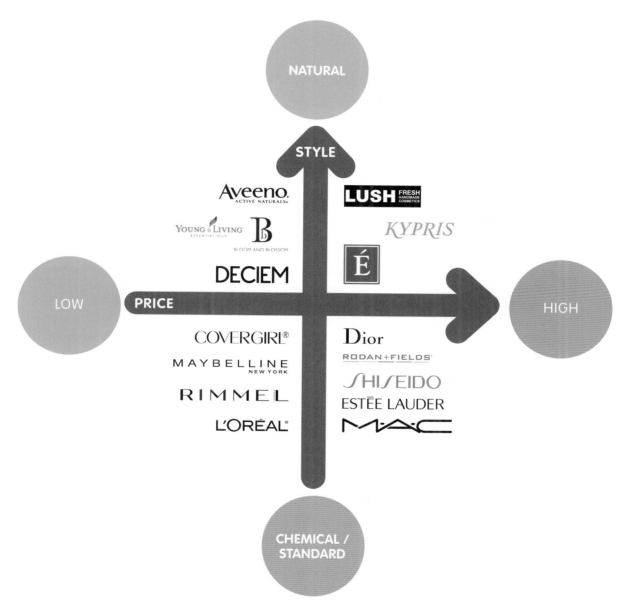

FIGURE 3.9   An Example of a Positioning Map

Once the positioning strategy is selected, it guides decisions in all areas of the marketing mix. In other words, the offer operationalizes the brand's desired position.

ING'S YOLT MOBILE BANKING APP TARGETS MILLENNIALS

Mobile banking is among the most popular smartphone activities, offering customers the convenience to bank anywhere, anytime without visiting a bank branch. By 2023, 72% of adults in the UK will use a smartphone banking app to manage their accounts (Croxford, 2018). That figure is already near 90% among millennials. Estimates are similar in the US. The popularity has in part been spurred by open banking, a UK policy that allows banks to share customer financial data with other service providers (other financial services organizations as well as providers of energy, telecom, and so on).

There's no doubt that mobile banking customers want convenience and functional capabilities like depositing a check with a photo, checking account balances on the go, and paying with the phone. But what about the banking brands? Though most mobile banking apps are quite similar, mobile banking customers are less likely to switch banks. Thus, banks can better retain customers by offering a mobile app and encouraging customers to use the app. A study of the reasons behind mobile banking apps found that 29% of banks wanted to retain existing customers, 24% needed to maintain competitive parity, 23% sought to acquire new customers, and 21% used the app to signal their market leadership in technology (Magids and Leemon, 2017).

ING, a Dutch bank operating in more than 40 countries and serving more than 35 million customers, is performing significantly better than many other financial institutions in terms of profitability, innovation, customer growth, and customer satisfaction (Muijs, 2016). Yolt, ING's mobile banking app, is certainly one of the reasons for the company's success. Yolt can combine all of a user's finances in one mobile platform, including checking, savings, credit card, and investment accounts and even from multiple organizations with open banking (Visser, 2018). Integrating financial data from different bank accounts provides Yolt with an extensive data set from which the application can analyze financial behavior. In this way, the app can predict balances, make budgeting recommendations, and explain spending patterns – all of which helps customers have more control over their money. The app is already used by more than 500,000 customers (Mobile Payments Today, 2017).

When so many banks offer mobile banking apps, how did ING effectively segment the market, understand the target markets, and position its app? Several distinct, mobile banking customer segments were identified. One was selected as a target market priority. Insights derived from a persona were used to position Yolt as the smartest money platform.

Yolt, like other ING products, was designed with the intent to provide a distinctive, strong, and positive customer experience. In so doing, ING believes customers will choose ING as their primary bank relationship (even if they have secondary relationships with credit card brands, brokerage accounts, and so on). ING encourages customers to use multiple ING products and services because this enhances ING's data analytics and subsequent ability to personalize services to meet customer needs.

Table 3.5 lists the relevant segmentation variables by segmentation base selected for the segmentation analysis. Figure 3.10 describes the characteristics of the four segments identified by the segmentation analysis: 1) Aspirational Affluents, 2) Social Strugglers, 3) Secure Self-service, and 4) Cautious Conservatives.[2]

TABLE 3.5   Selected Segmentation Bases and Variables

Demographics	Psychographics	Geographics	Behavior	Benefits Sought/JTBD
Age	Security concerns	Country	Mobile app usage	Deposit checks
Income	Trust in technology	Proximity to bank branch	Bank branch visits	Prevent fraud
Gender	Financial literacy	Proximity to ATM	Banking activities	Track/control spending
Education	Financial locus of control	Location, bandwidth/connectivity	Online bill paying	Feel smart
Occupation	Time-starvation	Population density	Monitoring finances	Make good financial decisions
Ethnicity	Financial self-efficacy	Ratio of region's physical store sales to online sales	Use diversity of smartphone functions	Reduce debt
Amount of debt	Communication preferences	Payment modes commonly accepted in region	Time spent online/on smartphone	Build long-term wealth
Financial literacy level	Willingness to share personal data	Climate	Payment methods	Save time
Family life cycle stage	Financial aspirations	Zip code characteristics	Online shopping	Help society

[2]Hypothetical segments and persona examples are drawn from information and personas described in Dintrans, Fuloria, Craver and Winitz (2013); Marous (2015); Ross and Srinivas (2018).

(Continued)

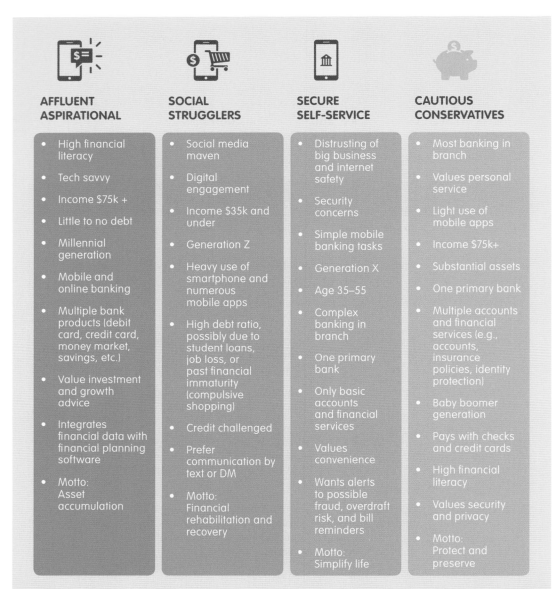

FIGURE 3.10   Segments Identified

Yolt followed a segmentation approach called BYOP, bring your own persona. The term is meant to emphasize the importance of including digital communication preferences, digital competencies using latest technology (e.g., apps, chatbots, location services, digital wallet payments), and degree of trust in sharing personal information via digital channels in persona descriptions (Marous, 2015; Cocheo, 2018; Marous, 2018). Figure 3.11 illustrates a persona developed for the Affluent Aspirational segment. This segment was selected as

Persona: Affluent Aspirational

"Success and achievement measured by accumulation of wealth.
    Show me the money."

AGE: 23–37 (millennial)

INCOME: $75k+

WORK: Knowledge worker (e.g., analyst, marketing manager, programmer)

FAMILY: 23–30 Single but may co-habit 31–37 Married, family

LOCATION: Global, 66% in Asia

CHARACTER: Optimistic, risk-averse, DIY decision-maker, tech-savvy, active on social media, value relationships, purpose-driven

PERSONALITY

Introvert	Extrovert
Thinking	Feeling
Sensing	Intuition
Judging	Perceiving

Online Social Premium Personal

TOP FINANCIAL GOALS

- Increase income
- Repay student loans
- Buy a home
- Repay credit card or other debt
- Save/invest for retirement

FRUSTRATIONS

- Biggest financial challenge is not knowing where to obtain information to make an educated financial decision
- Majority report dissatisfaction with available banking services and past experience
- Don't trust banks–banks are just trying to sell to get fees and commissions
- 75% worry banking systems will be hacked and their data will be stolen

FAST FACTS

- Considered the heart of the financial services market.
- Most report high levels of financial literacy but tests suggest a knowledge gap.
- Only 45% maximize contributions to 401k and other tax-deferred investment vehicles.
- Only 52% maintain an emergency fund that can cover six months' living costs.
- 81% believed they will be more financially successful than their parents.
- 78% of millennials believe that their finances will improve.
- Just 15% use a professional financial advisor, while others follow DIY decisions, ask friends for advice, and use automated recommendations engines.

MOTIVATION

Security

Fear/Desire to avoid risk

Achieve wealth as indication of success

Affiliation/Social relationships

Societal contributions

BRANDS & INFLUENCERS

amazon   UNDER ARMOUR

BBC   Waitrose

BMW

Uber   ZARA

PREFERRED CHANNELS

Mobile only

Branch only

Online-dominant, hybrid

Guerrilla Efforts & PR

FIGURE 3.11   Target Segment Persona: Affluent Aspirational

The original file is here: https://app.extensio.com/5549hzyp

(Continued)

a target, because of the potential profitability of the segment, the segment's demand for mobile banking services, the segment's characteristics as tech-savvy, connected, smartphone-reliant, and willingness to share financial data in exchange for personalized and convenient financial services. While still in the early years of wealth accumulation, the size of the segment (40% of the global adult population are millennials and 13% are affluent millennials) makes them important to the banking industry. According to Deloitte, the aggregated net worth of global millennial populations is expected to more than double by 2020, with estimates ranging from $19 trillion to $24 trillion (Marous, 2018).

Other key insights gleaned from the segmentation analysis and persona development provided guidance for Yolt's positioning strategy.

- People want to be in *control* of their finances and *financial health* but they'd rather spend time on other priorities like career, personal relationships, and *enjoying life*. How could Yolt make money management effective and enjoyable?

- Many are *intimidated* by the *perceived complexity* of finances and budgeting. People can feel *fearful* that they'll make bad decisions, lose money, make mistakes like overdrawing an account, or fall prey to fraud. How could Yolt make money management *simple, easy, error-proof, and safe*?

- People use money every day in many forms (pay apps, cash, check, credit card, debit card, bitcoin) and diverse situations. How could Yolt create solutions in the app that are designed for *real-life situations*?

- Some banking segments have a relatively low profitability level. How could Yolt automate and digitize repetitive, low-value, and low-risk processes to increase *efficiency* and lower costs for ING? (Whitehouse, Goslinga, Michna, Gawinecki and Menier, 2016).

- Research into the most profitable banking customers revealed that customers who feel an *emotional connection* to their bank are six times more valuable and five times less likely to switch banks than even customers who are highly satisfied but do not feel emotional attachment. An emotional connection occurs when customers connect their deepest motivations, values, and aspirations to a brand. Customers who were categorized as emotionally connected tended to use four or more bank products, conduct most financial business with one primary bank, and make seven times more transactions compared to other customers. To reap the benefits, Yolt needed to discover what features and benefits could build emotional connections with customers.

- Because mobile banking apps are comparable, Yolt needed to build in *unique, value-added benefits* to differentiate the brand and encourage app usage. Some of the most valuable app services include checking account balances, transferring money between accounts (and other people), depositing checks, searching for information like interest rates, budgeting, analyzing spending patterns, tracking receipts for tax-deductible or reimbursable expenses, and alerting users to fraud (Ross and Srinivas, 2018).

Frank Jan Risseeuw, Yolt's CEO, said: "In modern life, the phrase 'time is money' has never felt more apt, but fewer people have either the time or the desire to actually look after their money effectively. Instant gratification is the norm. People want convenience, speed, and personalization. Yolt understands that. We make it easier for people to concentrate on the other things in life" (RFi Group, 2017).

YOLT'S POSITIONING STRATEGY

The target persona and other insights informed Yolt's positioning strategy, including the features necessary to deliver the desired benefits and a brand identity to reinforce the desired perception in the minds of target customers. Of course, Yolt's design ensured mandatory points of parity were present in the app. The open banking platform capable of incorporating personal data from multiple accounts and third-party service providers was a point of differentiation, because Yolt was the first open banking mobile app. To address the gap between Affluent Aspirationals' perceived financial knowledge and actual financial literacy, a financial literacy education program was embedded in the app, featuring learning paths, lesson plans, high-quality video-shorts, gamified "test your knowledge" quizzes, and achievement badges to reward success. These features optimized the financial management benefits of the app and primed customers for higher order intangible values. The brand messaging sought to establish an emotional connection by activating the target market's esteem needs. You can see these feelings in the keywords chosen in Yolt's positioning statement.

> For Affluent Aspirationals, Yolt's *money platform* [comprehensive, value-added service capabilities, security] is built to give *everyone* [inclusivity and social respect] the *power* [self-determination, control, independence] to be *smart* [confidence, self-efficacy, financial literacy] with their money, allowing them to "*unthink money*" [stop worrying, no fear] and *live life to the fullest* [terminal value – happy, fulfilling life]. The slogan reinforces the position – "unthink money".

PRME BOX

SEGMENTATION AND TARGETING FACILITIES: SUCCESSFUL CLIMATE CHANGE INITIATIVES

Climate action is one of the sustainable development goals. The size of the consumer market motivated to prioritize climate protection in their consumption behaviors is growing. As the market becomes more substantial, organizations

(Continued)

targeting the market will position themselves to address climate change concerns in their product offerings, distribution decisions, and marketing communications. They are implementing more efficient technology and resource management practices in operations and supply chains, and developing products that enable consumers to reduce their carbon impact. Marks & Spencer is an example of a company dedicated to business practices that protect the climate, evidenced by its Plan A initiative. In addition to climate change, M&S's Plan A also includes food and health and ethical sourcing goals.

While it might seem like brands should be eager to embrace business decisions that protect against climate change, the STP model sheds light on the complexities facing brands. Climate concerns are part of a trend known as purpose-led purchasing. Consumers and organizations can participate in mitigation and adaptation actions to protect against climate change effects. Mitigation actions reduce greenhouse gas emissions, while adaptation refers to activities that reduce harm or risk of harm, or realize benefits associated with climate variability and climate change. Consumers participate in adaptation activities in part by choosing to buy from "green" organizations. The prevalence of sustainable shopping varies by region of the world. For example, 53% of shoppers in the UK and 78% in the US say they feel better when they buy products that are sustainably produced, but that number rises to 88% in India and 85% in Brazil. Why the differences? One reason is direct exposure to the negative impact of unsustainable business practices, such as water and energy shortages, food poverty, and poor air quality (Unilever, 2017). A segmentation analysis of British consumers and their attitudes toward climate change mitigation identified seven segments: Positive Greens, Waste Watchers, Concerned Consumers, Sideline Supporters, Cautious Participants, Stalled Starters, and Honestly Disengaged (Hine et al., 2017).

M&S's Plan A explains its commitment to mitigation and adaptation activities in its business practices. But brands are driven by return on investment. Ideally, positioning the M&S brand as one committed to sustainability will drive sales and brand loyalty among green target segments. The company identified four segments:

1. Green Zealots: people who actively seek out the most ethically and environmentally responsible products. Climate change is a particularly important issue to these people.

2. Concerned Consumers: people who are interested and concerned, but also feel uncertain as to how to shop to achieve their ethical objectives.

3. Sidelined Supporters: people who are aware of the problem, but aren't convinced that their personal actions have an impact.

4. Disengaged: people who do not prioritize sustainability issues (Goodall, 2007).

M&S believes its Plan A initiative is the right commitment for the company, but the segment most motivated to buy from green brands (the Green Zealots) makes up only

5–10% of the market. Further analysis of the segments revealed millennial consumers are a large portion of the Green Zealot segment. With that insight, M&S joined Collectively, a global movement launched to engage millennial consumers in new approaches to consumption. Collectively intends to enable audiences to raise awareness and inspire millennials to adopt a more sustainable way of living (M&S, n.d.). It focuses on things millennials feel passionate about – food, fashion, design, and technology. M&S developed its Limited London collection to show that sustainable fashion can look good and protect against climate change. Every garment is made from recycled fabric in a factory that meets environmental and ethical best practice standards (Hobbs, 2016).

online resources

Visit **https://study.sagepub.com/tuten** for free additional resources related to this chapter.

CHAPTER SUMMARY

The STP model exists to balance the trade-off marketers must make between the effectiveness in treating consumers like unique individuals and the efficiency in treating every customer similarly. Segmentation is important when marketing to a group because it allows marketers to formulate strategies to reach multiple consumers, but with an offer seemingly designed for the needs and wants of each individual in that group. Today's marketers must move beyond the classic bases for segmentation – demographic, geographic, psychographic, etc. – toward a more dynamic segmentation based on nuanced variables like consumer empowerment and the outcome consumers are seeking when looking for products and services. Correctly identifying segments and effectively targeting those segments helps marketers to maximize return on investment (ROI). After segmenting the market, each target segment has to be assessed for strategic fit with the sales and marketing goals of the organization. Those that "fit" are then distilled into usable buyer personas and out of these personas flows the design of offers that appeal to the chosen target segments relative to the competition. Think of this task as physically placing the product or service next to all its competitors and identifying a way to differentiate it, positioning how your buyer personas perceive the offer in comparison to similar offerings. In this final step the marketer conceptually maps the position of the brand's offer to create the positioning statement. It is important to remember that the STP model is a holistic approach with each step building upon, and relying on the validity of, the step before.

REVIEW QUESTIONS

1. What is segmentation? What benefits do marketers gain from segmentation analyses?

2. What are the bases of segmentation? Why is demographic segmentation declining in popularity?

3. What are the steps in the segmentation procedure?

4. How do marketers select the variables upon which to base segmentation analysis?

5. What targeting approaches can marketers choose?

6. What characteristics are used to select target segments?

7. Why are personas and customer journey maps relevant in the STP process?

8. What is a brand position? How do marketers choose a positioning strategy?

KEY TERMS

1. **A priori market segmentation** – classifies the market using a basic understanding of the chosen segmentation variables but does not utilize primary data analysis.

2. **Buyer persona** – snapshot of a prototypical customer in the target segment.

3. **Competitive frame of reference** – the set of brands offering substitutable products and competing for the target market's business.

4. **Compiled data** – off-the-shelf data that can be purchased from data aggregators such as credit agencies.

5. **Concentration strategy** – only targeting one segment (a niche).

6. **Deterministic data** – identifies a single user across a range of situations, devices, and environments.

7. **First-party data** – captured over the course of a direct relationship with a customer, as part of a company's customer relationship management system.

8. **Geocoding** – matching data to a specific latitude and longitude.

9. **Geospatial data** – often used to describe address-related data.

10. **Hybrid segmentation** – utilizes multiple data sources drawn from a combination of different types of consumer data to build a picture of the market.

11. **Job map** – depicts the eight process stages people experience to complete a job.

12. **Jobs-To-Be-Done (JTBD) theory** – holds that to create a product or service that customers will want to buy, marketers must understand the outcomes prospective customers are seeking.

13. **Market segmentation** – the process of dividing the total market into a number of smaller, more homogeneous sub-markets, called market segments.

14. **Mass marketing** – covering the market with one offer.

15. **Multi-segment strategy** – positioning differentiated offers for each targeted segment.

16. **Outcome-Driven Innovation (ODI)** – a strategy and innovation process that ties customer-defined metrics to the "job-to-be-done", making innovation measurable and predictable (Strategyn, n.d.).

17. **Points of differentiation (PODs)** – creating differences in the brand's offer that are perceived as unique relative to the competition.

18. **Points of parity (POPs)** – attributes that are similar across competitors and considered necessary to compete in the product category.

19. **Positioning statement** – communicates the strategy to internal audiences who make marketing decisions.

20. **Second-party data** – obtained through a direct relationship with a non-competitive brand partner, such as Google or Facebook.

21. **STP model** – helps marketers organize a large, heterogeneous market into meaningful, homogeneous groups and optimize marketing decisions by targeted group.

22. **Tagline** – a short and memorable phrase that captures the essence of the brand promise.

23. **Unique selling proposition** – a point of differentiation that is a tangible characteristic.

24. **Value proposition** – an assertion of the reasons the target market should choose the brand's offer.

Chapter 4

MARKETING RESEARCH AND ANALYSIS

In this chapter, we study the value, design, and use of effective market research. We'll learn the answers to the following questions:

1. What is marketing research and why is it valuable for marketers?

2. How do companies use marketing information systems (MISs), what are the components of MISs, and what can such systems accomplish?

3. What kinds of data can be gathered with market research?

4. What are the steps in the marketing research process and how are they applied?

5. How can a marketing manager assess the quality of research?

INTRODUCTION

Successful marketing means strategically planning and implementing the right offer for the right target segments in the market. To do this, marketers make a lot of decisions – ranging from what objectives and opportunities to pursue, which segments to target, the value proposition the brand will offer, how the brand will differentiate itself, to the tactical decisions related to the marketing mix.

Such decisions involve uncertainty and risk. Uncertainty is a state of having limited knowledge of current conditions or future outcomes. It is a major component of risk, which involves the likelihood and scale of negative consequences. To minimize the risk that their decisions will lead to undesired outcomes, marketing managers strive to reduce uncertainty whenever possible. Marketing research is the first line of defense when faced with uncertainty (Courtney, Kirkland and Viguerie, 1997).

By the end of the chapter, you'll be equipped with tools to use throughout your marketing career. You may never be part of a research team – but that doesn't mean that you won't be working with market research. Whether you work in a design lab creating new products, on the pricing team setting price points, in the e-commerce command center monitoring inventory and sales, in finance deciding which strategies to back, or in a host of other business activities, you will work with market research reports. This chapter will ensure that you can commission those reports when needed, understand the process, and evaluate their quality – before you make your decisions.

OPENING VIGNETTE

UNDERSTANDING ATTITUDES AND BEHAVIORS ABOUT STUDENT LOAN DEBT

As a university student, chances are good that you hold some student loan debt. Tuition for attending university varies. In some countries like Brazil or Germany, tuition may be free, but in others, like the United States and United Kingdom, tuition may be thousands of dollars a semester. The average student loan debt is $37,000 in the United States and $55,000 in the United Kingdom (Chamie, 2017). Even students in Sweden, where tuition is free, leave with an average debt of about $20,000. Though the United States isn't alone in its struggle with student loan debt, its growth rate in student loan debt has outpaced all other forms of consumer debt.

Financial companies like Credible, Citizens Bank, and Wells Fargo, among others, offer loan consolidation programs designed for people with student loan debt, but the adoption rate in the industry is slow. In the classic sense of understanding needs and offering benefits, this doesn't make sense. Loan consolidation is widely accepted as the best strategy for managing student loan debt, saving money over the total cost of the loan, paying off the loan more quickly, and lowering monthly payments.

Faced with the need to improve its offering to drive sales of loan consolidations, Citizens Bank turned to marketing research. Citizens Bank hired TNS, a market research firm, to conduct a survey of college graduates between the ages of 18 and 35 years who currently have student loan debt. The findings helped Citizens Bank understand the special concerns and needs of the target audience.

- The average graduate with student loan debt spends 18% of his or her salary on student loan payments.
- 60% expect they will be in their 40s before they can pay off their loans.
- Student loan payments interfere with their purchases of other products and services – respondents reported limiting travel, eating out and entertainment, and clothing purchases.

When brands underperform, a common assumption for marketers to make is that there wasn't enough *awareness* among the target market. If that were true, Citizens Bank's marketing department might launch an advertising campaign to drive awareness. Citizens Bank's survey negated this as a possible explanation. More than 60% reported that they were aware of refinancing programs, but only 30% had taken action to refinance their student loans. When asked *why* they had not refinanced, 25% reported that while they were aware of student loan refinance plans, they did not understand how to do so! An additional 20% were afraid of the risk of higher payments if the refinance made them ineligible for a repayment plan based on their income. Citizens Bank's survey also included questions about what benefits were most desirable in a student loan refinancing plan. The most valuable benefits were lower monthly payments and lower interest rates.

Armed with this knowledge of the target market, Citizens Bank designed a portfolio of products and services for the market. The product portfolio now includes a range of borrowing options for credit-qualified students and graduates and their families, including the Citizens Bank Student Loan, the Citizens Bank Student Loan with Multi-Year Borrowing, and the Citizens Bank Parent Loan. The average borrower saves over $1,700 per year with a student loan refinance plan through Citizens Bank. To address the perceived complexity of securing the loan and the fear associated with debt, the program provides for credit counseling and financial coaching and participants receive an annual "report card" to reinforce the progress they are making toward financial goals.

The market research enabled Citizens Bank to design a better marketing offer for its target audience. The survey findings directly influenced the design of its products and services and will also be useful in designing effective marketing communications.

THE ROLE OF MARKET RESEARCH IN MARKETING DECISION-MAKING
MARKET RESEARCH DEFINED

What is market research? According to ESOMAR (World Association of Opinion and Marketing Research Professionals), market research, which "includes social and opinion research, is the systematic gathering and interpretation of information about individuals or organizations using the statistical and analytical methods and techniques of the applied social sciences to gain insight or support decision making" (ESOMAR, 2009).

As we saw in the opening vignette, marketing research can help marketers make better decisions. Market research is about listening to people, analyzing the information to help organizations make better decisions, and reducing the risk of those decisions. It is about analyzing and interpreting data to build information and knowledge that can be used to predict, for example, future events, actions, or behaviors. This is where the real skill and value of market research lies. In fact, at any stage of the strategic planning process (which you'll learn more about in Chapter 5), research can be useful. Whether analyzing the environment, developing competitive intelligence, or seeking consumer insights to use when designing elements of the marketing mix, research is the process or source marketers use to get the information they need.

Let's take a look at some recent brands that turned to marketing research to address a marketing problem:

- How did Sephora retain store customers at the point of purchase? When research revealed that shoppers were checking retail competitor prices on their smartphones while looking at products in Sephora's aisles, Sephora decided to leverage that behavior. It designed its own smartphone app with benefits for in-store shopping, store loyalty, and usage. The research resulted in a marketing decision that enabled Sephora to retain prospective customers in-store at the point of purchase.

- How did Red Roof Inn increase its bookings at locations near airports? Research highlighted an increase in delayed and cancelled flights at airports in some geographic locations. Perhaps not surprisingly, consumer research revealed strong negative attitudes and emotions among weary travelers who find themselves stuck in a transit airport overnight. Acting on these insights, Red Roof designed a system to alert hotel managers in real-time when nearby airports experienced flight cancellations. The system was complemented by mobile advertising on travel sites which highlighted special pricing for stranded passengers. The timing coincided with the airport delays to ensure a high degree of relevance for the target market. The research resulted in marketing decisions that drove a 600% increase in reservations at the targeted hotel locations.

- What insight might have led to Geico's Gecko Baseball Game on its mobile app? When research revealed that smartphone app users spend more time with apps that give them "me time", Geico saw an opportunity to enhance the benefits of its app in a way that would increase user satisfaction, support the brand's image, and encourage users to spend more time using the app. The app still performs all the functions important for an insurance customer – but now users can also play a game of baseball with Geico's Gecko.

- Why did Heineken add non-alcoholic beverages to its product line? In market research commissioned by Heineken, which polled 5,000 people between the ages of 21–35 years in five countries (Heineken, 2016), 75% reported that they actively moderate their alcohol consumption, some foregoing alcoholic beverages entirely. The primary reasons included attitudes toward health and natural ingredients, the desire to feel in control, and fear of bad behavior living on in social media channels. Heineken acted on the survey results by developing new products and creating an ad campaign, called Moderate Drinkers Wanted, to reinforce the trend toward moderation. The new products, Radler and 0.0% MAXX, have been launched in 42 markets. Acting on the research has paid off for Heineken. Revenues from its non-alcoholic beverages grew 7.7%, outpacing the 3.3% growth in revenue for the company overall (Berman, 2017).

All of these successes were built upon a solid foundation of market research. In this chapter, we'll discuss the why and how of marketing research, including several of the methods and tools used.

Keep in mind as we move forward that no research method is perfect. Marketing researchers must choose the methods that best meet the needs of the marketing manager, including gathering the necessary data while managing constraints like budget, cost, and viability. Marketers don't always utilize market research. There may not be enough time or funding for the research, or the expected value of the information may not be sufficiently high to warrant the expense. This is known as making a cost–benefit analysis.

THE VALUE OF MARKET RESEARCH

When feasible, market research provides diagnostic information to guide marketing decisions. Marketing managers use research to identify trends, reduce risk and uncertainty, inform marketing mix decisions, and assess the effectiveness of marketing activities. On which types of marketing information do marketers spend the most of their research budget? Figure 4.1 identifies specific types of research projects by funds spent.

MARKETING INFORMATION SYSTEMS

Organizations use marketing information systems to gather, store, sort, analyse, and distribute information to marketing decision-makers. The marketing information system (MIS) was defined by Harmon (2003) as a series of procedures and methods for the

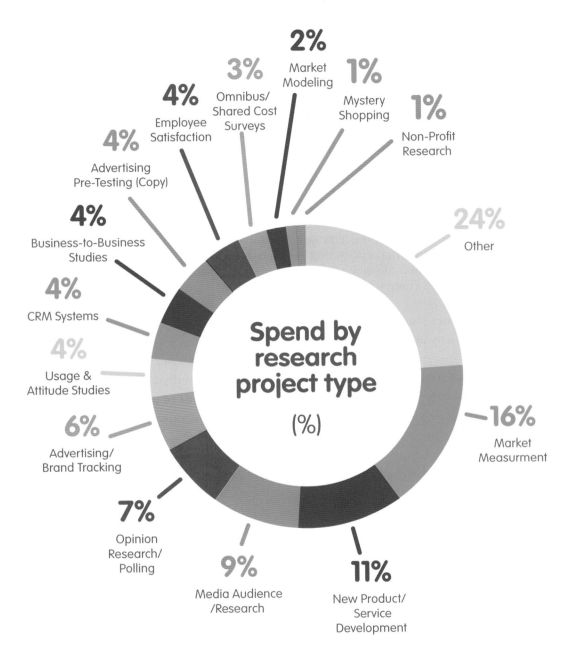

FIGURE 4.1   Global Spending by Research Project Type

Source: Copyright © (2017) by ESOMAR – The World Association of Research Professionals. This information first appeared in the ESOMAR Global Market Research Report (2017) published by ESOMAR (www.esomar.org).

regular, planned collection, analysis, and presentation of information for use in making marketing decisions. The MIS should be an interactive structure of people, equipment, methods, and controls, designed to create a flow of information able to provide an acceptable base for the decision-making process in marketing. Both strategic decisions such as segmentation and positioning as well as operational decisions about the marketing mix can be guided by information from an organization's MIS. Depending upon an organization's information needs, resources, industry, and maturity, the MIS design, capability, and power may range from simple to sophisticated (Al-Weshah and Deacon, 2009).

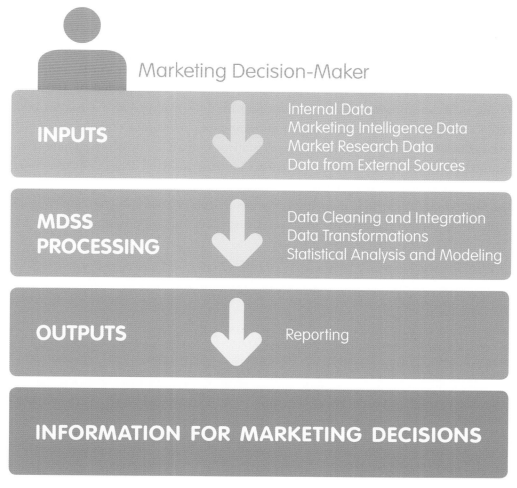

FIGURE 4.2   The Marketing Information System

COMPONENTS OF THE MIS

A marketing information system consists of two primary components: 1) information inputs and 2) a marketing decision support system. The inputs in the MIS may be sourced from 1) internal records, 2) marketing intelligence, and 3) marketing research. The data sources may be structured or unstructured, qualitative and/or quantitative, and sourced from both internal records and/or external sources of data. The marketing decision support system (MDSS) is the term used for the data management, analyzing, modeling, and reporting processes by which the data is transformed into information and marketing knowledge. Figure 4.2 illustrates the MIS components.

MARKETING DECISION SUPPORT SYSTEM

An effective MDSS will be capable of harmonizing data from different sources with disparate characteristics such as detail and quality by cleaning and aggregating data. This is an important capability. Without it, data from internal records, external records, and research cannot be utilized in a single analytical model. The MDSS is supported by software for analyzing data, interpreting results, and turning the information into a basis for making decisions. The statistical tools in the MDSS allow analysts to examine complex relationships among variables in the system. The types of statistical analyses possible include (but are not limited to) descriptive, correlation, regression, discriminant, factor, cluster, conjoint, and multi-dimensional scaling analyses.

The MDSS may also include modeling software capable of answering "what-if" questions. Examples of questions that can be answered using modeling are provided in Table 4.1.

TABLE 4.1   "What-If" Questions and Modeling

Budget Optimization	Sales Promotion Optimization	Price Optimization	Segmentation	Brand Equity Modeling
If we increased our marketing budget, what would be the most profitable place to make additional investments?	How do my promotional events compare across products? Across markets?	What price thresholds are relevant in making price shifts?	What are my customer segments and how are they defined?	Which paid, owned, and earned media drives increases in brand health?
Can we improve total revenue/profits by reallocating marketing or sales resources from one brand to another within a portfolio of products?	Are my promotions cannibalizing future sales?	If we increase price by 5%, what will be the impact on sales, revenue, and profitability?	What customer segments deliver the most revenue and profit?	What is the marketing cost and ROI to increase brand equity by 1%?

Budget Optimization	Sales Promotion Optimization	Price Optimization	Segmentation	Brand Equity Modeling
Can we improve global profit performance by moving marketing resources from one country to another geographic region?	Which of my promotional strategies are responsible for the greatest ROI for my business?	How will a price increase affect our revenue, volume, penetration, and buy rate?	Which consumers tend to shop/interact exclusively online and why?	How much does brand equity contribute to sales?
If we have to cut marketing expenditures by 5%, which component should we eliminate to have the least impact on our sales?	Should I promote more or less often?	How should we strategically price the different segments and brands in our portfolio to drive growth?	Where should we apply our CRM resources to deliver the best lift to customer lifetime value?	What is the relative influence on our brand health for individual campaigns, message attributes, product developments, pricing, and distribution?

SOURCES OF INFORMATION FOR MISS

Without data, the MIS cannot produce insights that meet the needs of the organization's marketing decision-makers. Let's take a closer look at the types of information the system can use.

1. *Data from Internal Records.* Organizations can use the data from their internal record systems as an information source. Organizations maintain records on customer relationships, past sales, customer service records, salesforce reports, inventory levels, traffic to physical locations and organizational websites and more. This data can be mined for answers to many common marketing questions such as: Who are my most valuable customers? How much inventory do I need to carry in my retail locations versus offered only online? How did my sales vary during different promotional periods?

2. *Marketing Intelligence.* While the internal report system pulls existing data from internal operations, the marketing intelligence system provides information from the external environment. Information is obtained through environmental scanning on an ongoing basis. Marketing intelligence can be gathered by reading publications, watching television, searching the Internet, talking informally with customers and suppliers, attending trade shows and industry conferences, and auditing the websites and facilities of competitors. Marketing intelligence activities are primarily unstructured, but because the scanning of environmental information is a continuous activity, it can enable marketers

to respond quickly to environmental changes like competitive actions and customer problems.

3. *Marketing Research.* The third data source in the MIS, and the primary focus of the chapter, is marketing research. Marketing research is the function or process by which information is gathered to meet the needs of a marketing decision-maker. Marketing research redefines the marketer's problem as research questions, designs the methods for collecting the information, manages and implements the data collection process, analyzes the results, and communicates the findings.

MOVING FROM MARKET DATA TO MARKET WISDOM

The real power of an MIS lies in combining the data and the processes to create a holistic and complete view of the market (Crowley, 2004). Research suggests that companies that use data and business analytics to guide decision-making are more productive and experience higher returns on equity than competitors that don't (Brynjolfsson, Hitt and Kim, 2011). Perhaps Marion Harper, Jr., one of the most influential advertising researchers in history, stated it best: "To manage a business well is to manage its future, and to manage the future well is to manage the information" (AdAge, 1999b). While marketing managers seek knowledge and wisdom, market research produces data and information. Ultimately, it is up to the marketer to identify the implications of the information gleaned from research and use the knowledge to take appropriate action. Table 4.2 explains the basic differences between data, information, knowledge, and wisdom.

TABLE 4.2   From Market Data to Market Wisdom

Level	Definition	Key Functions
Data	Collecting raw facts	Recording and storing data
Information	Transforming the raw data into meaningful, useful data	Giving form and functionality in the organization and presentation of data patterns
Knowledge	Understanding of implications	Analyzing and synthesizing the meaning of patterns and relationships
Wisdom	Applying the knowledge to the marketing problem	Discerning the implications of meaning and applying insights to marketing problems

THE MARKETING RESEARCH PROCESS

In this section of the chapter, we'll review the marketing research process. Figure 4.3 illustrates the steps in the marketing research process.

FIGURE 4.3   The Marketing Research Process

STEP 1: DEFINE THE MARKETING PROBLEM AND RESEARCH OBJECTIVES

The first step in the market research process is to define the decision problem and its research problem and objective. This may sound simple, but marketers must be careful not to oversimplify or unnecessarily complicate the decision they face. The marketer's goal is to get the information needed to make a better decision. The research problem is the articulation of what information is needed and how it can be obtained efficiently and effectively. Importantly, though we refer to this step as defining the problem, this doesn't necessarily mean that something is wrong. Rather, it refers to the overall questions the marketing manager needs answering. Let's revisit the Citizens Bank example from the opening vignette. From a marketing manager's perspective, the occurrence of student refinancing was lower than expected. Despite designing a product that should have been desirable for the target audience, adoption of that product was lower than expected.

The marketing manager then answers the question, *"What research objectives must be accomplished in order to provide the information needed to solve the problem?"* Research has three general roles: 1) descriptive, 2) diagnostic, and 3) predictive. When research seeks to describe, the goal is to gather factual statements. When research seeks to diagnose, the goal is to explain data and the relationships between variables. When research seeks to predict, the goal is to address "what-if" questions. In the Citizens Bank example, the research objective was descriptive – it sought to identify the reasons why graduates with student loans were not refinancing their loans despite the benefits of doing so.

As you set these objectives, be careful not to be overly ambitious in the number of research goals. The most successful research projects are focused on only one or two high-level goals. Of course, under that level, there can be several subgoals. For example, in the student loan research, the primary goals were likely to be 1) to measure awareness of loan refinancing options among the target audience, and 2) to identify the factors influencing the choice to refinance among those who were already aware of the option. Appropriate subgoals might have been (a) to understand how awareness varied by demographic or geographic subgroups and (b) to examine the relative importance of influence factors. Note that in the process of defining the problem and research objectives, we have specified the population of interest. Once the specific goals are outlined, agreed upon, and documented, and the decision to pursue market research is made, you can proceed to the next step – determining whether secondary research exists that can address your research needs.

STEP 2: DETERMINE WHETHER SECONDARY RESEARCH IS AVAILABLE

In this stage of the process, the organization determines whether the information they require to make a decision already exists. Secondary research sources are information sources created for some other purpose. Note that we are distinguishing between secondary research and secondary data. Because secondary data can be acquired and used in primary research, we discuss secondary data in step four. In the Citizens Bank example, there are several studies published that relate to student loan decisions. If the information provided from those studies can answer the research question, then primary research is not needed.

When secondary research that answers the research questions is available, it can save the organization time and money.

There are many sources of secondary research, some of which are highlighted in Table 4.3. These include published research on the state of the industry from trade organizations, studies from syndicated research firms like Experian Simmons, government reports, journal and trade articles, databases, and other sources. Syndicated research is general information related to specific topics or industries which specialized firms collect on a regular basis and sell to other firms. EuroMonitor International, a global market research firm with headquarters in the UK, creates more than 17,000 syndicated research reports each year covering more than 200 markets, 25 industries, and thousands of companies. For example, EuroMonitor International recently published a report on Unilever's (the company featured in this chapter's PRME case) marketing of packaged foods in global markets (EuroMonitor, 2019). The report explained the wisdom behind Unilever's acquisition of Graze, the UK's leading healthy snack brand, to fill a gap in its product portfolio. Though Unilever is the sixth largest packaged food company in the world, it lacked a popular snack offering. EuroMonitor also maintains a market research database, called Passport, with which clients can run customized market research reports on market context, competitor insights, and trends analysis.

TABLE 4.3   Secondary Sources of Market Information

Source	Example of Resources	Learn More
Government	Census data (US), European Data Market Monitoring Tool	www.census.gov http://datalandscape.eu/
Trade associations	The Chartered Institute of Marketing (CIM), American Marketing Association (AMA), Small Business Association (SBA)	www.cim.co.uk/ www.marketingsource.com/association www.sba.gov/offices/headquarters/oee/resources/2836
Periodicals/Journals	ABi/Inform, LexisNexis	www.proquest.com www.lexisnexis.com
White papers and branded research reports	eMarketer, Forrester Research, Bain & Company, Nielsen	www.emarketer.com www.forrester.com www.bain.com www.nielsen.com
Syndicated research reports	IDC, EuroMonitor International	www.idc.com www.euromonitor.com

While marketers can benefit from syndicated research and secondary sources, custom surveys are still considered the most important data source for the creation of insights today (Greenbook, 2016). If sufficient secondary research is not available to answer the research questions specified in step one, the organization will continue to step three.

STEP 3: DETERMINE WHETHER PRIMARY RESEARCH IS NEEDED, THE SCOPE OF WORK, AND HOW THE RESEARCH WILL BE SOURCED

If the choice is to conduct primary market research, the organization will need to decide whether it will be managed in-house, rely on a market research company, or some combination of the two. Organizations spent more than $40 billion on marketing research globally. Organizations may have their own consumer insights departments, commission custom research from marketing research agencies or freelance research professionals, and/ or purchase syndicated research.

Companies that conduct market research as an ongoing process may have in-house capabilities. What if the organization doesn't have full-service research capabilities? Organizations may still decide to DIY the project. Working with a market research agency is a big investment. Depending on the scope of the project, costs could exceed $100,000 or more. Still, depending upon the risk tolerance and budget set in step one, and the capabilities

TABLE 4.4   Top Market Research Organizations Worldwide

1–12	13–24	25–36	37–50
Brainjuicer	SSI	SurveyMonkey	Facebook
Ipsos	Gutcheck	Communispace	Hall & Partners
Insites Consulting	Research Now	iModerate	Incite
Nielsen	Kantar Media	Added Value	TRC
Gfk	Tolune	Cint	AYTM
TNS	Hotspex	Happy Thinking People	Discuss.io
Vision Critical	RIWI	Sentient Decision Sciences	Forrester
LRW	2020 Research	YouGove	Joint the Dots
Milward Brown	Focus Vision	InfoScout	Lucid
Goole	Intage	Odin Text	Metrix Lab
ZappStore	Lightspeed GMI	IBM	Forbes Consulting Group
Qualtrics	MartizCX	Instant.ly	Vaxpopme

that exist in-house, it could be far wiser to retain a research firm. Develop a realistic scope of work and then assess whether the organization has the required tools, skills, and time to manage the project. Web survey options like SurveyMonkey and Google Surveys make simple survey projects feasible without the aid of a research firm. If some or all of the project is beyond the organization's capabilities, it's time to hire a market research agency.

Market research firms can provide full-service options and a la carte research needs. Table 4.4 lists the 50 top market research organizations in the world (Greenbook, 2016).

There are several reference guides for identifying research providers: 1) the Marketing Research Association's Blue Book, 2) the MRA's online database of members, and 3) Greenbook. Unless you have an existing relationship with a research provider, you'll write a request for proposal, known as an RFP, to describe the scope of work and request proposals from qualified professionals. As a minimum, a market research RFP states the project parameters and requests responses to the basic questions that will allow the client organization to evaluate the proposals and choose the research provider. RFPs typically include the following:

- statement of research objectives (from step one)
- target population parameters
- statement of preference for qualitative or quantitative methodologies, if any
- deliverables required at project conclusion
- timeline requirements
- qualifications required
- instructions for proposal submissions.

A well-written RFP will result in proposals that will help you choose the best research partner for your needs. Read on to learn about the elements of a successful RFP. A sample RFP is illustrated below.

CASE STUDY

REQUEST FOR PROPOSAL: HEALTHY, MOBILE FOODS STUDY

RFP Responses: Please submit proposals in electronic format to research@company.com by January 15, 2019. Only complete responses will be considered.

Objectives: Our goal is to identify customer groups that would be most likely to try a new food bar product with specific flavor characteristics. To do this, we want to

(Continued)

measure satisfaction with, and purchase behaviors for, the food bar sector. Which food bars are best liked? Which are liked primarily because of their flavor? Are people loyal to their preferred bars, or are they strongly influenced by price promotions? Are certain flavor and ingredient combinations likely to entice them to try a new bar?

Hypotheses: We believe that brand switching potential varies notably by gender, income, and urban versus suburban households. We think that interest in specific new flavor and ingredient combinations will vary by gender, age, and activity profiles.

Geographic Scope: This is a US study, although we would like an option to conduct a follow-up phase in Canada.

Sample Source: To be provided by the agency.

Population: We are interested in conducting this research with adults who are physically active (engage in exercise at least three times per week), between the ages of 21 and 65 years. We want a mix of runners, bikers, rock climbers, skiers, and triathletes.

Methodology: We are open to agency recommendations for methodology, but we have a slight preference for quantitative research because we want some hard numbers as input to our marketing plan.

Deliverables Required: Upon completion, we will want a brief report in Keynote, a complete set of data tables, and an on-site presentation.

Qualifications: Please describe your experience in the specialty foods business that may be relevant. Include the biographies of proposed project staff.

Fee: Please state your fee as a total fee, and with an option for tables only (no slide deck). Also provide a separate option for adding Canada as a Phase 2.

Timeline: Please state your proposed timeline by stage (definition/kickoff, design, data collection, analysis/reporting).

STEP 4: DESIGN THE RESEARCH PLAN

The next step is to design the research plan. If the organization is using a full-service research provider, the design will be developed by the researcher (and submitted as a proposal in response to the RFP) or in consultation with the client organization once hired. If the organization will complete the project in-house, in-house staff will design the research plan. To develop the research plan, we will make several decisions including the most appropriate research approach, the sampling plan, the data collection mode, and the research instruments needed to measure the variables of interest.

WHAT PRIMARY RESEARCH DESIGN IS THE BEST APPROACH?

If primary research is needed, we must decide what is the best approach. Figure 4.4 provides a decision guide. Depending upon what kind of information is needed and whether the objective is exploratory or descriptive, the guide provides the options that will best fit the research objective.

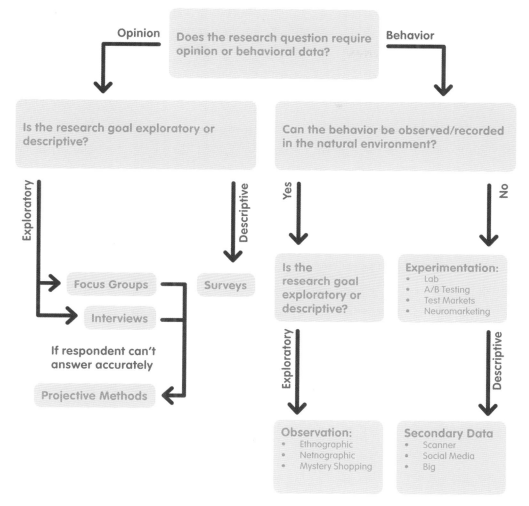

FIGURE 4.4   Flowchart for Determining Research Plan

Really, the first question for primary data collection is – are we interested in measuring what people say or what people do? Then we must decide whether the research is exploratory or descriptive. In part the answer to this question will control whether the research will be qualitative or quantitative and whether the research method will seek to use existing sources of behavioral data or will collect primary data.

In today's digital age, there is so much information available that it can be useful to think through the options using the two-by-two matrix shown in Figure 4.5. The figure is based on whether we need to know about the unit of interest's behavior or whether we need to understand attitudes and opinions. It is important to note that we can observe and capture behavioral data and analyze it qualitatively or quantitatively, and likewise, we can collect data directly from participants and analyze that data qualitatively or quantitatively. Figure 4.6 organizes some of the many options we have as market researchers.

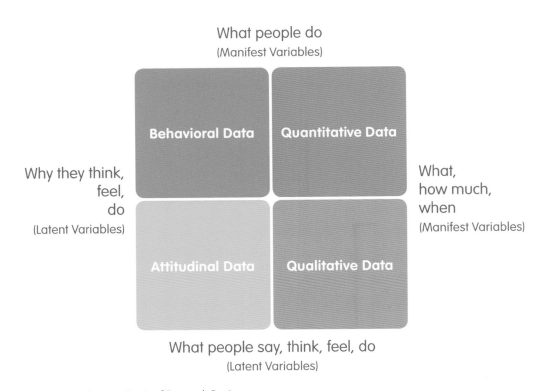

FIGURE 4.5   Two-by-Two Matrix of Research Designs

EXPLORATORY RESEARCH

We refer to most exploratory research as qualitative studies: that is, the results of the research project tend to be verbal or visual information about consumer's attitudes, feelings, and behaviors. These qualitative studies generate data about behaviors or attitudes based on observing them directly or questioning directly, whereas in quantitative studies, the data about the behavior or attitudes in question are gathered indirectly, through a measurement or an instrument such as a survey or an analytics tool. Analysis of exploratory data is not based on mathematics but based on the insight we can derive from observing what happens as people use the product. By contrast, insights identified by descriptive, quantitative methods are typically derived from mathematical analysis.

Qualitative approaches tend to be best for answering why questions (exploratory questions) while quantitative methods tend to be best for answering descriptive questions

Behavioral Data / Qualitative

- UX Studies
- Product Usage Studies
- Observations

Behavioral Data / Quantitative

- A/B Testing
- Neuromarketing Studies
- Physiological Studies (e.g. Eye Tracking)
- Data Modeling with Data Sets
- Experiments

Attitudinal Data / Qualitative

- IDIs
- Focus Groups
- Projective Methods

Attitudinal Data / Quantitative

- Surveys

FIGURE 4.6   Research Designs by Data Type

(how much, when, what). As much as we can learn from behavioral, quantitative data, that data cannot explain why something happened. We will always need other forms of market research to explain the why. Some marketing firms, like design consultancy IDEO, rely heavily on exploratory research regardless of the marketing objective. David Gilmore, former User Experience Research Lead at IDEO, explains that ethnographic design research is not about rational arguments about business goals. Rather it is about enabling someone to see that there is a different perspective. Ethnographic research shouldn't be thought of in opposition to quantitative approaches, but rather complements quantitative approaches by sharing the story in the data (Gilmore, 2002).

There are many advantages of qualitative research, but the market researcher must be sure that the marketing manager will benefit best from these advantages and be comfortable with the limitations of the approach. If your use of the flowchart in Figure 4.4 led you to consider qualitative approaches, you should next ask the following questions before moving forward:

- Are you looking for rich insights filled with descriptions of participant thoughts and behaviors?

- Is it desirable that data collection be completed quickly?

- Do you have access to trained interviewers and observers?

- Is it acceptable, given the nature of the project, to use a small sample?

- Will you have sufficient access to qualified participants?

- Must the data be generalizable to the population of interest?

- Must you estimate the magnitude of the phenomenon you are studying?

- Must data be objective rather than subjective?

Let's take a closer look at the two primary designs for gathering exploratory, attitudinal data: focus groups and interviews.

Focus Groups and Interviews

Focus groups refer to interactive discussions about a topic or concept among a small group of people who are led by a professional moderator. The intensive interview, also referred to as an in-depth interview or IDI, is a one-on-one interview that follows a semi-structured series of questions.

The focus group is the technique that marketing researchers use most often for collecting exploratory data. They are the "workhorses" of qualitative data collection, making up 11% of total global market research and more than 50% of exploratory studies (ESOMAR, 2015). Focus group and interview research might stand alone for a project that seeks to develop rich insight into a sample of individuals. They are also frequently used alongside quantitative studies to prepare researchers prior to a project, to assist them in understanding unexpected or unclear results after it, or to offer a deeper picture of the phenomenon of interest.

Focus groups and interviews have most commonly been conducted in face-to-face settings, but increasingly online options including video conferencing and digital chat rooms make it possible for market researchers to reach customers in other geographic areas without the cost of travel. These qualitative techniques help researchers to understand participants on their own terms and in their own words.

Focus groups typically include 6 to 12 consumers who have been recruited because they share certain characteristics that relate to the target audience. They may use the product, or fit the demographic characteristics. In our Citizens Bank example, a focus group would have included students who have used student loans to fund their education. Discussions are semi-structured (following an outline known as an "interview guide" or a "moderator's guide") and typically last 90 minutes to 2 hours. The moderator's objective is to encourage group members to talk in detail about the topics posed while the moderator draws out experiences, ideas, and emotions from the group.

The basic stages of the focus group process include 1) planning, 2) conducting, and 3) analyzing/writing. In planning, the researcher must develop the moderator's guide, select the best location for the discussions (which may be online or offline), and select and recruit participants. Focus groups can be held in a variety of locations (including online) such as a conference room, a meeting room in a church or civic organization, an office, a hotel meeting room, or even the moderator's home. While all of these sites may be appropriate, professional focus groups commonly meet in a focus group facility equipped with a conference table and comfortable seating, an observer viewing area with a one-way mirror, and built-in audiovisual recording equipment. Online focus groups offer the benefits of traditional focus groups as well as other benefits not commonly associated with in-person groups. Though more focus groups are held in person than online, we expect more online focus groups to be held as video conferencing and digital chat technologies improve. Participants should reflect the primary characteristics of the target audience of interest in the research problem. Recruiting may involve a variety of methods, such as using established lists of willing participants, advertising for participants, or even telephone recruiting. The focus group discussion will be recorded and transcripts created from the recordings for use in content analysis.

Projective Techniques

Projective techniques are used when a consumer may not be able to share their attitudes with the researcher. Projective techniques involve the "use of stimuli that allow participants to project their subjective or deep-seated beliefs on to other people or objects" (Morrison, Haley, Sheehan and Taylor, 2011: 63). Projective techniques facilitate the articulation of otherwise repressed or withheld thoughts by allowing the research participant to "project" their own thoughts onto someone or something other than themselves. Projective techniques are thus techniques that enable research participants or subjects to respond in ways in which they would otherwise not feel able to respond (De Jong, Hoofstede, Van Hoof and Walenberg, 2007). These techniques are often used within a focus group or interview. For a review of the validity and reliability issues with projective techniques used for market research, see Boddy (2005).

Though there are many variations of projective techniques, they can typically be categorized into one of five types: 1) methods-association, 2) completion, 3) construction, 4) choice ordering, and 5) expressive. Association tasks require respondents to respond with the first image or thought elicited by the presentation of a stimulus. Completion tasks require participants to complete an incomplete stimulus, which may be a story, sentence, argument, or conversation. Expressive tasks require participants to draw, enact, or role play a specific concept or situation. Table 4.5 lists some of the most popular variations used in market research.

TABLE 4.5   Projective Techniques

Technique	Description
Word associations	Ask participants what words come to mind when they hear or see a stimulus.
Bubble story-telling	Ask participants to complete a story by filling in conversation "bubbles".
Modified Thematic Apperception Test	Ask participants to build a story around visual stimuli such as a logo or ad.
Laddering	Ask participants a series of "why" questions until underlying motives and emotions are reached.
Mind-mapping	Ask participants to identify associations, mapping new associations as they are triggered.
Brand personification	Ask participants to describe the brand as a person, including where it lives, what it wears, and how it spends time.
Role-playing	Ask participants to assume a character role.
Third-party projections	Ask respondents to describe what other people are doing, thinking, feeling, believing, and saying.
Zaltman Metaphor Elicitation Technique (ZMET)	Ask participants to select images to represent their thoughts and feelings about the research topic and use these to create a collage.

Exploratory Studies – Behavioural Observation

Remember earlier we talked about the Sephora market research? That all started when employees noticed customers were price-checking products using their mobile phones in the store aisles. Sephora took that initial observation further to plan for systematic research, but it all started with a simple observation. Researchers can gather data by unobtrusively observing people while they use products or shop for products (online and off). These approaches can provide deep insights into the target audience.

When marketing researchers want to understand how "real" consumers use their products, they may conduct field research where they visit people's homes and offices to observe them as they go about their everyday lives; this is known as ethnographic research. For example, a team of researchers that wanted to learn about how teenage girls actually talk about beauty care products sponsored a series of sleepovers where they sent researchers to hang out overnight and record what they learned when conversation turned to cosmetics and skin treatments. Now, some social scientists adapt these methods to rigorously study online communities.

Netnography is a rapidly growing research methodology that adapts ethnographic research techniques to study the communities that emerge through computer-mediated communications. Like monitoring, the approach uses information available through online forums such as chat rooms, message boards, and social networking groups to study the attitudes and behaviors of the market involved.

How can we use netnography? One researcher recommends the following steps:

- Identify online venues that could provide information related to the research questions.

- Select online communities that are focused on a particular topic or segment, have a high "traffic" of postings, have a relatively large number of active posters, and appear to have detailed posts.

- Learn about the group culture, including its characteristics, behaviors, and language.

- Select material for analysis and classify material as social or informational and off-topic or on-topic.

- Categorize the types of participants involved in the discussions to be analyzed.

- Keep a journal of observations and reflections about the data collection and analysis process.

- Be straightforward with those in the online community about your purpose for participation by fully disclosing the researcher's presence in the community as well as his/her intent.

- Utilize "member checks" following content analysis of the discourse to ensure that members feel their attitudes and behaviors have been accurately interpreted.

Mystery shopping also fits into this category of research and can be useful for customer service evaluations as well as for competitive intelligence gathering. Mystery shopping is a research method that collects data from researchers posing as customers. It can be useful for competitive intelligence, checking for conformance standards for franchise locations, and assessing service quality. Mystery shoppers can report on processes like returning merchandise, making special requests, and the availability of advertised promotions. They can be used to report on bathroom cleanliness, customer service, and the condition of store shelves and displays.

DESCRIPTIVE STUDIES

Behavioral Data – We Use the Data

When the phenomenon being examined is behavioral and can be recorded, market researchers can use the data. Scanner-based research is an example. It evolved as a system for gathering information from a single group of respondents by continuously monitoring the advertising, promotions, and pricing they are exposed to and the things they buy. The consumer's shopping record is combined with demographic information (e.g., income, educational level of adults in the household, occupations of adults, ages of children, and whether the family owns and rents their home) and the family's television-watching habits and other media habits. The data is kept in databases and available for analysis for a variety of purposes. The two major scanner-based suppliers are Information Resources Inc. (IRI) and A.C. Nielsen Company.

Access to data related to the buying process has evolved into shopper marketing, a form of marketing that uses data to make decisions to improve the shopping experience and better meet shopper needs and wants. With dozens of digital shopping tools now available to shoppers, the journey buyers take from need recognition to purchase and beyond is more complex. Shoppers are Googling prices, posting pictures to Pinterest, scanning QR codes, and pulling digital coupons. Shopper marketing research measures how shoppers access information related to their buying decisions, what digital advertising message inspired action, whether they downloaded coupons, whether they purchased and if so via what channels and websites.

Neuromarketing Research

Neuromarketing research studies how people respond to stimuli by measuring biometrics such as heart rate, brain waves, and eye movement patterns. Researchers use technologies such as functional magnetic resonance imaging (fMRI) to measure changes in activity in parts of the brain, electroencephalography (EEG) and steady state topography (SST) to measure activity in specific regional spectra of the brain response, or sensors to measure changes in one's physiological state. These biometric indicators, including heart rate, respiratory rate, and galvanic skin, can show why consumers make the decisions they do, and which brain areas are responsible.

For example, Frito-Lay hired a neuromarketing firm to look into how consumers respond to Cheetos, the top-selling brand of cheese puffs in the United States. Using EEG technology on a group of willing subjects, the firm determined that consumers respond strongly to the fact that eating Cheetos turns their fingers orange with residual cheese dust. The EEG patterns of participants indicated "a sense of giddy subversion that consumers enjoy over the messiness of the product" (Nobel, 2013). Frito-Lay moved ahead with an ad campaign called "The Orange Underground", featuring a series of 30-second TV spots in which the Cheetos mascot, Chester Cheetah, encourages consumers to commit subversive acts with Cheetos. In one commercial, an airline passenger quietly sticks Cheetos up the nostrils of a snoring seatmate.

Descriptive Studies – We Ask Them – With Survey Research

We've seen that marketers have many tools in their arsenal, including focus groups and interviews to help them better define a problem or opportunity. These are usually studies of a small number of people, enough to get some indication of what is going on but not enough for the marketer to feel confident about generalizing what they observe to the rest of the population of interest.

Either as a complement to qualitative research, or in lieu of it, market researchers may conduct descriptive research. This kind of research probes systematically into the marketing problem and bases its conclusions on a large sample of participants. To do this, companies undertake surveys to assess people's beliefs, feelings, and behaviors and to do so with an approach that can produce quantitative data that can be analyzed using statistics.

Surveys use questions (formulated as the research instrument) to measure the variables of interest. The surveys may be completed with a researcher and the participant, but most market research surveys are "self-completed" – meaning that the participant is able to read the questions, and record their answers without the direct aid of a researcher. Results typically are expressed in quantitative terms – averages, percentages, or other statistics – that result from a large set of measurements. The research may be as straightforward as reporting simple percentages of responses to a question or as complex as assessing multiple variables across thousands of individuals.

Marketing researchers who employ descriptive techniques most often use a cross-sectional design. This approach usually involves the systematic collection of responses to a survey instrument (e.g., questionnaire) from one or more samples of respondents at one point in time (unless the study is longitudinal and involves collecting data at multiple time points). Market researchers have relied upon consumer panels to address some of the limitations of survey research. Today, much of the research results rely upon panel data.

DATA COLLECTION MODE

The mode of data collection is a major issue for marketing researchers using surveys. According to ESOMAR, 74% of the market research conducted globally is quantitative and

16% is qualitative. Once upon a time surveys would have used mail or telephone to collect data, but more surveys now are conducted online. Traditionally, surveys were conducted by telephone or sent by mail, but today just 3% of market research uses mail and 9% is conducted by telephone. When the population of interest can be reached online, researchers will choose online survey options for their many efficiencies. Table 4.6 reviews some of the characteristics associated with mode for surveys.

TABLE 4.6   Which Data Collection Mode Do I Choose? A Comparison of Choice Considerations for Forms of Survey Research

Mode	Cost	Time Span	Demonstration Ability	Need for Interviewer	Data Quality Control	Ability to Handle
Online	Low	Fast	High	No	High	High
Online panel	Low	Fast	High	No	High	High
Mail	High	Slow	Moderate	No	Moderate	Moderate
Mail panel	Moderate	Moderate	Moderate	No	Moderate	Moderate
Telephone	Moderate	Moderate	Low	Yes	Moderate to high	Low
Intercept	Moderate	Moderate	High	Yes	Moderate	Low
Interview	High	Slow	High	Yes	High	Moderate
Mobile	Low	Moderate	Low	No	Low	Low

SAMPLING PLAN

What kind of sample should be selected to best approximate the population, taking into account any constraints which might exist? One of the first decisions we must make (after we identify the need for research information and our research approach) is to establish the population from which we need to collect data. If we were collecting primary data using survey research or interviews, we would specify the units of interest, likely the people or families to which we wish to generalize the study results. This is known as defining the population. That's because we would want to ultimately select participants for our study who represent the people in our population. If we studied the whole of the population, rather than a subset (known as a sample), this would be called a census (like the ones conducted by the UK and US governments). We would then define a sample frame, an available list that approximates the population and from which we draw a sample to represent the population.

In some situations, it may not be possible to identify unique people as units in a defined population, though we still want to ensure that ultimately our content is representative.

For instance, in social media research, we could define the population as the social communities to which our audience belongs. We create a sampling frame of selected social communities and websites based on their descriptions; these include membership demographics, purpose, location, and activity. In other words, rather than identifying a population of consumer units that matches our target audience and then defining a sampling frame that provides a list from which to draw access to that population, we define a population of relevant communities for those consumer units.

The sample refers to the units of content we draw from the frame for inclusion in data analysis. In this case the sampling plan should also include specifications on identifying relevant content and the time period in which content is drawn. For example, let's say we want to understand how our new video game product fares in relation to other games that are similar. We define our population as members of gaming sites such as GamesForum and Gaming Bay. Our sampling frame could be all members who post on these two forums over a four-week period including two weeks prior and two weeks post video game launch. A well-devised sampling plan helps us to ensure that a small portion of the data in the sampling universe can provide an accurate depiction of the truth. Table 4.7 defines the primary types of sampling designs used in market research.

TABLE 4.7   Types of Samples

Sample Type	Definition
Probability Samples	
Simple random sample	Every member of the population has a known and equal chance of selection.
Stratified sample	The population is divided into mutually exclusive groups and then random samples are drawn from each group.
Cluster sample	The population is divided into mutually exclusive groups and then a random set of clusters is selected.
Systematic sample	A list of the population is obtained. A skip interval is determined. The first number is randomly selected and then the skip pattern is used to continue to select units for the sample.
Non-Probability Samples	
Convenience sample	Population members who can be accessed most easily are selected for the sample.
Judgment sample	The researcher chooses population members who have appropriate characteristics given the researcher's judgment.
Quota sample	The sample is selected to ensure a desired ratio of characteristics.
Snowball sample	Respondents refer others who may meet the desired characteristics for participants.

STEP 5: COLLECT THE DATA

Step 5 is the collection of data following the chosen methods.

STEP 6: ANALYZE THE DATA

In step 6, the data is cleaned and analyzed. With the data in a form that is now useful, the researcher can begin the process of analyzing the data to determine what has been learned.

DESCRIPTIVE DATA ANALYSIS

Not to be confused with descriptive research, descriptive analysis, as the name implies, is used to describe the results obtained. In most cases the results are merely used to provide a summary of what has been gathered (e.g., how many liked or disliked a product) without making a statement of whether the results hold up to statistical evaluation. For quantitative data collection the most common methods used for this basic level of analysis are visual representations, such as charts and tables, and measures of central tendency including averages (i.e., mean value).

INFERENTIAL DATA ANALYSIS

While descriptive data analysis can present a picture of the results, the research may have other goals such as:

- using information obtained from a small group (i.e., sample of customers) to make judgments about a larger group (i.e., all customers)
- comparing groups to see whether there is a difference in how they respond to an issue
- forecasting what may happen based on collected information.

To move beyond simply describing results requires the use of inferential data analysis, where advanced statistical techniques are used to make judgments (i.e., inferences) about some issue (e.g., is one type of customer different from another type of customer). The "what-if" scenarios shown in Table 4.1 all require analysis using inferential statistics.

STEP 7: REPORT THE FINDINGS

The purpose of a research report is to not only present the results, but to do it in a way that is easy for the marketer to understand the key findings. Kimberley Bell advises that all research reports should have three key elements: 1) interpretation, 2) clarity, and 3) implications (Bell, 2016).

1. *Interpretation*. A client isn't interested in a list of results with no meaning. What they want to know is how the findings relate to the marketing decisions at hand. For instance, in a study of how people use their mobile phones (*Moments That Matter*, Forrester Consulting, 2015), the results showed that smartphone users spend the most time on their phones using apps for "me time". What might this result mean for an app marketer? The researcher should look for patterns in the data. One of the patterns identified in the Mobile Moments Study is that smartphone users use their phones at home. Now that this pattern is identified, the marketing decision-maker can identify what actions might be possible to take advantage of the pattern.

2. *Clarity*. It is essential for the report to be clear and relevant to the original objectives of the research. Why was the research conducted in the first place? Focus on supporting the findings with statistics and with graphs and diagrams.

3. *Implications*. Now that the results have been presented, how can their business benefit from this insight and apply it? Keep in mind that the researcher is not a decision-maker. The role of the researcher is to deliver the information and guide the client to a decision of their own.

STEP 8: MAKE THE DECISION

At this stage, the research report has made its way back to the marketing manager who initially determined the research problem. Before making a decision based on the research findings, the decision-maker should take the time to evaluate the quality of the research report (Acito, Day and Lee, 1987).

EVALUATING RESEARCH QUALITY

As a marketing manager, you won't typically have the expertise of marketing researchers in the areas of research design and analysis. Still, you'll want to evaluate the quality of the research before you make decisions based on research findings. Failing to assess the validity and reliability of that data could lead to inaccurate analyses and poor business decisions.

Basically, validity boils down to whether the research is really measuring what it claims to be measuring. For instance, if a marketer has commissioned custom research on how consumers perceive the brand's position relative to the top competitor in the market, the marketer should understand how the data was gathered to help determine whether the research really captures the information the way the research company says it does. Always ask this simple question: *Is the research measuring what it is supposed to measure?*

Reliability is chiefly concerned with making sure the method of data gathering leads to consistent results. For some types of research this can be measured by having different researchers follow the same methods to see whether results can be duplicated. If results are similar, then it is likely that the method of data gathering is reliable. Replicating research is likely not within the marketer's budget for research though. So in lieu of that option, consider whether the research design, data collection, and analysis appear to have been conducted with sound decisions and professional standards.

Consider the following questions when evaluating market research before using the results in your own business decisions:

- *If the research report is secondary research, what was the purpose of the original research?* Based on why the data is presented, the provider might have had a biased reason to post the information. Commercial businesses and even political parties post information online that might favor them in some way or represent their own interests.

- *Who collected the data?* Reliability of data can be impacted by who collected it. Data from a government agency is going to be much more reliable than data found on a personal website or blog. Were the researchers established experts?

- *Does the report include sufficient information on the research design for you to evaluate the research decisions and make a personal judgment about the likely accuracy of the results?* The completeness of the survey report is one indicator of the trustworthiness of the survey and the professionalism of the expert who is presenting the results of the survey. A survey report generally should provide in detail:
  - the purpose of the survey
  - a definition of the target population and a description of the population that was actually sampled
  - a description of the sample design and selection method
  - the research technique and data collection mode
  - the defined measurement for the study variables (including the exact wording of the questions used for survey or interview designs)
  - detailed findings on the analysis of study variables
  - supporting documentation such as the questionnaire (if relevant), statistical analyses, tables, etc.

From detailed reports, marketing decision-makers can then consider whether the results are likely to be reliable and valid (based on Diamond, 2011 and Stewart, 2014).

CASE STUDY

ITV USES MARKET RESEARCH TO DESIGN VIDEO STREAMING SERVICE

Video streaming is all the rage. Viewing of live television programs is declining worldwide and streaming of programming online and through subscription services like Netflix and Hulu are on the rise. Research shows that in the UK, the time spent streaming television online has doubled from that just a year ago.

A study from consulting firm Deloitte found that consumers are more inclined to stream entertainment from an Internet service than tune in to live TV. The study also found that more than 50% of television viewers stream movies and television shows monthly. What's more – among the services associated with video viewing – 72% cited streaming as one of the most valuable services (Deloitte, 2017b).

Viewers have spoken – they want streaming video! But there's also a lot of competition in the market – Netflix, Prime Video, Hulu. Viewers can stream from many providers – some paid, some free, some streaming only, some a mix of live television and streaming. One such company is ITV.

ITV is the oldest commercial media broadcaster and producer in the UK across TV and digital channels. You may have watched some of its most popular shows, including *Mr Selfridge, Coronation Street, Dancing on Ice* and *Broadchurch*. ITV broadcasts traditional television, but it also offers on-demand streaming. That means it competes with other streaming providers both directly and indirectly. ITV had a total viewing share of 21.2% in 2015, the largest audience of any UK commercial broadcaster, with programming primarily funded through television advertising.

But as viewers increasingly turn to streaming content, ITV wants to provide its viewers with the content they want, when they want, and via the medium they want. "With new competing video streaming services entering the market, ITV's streaming HUB service must delight and amaze. We need research that will tell us what to fix and what to innovate to gain new ITV viewers and to ensure current ITV viewers to spend more time with ITV Hub", said Adam Crozier, ITV's CEO (FlexMR, n.d.).

To learn what the target audience wanted, ITV turned to UK-based market research provider, FlexMR. Market research was especially important because the ITV Hub improvements being planned included the introduction of the ITV Pay Player (a fee-based curated archive of iconic programs) as well as changes to the current streaming system that would impact the user experience. What's more, ITV had a tight timeline.

FlexMR provided a full-service, custom market research program incorporating several methods to answer the research questions posed by ITV. It developed a short-term community of 500 trial users to provide feedback on the ITV Hub experience. This was a qualitative approach that ensured relevant insights from the user experience could be collected. Not only did these users share experiences and attitudes, they also were given access to a "Problem Box" where system bugs could be reported. The research also included customer journey research for specific market segments, including casual users, frequent viewers, and new audiences. Dedicated online forums (focus group research) enabled discussions on the ITV Player features and the programming offered. UX-based smartboards prompted image-led discussions on layout, supported by a range of sentiment-led analysis.

Multiple methods were used – both qualitative and quantitative. Overall, this balance of qualitative and quantitative research methodology guided the day-to-day developments of the ITV Player platform. What did FlexMR and ITV learn?

(Continued)

- ITV's intended payment model was a single, flat-rate subscription fee. However, in-depth community discussion revealed that consumers preferred a tiered model of payment in order to suit low- and high-volume users.

- User diaries confirmed ITV's belief that viewers have a strong appetite for accessing iconic material from the ITV archive. This content was worth paying for.

- Though users could view from multiple devices, mobile features needed to be easier to navigate and desktop features needed to be expanded.

- Viewers need customer support – at least they want to know that it is available if they need it. In response, ITV expanded its customer service and added a live chat system.

"Through working with FlexMR we were able to get a clear understanding of how consumers used ITV Player. This helped us fine tune it before launch" (FlexMR, n.d.). Marketing decisions based on the research included how the payment portal for premium options operated, customer service experiences/training, bug fixes and patches in the product itself prior to launch. The insights from the marketing research enabled the ITV Player development team to create a world-class digital content delivery system.

PRME

UNILEVER RESEARCH SHOWS PEOPLE WANT SUSTAINABLE LIVING BRANDS

Unilever commissioned market research to learn how sustainability issues affect people's purchasing behavior (Sustainable Brands, 2017). The study surveyed 20,000 adults in five countries. The results showed that over half of all consumers already buy or want to buy sustainably. One in three (33%) already choose to purchase brands that they believe are doing social or environmental good. Another 21% do not currently base purchase decisions on brand commitment to sustainability but would like to do so. Moreover, one in five say they would choose a brand if its sustainability credentials were made clear on packaging or in advertising. The research backs up Unilever's belief that sustainability is an increasingly important part of consumers' purchasing decisions. In the past, there has been a "say-do gap", meaning that people will say sustainability matters but still choose a brand based on price rather than sustainability. Unilever's research and sales data show the gap is closing. The trend is stronger among consumers in emerging markets rather than those in developed countries. While 53% of shoppers in the UK and US said they feel better when they buy sustainable products, 88% said so in India and 85% in Brazil. People in emerging markets are more likely to be exposed to the negative impacts of unsustainable business practices such as poor air quality or water shortages.

Unilever has made sustainable living the cornerstone of its purpose. The brand seeks to "help create a world where everyone can live well within the natural limits of the planet. We're putting sustainable living at the heart of everything we do including through our brands and products, our standards of behavior within and beyond Unilever, and our partnerships which are driving transformational change across our value chain" (Unilever, n.d.). The Unilever Sustainable Living Plan includes steps that contribute to many of the UN's sustainable development goals with SDG 3, with good health and well-being chief among them. According to Paul Polmon, Unilever's CEO, business needs to "Put the SDGs at the core of business strategies. This means applying an SDG lens to every aspect of strategy: appointing the right leaders, innovating to create sustainable solutions, marketing products and services that inspire consumers to make sustainable choices, and using the goals to guide leadership development and women's empowerment at every level" (Polman, 2017).

Unilever's five biggest brands – Knorr, Dove, Persil, Lipton and Hellmann's – are designated as Sustainable Living brands. They combine a strong social and/or environmental purpose that contributes to achieving the Unilever Sustainable Living Plan goals. Their success points to the business case for sustainability. These brands grew 50% faster than the rest of Unilever's business.

Since the launch of its Sustainable Living Plan, Unilever has helped around 600 million people to improve their health through programs on handwashing, safe drinking water, sanitation, oral health, and self-esteem. The Domestos brand toilet cleaner helped over 10 million people to gain improved access to a toilet. The Vaseline Healing Project reached 2.6 million people last year. Pureit, a water purifier, provided 96 billion liters of safe drinking water to more than 55 million people last year. Pureit removes harmful viruses, bacteria, parasites, and other impurities from water without boiling at a cost of about a penny for 3.2 liters of drinking water. There's no need for gas, electricity, or for a continuous water supply, meaning anyone, anywhere, can use it. Lifebuoy's School of 5 teaches children and their families to adopt healthy handwashing with soap habits using in-person volunteers or via mobile phone calls. Signal toothpaste provides free dental camps, ensuring kids get an annual check-up and treatment from a dentist. Unilever is so committed to its purpose that it is even considering registering as a "B corporation". B corporations incorporate social responsibility goals in their governing documents and set impact goals in addition to profitability goals. Unilever's market research suggests that the company will do well by doing good.

online resources

Visit **https://study.sagepub.com/tuten** for free additional resources related to this chapter.

CHAPTER SUMMARY

Understanding the components of marketing information systems, and the scope of data sources each component provides, is essential for all marketing decision-makers. Knowing how to gather, sort, and analyze the data helps marketers to make informed decisions regarding consumers, trends, and the marketing mix. Having good data that allows marketers to be confident in their decisions reduces the risk associated with these decisions. In addition, while marketers rarely conduct their own research, they must know the steps in the market research process in order to better judge whether research results presented to them are valid, reliable, unbiased, appropriately controlled, and ethically collected. It is important to remember that data alone is not enough to make informed decisions. Marketing managers must utilize the data as a tool, combined with their own insights gained from experience, to understand the implications of the information extracted from that data and to apply that understanding to the marketplace and the decisions at hand.

REVIEW QUESTIONS

1. Why is market research valuable for marketers?

2. What information inputs are used in marketing information systems?

3. What is the difference between marketing research and the other MIS inputs?

4. What are the steps in the market research process?

5. When should qualitative research be chosen rather than quantitative methods?

KEY TERMS

1. **Cost–benefit analysis** – there may not be enough time or funding for the research, or the expected value of the information may not be sufficiently high to warrant the expense. Marketing researchers have to choose the methods that best meet the needs of the marketing manager, including gathering the necessary data while managing constraints like budget, cost, and viability.

2. **Cross-sectional design** – usually involves the systematic collection of responses to a survey instrument (e.g., questionnaire) from one or more samples of respondents at one point in time (unless the study is longitudinal and involves collecting data at multiple time points).

3. **Descriptive analysis** – used to provide a summary of what data has been gathered without making a statement of whether the results hold up to statistical evaluation.

4. **Descriptive research** – probes systematically into the marketing problem and bases its conclusions on a large sample of participants.

5. **Ethnographic research** – seeks to understand how "real" consumers use their products by observations or interviews conducted in their real-life environments.

6. **Inferential data analysis** – advanced statistical techniques are used to make judgments about some issue.

7. **Market research** (also **marketing research**) – the function or process by which information is gathered to meet the needs of a marketing decision-maker. Marketing research redefines the marketer's problem as research questions, designs the methods for collecting the information, manages and implements the data collection process, analyzes the results, and communicates the findings.

8. **Marketing intelligence** – a process that constantly captures, assesses, and uses information from multiple sources during the ongoing business decision-making process.

9. **MDSS (Marketing Decision Support System)** – the term used for the data management, analyzing, modeling, and reporting processes by which the data is transformed into information and marketing knowledge.

10. **Mystery shopping** – a research method that collects data from researchers posing as customers in order to gather observational data about the subject and interactions with employees.

11. **Netnography** – a rapidly growing research methodology that adapts ethnographic research techniques to study the communities that emerge through computer-mediated communications.

12. **Neuromarketing research** – a field of marketing research that studies consumers' sensorimotor, cognitive, and affective responses to marketing stimuli.

13. **Panels** – address some of the limitations of survey research by recruiting participants who represent a market.

14. **Primary data** – data collected for the current research problem.

15. **Qualitative studies** – generate data about behaviors or attitudes based on observing them directly or questioning directly, answering exploratory questions (why).

16. **Quantitative studies** – generate data about the behavior or attitudes based on observing them indirectly, through a measurement or an instrument such as a survey or an analytics tool, answering descriptive questions (how much, when, what).

17. **Reliability** – making sure the method of data gathering leads to consistent results.

18. **RFP (request for proposal)** – as a minimum, a market research RFP states the project parameters and requests responses to the basic questions that will allow the client organization to evaluate the proposals and choose the research provider.

19. **Scanner-based research** – evolved as a system for gathering information from a single group of respondents by continuously monitoring the advertising, promotions, and pricing they are exposed to and the things they buy.

20. **Secondary data** – data that was collected for a previous purpose.

21. **Secondary research** – includes pre-existing sources of information already created for other purposes that may save the organization time and money compared to primary research. Sources may include published research from trade organizations, syndicated research firms, journal articles, trade articles, and government organizations.

22. **Shopper marketing** – a form of marketing that uses data to make decisions to improve the shopping experience and better meet shopper needs and wants by measuring how shoppers access information related to their buying decisions, what digital advertising message inspired action, whether they downloaded coupons, whether they purchased, and if so via what channels and websites.

23. **Syndicated research** – general information related to specific topics or industries which specialized firms collect on a regular basis and sell to other firms. Examples of syndicated research reports include Nielsen's television ratings and Arbitron's radio ratings.

24. **Uncertainty and Risk** – *uncertainty* is a state of having limited knowledge of current conditions or future outcomes. It is a major component of *risk*, which involves the likelihood and scale of negative consequences.

25. **Validity** – whether the research is really measuring what it claims to be measuring.

Chapter 5

MARKETING STRATEGY

In this chapter, we'll learn the answers to the following questions:

1 What is marketing strategy? How do marketing strategies relate to business and corporate strategies?

2 What are the steps in the strategic planning process?

3 How do these relate to the elements in a marketing plan?

INTRODUCTION

Marketing is central to an organization's success. It is tasked with understanding market needs, identifying, designing, delivering, and communicating an offer capable of meeting those needs (and doing so with a competitive advantage), and successfully producing stakeholder value. Thus far, you've learned about buyer behavior, segmentation, targeting, and positioning, and how to use market research to get the market intelligence you need to plan marketing strategy. Marketing strategy and the strategic planning process are the focus of Chapter 5.

OPENING VIGNETTE

NETFLIX – APPLYING THE STRATEGIC MARKETING PLANNING PROCESS

Netflix, the world's leading Internet television network, has disrupted the entertainment industry twice in its 20-year history. Back in the mid-1990s, Blockbuster was America's sweetheart for movie entertainment enjoyed at home. People browsed movies (including recent "blockbusters", hence the brand name) in Blockbuster retail stores and rented movies to watch at home. In 1998, Netflix launched as an online DVD rental and sales site, Netflix.com. Customers could make selections online and receive the movies by mail.

Netflix disrupted the industry by eliminating the need for physical retail stores, an innovation in *distribution*. You see, Netflix competed against Blockbuster with the same *product* – home movie rentals. But by using the Internet to distribute movies directly to customers, Netflix provided a value proposition with a competitive advantage. Customers could have the same at-home movie experience but with less friction. Even the name, "Netflix", points to the initial disruptive innovation – the company used the Internet (the "net") to distribute movies (the "flix") directly to customers. Netflix's acquisition of customers came at Blockbuster's expense, as Blockbuster customers switched to Netflix.

In 1999, Netflix's marketing strategy was based on an industry innovation in pricing. The company debuted a subscription service of unlimited DVD rentals for one low price, making the value proposition even better! Why? That's because Blockbuster customers were charged late fees when movies weren't returned on time – and this happened a lot! In fact, late fees, amounting to hundreds of millions of dollars, made up more than 15% of Blockbuster's annual revenues! The Netflix subscription plan meant customers could keep a movie as long as they wanted without penalty.

Netflix's early marketing strategies focused on building market share against an industry incumbent, Blockbuster. But over time, the environment changed. Internet speeds and bandwidth costs made it possible to stream video at scale. More people than ever had Internet access and mobile devices. In 2007, Netflix once again innovated in the distribution of movies, by adding a streaming service with a small library of titles. People could still rent DVDs (from a library of about 100,000 titles), but Netflix wisely anticipated the demand for streaming entertainment.

Interestingly, it wasn't until 2011 that Netflix's marketing strategy focused on product innovation. It was then that Netflix experimented with producing its own original shows, beginning with Lilyhammer. Though Netflix continues to invest heavily in technology to support and improve its online distribution channel, creating original content is the linchpin of Netflix's marketing strategy. Subscribers stream more than 150 million hours of TV shows and movies per day! Perhaps it's not surprising then that Netflix has allocated billions of dollars to produce 700 original shows in 2018. The company's goals for new customer acquisition and customer retention are tied to the company's ability to offer a sufficient quantity of high-quality, original content. So far, the strategy is working! Now, more than 125 million people in 190 countries – everywhere except China, North Korea, Crimea, and Syria – stream video entertainment on-demand using a smartphone, laptop, desktop, or connected television (Netflix, n.d.).

MARKETING STRATEGY
WHAT IS MARKETING STRATEGY?

Marketing strategy is defined as an integrated pattern of decisions specifying choices of markets to serve, market segments to target, marketing activities, and the allocation of resources to create, communicate, and deliver a product that offers value to customers in exchanges with the organization, and thereby results in organizational goal achievement (Varadarajan, 2012). If you take a close look at the definition, you can see that marketing strategy relates to our work as marketers. Which markets will we serve? What are the needs of those markets? Which segments should we target? How do we position the offer with a value proposition and competitive advantage? How should we design the offer to create the value we've promised in the value proposition in terms of product, price, place, promotion, people, process, and presence? How can we accomplish all this such that we also achieve our goals and objectives? Some say it is difficult to define the word strategy. Any and all possible answers to these questions fall into the broad scope of marketing strategy.

HOW DO MARKETING STRATEGIES RELATE TO THE LEVELS OF AN ORGANIZATION?

Organizations use a planning system based on a strategy hierarchy, in which corporate strategy guides business unit strategies and business unit strategies guide functional tactics (Hamel and Prahaland, 2005). Corporate strategy is concerned with the organization's scope and direction, taking a portfolio approach to creating and earning value. Corporate strategic planning defines the corporate mission, identifies growth opportunities, and assigns resources. A mission statement is a clear and concise expression of the organization's reason for being. The statement guides the organization's strategic perspective. Organizations may also state a vision, an aspirational statement. For instance, IKEA expresses its vision as "to create a better everyday life" for people. These statements are meant to be internal documents used to guide decision-making, but they also point to a meaningful purpose – something that can resonate with customers and serve as a foundation for brand meaning. You can see this in these examples:

- Virgin (capital conglomerate): to embrace the human spirit and let it fly.

- Soma (water-filter company): to hydrate the world.

- Casper ("bed in a box" mattresses): great sleep, made simple.

- Google (search engine and online advertising): to organize the world's information and make it universally accessible and useful.

- Headspace (meditation app): to improve the health and happiness of the world.

Business leaders are increasingly recognizing how a strong sense of purpose can help companies meet challenges and some are embracing "purpose-led branding", which we will discuss in-depth later in the book. Figure 5.1 illustrates the relationship between purpose, vision, mission, and corporate sustainability efforts (Sable and Jones, 2018).

Historically, strategy theorists have advised marketers to seek a strategic fit, which means to match resources to ambitions. However, companies that have disrupted industries and risen to positions of global leadership pursued stretch goals that were beyond their resources and capabilities. These organizations created a strategic intent, an obsession for winning that infiltrated every level of the organization, and used innovation to change the competitive landscape (Hamel and Prahaland, 2005).

Each business in an organization's portfolio is a strategic business unit (SBU). SBUs follow a business model, which is essentially the way an organization makes money. Business models have three elements: 1) a value proposition, 2) a profit formula, and 3) the resources and processes needed to deliver the value proposition (Johnson, Christensen and Kagermann, 2008). As we learned in Chapter 3, a value proposition is the promise of value customers will receive (the benefits). The profit formula defines revenue expectations, cost structure, and margin contributions (Johnson et al., 2008). The processes needed to deliver the value proposition are part of a system of interdependent organizational functions called a value chain (Amitt and Zott, 2010). Though the functions are interdependent, each function will have its own specialized strategic plan as to how the function will

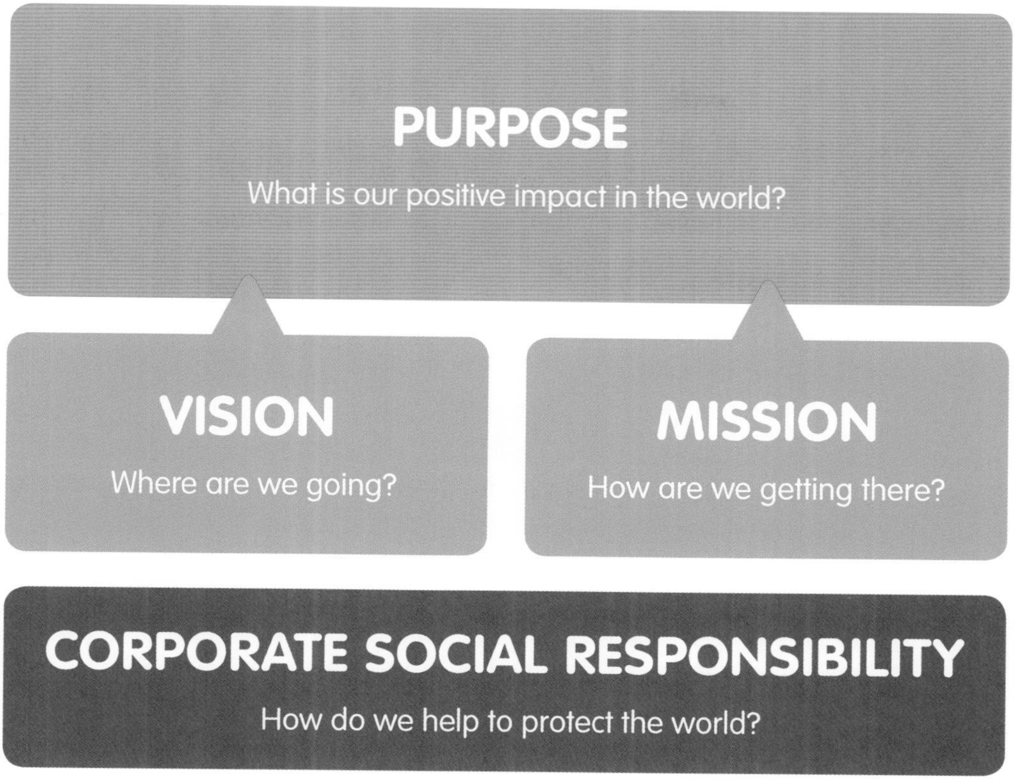

FIGURE 5.1   The Relationship Between Purpose, Vision, Mission, and Sustainability Efforts

Source: Adapted from Sable and Jones (2018: 13)

contribute to the overall success of the business. Some functions may be outsourced, but core competencies will be nurtured. At the operational level of the organization, tactical plans are developed for each plan element. Corporate strategists may use a business model canvas template like the one shown in Figure 5.2 as a planning tool (Osterwalder, 2013).

Whether planning marketing strategy at the corporate, business, or operational level, there are commonalities to the concept of strategy: strategy as 1) perspective (direction), 2) position (competitive advantage), 3) pattern (design), and 4) plan (roadmap) (Mintzberg, 1994). Ultimately, strategy answers "how" questions (Watkins, 2007). For marketers like those at Netflix, strategic planning is the process of analyzing the situation, identifying objectives to accomplish, deciding how to accomplish those objectives with specific strategies and tactics, planning for implementation, and defining how effectiveness will be assessed.

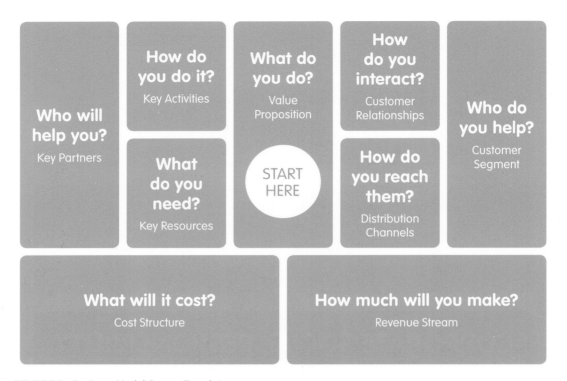

FIGURE 5.2   Business Model Canvas Template

Source: Based on the tool designed by Alexander Osterwalder (2013)

Why should we take the time to plan? Some experts warn that the strategic planning process acts as a "feasibility sieve" and can result in "recipes" for marketing strategy (Hamel and Prahaland, 2005). These recipes limit ambition, innovation, and future competitive advantage. Despite these warnings, there is tremendous value in planning. Planning ensures that an organization understands its markets and its competitors. It helps to ensure that organizations are aware of the changing marketplace environment. It provides for assessing contingencies, if–then scenarios that could occur and influence the likelihood of success. When organizational partners participate in the planning process, they are better able to communicate and coordinate activities. Planning requires that objectives are set and agreed upon, which improves the likelihood of those objectives being met. It enhances the ability of managers to allocate limited resources using established priorities. Perhaps most of all, planning enables success to be defined. Success or the lack thereof becomes a measurable outcome that can guide future planning efforts.

THE STRATEGIC PLANNING PROCESS
WHAT ARE THE STEPS IN THE STRATEGIC PLANNING PROCESS AND HOW DO THEY RELATE TO THE ELEMENTS OF A MARKETING PLAN?

The strategic planning process includes the following steps:

1. Conduct a situation analysis.
2. Identify a strategic opportunity.
3. Determine the marketing objectives.
4. Describe the target market.
5. Formulate a marketing strategy.
6. Establish the implementation plan.
7. Determine evaluation and control parameters.

STEP 1: CONDUCT A SITUATION ANALYSIS

The first step in the planning process is a situation analysis. The situation analysis details the current problem or opportunity the organization faces. It includes analysis of the organization's internal and external environments such that the organization's resources and capabilities can be considered along with competition, customers, and environmental issues. The situation analysis is useful for identifying opportunities (options for growth), evaluating strategic fit (matching strengths to opportunities), and anticipating threats for contingency planning. Three models are prevalent in conducting situation analyses: 1) SWOT analysis, 2) PESTLE analysis, and 3) Five Forces analysis.

SWOT ANALYSIS

The SWOT acronym refers to strengths, weaknesses, opportunities, and threats that the firm should consider as it crafts a strategy. The internal environment refers to the strengths and weaknesses of the organization – the controllable elements inside a firm that influence how well the firm operates. The external environment consists of those elements outside the organization – the organization's opportunities and threats – that may affect its choices and capabilities. Unlike elements of the internal environment that management can control to a large degree, the firm can't directly control these external factors, so management must respond to them through its planning process. Figure 5.3 illustrates the organization of a SWOT analysis.

Strengths	Weaknesses
• Core competences • Resources • Successes	• Skill weaknesses • Missing resources • Failures
Opportunities	**Threats**
• Macro or micro environmental state to leverage	• Macro or micro environmental state to protect against

FIGURE 5.3   SWOT Analysis

Using the results of the SWOT analysis, strategists can then consider opportunities that make use of the organization's strengths, identify any weaknesses that must be overcome to pursue chosen opportunities, and/or prepare to avoid or overcome threats using organizational strengths.

PESTEL ANALYSIS

To adequately assess opportunities and threats for a SWOT analysis, analysts may use the PESTEL model to review the major macro-environmental factors affecting an organization's situational context.

- *Political.* The political environment includes taxation policy, government stability, and foreign trade regulations.
- *Economic.* The economic environment includes general state of the economy, consumer confidence, unemployment, disposable income, interest rates, and exchange rates.
- *Social.* The social/cultural environment includes demographic patterns, lifestyle trends, norms and values, and elements of shared culture.
- *Technological.* The technological environment is influenced by new discoveries and capabilities.

- *Ecological.* The ecological environment captures concerns related to the state of the environment, environmental changes, and minimizing environmental damage, such as water, air, land, and energy issues.

- *Legal.* The legal environment covers issues such as regulations related to production, distribution, employment, and taxation.

PORTER'S FIVE FORCES MODEL

Porter's Five Forces model is an analysis of the micro-environment in which an organization operates. It reveals which players have power and therefore is useful for assessing threats and identifying possible partnerships. Figure 5.4 illustrates the forces and their influence on the attractiveness of the market.

We can see Porter's Five Forces at play in the Netflix example. The company has faced intense industry rivalry in recent years. When Netflix first came to market, it was the only option for online distribution of video entertainment. The threat of new entrants was high and many competitors have entered the market following the "Netflix model". Competition includes Amazon Prime Video, Hulu, CBS All Access, and others. Disney plans to launch its own streaming service featuring its content in the near future. Netflix licenses content from suppliers like CBS, but many of those suppliers have begun their own streaming services and become competitors. But other content suppliers lack power in that there are relatively few companies with the financial resources to commission high-quality video content. In fact, some Hollywood insiders have expressed a fear that Netflix will have a monopoly on creative video content (Masters, 2016). Buyers should have power because of the many alternative services available, but the low price point of these services results in many customers viewing competitors instead as complementary services. Many subscribe to more than one service. The most popular combination is Netflix and Amazon Prime Video.

FIGURE 5.4   Porter's Five Forces Model

STEP 2: IDENTIFY A STRATEGIC OPPORTUNITY

The organization must determine the strategic opportunity it wishes to pursue. This may be a new business model, new target market, new products to offer, or tactical shifts to increase margin, market share, and/or sales and profitability. Two models are especially useful: 1) Ansoff's matrix and 2) the Jobs-To-Be-Done Growth Strategy Matrix.

ANSOFF'S MATRIX

Ansoff's matrix, shown in Figure 5.5, classifies strategies according to whether they involve the organization's existing products or new products and the organization's existing target markets or new markets, resulting in four strategic options: 1) market penetration, 2) product development, 3) market development, and 4) diversification.

FIGURE 5.5 Ansoff's Market Opportunity Matrix

The options must be considered in light of whether they are suitable for pursuing the organization's strategic position, acceptable given the organization's mission, and feasible given the organization's resources. In other words, these opportunities must be evaluated alongside the results of the situation analysis.

Market penetration is a strategy by which a company seeks to increase revenues from sales of its present products in its existing markets. This strategy may be aimed at increasing usage and turnover, increasing margins by increasing prices and/or lowering costs, and/or building market share and sales by attracting new customers with lower prices and/or advertising. Thus, market penetration can include both objectives of acquisition and retention of customers. Market penetration becomes more difficult when the market is saturated, the product is perceived as a commodity, and/or when competitors have a competitive advantage. Some have suggested that Netflix's growth will slow because of market saturation, especially in the United States. In the United States, market penetration is still feasible as more and more people become "cord-cutters", a term that refers to people who have cancelled cable entertainment services and rely totally on streaming entertainment. Margin can also be increased with price increases. Further, Netflix's global markets have substantial potential for market penetration. Even though market penetration is seen as the least risky of Ansoff's options, don't assume it is without risk.

Product development seeks to increase revenues by developing products in the organization's product portfolio while targeting the existing market. New product development is a broad term in that it encompasses the development of innovative "new to the world" products and simple modifications and improvements to existing products. We'll discuss this strategy further in Chapter 6. For instance, Netflix has improved its service by enabling customers in areas with limited Internet access to download some of its program titles to watch offline. Some of the tactics used to implement this strategy include developing new product features, different quality versions of the product, or different models and sizes. Product development can be useful for creating up-sell and cross-sell opportunities for existing customers and for encouraging switching behaviors among competitor's customers. For example, Netflix is partnering with Target to offer themed toys and other merchandise celebrating its most popular shows (AdAge, 2017). Fans of the hit show *Stranger Things* will be able to buy t-shirts, coffee mugs, and other themed items. Netflix is also considering the possibility of buying movie theaters. Doing so would expand the current service to include in-theater entertainment (AdAge, 2017). New technology drives product development whether through improvements to existing products or the creation of entirely new innovations.

Market development (sometimes called market creation) seeks to increase sales by offering existing products to new markets. New markets may become viable when disposable income moves into the hands of new groups of buyers, when economic growth or consumer trends favor new geographic locations, and when changing values and lifestyles open up a new market. Netflix followed a market development strategy between 2014 and 2017, during which the company expanded into more than 130 new geographic markets. It is now in every location in the world except China, North Korea, Crimea, and

Syria. Even in China, the company is exploring a partnership that will facilitate access to the Chinese market.

Diversification involves offering new products in new markets. It is the most risky of the opportunities in the matrix, but related diversification is less risky than unrelated diversification. Related diversification means that the new product is related in some way to the organization's existing business. There are two types of related diversification: 1) vertical integration (expanding along the supply chain) and 2) horizontal diversification (expanding into parallel products). Experts advise that organizations seek diversification opportunities that utilize their existing core competencies, even creating offer portfolios based on core competencies rather than products (Moreno, Rodríguez and Zambrana, 2014). Netflix followed a vertical integration strategy when it began developing Netflix Originals. Doing so provided Netflix more power and control over the pipeline of content needed to deliver on its value proposition. Netflix also acquired Millarworld, a comic book publisher (Netflix, 2017a). The acquisition is part horizontal diversification and part vertical diversification in that Millarworld will continue to publish comic books for its customer base, but the characters and stories can also be developed into video content for Netflix.

According to the latest CMO Survey results, companies are investing 52% of marketing spending in market penetration strategies, 24% in product development, 13% in market development, and about 11% in diversification (Moorman, 2018).

JOBS-TO-BE-DONE GROWTH STRATEGY MATRIX

We reviewed the value of the Jobs-To-Be-Done theory in Chapter 2 as an approach to understanding customer needs and in Chapter 3 as a segmentation base. Remember, the fundamental basis of JTBD is that people buy products to help them get a job done. Analysis of company successes and failures reinforces the belief: successful brands are those that help customers do a job better and/or cheaper. This observation resulted in the creation of the Jobs-To-Be-Done Growth Strategy Matrix (Ulwick, 2016b). Figure 5.6 illustrates the JTBD growth strategy matrix, which explains that organizations can offer products that, relative to the competition, are 1) better and more expensive, 2) better and less expensive, 3) worse but less expensive, and 4) worse and more expensive.

A differentiated strategy offers a better product at a higher price. This strategy works when there are customers willing to pay more to meet previously unmet needs. Examples include the Nest thermostat and Nespresso's coffee machines.

A dominant strategy offers a product that gets a job done significantly better and for significantly less money. This strategy offers a relative advantage in benefits provided and cost. Netflix used this strategy. Other examples include Uber and many of Google's products such as Search, Maps, and AdWords.

	Higher Price	Lower Price
Job Done Better	Differentiated Strategy (underserved customers)	Dominant Strategy (all customers)
Job Done Worse	Discrete Strategy (customers with few alternatives)	Disruptive Strategy (non-customers and overserved customers)

FIGURE 5.6   Jobs-To-Be-Done Growth Strategy Matrix

A disruptive strategy targets a population of overserved customers or non-consumers with a new product that is cheaper but not as good as competing solutions. Examples include Google Docs (relative to Microsoft Office), Dollar Shave Club (relative to Gillette), and Coursera (relative to universities). A discrete strategy offers an inferior product that costs more to a market of customers with limited alternatives. The expensive and unhealthy food options in airports are an example. Organizations may also follow a sustaining strategy, which is offering a product that is only slightly better and/or slightly less expensive. This is a common strategy but not one that offers a competitive advantage.

STEP 3: DETERMINE THE MARKETING OBJECTIVES

In this stage of the planning process, the planner elaborates on what is expected of the strategy. What are some examples of the basic objectives marketers pursue? Here are some important ones:

- increase brand awareness
- improve brand or product reputation
- increase website traffic
- amplify or augment public relations work
- improve search engine rankings
- improve perceived customer service quality
- generate sales leads
- reduce customer acquisition and support costs
- increase sales/sales revenue.

Objectives should be stated using the SMART characteristics: 1) Specific, 2) Measureable, 3) Action-oriented, 4) Relevant, and 5) Time-lined. For example, Netflix may have set a SMART objective for its market development strategy. Hypothetically, the objective may have read: "Establish distribution in France, Germany, Austria, and Belgium including country-specific Netflix websites by December 2015", and "Acquire 500,000 new streaming customers in each country market by March 2016". The tactical plans would incorporate objectives for each tactic used to pursue the strategic objectives. For instance, Netflix pursues a customer-retention strategy. A hypothetical objective might be "to retain 95% of customers month over month". Netflix's tactical objectives might be "to encourage customers to watch a minimum of 5 hours but preferably 15 hours or more of Netflix content per month". Why? For customer retention, Netflix knows that people are unlikely to cancel if they watch 15 hours of content or more per month, but likely to cancel if they watch less than 5 hours (Bulygo, n.d.).

Note that the content of the objective will vary based on the situation, the problem at hand, and the chosen strategy. For instance, Netflix's position has historically focused on scripted television programs and movies. It has expanded its library to include recordings of live comedy performances, but the market lacked awareness of this new benefit. Netflix used an advertising campaign to deliver the message "Netflix is a joke", and reposition the brand to include comedy (Vena, 2017). The objectives for the repositioning strategy might include "Reach 80% of fans of late-night comedy shows with advertising message in the third quarter", or "increase search for comedy-related titles on Netflix.com by 155% within 6 weeks of campaign launch".

STEP 4: DESCRIBE THE TARGET MARKET

Marketing plans must target the desired audience in a meaningful and relevant manner. We have already covered buyer behavior in Chapter 2 and segmentation and targeting in

Chapter 3. In those chapters, you learned how to develop a persona and customer journey to capture key insights about the target market. In the strategic planning process, you'll turn to those insights to inform strategy decisions. Recall that organizations may target a mass market typically with an undifferentiated approach, multiple segments with a differentiated approach, a concentrated, niche approach, or a personalized, one-to-one approach. KANTAR Consulting believes digital technology is driving a shift to more personalized, niche target markets: "The mass market is dissolving into a proliferation of small niches outside the comfort zone of established businesses, ultimately headed to digitally enabled personalization" (Walker Smith, 2018: 8).

What kind of targeting approach does Netflix take? Well, that's an interesting question. We could argue that Netflix pursues a mass market approach for customer acquisition, offering the same basic service (streaming video entertainment), via the same channels (any connected device to Netflix service), at the same monthly subscription price. The basic marketing mix does not vary by segment. In its customer acquisition efforts in new geographic markets, Netflix reported it targeted consumers with three simple characteristics: affluence, international credit cards, and smartphones (Netflix Investors, 2018).

When it comes to customer-retention efforts, Netflix uses its enormous library of content and recommendation algorithms to use a concentration, niche targeting approach. The company foregoes typical demographic and geographic segmentation variables (despite its vast global reach). Todd Yellin, VP of Product, said, "Geography, age, and gender? We put that in the garbage heap" (Morris, 2016). Instead, Netflix uses big data and advanced data analytics, including predictive modeling, to deliver personalized content recommendations and even personalized trailers! That's right. Not everyone sees the same image or trailer for *Stranger Things*. There are thousands of variations possible and Netflix's algorithms select what to reveal based on its segmentation data. Netflix also uses human and artificial intelligence to content-code and categorize programs to facilitate insights and predictions. There are more than 76,000 genres (Madrigal, 2014) (such as period pieces about royalty based on real life) in the Netflix library (Titcomb, 2018). This is why Joris Evers, Director of Global Communications, said, "There are 33 million different versions of Netflix" (Bulygo, n.d.).

STEP 5: FORMULATE A MARKETING STRATEGY

The next step in strategic planning is to determine the marketing mix decisions that will operationalize the overall marketing strategy. As we discussed in Chapter 1, the marketing mix decisions include product, price, place, promotion, people, process, and presence. Figure 5.7 highlights some of the decisions that may be made when formulating the marketing mix.

FIGURE 5.7   The Marketing Mix

Each of these will be covered further in later chapters. The decisions made will need to be aligned with the organization's mission and identity and be valuable for achieving the plan's objectives. Because of the contingencies identified in the situation analysis and required by the selected strategic opportunity, the mix decisions may represent minor shifts or substantial design changes. For example, if Netflix pursues a market penetration strategy, its marketing mix may be stable with the exception of promotion, which may be emphasized with advertising and free trial sales promotion offers. Netflix's market development strategy, pursued avidly in recent years, required substantial place (distribution to new geographic markets) and promotion plans as well as minor adjustments to both product (library of titles available in different markets, translation of language for chosen titles, ability to download for offline viewing) and price (to adjust to economic conditions and exchange rates). Netflix is also committed to vertical integration into content creation, a strategy that directly affects product, promotion, and process strategies. Thus far, Netflix has remained committed to one low price, but it is under pressure from investors who see the potential for price increases. As Netflix considers diversification into movie theaters, a place decision, other marketing mix elements will be impacted as well.

STEP 6: ESTABLISH THE IMPLEMENTATION PLAN

Once the plan is developed, it has to be acted upon. In practice, the implementation plan may actually represent action plans for each element of the marketing mix and possibly even sub-elements. For instance, the promotion strategy may be operationalized as an advertising campaign plan, social media marketing plan, and public relations plan. Place decisions, particularly in this omnichannel environment, may incorporate action plans to guide retail merchandising, data capture throughout the distribution process, and so on.

STEP 7: DETERMINE EVALUATION AND CONTROL PARAMETERS

The final step of the strategic planning process is to establish guidelines for evaluating the strategy and tactics and using the information to make adjustments as needed. This means that the organization defines a process for measuring performance, comparing the performance to the stated objectives, and making adjustments to strategy based on the results. We discuss measurement and marketing metrics in depth in Chapter 12.

Organizations sometimes fail to properly measure results. Marketing consultant Tom Peters famously observed that "What gets measured gets done". Marketing has at times been accused of focusing on creative ideas to the exclusion of objective evidence of success. In the long term, that's just not good enough. For organizations to succeed in marketing, measurement is critical. Measuring outcomes ensures that the organization is learning from what worked and what didn't. Importantly, as organizations choose how to allocate limited funds to different tactics, marketing managers can use comparisons on metrics such as ROI (return on investment) to determine which choices provide the best bang for the buck.

THE MARKETING PLAN

HOW DO THE STEPS IN THE MARKETING STRATEGIC PLANNING PROCESS RELATE TO THE ELEMENTS IN A MARKETING PLAN?

The key insights derived from the analysis and decisions made in the stages of the strategic planning process are communicated in a marketing plan. A marketing plan is a written document expressing the analysis and recommendations developed during the strategic planning process. The plan explains the situation analysis, states marketing objectives, specifies the target markets, recommends marketing strategy and marketing mix decisions, and addresses implementation and evaluation requirements. Table 5.1 provides a sample of an overall marketing plan structure.

TABLE 5.1   The Structure of a Typical Marketing Plan

The Marketing Plan OUTLINE	QUESTIONS the Plan Addresses
PERFORM A SITUATION ANALYSIS 1 Internal environment	• How does marketing support my company's mission, strategic intent, objectives, and growth strategies? • What is the corporate culture and how does it influence marketing activities? • What has my company done in the past with its: Target markets? Products? Pricing? Promotion? Supply chain? People? Process? Presence? • What resources, including management expertise, does my company have that make us unique? How has the company added value through its offerings in the past?
2 External environment	• What is the nature of the overall domestic and global market for our product? How big is the market? Who buys our product? • Who are our competitors? What are their marketing strategies? • What are the key trends in the economic environment? The technological environment? The regulatory environment? The social and cultural environment?
3 SWOT analysis	• Based on this analysis of the internal and external environments, what are the key Strengths, Weaknesses, Opportunities, and Threats?
IDENTIFY STRATEGIC OPPORTUNITY	• What opportunity should we pursue? Is there an underserved market? Are we building primary demand or secondary demand?
SET MARKETING OBJECTIVES	• What does marketing need to accomplish to support the objectives of my firm?
DESCRIBE TARGET MARKETS	• How do consumers and organizations go about buying, using, and disposing of our products? • Which segments should we select to target? If a consumer market: What are the relevant demographic, psychographic, and behavioral segmentation approaches and the media habits of the targeted segments? If a business market: What are the relevant organizational demographics? • How will we position our product for our market(s)?
FORMULATE MARKETING STRATEGIES Product strategies	• What is our core product? Actual product? Augmented product? • What product line/product mix strategies should we use? • How should we package, brand, and label our product? • How can attention to service quality enhance our success?

The Marketing Plan OUTLINE	QUESTIONS the Plan Addresses
Pricing strategies	• How will we price our product to the consumer and through the channel? How much must we sell to break even at this price? What pricing tactics should we use?
Promotional strategies	• How do we develop a consistent message about our product? How do we best generate buzz? • What approaches to advertising, public relations, sales promotion, and newer forms of communication (such as social networking) should we use? • What role should a salesforce play in the marketing communications plan? How should direct marketing be used?
Channel strategies	• How do we get our product to consumers in the best and most efficient manner? • What types of retailers, if any, should we work with to sell our product? • How do we integrate supply chain elements to maximize the value we offer to our customers and other stakeholders?
People	• How can our people better represent the brand's position? What characteristics will help deliver the value proposition?
Process	• Can the process be blueprinted to identify ways to remove friction in the customer journey? • How can the process better deliver value?
Presence	• What are the sensory elements we can develop to support the brand position and desired customer experience?
DETERMINE IMPLEMENTATION PLAN Action plans (for all marketing mix elements)	• How do we make our marketing plan happen?
Responsibility	• Who is responsible for accomplishing each aspect of implementing the marketing plan?
Time line	• What is the timing for the elements of our marketing plan?
Budget	• What budget do we need to accomplish our marketing objectives?
MEASUREMENT	• How do we measure the actual performance of our marketing plan and compare it to our planned performance and progress toward reaching our marketing objectives?

DOES NETFLIX NEED A NEW BUSINESS MODEL? THE CASE OF NETFLIX'S STRATEGIC POSITION

Netflix doesn't have a published mission statement. Despite this, the company's actions speak to strategic intent. Once the company began creating original content, it set an aspirational target to "become HBO faster than HBO can become Netflix" (Condliffe, 2013). Over time, Netflix's strategic intent has grown. Some say the new aspiration is to be like Disney (Bishop, 2017). But Netflix's relentless pursuit of Hollywood's best directors, producers, writers, and actors as well as awards for its original content suggest Netflix wants to be the next great Hollywood studio (Lazaroff, 2017). While Netflix began by innovating distribution, Ted Sarandos, the Netflix Chief Content Officer, has said that Netflix is committed to the art of cinema, which is not defined by distribution (Sims, 2018).

Netflix has three business units: 1) domestic DVD, 2) domestic streaming, and 3) international streaming. All follow the same basic business model. The value proposition Netflix promises subscribers is the value of flexibility, freedom, fun, and finds at a low monthly price.

- *Flexibility*: members watch as much as they want, anytime, anywhere, on nearly any Internet-connected screen.

- *Freedom*: there are no commercials and no contract commitments. Members can cancel at any time for any reason, but why would they when the cost is so low?

- *Fun*: the Netflix library includes more than 1,500 TV shows and 4,000 movies (with some variation by geographic region) covering virtually every imaginable genre (Clark, 2018).

- *Finds*: a find is a discovery of something valuable and that's just what Netflix promises. Personalized recommendations help members discover content that will truly delight.

Netflix earns revenues from the price customers pay for monthly subscription fees. The more subscribers, the more revenues earned. There are direct and indirect costs to deliver the value proposition, including substantial costs to license and produce video content. In fact, its content obligations top $17 billion per year with an estimated $8 billion for producing original shows. For now, costs exceed revenues, a choice Netflix justifies because of the strategic importance of content development. Analysts question the use of debt to fund such aggressive content production and suggest the situation is not sustainable. For now, it appears investors agree. Netflix's stock price has been on a decline since news that the company failed to meet subscriber growth goals.

PRME

NETFLIX'S ENERGY PROBLEM

Energy is among the UN's Sustainable Development Goals. Affordable and clean energy is SDG 7, but it also plays a role in other goals such as climate action (SDG 13), industry, innovation, and infrastructure (SDG 9), and life on land (SDG 15). Many companies have committed to clean energy and improvements to protect against the negative impact of energy use. Unfortunately, according to Greenpeace, Netflix's commitment has fallen short compared to other industry organizations.

The report, *Clicking Clean: Who Is Winning the Race to Build a Green Internet?* (Cook et al., 2017), explains that Internet use accounts for 7% of the world's electricity and video streaming is 63% of global Internet traffic. What's more, Netflix alone is responsible for a third of downstream Internet use.

Electricity is the largest component of Netflix's carbon footprint. Netflix explained its electricity use incorporates not only its own operations but also electricity used by its partners, especially Amazon Web Services and Google Cloud Platform, and its customers. Most of the energy use related to Netflix's business is indirect. Netflix reported that energy use from its partners was estimated to be 100,000 MWhs, and when combined with the company's direct energy use, the total electricity footprint is 140,000 MWhs (Netflix, 2017b).

Netflix purchases renewable energy certificates to match its non-renewable energy use and fund renewable energy production from sources like wind and solar. The company also joined the EPA's Green Power Partnership program, a voluntary program where businesses commit to use green power for some or all of their annual electricity consumption.

However, Green Peace's report scored Netflix's energy grade as a D. The report evaluated companies on energy transparency, commitment to renewable energy, efficiency, renewable energy procurement, and energy advocacy. Netflix scored an F on energy transparency, F on commitment to renewable energy, C on efficiency, D on renewable energy procurement, and F on energy advocacy, for an overall grade of D (Cook et al., 2017).

The report emphasized that Netflix does not regularly provide energy consumption data, unlike Apple, Facebook, and Google. Netflix has not made a public commitment to renewable energy. The company claims to have improved energy efficiencies through innovation and improvements, but without transparency, these claims are difficult to evaluate. Netflix relies heavily on purchased renewable energy certificates to offset its carbon footprint.

Netflix retorted that video streaming is greener than breathing! That's right. Netflix said its infrastructure generated significantly fewer carbon emissions for each hour

(Continued)

of streaming than the average human emits in an hour while breathing. Or consider this quote from the Netflix blog post: "A viewer who turned off their TV to read books would consume about 24 books a year in equivalent time, for a carbon footprint around 65kg CO2e – over 200 times more than Netflix streaming servers" (Greenberg, 2015). In other words, streaming is greener than reading.

How do you feel about Netflix's position? Whether or not you agree, there is a carbon impact from the binge-watching people engage in. While you binge-watch *The Crown*, Amazon Web Services' cloud infrastructure, Netflix's content servers, ISPs, your WiFi router, and laptop or TV all consume energy. And, in a time when many companies have adopted corporate social responsibility programs and integrated those programs into marketing strategies, Netflix has not.

 Visit **https://study.sagepub.com/tuten**
for free additional resources related to this chapter.

CHAPTER SUMMARY

Marketing strategy is defined as an integrated pattern of decisions specifying choices of markets to serve, market segments to target, marketing activities, and the allocation of resources to create, communicate, and deliver a product that offers value to customers in exchanges with the organization, and thereby results in organizational goal achievement. Organizations develop strategies at the corporate, business, and operational levels. These are hierarchical in that corporate strategy is supported by business strategy, and so on.

The steps in the strategic planning process are

1. Conduct a situation analysis.
2. Identify a strategic opportunity.
3. Determine the marketing objectives.
4. Describe the target market.
5. Formulate a marketing strategy.
6. Establish the implementation plan.
7. Determine evaluation and control parameters.

The situation analysis may utilize a SWOT analysis, PESTEL analysis, and/or Porter's Five Forces analysis. Strategic opportunities may be identified using Ansoff's marketing opportunity matrix and/or the jobs-to-be-done growth strategy matrix. Marketing objectives should be expressed as SMART: Specific, Measureable, Action-oriented, Relevant, and Time-lined. The target market is evaluated using customer journey maps and personas. The marketing mix design specifies the product, place, price, promotion, people, process, and presence decisions that are necessary to operationalize the strategy. Implementation plans specify the actions required, timing, budget, and responsibility assignments. Evaluation ensures that the organization can measure the relative success and effectiveness of the plan and its elements.

The key insights and decisions of each stage of the strategic planning process are communicated in the marketing plan. Table 5.1 detailed the specific sections covered in a marketing plan.

REVIEW QUESTIONS

1. What is marketing strategic planning?
2. How does strategic planning vary at each level of an organization?
3. What is strategic intent? How is it different from a mission statement?

4. What models are useful for performing a situation analysis?

5. What are the differences in the scope of opportunities and threats versus strengths and weaknesses?

6. How do the PESTEL analysis and Five Forces analysis contribute to the SWOT analysis?

7. What models are useful for identifying and analyzing possible strategic marketing opportunities?

8. Why is the evaluation component of the marketing plan necessary?

KEY TERMS

1. **Business model** – includes a value proposition, a profit formula, and the resources and processes needed to deliver the value proposition.

2. **Corporate strategy** – concerned with the organization's scope and direction, taking a portfolio approach to creating and earning value.

3. **Differentiated strategy** – offers a better product at a higher price.

4. **Discrete strategy** – offers an inferior product that costs more to a market of customers with limited alternatives.

5. **Disruptive strategy** – targets a population of overserved customers or non-consumers with a new product that is cheaper but not as good as competing solutions.

6. **Diversification** – involves offering new products in new markets.

7. **Dominant strategy** – offers a product that gets a job done significantly better and for significantly less money.

8. **Market development** (sometimes called **market creation**) – seeks to increase sales by offering existing products to new markets.

9. **Market penetration** – a strategy by which a company seeks to increase revenues from sales of its present products in its existing markets.

10. **Marketing plan** – a written document expressing the analysis and recommendations developed during the strategic planning process.

11. **Mission statement** – a clear and concise expression of the organization's reason for being.

12. **Product development** – seeks to increase revenues by developing products in the organization's product portfolio while targeting the existing market.

13. **Profit formula** – defines revenue expectations, cost structure, and margin contributions.

14. **Strategic business unit (SBU)** – each business in an organization's portfolio.

15. **Strategic fit** – matching resources to ambitions.

16. **Strategic intent** – an obsession for winning that infiltrates every level of the organization, and uses innovation to change the competitive landscape.

17. **Sustaining strategy** – offers a product that is only slightly better and/or slightly less expensive.

18. **Value chain** – the processes needed to deliver the value proposition are part of a system of interdependent organizational functions.

PART III

The Marketing Mix

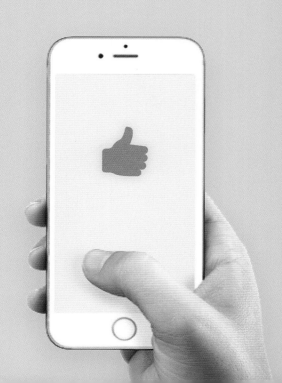

Chapter 6

CREATING VALUE: PRODUCTS AND SERVICES

In this chapter, we'll learn the answers to the following questions:

1   What is a product and what product levels create value for customers?

2   How and why are products classified? How are services different from goods?

3   What is product portfolio management?

4   What is the process by which new product innovations are developed? How does design-to-value facilitate new product development?

5   How does the product life cycle inform marketing decisions?

6   How does product design influence the adoption of new products?

INTRODUCTION

When buyers think about how to meet their needs – how to get the job done – they typically think of the products that will provide a solution and offer the benefits they need. As marketers, we tend to do the same. We think about what product we want to bring to market and how to differentiate our products from those of competitors. Product reigns supreme, even though the value proposition is delivered through the offer – including all elements of the chosen marketing mix. Product decisions can be risky. It's a long-understood fact that most new products fail. But if we fail to innovate, we risk being stuck in the sustaining strategy mode – with only marginal advantages to offer customers. Advances in technology offer a seemingly infinite number of possibilities. For this reason, some suggest that marketers are facing digital Darwinism (Ingledew, 2017). Only those organizations that can integrate technology to add real value for customers and the organization's value chain will survive and thrive.

Industry 4.0 technologies can transform product design, resulting in new business models, new products, and product improvements. The process of product design and development can also be enhanced in speed and quality with rapid prototyping and testing made possible with IoT sensors, machine learning, additive manufacturing and digital twins, robotics, and analytics. Connected products can also provide added customer benefits like personalization, interactivity, predictive service and maintenance, and trust certification of ingredients. For the organization, they provide data that can be used to improve processes and/or be monetized as an asset to sell to business partners.

Digital technology is driving innovation in the products available in the market and in the design and development of products.

OPENING VIGNETTE

VOLVO'S INNOVATION IN CONNECTED CARS AND TRANSPORTATION PRODUCT DESIGN

Technology is changing the transportation industry. Today, there are hundreds of thousands of "connected cars" already on the road. More will be available soon as many companies have prototypes for connected cars, including autonomous vehicles like Volvo's Autoliv. Connected cars primarily utilize IoT technologies. Embedded, connected sensors provide wired and wireless connectivity, cloud computing, and artificial intelligence capabilities. Connected cars are capable of vehicle-to-infrastructure communication (V2I) and vehicle-to-vehicle communication (V2V), which are services that allow automobiles to continuously exchange information with their environments.

What's possible in a connected car? These are just a few of the benefits:

- The car can complete payment for gas and other purchases.
- The navigation system can anticipate traffic hazards and provide warnings, or even make adjustments to avoid the hazard.
- The car can transmit performance and maintenance data to the dealer service department, enabling the mechanic to provide remote diagnostics and preventive maintenance and/or schedule service appointments seamlessly.
- If the car experiences a crash, real-time data can be automatically sent to emergency teams.
- The car can access streaming entertainment, including music, games, radio, and video, and connect to social networks.

Tom Rivers, an automotive connectivity specialist with Harman, put it this way: "Connectivity will have a more dramatic effect on cars than any other automotive technology in the last century. That's because the car is a great 'data centre' with the potential to collect and share information from a huge range of sources. It will know where you shop, work, when you drive and even what you do on your weekends off. Cars will therefore become much smarter and understand you and respond to you in a way that in the past was considered science fiction" (Bashford, 2017).

Volvo's connected cars use the IoT to connect drivers with their cars and beyond via Volvo's Sensus system. Some of the product benefits include guiding drivers to parking spots and paying for parking, sharing location and arrival times, searching for points of interest nearby, and using the car as a WiFi hotspot. In some areas, Volvo owners can even enable the car as a delivery point for groceries and Amazon deliveries! Volvo also offers co-piloting technology and is working actively to bring a fully autonomous, self-driving car to the market.

Volvo approached digital innovation with an intent of establishing "digital building blocks" that could be applied in multiple ways (Svahn, Mathiassen, Lindgren and Kane, 2017). An example of the benefits is the application of autonomous vehicles across several of Volvo's strategic business units – consumer cars, city buses, and trucks used in industries such as mining. Volvo buses are already the leader in providing communities with buses designed to manage urban mobility challenges. The autonomous buses will expand on the benefits, improving energy efficiency, safety, and passenger comfort.

Technology also plays a major role behind the scenes in Volvo's product research and design. For instance, a team of Volvo Group engineers recently succeeded in building and running an engine built from 3D-printed components. Using additive manufacturing technology enabled the team to reduce the number of engine parts required and the engine's weight, which could lead to better energy efficiency (Volvo Group, 2018).

PRODUCTS, PRODUCT LEVELS, AND VALUE
DEFINING PRODUCT

At its most basic level, a product is something that is *produced* and offered for sale in the market. We learned in Chapter 1 that products include goods and services (and hybrids with elements of goods and services), ideas, experiences, destinations, people, and so on. Essentially, anything that can be offered for exchange and can satisfy buyer needs is a product. A pure good is tangible, whereas a pure service is intangible. Intangible means that the product has no physical existence but exists in the synchronous moments of production and consumption.

There is really no such thing as a pure physical good or a pure service (Hill, 1986). Many products exist along a good–service continuum (Shostack, 1982) and increasingly are hybrids that are neither a pure tangible good nor a pure service. Rather, most products include both tangible and intangible elements. A connected car, for example, is a tangible good but also includes benefits of connected entertainment, navigation, safety, maintenance, and so on. In other words, products are bundles of features and attributes that promise to provide benefits that will meet customer needs.

DIGITAL TECHNOLOGIES LEAD TO NEW PRODUCT MODELS

Digital technologies have made new forms of products possible. Examples include "products as a service", "software as a service", and product sharing. These examples mark a shift from ownership to usership. In each variation, buyers pay to use the product but don't assume ownership of the product. **Software as a service** (SaaS) was an early iteration of this phenomenon, with wide acceptance. Customers can pay to use software by usage rental or subscribe. It's likely you've used SaaS services – Google apps, Dropbox, and Zoom are all examples. Products as a service function much the same way – except that the customer rents use of the product. Rental services in the construction industry now account for 50% of the market in the US. Daimler and BMW launched Car2Go and DriveNow as car-sharing services, respectively, and both are generating double-digit growth rates (Emprechtinger, 2018). Currently, 2.1 million customers in Germany alone use car sharing.

In B2C markets, the sharing economy has created a product variation. Businesses provide apps and/or platforms to facilitate peer-to-peer sharing. You might rent an apartment for a holiday and/or rent yours using Airbnb. Uber and Lyft can connect you with a driver for a ride. These sharing platforms provide services to both parties, collecting fees to facilitate the match.

PRODUCT LEVELS AS LAYERS OF VALUE

Products are bundles of features and attributes that can be best understood by viewing products as layers of value. As Figure 6.1 illustrates, we can distinguish three product layers, each of which includes elements of value for target buyers: 1) core product,

2) actual product, and 3) augmented product. When we design product offers for a target market, we can use these layers to develop a product with a strong value proposition that differentiates the product from the competition and fits the brand's positioning strategy. Figure 6.1 illustrates these layers.

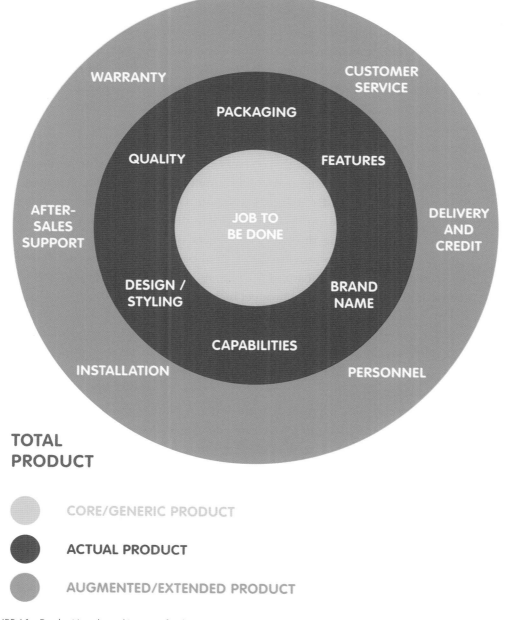

FIGURE 6.1   Product Levels and Layers of Value

The core product refers to the utility the customer is buying. Jobs-to-Be-Done theory is a useful lens with which to identify the core product. It approaches marketing from the perspective of understanding what job the customer needs to do and the role a product can play in that. The value of a product does not directly come from the product's attributes themselves, but through the perceived benefits that the product provides to consumers. Think of any product you've purchased recently. What were you really after when you made the purchase?

The actual product is the physical good or service process that supplies the benefit sought. Brands distinguish their actual products through branding, product quality, packaging, design features, and product capabilities. The augmented product consists of the added value created by features beyond the basics. For goods, augmentations may include support services like installation, delivery, financing, maintenance and repair, and so on. Volvo's connected car systems are a type of product augmentation.

The actual and augmented product should be designed in such a way as to provide the values desired by the target market. Marketers study target market needs and wants, drawing upon buyer behavior insights and the target market persona. Drawing upon Maslow's Hierarchy of Needs (discussed in Chapter 1), met needs can be viewed as customer-received value. These product levels relate directly to the tactical decisions marketers make when designing the product element of the marketing mix. The core product is the primary benefit to provide. The actual product includes product attribute decisions such as product quality, features and capabilities, style and design, packaging, labeling, and branding. The augmented product includes support services like installation, delivery, maintenance, and report and "value-add" elements like mobile apps, loyalty programs, service quality, warranties and guarantees, and customer experiences. Generally, you can think of the actual product as providing functional value (in that it operationalizes the core product) and the augmented product as providing psychological, financial, temporal, and experiential value.

Bain, a consulting company, identified 30 elements of value relevant for end consumers and 40 elements affecting B2B buyers. The elements suggest opportunities for marketers to improve actual and augmented product offerings in ways that will provide competitive advantage. The B2C Elements of Value model is organized in four categories:

1. Social impact – what value to society does the product provide?

2. Life-changing elements – how does the product change my life?

3. Emotional elements – how does this product make me feel?

4. Functional elements – what problem does the product solve and what costs does it prevent?

The B2B Elements of Value model includes five categories:

1. Inspiration – does the brand contribute to purpose and social responsibility?

2. Individual impact – does the brand contribute to buyer's personal career growth?

3. Business value – does the brand enhance productivity, access to resources and/ or markets, and build relationships?

4. Functional elements – what outcomes such as performance, cost savings, and innovation benefit are derived from the brand?

5. Table stakes – to what extent does the brand meet mandatory requirements for product specifications and regulatory, ethical, and quality compliance?

To test the model, Bain surveyed more than 10,000 consumers in the US as to their value perceptions of 50 brands. The results showed that brands whose products provided eight or more value elements performed significantly better than brands with fewer than eight value elements.

Some of the values identified are tied to operational standards and even brand purpose, more so than product design. But other value elements can be offered by adding to the number of product features. This is a common approach when brands follow an incremental new product development strategy or sustaining strategy. You can see this in the smartphones available on the market today. Each new iteration touts a new feature – facial recognition, infinity screen, low-light camera, and so on. Despite Bain's advice, adding features to a product isn't always a good idea. Experts warn against "feature fatigue" (Keane and Stamm, 2005). Technological advances make it possible to load on added features, oftentimes at little additional cost to produce. Customers may purchase feature-laden products because of expected utility, but ultimately suffer lower experience utility. Why? Customers may not actually use many of the features. Think about it. How many features of your smartphone do you use? How many is the smartphone actually capable of? Customers who experience lower levels of utility due to feature fatigue are less likely to buy the same brand in the future. In other words, the brand won the customer in the short term, but lost out on customer retention and loyalty. Feature fatigue is alive and well in today's competitive environment.

A product, therefore, is more than a simple set of tangible features. Consumers see products as complex bundles of benefits that satisfy their needs. Most important is how the customer perceives the product. Factors like aesthetics and styling, durability, brand image, packaging, service and warranty, and experience help to improve the value proposition and set the brand apart from the competition. As you consider product design in the marketing mix, pay special attention to customer experience. We emphasized customer experience management across the customer journey and during the moments of truth and micro-moments in Chapter 2. Increasingly, customer experience is a product attribute. Chris Janiszewski, former president of the Association of Consumer Research, captured this well, saying "Benefits are not in the products. Benefits are in the consumer experience" (Janiszewski, 2009).

PRODUCT CLASSIFICATIONS

Products can be classified in many ways, such as for consumer or business use, durability, location along the good–service continuum (covered in Chapter 10), and involvement.

DURABILITY

Marketers classify consumer goods as durable or nondurable depending on how long the product lasts. A car will last many years, but a tube of mascara will last only a few months. Durables are products that provide benefits over an extended period of time, while nondurables (sometimes called disposables) provide short-term benefits. Durables tend to be more expensive than nondurables and consequently tend to be high-involvement purchases. However, this isn't always the case. For instance, the benefit of a concert ticket is primarily limited to the time spent experiencing the concert, but the ticket may still be relatively expensive. For shared products, durability matters. Citybike Vienna, a public bike-rental system, found that its bikes needed heavy-duty frames and high-quality tires.

INVOLVEMENT

Consumer products are sometimes categorized as convenience, shopping, specialty, or unsought products. Convenience products are nondurable, low-involvement products that are purchased frequently. Consumer-packaged goods (CPG) like soft drinks, snacks, toilet paper are convenience goods. Typically, convenience products are inexpensive and widely available. Convenience products include staples, impulse buys, and emergency purchases.

Staple products such as toilet paper, milk, and gasoline are necessary items that are available almost everywhere. Impulse products are unplanned purchases. Emergency products are purchases tied to a situation or crisis occasion, like if you find yourself in a rainstorm but didn't bring your umbrella. Marketers are sometimes criticized for earning a profit during emergency situations, but emergencies also provide an opportunity for brands to build brand equity and goodwill. That's what Budweiser did when it created Budweiser Water. As part of Budweiser's commitment to SDG 6, Budweiser created the "Water for a Better World" campaign (Monllos, 2018). The company even switched over some of its production lines from beer to water to provide water for disaster relief in areas like Puerto Rico. The company has donated millions of cans of water for disaster relief (Monllos, 2018).

Shopping products are those that inspire the buyer to gather information and make comparisons among competing brands. Thus, while convenience products have an abbreviated decision journey, the journey is extended for shopping products. The micro-moments and zero moments of truth (ZMOT) we discussed in Chapter 2 are relevant.

Specialty products are typically high-involvement purchases with an extended customer journey. These products may be expensive and may have limited distribution. Like the journey for shopping products, the moments of truth may play a role. But if a brand has earned loyalty, the "loyalty loop" in the journey may result in an abbreviated purchase process. That's a definite benefit to brands and a key reason brands focus on customer satisfaction.

Unsought products are those for which prospective buyers lack awareness of the product and its benefits and therefore do not actively move through the purchase process.

Products can be substitutable or non-substitutable. A product is substitutable if an alternative can be found that meets the buyer's needs equally well and the cost to switch is low. Generally, convenience and shopping products are considered substitutable while specialty products are not. Brands also try to create ecosystems to increase buyer commitment and the perceived cost of switching. The most successful businesses create a cluster of products and services that complement each other and work symbiotically (Marketing Science Institute, 2012).

USE

Products used by businesses for operations and/or manufacturing include raw materials, component parts, materials for maintenance, repair, and operations, equipment, installations, and business services. Like consumer products, raw materials, component parts, and materials are frequently purchased, whereas installations and business services are higher involvement decisions. SaaS and "products as a service" products have also grown in business markets. In fact, many MarTech vendors provide the marketing software solutions we discussed in Chapter 1, such as marketing automation, content marketing, programmatic advertising, and customer relationship management, using the SaaS product model.

In principle, shared use products can be anything to which access is enabled. Products available thus far can be categorized by the brand role and other parties involved in the exchange. The product categories are 1) product as a service (company-provided service), 2) mutualization enabled by a digital product platform (peer-to-peer service supported by company platform), and 3) redistribution markets (company platforms enabling peer-to-peer reownership of products). Product as a service may include selling the use of a product rather than ownership, or providing services by rental or subscription such as marketing automation or equipment maintenance (Maltzer, Veider and Kathan, 2015).

PRODUCT PORTFOLIO MANAGEMENT

Companies frequently manage a portfolio of products. Doing so allows companies to leverage the strength of their brands through brand extensions and target multiple market segments with different offers. There are common terms that you may find mentioned when discussing product portfolios.

- **Product portfolio**, also called a **product mix**, is the number of product lines being offered by a company.

- **Product line** is any one type of product in the product mix.

- **Product line length** is the number of products in a product line.

- **Product line width** is the number of product lines in a product mix.

- **Product line depth** is the number of sub-products in a line.

- **Product line consistency** is the degree of variation between the products within the product line.

Companies may need to expand, reduce, or invest in their product portfolios depending upon the chosen marketing strategy and the environmental situation. Knorr and Arm & Hammer both followed a product development strategy based on brand extensions. Both companies were successful with their flagship products and saw an opportunity to extend their brands. Knorr started with bouillon cubes but now offers side dishes and spice packets for specific recipes. The Arm & Hammer brand began with its original baking soda but extended into a $1 billion mega-brand in a dozen categories, including toothpaste, kitty litter, and laundry detergent.

Product development can also be valuable when market trends change. Coca-Cola acquired products to diversify and address the decline of soft drink sales and popularity of healthy beverages. For instance, Coca-Cola bought Innocent Drinks, a UK brand of smoothies, sparkling juices, and coconut water (Soundrarajan and Veldhoen, 2017). It acquired Glaceau water, Fuze vitamin-enriched beverages, Odwalla juices, and Honest Tea bottled teas. Coca-Cola targets brands that are niche market leaders and then positions the products as premium beverage with a market-penetration strategy.

Frito-Lay, a major player in the potato chip category, responded to the popularity of artisan chips with a new product. Lay's potato chips brand holds the position of "category captain" among traditional flat potato chips. Its market share gave Frito-Lay the power to influence product placement in grocery stores and supermarkets. But artisan chips have grown in popularity, especially when shoppers are buying for a special occasion. Lay's introduced a new product to its line, Lay's Kettle Cooked, and priced it lower than the category leaders, Cape Cod and Kettle Chips. Lay's Kettle Cooked chips quickly outpaced sales of the Cape Cod and Kettle brands.

Product development may also be necessary to adjust to local tastes. For example, Colgate has more than 65% penetration around the world because it has customized products and flavors for local markets. In India, Colgate's toothpaste line includes Active Salt Neem, Clove, and Cibaca Vedshakti, a herb used in Ayurvedic medicine.

Not all companies invest in their own research and development or even manufacture their own products. Rather, they partner with manufacturers or buy products from third-party providers. They can accomplish their goals using white labeling. A white label is something that is produced by one company and then repackaged and sold by other companies under their brand name.

Increasingly, brands are developing product ecosystems. A product ecosystem is a suite of complementary products. By developing an ecosystem, the products are synergistic. As customers develop brand loyalty, they adopt more of the ecosystem. The ecosystem also supports partner organizations providing the organization with more power in the micro-environment.

Apple is an ecosystem brand. Apple's hardware products (iPhone, iPad, Mac, and Apple TV) drive consumption of its software, retail business, and partner products. The iPod device drove adoption of Apple's iTunes music and video store. The iPhone continues to do so and has also driven more than $25 billion in mobile app purchases. It's no coincidence that GAFA (Google, Amazon, Facebook, and Apple) all market product ecosystems. By creating ecosystems, they made their brands indispensable in the lives of customers, thus driving customer retention and customer lifetime value. Just like other product development, ecosystems may be built via partnerships, white labeling, or in-house innovation development.

INNOVATIONS AND NEW PRODUCT DEVELOPMENT
TYPES OF INNOVATION

From a marketing standpoint, an innovation is anything that customers perceive as new. The degree of innovation may be incremental or radical (Clark and Henderson, 1990). Radical innovations introduce a truly new design that displaces previous design. Discontinuous innovations are "new to the world" products. These innovations may take some time to reach the marketplace. For instance, Oculus offers virtual reality headsets you can use at home. 23andme offers DNA kits and reports. 3D printers are still primarily used in manufacturing, but as prices come down more people are buying them for at-home use. Just think of some of the aspects of daily life that we take for granted but once upon a time were radical innovations – electricity, air travel, radio, television, computers, the Internet. Radical innovations may also be *disruptive*. The Netflix case we discussed in Chapter 5 followed a disruptive strategy. But how can we clarify what makes an innovation discontinuous versus what makes it disruptive?

A disruptive innovation occurs when a new entrant in a market offers a functional alternative to the underserved, oftentimes at a lower price. Over time, the main market adopts the new product, completing the disruption (Christensen, Raynor and McDonald, 2015). The new competitor is pursuing the disruptive strategy in the jobs-to-be-done growth strategy matrix, defined as a worse product for a lower price. The disruptive innovation model explains that the disruption is in part predicated on the use of a sustaining strategy by the competing incumbents (Christensen et al., 2015). Because the incumbents focus on incremental innovations with only minor advantages, they leave an opening for new entrants to gain market share. Over time, the new entrant improves product performance and gains market share, ultimately changing the marketscape (Christensen et al., 2015). For example, when the gaming market was only focused on hardcore gamers and dominated by Sony and Microsoft, Nintendo introduced Wii for casual gamers, with an inferior technology, and soon took over the market. Uber and Lyft disrupted the taxi service. Airbnb disrupted the hotel industry. Google disrupted the advertising industry. Do you notice a theme? Disruptive innovation is oftentimes driven by new technologies that make process innovation as well as product innovation possible.

Though it's exciting to think about discontinuous innovations, most new products are continuous innovations. In other words, the innovation is an incremental change in product design, product components, and/or related processes. We're accustomed to seeing "new and improved" touted on product packaging. For instance, mobile phones experienced several incremental innovations as new features were incorporated. What once was truly and simply a mobile phone, over time, became a camera, organizer, calendar, and connected device for email, social networking, and web surfing and searching. These improvements occurred gradually and new features continue to be developed and added. Some incremental changes are small adaptations to address social-cultural trends. For instance, Nestlé plans to reduce sugar in its chocolate bars by 40% to address global concerns about obesity.

Many innovations are co-created. That's one of the reasons we say that marketing is now in the era of marketing convergence. Consumers sometimes contribute to product ideas, funding, and creation. For instance, consumers proposed an idea for dress yoga pants – yoga pants designed to look like dress pants. Funding for the design and manufacturing was crowdsourced on Betabrand and now dress yoga pants are one of the company's most popular products!

When innovation is co-created by stakeholders for the long-term benefit of society it is called social innovation (Voorberg, Bekkers and Tummers, 2014). Social innovation is defined as new solutions for social issues that are more efficient, effective, and sustainable than the existing ones. Take the development of HelpUsGreen as an example (Prasad and Manimala, 2018). Ankit Agarwal and Karan Rastogi, the founders of HelpUsGreen, were childhood friends who grew up in Kanpur on the banks of the Ganges in India. The Ganges is severely polluted, but HelpUsGreen combats river pollution. The HelpUsGreen team collects discarded flowers to keep them out of the river, then "flower-cycles" them into organic fertilizer and incense. The social enterprise reduces river pollution and provides economic benefits by employing women to collect the flowers. There are two main phases required for social innovation to occur: 1) bricolage and 2) contagion. Bricolage is the ideation and design of the social innovation. Contagion is the process of adoption and diffusion (Yang and Sung, 2016).

NEW PRODUCT DEVELOPMENT PROCESS

When it comes down to it, the new product development process is much like that required for social innovation. There must be a viable idea and its success is determined by whether it is adopted by the market. Figure 6.2 illustrates the major steps in the new product development process.

What happens in each step in the process?

- Ideation or idea generation is the stage during which the organization comes up with new product ideas. Companies like Lego rely heavily on customer input during this stage. After all, sometimes customers know what they want! Design consultancies like IDEO provide ideation and market research services for new product development. Historically, product innovations have come from new technological knowledge or from new market knowledge about the needs and wants of prospective customers and/or competitive offers (Nerkar, 2003).

- In the second phase, the idea's viability must be assessed. Is the concept technically feasible? Does it already exist? Is the total available market sufficiently large to make it attractive? How costly will the concept be, generally speaking, to bring to life?

- Assuming that the concept is viable, the third phase is the development of the concept into a prototype that can be further tested and assessed. If there are similar products offered by competitors, a "competitive teardown" may provide insight into competitive design, quality, and materials. If the concept is a service, process mapping (blueprinting, discussed further in Chapter 10) will be conducted. If the concept is good, drawings will be rendered and eventually a physical prototype will be created.

- Once the prototype is developed and tested, branding decisions including brand name, logo, and visual identity decisions will be made. Part of this process will include checking registered trademarks to ensure the preferred brand name and logo are available and protectable. The package will be designed, including labeling decisions, and a package prototype created. If funding and approvals are sought (whether from investors, partners, angel investors, or crowdsourcing), a business case and/or video proposal will be developed at this stage. The marketing strategy and tactics are planned.

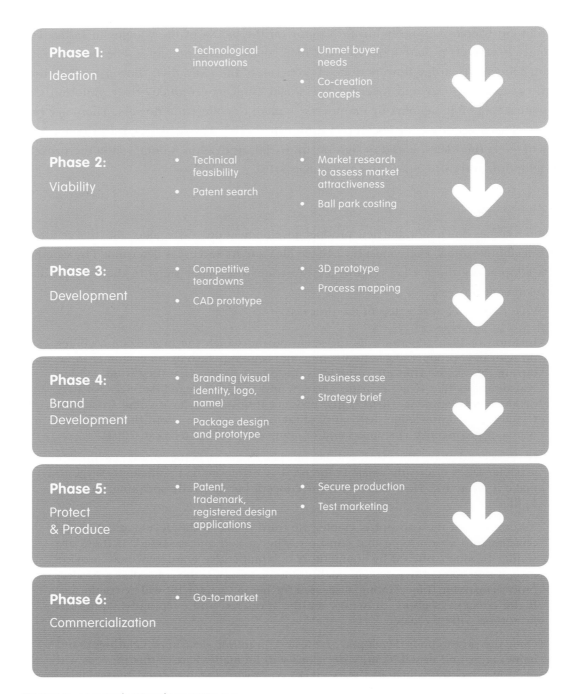

FIGURE 6.2   New Product Development Process

- In the fifth phase, the concept and related materials must be protected and produced. Applications for patents, trademarks, and registered designs will be filed. Test marketing, if planned, will be implemented to guide commercialization decisions. Production will begin. Companies may manufacture the new product themselves or may partner with manufacturers or other businesses to secure the new product in its portfolio.

- The final phase is commercialization. In this phase the marketing strategy and tactical plan are implemented and the product is available in the market.

The early stages of the new product development process may utilize agile methods and/or design-to-value methods. Agile innovation, described by Ernst & Young as "the art of making hard things easy and creating new viable business offerings faster" (EY, 2014), is a valued approach to new product development. The agile approach is based on the *agile manifesto*, a philosophical statement on agile innovation which includes 4 values and 12 principles (Manifesto for Agile Software Development, 2001). The approach enables new product development through collaboration while also remaining responsive to market changes (Rigby, Sutherland and Takeuchi, 2016a). This means agile is not just about creating new products but also focuses on how these developments can be sustainable. The approach helps firms achieve the optimal efficiency and effectiveness from their innovation activities (Doz and Wilson, 2011). Agile innovation relies on a method called scrum, which emphasizes creative and adaptive teamwork in solving complex problems, lean development, and Kanban (reducing lead times and the amount of work in process). The fundamentals of scrum are relatively simple (Rigby, Sutherland and Takeuchi, 2016b). To tackle an opportunity, the organization forms and empowers a small, cross-functional, self-managing team with all the skills necessary to complete its tasks.

DESIGN-TO-VALUE (DTV)

Design-to-value (DTV), an integrated approach to product development that considers what customers want, what competitors offer, and what it costs to manufacture and distribute an end product, may also be used in new product development. The concept of designing for value is key. There are many possible ways to add value even when designing incremental improvements to existing products. For instance, value could be tied to sustainability contributions, product safety, cost of ownership, or augmented services. Figure 6.3 highlights the information used in DTV.

The DTV process uses data from customer research, competitive intelligence, and cost analysis to ensure objectivity in design decisions. The customer research focuses on developing a deep understanding of customer value drivers and quantifying their worth. In other words, it considers not just what customers want but how much they are willing to pay for specific product features. Journey mapping and other customer research approaches like

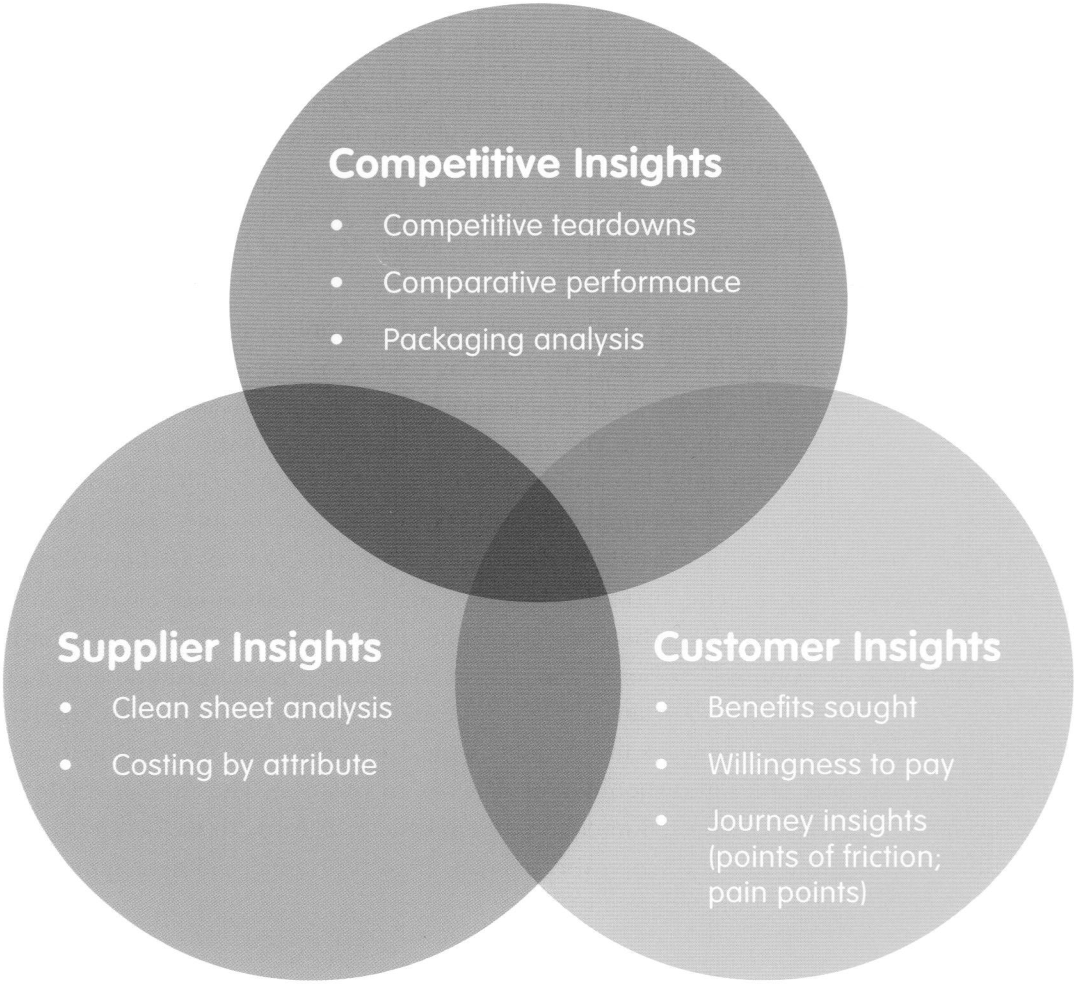

Competitive Insights
- Competitive teardowns
- Comparative performance
- Packaging analysis

Supplier Insights
- Clean sheet analysis
- Costing by attribute

Customer Insights
- Benefits sought
- Willingness to pay
- Journey insights (points of friction; pain points)

FIGURE 6.3   Sources of Insight for DTV

Source: Exhibit from "The consumer decision journey", June 2009, *McKinsey Quarterly*: www.mckinsey.com. Copyright © 2019 McKinsey & Company. All rights reserved. Printed by permission.

ethnography, focus groups, and empathy mapping are useful. Competitive teardowns refer to the disassembling of competing products to document technical and functional differences, and identify strategies for reducing costs or optimizing features with a differential advantage. Teardowns are often part of a teardown workshop because seeing the competitors' products side by side can produce transformational design ideas. Clean sheet modeling involves determining what products should cost given different parameters such as design choices, raw material and component quality, and so on. Clean sheet analysis is critically important for assessing opportunities for the product design to facilitate sustainability initiatives like those identified in the UN's SDGs. For instance, the costs of reducing packaging, utilizing renewable materials, and the energy use tied to production, shipping, and so on can be assessed and compared. The result of DTV is a list of specific and pragmatic ideas that companies can implement to increase customer value and improve competitive advantage, while reducing product costs (Henrich, Kothari and Makarova, 2012).

Design-to-value is most commonly part of product development teams, but it's worth noting that the concept could be applied to the design of the entire marketing mix. For example, Bain's elements of value model points to several functional values such as saving money (pricing implications), simplifying and reducing hassles (channel and process implications), sensory appeal and design aesthetics (presence implications), affiliation (people implications), and motivation and meaning (promotional implications).

Further, companies that embrace design-to-value may do so as part of a strategic product value management initiative. Strategic product value management uses design-to-value and design-to-cost procedures to determine the ideal portfolio of products, develop detailed cost models for those products, and reduce costs throughout the value chain (Moebius and Stack, 2015). The design-to-value component ensures that the company's product portfolio meets customer needs and each product in the portfolio can offer a meaningful and deliverable value proposition. The design-to-cost component ensures that margins and profitability are not threatened by unnecessary expenses.

PRODUCT LIFE CYCLE MANAGEMENT
THE PRODUCT LIFE CYCLE

The life of a product from start to finish is described by the product life cycle. Most new products fail and consequently may experience an abbreviated life cycle. For successful products, the product life cycle can be useful for planning marketing strategy and tactics, because it suggests typical shifts in the marketing mix for each stage of the cycle. Importantly, the life cycle describes the life of the product, not the life of a brand's product offer. Each stage is marked by specific characteristics. Figure 6.4 illustrates the product life cycle.

When new products launch, they enter the introduction phase. Because the product is new, the focus must be on primary demand, which is demand for a product category. To drive primary demand, the market must be made aware of the product and educated on its value. There is little if any competition at this stage. Pricing is critical. The organization may price low to penetrate the market or price high to skim the market. We'll discuss pricing strategy further in Chapter 7.

If the product enters the growth stage, sales will increase and competition may decide to enter the market with an imitative product. During the growth stage, sales are increasing sufficiently to support multiple competitors. Brands will strive to differentiate their offers from those of competitors.

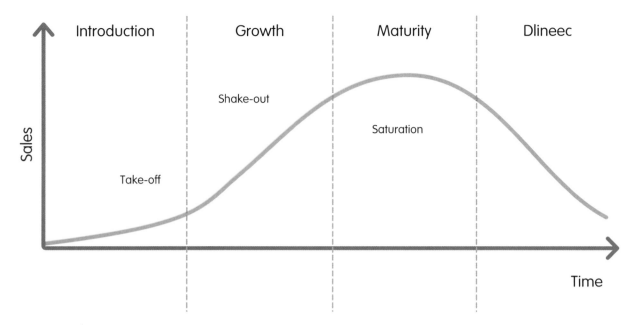

FIGURE 6.4   The Product Life Cycle

Source: Adapted from Claessens (2017)

In the maturity stage, sales continue to increase but they do so at a declining rate. The products on the market have been augmented and developed to enhance their value, but this also means that customers have choices. If the brands fail to differentiate themselves, the product may be perceived as a commodity. This puts downward pressure on prices. Some brands will innovate and/or reposition to reverse the life cycle progress (Moon, 2005). To reposition in the maturity stage, brands can use reverse positioning, breakaway positioning, or stealth positioning. **Reverse positioning** removes some product attributes while adding new ones. IKEA stores are completely unlike traditional furniture stores, for instance. In some ways, the entire smartphone market has used reverse positioning by focusing on features like cameras but not on the ability to make phone calls. **Breakaway positioning** associates the product with a different category. Swatch Watches treated its watches more like fashion jewellery that should be changed with different outfits. **Stealth positioning** disguises the product's true nature as it attracts new customers. Some products remain in the maturity stage for decades. For instance, the market for televisions is mostly saturated. Households may add televisions in different rooms or replace televisions from time to time. Televisions continue to evolve though, and people may choose to upgrade to the latest technology like curved screens and smart televisions.

If a product is no longer needed, it will enter the final stage of the product lifecycle, decline. Decline may be triggered by an innovation or by a change in the environment. For instance, the ability to use Google Maps on our smartphones drove the decline of portable GPS units. In fact, the evolution of smartphones has brought many products into decline – physical maps, mp3 players, cameras, pagers, and planners.

THE INNOVATION ADOPTION CURVE

The product life cycle shows how sales vary over time, but another view of the life of an innovation can be seen through the innovation adoption model. The innovation adoption model illustrates the diffusion of the innovation by the relative percentage of customers who adopt it at each stage. Product adoption is the process by which a consumer or business customer begins to buy and use a new good, service, or idea. The term diffusion describes how the use of a product spreads throughout a population (Muller, Peres and Mahajan, 2009). As Figure 6.5 illustrates, there are five categories of adopters. A small group of *innovators* (approximately 2.5% of the population) and *early adopters* (13.5%) give an innovation its start. Once the innovation begins to be adopted by the *early majority* (34%), sales increase rapidly and the *late majority* (34%) adopts. The most risk-averse, called *laggards* (16%), adopt last (KPMG, 2016). By the time laggards adopt a product, it may already be in the decline stage of the product life cycle.

The point between early adopters and early majority is called the "chasm" (Moore, 1991). This is a critical point, sometimes called the tipping point, because a product is unlikely to succeed if it cannot cross the chasm to reach the early majority. Innovators and early adopters are interested in new technologies and prone to try innovations. But the early majority will not adopt until the product is perceived as reliable and advantageous. They may also wait until prices drop.

Marketers strive to increase the rate of adoption to facilitate a product's success. There are five factors thought to drive adoption: 1) relative advantage, 2) compatibility, 3) simplicity, 4) observability, and 5) trialability. Relative advantage is the degree to which the innovation is perceived as better than the incumbent product (non-existent if no product met the need). The greater the relative advantage, the faster the adoption. Compatibility is the degree to which the product is compatible with any existing equipment and/or buyer values.

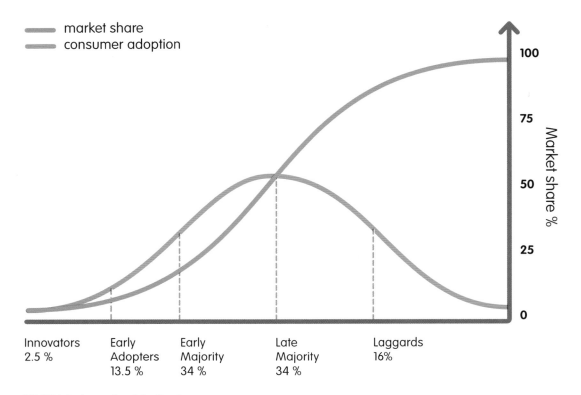

FIGURE 6.5   Innovation Adoption Curve

Source: Figure courtesy of Rogers, Everett, 2012. Accessed via wikicommons.

The greater the compatibility, the faster the adoption. Simplicity is the degree to which the product is easy to understand and use. The simpler the product is, the faster the adoption. Observability is the degree to which prospects are exposed to the product and can see others using the product. The more observable it is, the faster the adoption. Trialability is the degree to which the product can be used prior to making a commitment. The ability to try a product without risk and experience the product's benefits before purchase can increase the rate of adoption.

Maloney's 16% rule explains that marketers must speak differently to innovators and early adopters (the first 16% of people who will adopt an innovation) than they do to early majority and late majority (Maloney, 2010). Specifically, Maloney's 16% rule suggests that the first 16% to adopt are motivated to adopt by product scarcity (Maloney, 2010). Because the innovation is new and scarce, innovators and early adopters are motivated to be among the first to acquire the innovation. The remaining adopters though are persuaded by social proof. In other words, observing that others have adopted the innovation, they too follow suit.

THE HYPE CYCLE

Another model for understanding the diffusion of innovation is the hype cycle (Gartner, n.d.). Importantly, the hype cycle shows that organizations should not invest in new technologies just because they are hearing hype about the technologies. Introduced by Gartner, a consulting firm, the hype cycle illustrates the typical progression of an emerging technology from optimism and enthusiasm, through a period of disillusionment, to an eventual understanding of the technology's relevance and role in a market. As illustrated in Figure 6.6, the initial stage of the hype curve is driven by buzz, primarily from media speculating on the technology's prospects. Later the curve is driven by performance improvements and adoption.

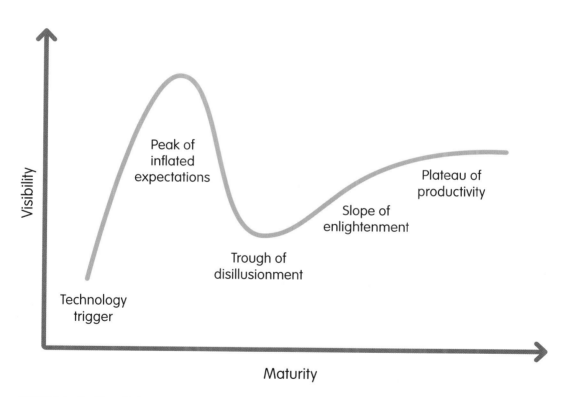

FIGURE 6.6   The Hype Cycle

Source: Figure courtesy of Kemp, Jeremy, 2007. Accessed via wikicommons.

The hype cycle shows five phases of a technology's life cycle. Just as there is value in overlaying the product life cycle and the innovation adoption curve, it can be valuable to view the hype cycle in the context of adoption and sales. Doing so makes it clear that for new products inspired by technology, the technology may have experienced its own life cycle challenges.

- In the first phase, a research breakthrough serves as a *technology trigger*.

- In the second phase, the *peak of inflated expectations*, there is a lot of buzz about the technology but the technology is unproven.

- The third phase is the *trough of disillusionment*, during which first-to-market products are introduced but many fail. Businesses want first-mover advantages but being first also comes with risk.

- The fourth stage is the *slope of enlightenment*, at which point practical benefits of the technology emerge.

- The fifth stage is the *plateau of productivity*, when the market is ready to adopt products with the new technology and mass adoption is feasible. This is when mass adoption really beds in and it's much easier for customers to commit to the new tech.

New products based on the technology will not be introduced until the technology reaches the third stage of the hype cycle, and even then, the introduction is risky. Only if the technology reaches the fourth stage are products based on it likely to succeed in the market. Both the innovation adoption curve and the hype cycle illustrate that market success is dependent upon a small band of people who are willing to take the risk on an unknown. Though the cycle is valuable for understanding the precursors to the product life cycle, not all technology gets hyped. Some technologies stay in stealth mode until they emerge in the mass market. Smartphones are an example. In contrast, virtual reality and wearables were overhyped (Desjardins, 2017). Virtual reality has been the next big thing for years but still has a relatively small consumer footprint. When Google Glass came out, people thought wearables would take off. But despite many wearable categories, most consumers have stuck with fitness wearables like FitBit. What does that mean for marketers trying to make decisions about new product development? Professor Mark Kennedy of Imperial College says, "Think of your business's innovations as a portfolio to be traded … Start to identify which are seeing changes in momentum and the highest potential impact – and therefore deserve capital investment" (KPMG, 2016). Apple is a good example of a company that has chosen not to pursue first-mover advantages in favor of lesser risk. Despite its perception as an innovative company, Apple is almost never first to a market. Instead, Apple waits for demand to support a product and then develops incremental innovation on an existing product to produce an offer with a differential advantage.

CASE STUDY

PRODUCT DEVELOPMENT IN THE SMART HOME INDUSTRY – AMAZON'S SMART HOME ECOSYSTEM

Smart home products include a wide range of categories – from voice-activated speakers, to thermostats that change the temperature when users are home or away, to refrigerators with touchscreens that let people watch TV and see their groceries from a mobile app, to security cameras that recognize familiar faces! The products are part of the aspiration of a truly smart home. Smart homes promise to anticipate and respond to their occupants' needs, intuitively and automatically, based on learned lifestyle patterns, and to empower people with better control of the home environment to increase comfort, awareness, convenience, and cost and energy savings.

Marketers are developing new connected products for the smart home market and increasing consumer adoption of available products. The smart home market includes several product categories: 1) artificial intelligence/voice assistants, 2) audiovisual entertainment, 3) security, 4) energy, 5) kitchen appliances, and 6) personal care and health.

The market is growing. In 2016 it was valued at $24 billion, but by 2022 it is expected to reach $53 billion (Ali and Yusuf, 2018). Smart home purchases have moved past the innovator and early adopter stages. For example, in connected US households, 32% own at least one connected device and more than half plan to buy a smart home device in the coming year. Of those who own a smart home device, 25% can control all or some of their smart devices with a single app. A third of consumers don't have a device that will control multiple home products, but use individual apps for discrete devices (Martin, 2018).

Some consumers have hesitated to adopt smart home products. Many smart home products are far more expensive than their dumb counterparts. For example, a Nest smart thermostat is several times the cost of a traditional thermostat. It can be complicated to install smart product systems and/or to fully utilize the promised functionality. And then there's the risk of obsolescence. New and improved smart home products seem to hit the market every day. Consumers worry they might buy something that will be obsolete before long. To minimize these risks, consumers considering smart home product purchases are relying on brands they have confidence in:

- 50% said they will purchase from a well-known, established brand
- 49% will choose brands that work with other products in their home
- 43% want to buy a brand known for innovation
- 35% will choose the same brand as another smart product they own
- 32% will buy the same brand as their smartphone brand.

(Continued)

Amazon is the market leader, with roughly 70% of smart home product sales. Its product development strategy is establishing a branded smart home ecosystem. Some of Amazon's new product offerings include a new and improved Echo Show, AmazonBasics microwave, AlexaGuard security system, and the Amazon Smart Plug (Moore, 2018). The Echo Show features a large, high-resolution display and a powerful microphone and sound system. AmazonBasics Microwave integrates Alexa into a compact countertop microwave retailing for less than $60. It includes dozens of quick-cook voice presets, so users can cook just by asking Alexa. Amazon Dash is built in, so you can also easily order groceries in case you're running low on microwave popcorn. There's also an Echo Wall Clock that connects to Echo via Bluetooth. Alexa Guard is a home security hub that manages lighting, doorbells, and security. For the devices not offered by Amazon, customers can simply use the Amazon Smart Plug! For under $25, the Smart Plug lets customers control any device they plug into it. All of these products have two commonalities: 1) they cost less than comparable products and 2) they only work with the Alexa voice assistant. These characteristics suggest that Amazon's product development strategy is meant to disrupt the industry. The product line's lack of compatibility with other AI voice assistants is essential to Amazon's product strategy – to make its product ecosystem a part of everyday life, whether people are listening to music, turning off the lights, or making dinner. Once a customer is invested in the ecosystem, the perceived cost of switching will decrease the likelihood of buying additional smart home products from a competitor. Amazon augments the product ecosystem with added value services like Music Unlimited for Echo, a streaming music subscription plan priced far below competing music services.

PRME

VOLVO'S CONTRIBUTION TO SUSTAINABLE CITIES AND COMMUNITIES

Managing the mobility of people and products is one of the most challenging issues of our time. By 2030, passenger traffic is expected to exceed 80,000 billion passenger-kilometers – a 50% increase – and freight volume will grow by 70% globally (Mohieldin and Vandycke, 2017). In places like India, China, sub-Saharan Africa, and Southeast Asia, the lifestyles of billions are rapidly improving along with expectations for the products associated with a better life. The number of vehicles on the world's roads is expected to double by 2050. Projects like China's One Belt, One Road will connect more than half of the world's population and nearly a quarter of the products transported through maritime links and roads. For these reasons, you might be surprised that the UN didn't identify transportation and mobility specifically among its target SDGs. Why? Transportation contributes to many of the challenges identified by SDGs (Project Breakthrough, 2017).

Transportation uses fossil-fuel energy, so it affects SDG 7 for affordable and clean energy. Transportation is indispensable for industry, innovation, and infrastructure, the focus of SDG 9. It is a major influence in the viability of sustainable cities and communities, the focus of SDG 11, whether by innovations in public transportation or roadways. Road access correlates to reduced poverty in rural areas, implicating SDG 1 and SDG 10. Transportation is necessary for the economic engine of commerce, which is tied to SDG 8. Mobility has the potential to improve the lives and livelihoods of billions of people including health, quality of life, and future opportunities. Transportation creates emissions that cause pollution and threaten the climate (SDG 13). One could argue that transportation and mobility have the potential to impact – for good or bad – all of the SDGs.

Transportation's role across the SDGs also means that transportation companies are in a position to initiate positive change. The UN worked with consulting firm KPMG to identify specific contributions companies in the transportation industry could make toward accomplishing each of the SDGs. The resulting report, the *SDG Industry Matrix: Transportation*, offers specific ideas for action and industry-specific practical examples (UN Global Compact and KPMG, 2016).

SDG 11 focuses on sustainable cities and communities, and seeks to make cities and human settlements inclusive, safe, resilient, and sustainable. It is an area in which Volvo makes a substantial contribution worldwide. Specific issues to address in creating sustainable cities include:

- improved road, rail, air, and marine safety
- solutions for managing mobility needs, including supporting city infrastructure and enhancing accessibility that may open up socio-economic opportunities
- efficient systems that reduce waste, emissions, traffic congestion, air pollution, and other issues.

Volvo contributes to the pursuit of sustainable cities by providing a product line of buses that use the latest technology to provide safe, efficient, and comfortable public transportation. Buses are the most common form of public transport in the world today. As the world's cities continue to expand rapidly, the demand for public transport is also increasing. The Volvo Buses product line now offers a range of electrified city buses in 22 countries, including hybrids, electric hybrids, and all-electric buses. Electric motors are energy efficient, reduce emissions, and minimize city noise. Volvo also collaborates with cities on BRT (Bus Rapid Transit) systems. BRT is a popular sustainable mobility concept that provides dedicated bus lanes to deliver an efficient and environmentally sustainable transport service to urban residents. Autonomous, self-driving buses will be available in the near future. The autonomous bus provides all of the benefits of Volvo's electric bus models but with enhanced safety and efficiency. IoT sensors monitor

(Continued)

the vehicle's environment to anticipate and prevent safety threats and provide information used to navigate the vehicle. Volvo believes automation, connectivity, and electromobility are the key enablers for change and this is reflected in Volvo's product design decisions – decisions that contribute to the sustainability of cities.

Visit **https://study.sagepub.com/tuten**
for free additional resources related to this chapter.

CHAPTER SUMMARY

Marketers must understand that a product's value proposition goes beyond the core product and actual product to the augmented product – differentiation can be found in added value. Nurturing of the product mix through investment and innovation is critical to cultivating and maintaining a strong foothold in the market relative to the competition. In this chapter we learned about the product life cycle and the role it plays in informing marketing decisions – as demand for a product changes throughout its life cycle, so too should the strategy to market that product, focusing increasingly on differentiation and innovation. We also learned that the innovation adoption curve adds another lens through which to view the "life" of a product where demand is measured by rate of adoption. Good marketers must drive adoption early on in a product's life cycle by successfully marketing to innovators and early adopters, critical consumer categories to crossing the "chasm". Of the five factors thought to drive adoption, relative advantage, compatibility, and simplicity all inform the product design process. This symbiotic relationship between product design and product promotion means that marketers are often a critical link in continued product innovation, making sure that companies design and redesign products that add value for consumers and stand apart in the competitive landscape.

REVIEW QUESTIONS

1. What is a product?
2. What are the levels of a product and why are they relevant in developing a value proposition?
3. What is the difference between secondary demand and primary demand?
4. What is design-to-value?
5. How are products and services different?
6. What is the new product development process?
7. What are the tenets of the design-to-value approach to innovation?
8. What is meant by the term agile innovation?
9. What are the stages in the diffusion-of-innovations process? What factors influence the rate of adoption of new products?
10. How does the product life cycle influence marketing strategy decisions?
11. What are the stages in the product life cycle?
12. What is the hype cycle?

KEY TERMS

1. **Actual product** – the physical good or service process that supplies the benefit sought.

2. **Adoption** – the process by which a consumer or business customer begins to buy and use a new good, service, or idea.

3. **Agile innovation** – enables new product development through collaboration while also remaining responsive to market changes.

4. **Augmented product** – consists of the added value created by features beyond the basics.

5. **Breakaway positioning** – associates the product with a different category.

6. **Chasm** – the point between early adopters and early majority; this is a critical point, sometimes called the tipping point.

7. **Clean sheet** – involves determining what products should cost given different parameters such as design choices, raw material, and component quality.

8. **Compatibility** – the degree to which the product is compatible with any existing equipment and/or buyer values.

9. **Competitive teardown** – refers to the disassembling of competing products to document technical and functional differences and identify strategies for reducing costs or optimizing features with a differential advantage.

10. **Continuous innovation** – incremental change in product design, product components, and/or related processes.

11. **Convenience products** – nondurable, low-involvement products that are purchased frequently.

12. **Core product** – refers to the utility the customer is buying.

13. **Design-to-value (DTV)** – an integrated approach to product development that considers what customers want, what competitors offer, and what it costs to manufacture and distribute an end product; may also be used in new product development.

14. **Diffusion** – describes how the use of a product spreads throughout a population.

15. **Digital Darwinism** – the concept that only those organizations that can integrate technology to add real value for customers and the organization's value chain will survive and thrive.

16. **Disruptive innovation** – occurs when a new entrant in a market offers a functional alternative to the underserved, oftentimes at a lower price.

17. **Durables** – products that provide benefits over an extended period of time.

18. **Innovation adoption model** – illustrates the diffusion of the innovation by the relative percentage of customers who adopt it at each stage.

19. **Maloney's 16% rule** – explains that marketers must speak differently to innovators and early adopters (the first 16% of people who will adopt an innovation) than they do to early majority and late majority.

20. **Nondurables** (sometimes called **disposables**) – provide short-term benefits.

21. **Observability** – the degree to which prospects are exposed to the product and can see others using the product.

22. **Primary demand** – demand for a product category.

23. **Product** – something that is produced and offered for sale in the market.

24. **Product ecosystem** – a suite of complementary products.

25. **Product line** – any one type of product in the product mix.

26. **Product line consistency** – the degree of variation between the products within the product line.

27. **Product line depth** – the number of sub-products in a line.

28. **Product line length** – the number of products in a product line.

29. **Product line width** – the number of product lines in a product mix.

30. **Product portfolio** (also called a **product mix**) – the number of product lines being offered by a company.

31. **Relative advantage** – the degree to which the innovation is perceived as better than the incumbent product.

32. **Reverse positioning** – removes some product attributes while adding new ones.

33. **Scrum** – emphasizes creative and adaptive teamwork in solving complex problems, lean development, and Kanban (reducing lead times and the amount of work in process).

34. **Shopping products** – products that inspire the buyer to gather information and make comparisons among competing brands.

35. **Simplicity** – the degree to which the product is easy to understand and use.

36. **Social innovation** – when innovation is co-created by stakeholders for the long-term benefit of society.

37. **Software as a service (SaaS)** – customers can pay to use software by usage rental or subscribe.

38. **Specialty products** – typically high-involvement purchases with an extended customer journey.

39. **Stealth positioning** – disguises the product's true nature as it attracts new customers.

40. **Strategic product value management** – comprehensive method using design-to-value and design-to-cost procedures to determine the ideal portfolio of products, develop detailed cost models for those products, and reduce costs throughout the value chain.

41. **Trialability** – the degree to which the product can be used prior to making a commitment.

42. **Unsought products** – those for which prospective buyers lack awareness of the product and its benefits and therefore do not actively move through the purchase process.

43. **White label** – something that is produced by one company and then repackaged and sold by other companies under their brand name.

Chapter 7

OFFERING VALUE: PRICE

In this chapter, we'll learn the answers to the following questions:

1   What is the role of price in the marketing mix?

2   What are the levels of price management? What marketing objectives are related to pricing strategies? What are the implications of algorithmic pricing?

3   What pricing orientations do marketers use to guide pricing decisions?

4   Why do marketers make price adjustments and how might they harm profitability?

5   What are the psychological influences that affect customer perceptions of value?

6   How are digital innovations benefitting price management in organizations?

INTRODUCTION

After product, pricing plays a key role in the marketing mix. The reason for this importance is that where the rest of the elements of the marketing mix are cost generators, price is a source of income and profits. It is the brand's opportunity for value capture. Through pricing, the organization manages to support the cost of production, the cost of distribution, and the cost of promotion. Any pricing decisions for a product need to be made through proper research, analysis, and an eye on strategic objectives for the organization and the product.

Simplistically, price is the value of the exchange. The buyer offers money in the amount of the price to gain something offered by the seller. That's simple, but choosing the right price can be challenging for marketers. Why? The pricing decision is affected by several internal and external factors. It affects the brand's position in the competitive marketplace and the product's role within the organization. Price must reflect the product's market strategy, the cost to produce and market the product, demand, competition, and the perceived value of the offer in the mind of the buyer. A price that is too high will result in fewer sales; one that is too low results in lower profit margins – leaving money on the table. The "right" price could be in a state of near-constant flux as circumstances change over time. The opening vignette explains how Philips managed pricing for one of its lighting products.

OPENING VIGNETTE

PHILIPS LIGHTING'S SMART PRICING

Philips Lighting was eager to sell its smart lighting solution for a new office building (Van Wyk, Brooke and Bornstein, 2018). The company already had recognition for its connected lighting system in the Edge, an innovative 40,000-square-meter multi-tenant office building in the Dutch capital of Amsterdam. The Edge demonstrated what a smart, sustainable lighting system could do. Philips Lighting had installed 6,500 LED luminaires over 15 floors to create a "digital ceiling", of which 3,000 were equipped with integrated sensors. These were linked to the IT network through 750 power-over-Ethernet switches that provided both power and connectivity. The sensors captured data on room occupancy, temperature, and natural light levels; this data was then used to tailor the lighting, heating, and cooling, and to organize cleaning services. Employees working in the office could control light levels and temperature for their own desk areas using a smartphone app. According to Philips Lighting, the system can provide hundreds of thousands of dollars in energy savings.

The prospective client saw value in developing a "smart building" with the lighting technology fully incorporated within the building's heating/ventilation/air conditioning, and security and fire systems, but was also hesitant to invest twice the price of a more typical lighting solution. Philips emphasized the substantial energy cost savings – as much as 50% of energy costs – that result from the system when viewing the price from the perspective of total cost of ownership. This example highlights a challenge facing manufacturers of innovative products. It can be difficult to articulate the benefits of the product innovation and justify premium pricing. Investments in innovations like smart lighting may also carry costs beyond the system itself.

One approach to pricing in such situations is the product-as-a-service model. Philips Lighting used the lighting-as-a-service model, charging for long-term maintenance contracts instead of for lighting fixtures. For example, Staci Italia, a logistics management company, wanted a lighting system that would significantly reduce their operating and maintenance costs, while complying with regulations, enhancing safety, and contributing to sustainability goals. Philips designed a lighting solution with an interactive management system. Lights are controlled by motion sensors and an automatic regulator with wireless control, which dims lights when not in use. For example, lighting zones activate automatically when staff unload deliveries, or when staff move stock from one part of the warehouse to another. Philips' contract maintenance program services the luminaires, sensors, and software to maximize product performance for the client. For Staci Italia, the result was 82% energy savings. The cost savings help to offset the service contract price Staci Italia pays Philips (Philips, 2016).

THE ROLE OF PRICE IN THE MARKETING MIX

While all elements of the marketing mix are part of offer design, price stands out because of its role in driving revenues, covering costs, and generating profits. Price is the assignment of value used to express the rate of exchange. Payment could be made by exchanging something of value, even non-monetary value. For instance, you exchange your time and attention for access to Facebook's services. As marketers, we assign price as a monetary value. There are many terms used to signify price, such as fee, premium, rent, toll, fare, and tuition. Some savvy marketers even refer to price as a buyer's investment!

Pricing decisions relate directly to the effectiveness of an organization's business model, and especially the profit formula. Revenues are a function of sales and price point. Profitability is the difference between revenues and the costs of doing business. Raising prices can increase revenues and profits if sales remain unchanged, but raising prices can also cause a decline in demand. Managing costs also contributes directly to profitability. The brand's value proposition is a major driver of buyer response to price.

Choosing the right price can boost profit far faster than efforts to increase sales volume and market share. A study of B2B industries found that a 1% improvement in realized price resulted in an 8% increase in earnings (Burns, McLinn and Porter, 2016). In contrast, increasing market share by 1% only increased earnings by 4%. According to McKinsey, a 1% price increase results in an 8.7% increase on average in operating profits assuming no loss of sales volume (Baker, Kiewell and Winkler, 2014). Despite the value to organizations, as much as 30% of pricing decisions made each year do not result in an optimal price. Warren Buffett, the legendary investor, put it like this: "The single most important decision in evaluating a business is pricing power. If you've got the power to raise prices without losing business to a competitor, you've got a very good business. And if you have to have a prayer session before raising the price by 10 percent, then you've got a terrible business" (Maxwell, 2015). Unfortunately, fewer than 5% of Fortune 500 companies have a full-time function dedicated to pricing (Petro, 2014).

Marketing's price-management function is responsible for evaluating industry shifts that may affect pricing, selecting a price strategy that aligns with the brand positioning and market strategy, and setting prices for specific products in the product portfolio in such a way as to achieve target objectives (e.g., profitability, market share). Marketers choose a price strategy which then guides price setting decisions. Price strategy is defined as a chosen and purposeful policy for price-setting designed to achieve objectives (e.g., sales, margin, product trial) while supporting market perceptions of value consistent with the product's positioning and value proposition. When we achieve the design of optimal pricing strategies, defined as "the sustainable price point that delivers the highest level of profitability, as measured by free cash flow" (Schmitt, n.d.), price decisions also contribute to the financial success of the business. Identifying a perfect pricing strategy is difficult to do because any individual product price decision takes place in the context of the brand's total marketing structure and ever-changing market dynamics. Still there are best practices for setting pricing strategies, guidelines for choosing tactics, and innovations in digital technology that can contribute to our success. Ultimately, as illustrated in Figure 7.1, marketers must consider how the target market perceives value, how competing prices compare, and the price implications relative to the costs to bring the offer to market.

PRICE-MANAGEMENT STRUCTURE AND PRICE SETTING

Before we consider how to choose the right price for a strategic marketing plan – one designed for a specific target market, to pursue a specific market opportunity, with a chosen brand positioning and value proposition to meet a target's needs with the right product, place, and so on – let's review how pricing decisions are managed in organizations. Price management is the organizational function responsible for supporting pricing-related processes, structuring roles and responsibilities, and putting necessary tools and systems in place to select price strategy, set prices, make price adjustments, measure performance,

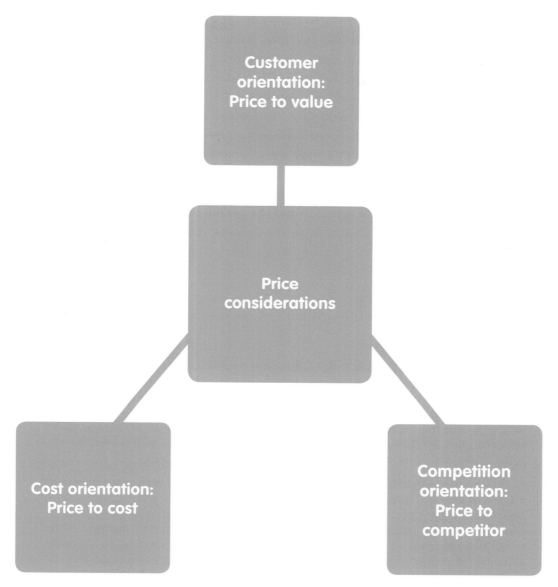

FIGURE 7.1   Primary Determinants Influencing Price

Source: Inspired by Gard and Eyal (2012)

and adapt pricing as needed. It is sometimes described as part of an organization's broader comprehensive value management (CVM) program (Dubey, Moeller, and Turner, 2015). CVM encompasses other organizational functions whose role affects price management. Why? Price is one of four profit levers. The others are sales volume, variable costs (costs that vary by production levels), and fixed costs (overhead costs). Price is typically set at a point somewhere between the price floor (break-even price at which total costs are covered) and the price ceiling (the highest price the market is willing to pay; demand elasticity would depress sales volume at higher prices). Thus, the price decision is directly affected by 1) costs incurred by product design, manufacturing, and supply chain operations and 2) sales volume levels driven in part by brand management, sales, and marketing communications.

For our purposes, we will focus on the elements of price management tied to price setting in marketing planning. The price-management functions rely on the organization's pricing infrastructure, which dictates the roles and responsibilities, processes, and the systems and tools put in place to support effective price management. Price strategy specifies pricing objectives and performance expectations, acknowledges the organization's pricing orientation, determines the price approach and any pricing tactics, and specifies the metrics used to evaluate performance (Baker, Marn and Zawada, 2010).

LEVELS OF PRICE MANAGEMENT

The pricing puzzle is more manageable when seen as components. Price management has three distinct but closely related levels: industry, product market, and transaction (Marn and Rosiello, 1992).

- At the *industry level*, pricing strategists assess supply and demand market-wide, product category performance, and trends like new technologies or lifestyle patterns. The goal is to understand the general context. Is market demand increasing? At what rate? Is supply scarce or plentiful? Are new competitors still entering the market? Are products viewed as commodities or are there opportunities for differentiation? Answers to these questions will determine the price orientation used to guide strategy at product market level.

- At the *product market level*, price strategy is determined. What pricing objectives are prioritized? Will the strategy be based on perceived customer value, competitive benchmarking, or cost? How differentiated is the product from those offered by competitors? How valuable is the value proposition to the target market? Is the target market price sensitive? How does the target market account for the total value of the product, defined as the sum of the benefits they will receive less the costs of acquisition including the product price and other intangible expenses like time and effort? What cost considerations could contribute to the profit formula by increasing margin? How will performance be assessed and used to adjust price strategy?

- At the *transaction level*, the exact price for each transaction is set. Pricing tactics are used to specify the transaction structure and price point. Any price adjustments (allowances and discounts) that may apply are set. At this level, specific price offers are made, possibly even personalized for individual prospective buyers. At the transaction level, pricing managers will assess performance in terms of average realized price (actual price after any discounts) and price leakage (lost revenue due to discounts and transaction-related expenses).

Price elasticity of demand is a relevant concept at all three levels of price management. It explains how sensitive the market is to price fluctuations. When demand is elastic, prospective buyers are sensitive to market fluctuations in price. When demand is inelastic, it does not vary in response to changes in price. Technically, you can calculate a precise value for price elasticity using this formula: price elasticity of demand is equal to the percentage of change in unit volume demanded divided by the percentage change in price. However, for marketers, it's more valuable to understand a product's general placement along the elasticity continuum from the two extremes of perfect elasticity and perfect inelasticity (Gallo, 2015). Marketers in situations of perfect elasticity are selling commodities. There will be little to no ability to differentiate on price; prices will tend to be low with little variance between competitors. In situations of perfect inelasticity, marketers are not constrained by price sensitivity and command high prices for differentiated products. In between these two extremes, marketers must solve the pricing puzzle – how high a price can be justified for a differentiated product without losing the sale.

PRICING OBJECTIVES

Before any pricing decisions are made, a company must identify the objectives it wishes to attain through pricing. The most common objectives are described in Table 7.1.

TABLE 7.1 Pricing Objectives

Objective	Explanation
Maximize profit	Mind revenue and costs to maximize profits; may involve setting high price in situations of weak competition and lowering costs.
Maximize revenue	Set price to optimize earnings.
Maximize sales growth/Gain market share	Set low price to capture market share.
Maximize profit margin	Increase the profit margin for each unit and don't focus on the total number of units sold.
Demonstrate product–quality leadership	Set premium price to demonstrate price–quality relationship.
Recoup product innovation costs	Follow market-skimming approach by setting high initial price while product is in introduction stage of the product life cycle.
Encourage product trial	Offer low or free initial price during trial period.
Demonstrate low-cost leadership	Set price beneath competitors.
Ensure survival	Drop price to gain market share, and/or only cover costs.
Maintain status quo	Maintain stable price to avoid competitive retaliation.

PRICING ORIENTATION

An organization's pricing orientation refers to the organization's strategic view of pricing in its marketing strategy as well as the methods used to reach pricing decisions that support a competitive advantage (Boland, Hinterbuber, Liozu and Perelli, 2015). There are three types of orientation: 1) competition-based, 2) cost-based, and 3) customer value-based. The customer value-based orientation is customer-centric, while the cost-based orientation is product-centric (Cross and Dixit, 2005). While perceived customer value is generally thought to be the preferred orientation, competitive strategy is more commonly used.

COMPETITION-BASED PRICING

This approach relies upon competitive benchmarking. In other words, it uses data on competitive price levels to set prices. It is valuable in specific situations such as when a brand is 1) competing against a limited number of successful competitors, 2) selling commodities, 3) establishing itself as the low price leader, and 4) trying to avoid a price war with the competition. It overlooks information on demand characteristics, market perceptions, and costs (Biscarini, Guerrini, Ferri, Jhunjhunwala and McCaleb, 2017). Boston Consulting Group reported that, in a study of executives working in sectors with commoditized products and little opportunity for differentiation, 90% used competitive benchmarking to set prices (Biscarini et al., 2017).

COST-BASED PRICING

Pricing decisions are influenced primarily by accounting data. Objectives are tied to achieving a target markup on costs, goal for return on investment, and/or margin. Cost-based pricing approaches include 1) cost-plus (markup) pricing, 2) target return pricing, and 3) break-even pricing. Total costs, the sum of variable and fixed costs, are determined for all three methods. In cost-plus pricing, the desired unit profit is added to the unit cost to determine the price. Target return pricing determines the price that would produce the target rate of return given unit costs, capital investments, and forecasted sales volume. Break-even pricing determines the price at which total costs would be recovered at the forecasted sales volume. While cost-based pricing ensures that companies are covering costs, it ignores demand characteristics, market perceptions, and competitive threats. Marketers may instead use total cost to set a price floor.

CUSTOMER VALUE-BASED PRICING

This orientation is the most valuable to pricing strategists but also the most misunderstood. It is sometimes confused with value pricing's everyday low-price tactic. Customer value-based pricing leverages the customer perception of value as a sum of both the benefits and costs of the product. For highly differentiated products, customer value-based pricing will typically produce a higher price setting than would have been recommended as a result of cost-based or competitive-based pricing. Margins will be healthier and the price serves as a perceptual cue to reinforce brand positioning.

Customer value-based pricing approaches are driven by a deep understanding of customers' needs, the value they anticipate when those needs are met, perceived costs associated with acquiring the product (including intangible costs like time and effort), and possible psychological influences. People think of value in relative terms, given alternatives, not absolute terms. They also recognize that value from the benefits and utilities of a purchase are acquired at a cost, meaning that a choice among a set of alternatives will be based on perceptions of which brand will maximize net value. The primary disadvantage of adopting a customer value-based orientation is the difficulty in accurately assessing the target market's perceptions of total value and assigning monetary equivalents to those perceptions. Peter Drucker explained that marketers are unlikely to know how their customers define value without asking, yet understanding customer-perceived value is essential if we are to price products effectively: "'What is value to the customer?' It may be the most important question. Yet it is the one least often asked. One reason is that managers are quite sure that they know the answer. Value is what they, in their business, define as quality. But this is almost always the wrong definition … The customer never buys a product. By definition the customer buys the satisfaction of a want. He buys value" (Drucker, 1973/1993: 83–84).

A COMBINED ORIENTATION

In differentiated product markets, it's easy to see how valuable it is to understand customer perceptions of value. But given that customer perceptions are relative, driven by comparisons to competing alternatives or reference prices, the best orientation may take a combined view. A study of marketing executives by Bain & Company found that 85% felt their company approach to price setting and getting needed improvement. The most effective companies utilized aspects of all three pricing orientations to create optimal pricing strategies. Specifically, they considered:

- the attributes and benefits that customers truly value, and how much value is created for them
- the substitutable alternatives and competitive intensity in the business
- the true profitability of the transaction after netting out leakage in areas such as rebates and shipping costs (Burns and Kermisch, 2018).

PRICE SETTING TACTICS AND PRICE ADJUSTMENTS

At the transaction level of price management, prices are set and managed. Importantly, marketers must set the desired list price, but they also need to monitor performance and make price adjustments as needed on an ongoing basis. It's a mistake to see price setting as a one and done task.

PRICE-SETTING TACTICS

When it comes to pricing, a long list of pricing tactics has evolved from customer value-based, competitive-based, and cost-based pricing strategies. Table 7.2 includes some of the most common tactics used.

TABLE 7.2   Pricing Tactics

Pricing Tactic	Description
Value (low-price leader) pricing	Set price to beat competition and/or be perceived as low-price leader in industry; not to be confused with customer value-based pricing.
Everyday low pricing (EDLP)	Set price low with promise to continue; no sales or discounts offered.
Keystone pricing	Set price at double the cost; commonly used in retailing.
Target-return pricing	Set price that yields desired return on costs and capital investments.
Cost-plus pricing	Set price based on cost per unit plus desired profit; also called markup pricing.
Subscription pricing	Price tied to ongoing access rather than ownership; common in software-as-a-service products.
Product line pricing	Offering portfolio of similar products at different price points for different levels of quality; also called price lining.
Penetration pricing	Set price low to gain market share; raise price over time.
Prestige pricing	Set price high to reflect high-quality and/or luxury image.
Going rate pricing	Match competitor price.
Price skimming	Set price high at product launch (introduction stage of product life cycle); lower price over time.
Discount pricing	Offer price reduction off list price; variations include discounts for volume purchases (quantity), buyer credentials (e.g., in related business), off-season merchandise, trade-ins, special events.
Freemium	Product offered free of charge, but price charged for related items and services.
Bundle pricing	Offer special price on a set of complementary products packaged together as a bundle.

Pricing Tactic	Description
Loss leader	Offer one product at a price below cost to draw store traffic; when loss leader is actually unavailable for purchase, it is known as baiting.
Negotiated pricing	Set price through bargaining.
Differentiated pricing	Setting different prices for same product for different markets.
Free lunch pricing	Offer free product to build user base; build revenue by selling data, advertising, etc., to third-party customers (e.g., Gmail).
Auction pricing	Let buyers bid on price they wish to pay.
Pay-what-you-want (PWYW) pricing	Let buyers set price based on what they are willing to pay; also called value-for-value pricing.
Group pricing	Set special deal when people purchase large volume as a group (e.g., Groupon).
Product as a service; share pricing	Price set for access to product rather than product ownership; product shared by buyers.
Pay as you go (PAYG) pricing	Price charged for resource usage, modeled after utility billing; price only for what buyer used; frequently used for cloud computing services
Odd/even pricing	End price in a 9 to suggest a good deal; end price with an even number to suggest product quality

PRICE ADJUSTMENTS

Prices may be adjusted, typically discounted from the list price, to increase sales during a promotional period and accommodate situations in which the brand is willing to make price concessions. Discounts are price reductions, sometimes called price-offs. They may be offered for seasonal events like holiday specials and high-volume purchases, and for trade partners (like members of an association or industry trade group). Promotional pricing may also be used to adjust prices. Some examples are cash or gift card rebate offers, special pricing for members of loyalty programs, warranty and service add-ons at no extra charge, and generous payment terms such as low- or no-interest financing and longer payment periods. In B2B markets, price allowances include discounts for early payment and allowances for services performed by the buyer (such as a retailer setting up in-store displays). Importantly, price adjustments reduce pocket prices (the price realized from the sale). Price adjustments are sometimes made at different points in the exchange process. The decline in price with each discount visually illustrated is called the pocket price waterfall.

FIRM CAPABILITY AND PRICING EFFECTIVENESS

The pricing capability grid captures the relationship between a firm's price-management capabilities and price effectiveness (Burns, McLinn and Porter, 2016). Price setting is guided by the pricing orientations discussed above. Organizations identify what they believe to be an optimal price strategy and set prices consistent with the chosen strategy. Performance though boils down to the actual price pocketed by the firm. When prices are adjusted using discounts and allowances, the pocket price will be less than the list price. The amount lost is called price leakage. To be effective, organizations must excel at price setting and price getting. Price getting, also called price realization, is the process of managing the gap between the price the company wants to charge and the price it can actually get. In other words, the most successful companies control the use of price adjustments to cut down on price leakage.

The pricing capability grid identified five types of company pricing performance based on these two dimensions: 1) organization's pricing orientation and 2) price realization (Hinterhuber and Liozu, 2012). Organizations that used customer-value-based pricing were scored as strong on price orientation. Those using competitive-based pricing were scored as moderate and those using cost-based pricing were scored as weak. Price realization was categorized as strong, moderate, or weak depending upon the organization's level of average profit loss attributed to price leakage. Table 7.3 summarizes the five types. The results point to the need for organizations to focus on price strategy at the product market level of its price-management program as well as price realization at the transaction level to truly succeed.

TABLE 7.3   Price Capability Grid

Price Type	Price Orientation	Price Realization	Description
Power zone	Customer value	Strong	Embraces price-optimization tools to estimate customer value, set prices to demand and value, effective price setting minimizes need for price adjustments like discounts.
Value surrender	Customer value	Weak	Understands customer value as most effective price orientation but weak in estimating value–price relationship and/or overly reliant on price adjustments to achieve sales.
Good intentions	Competition	Medium	Somewhat effective at getting price set but reliance on competitive-based pricing limits price-setting effectiveness.
Price capture	Cost	Strong	Excels at setting cost targets to achieve margin expectations and then sets static sales price.
White flag	Cost	Weak	Sets price based on cost but relies on discounts to achieve sales volume targets.

MANAGING THE GAP

Marketers tend to pay a lot of attention to choosing the right price strategy, but may miss opportunities for enhanced profitability at the transaction level. Pricing consultants with McKinsey analyzed the financial statements of the top 1,500 companies in the Standard & Poors (S&P) list (Marn, Roegner and Zawanda, 2003b). They found that raising prices by just 1%, assuming no change in sales volume, would result in an 8% increase in operating profits. The impact would be about 50% more than cutting variable costs by 1% and three times more than increasing sales volume by 1%. In other words, price is the most powerful profit lever we have.

There's a downside. If prices were decreased by 1%, operating profits would decline 8% assuming other factors remained stable. When it comes to price adjustments, strategists sometimes discount prices assuming that the subsequent increase in sales volume will produce better profitability. According to McKinsey, this is almost never the case. Sales volume would need to increase by 18.7% for profit to break even after a price cut of 5%. Even for products with elastic demand, discounts do not usually produce substantial increases in sales volume.

For pricing strategists, the implications are clear. There is value in using customer value-based pricing methods to support price strategies that can command higher prices. But that's not the only way to effect increases in price. If a brand is applying price adjustments, reducing the use of discounts will result in higher price realization (pocket costs), and affect the bottom line just as a list price increase would.

Remember Philips Lighting from our opening vignette? Pocket prices for lighting suppliers like Philips are usually lower than the list prices. Every product (and product as a service) has a standard list price, but after applying industry discounts and allowances, average invoice prices were more than 30% lower than the list prices for those products. Price leaks were coming from cash discounts for prompt payment, the cost of carrying accounts receivable, cooperative advertising allowances, rebates based on annual volume, and freight expenses. The company was able to set rules to guide its use of price discounts and allowances and reduce discounting overall. In the end, they were able to increase the average invoice pocket price by more than 15% – resulting in substantial increases in operating profits (Marn, Roegner and Zawanda, 2003a).

PSYCHOLOGICAL INFLUENCES AND CUSTOMER VALUE-BASED PRICING

Earlier we introduced the three price orientations marketers may use in price decisions. Customer value-based pricing is useful, but it can also be a challenge to understand target markets, their views of value, and decisions that can sometimes appear irrational.

What really matters when it comes to using a customer value-based pricing approach is the trade-off between the benefits a customer will receive from a purchase and the price paid (Leszinski and Marn, 1997). When we look at pricing strategy through a jobs-to-be-done lens, we see that customers aren't paying for products. They are paying to get a job done. What we need to know is what it's *worth to the customer* to get that job done (Strategyn Pricing Strategy, n.d.).

So despite the price tag, customers do not buy solely on low price. They buy according to a perception of the value they will receive. Customer value can be thought of as an equation; it equals customer-perceived benefits minus customer-perceived price. So, the higher the perceived benefit and/or the lower the price of a product, the higher the customer value and the greater the likelihood that customers will choose that product.

Not only do customers define value differently from price, they also define costs differently. Customer costs go beyond the price of the product. They include any expenses the customer will incur because of the purchase. In other words, buyers view value as the sum of all consequences, positive and negative, associated with the purchase (Alvarez, 2009). There are three primary cost drivers that customers may consider when evaluating "what something costs": 1) monetary expenses (price of the product, sales tax, shipping costs), 2) time and effort required (to shop, choose, order, pay, and acquire the product), and 3) mental energy (cognitive effort required due to complexity of decision) (Laja, 2018).

These estimates are not absolute. Value is relative. Relative to what? Just as a brand's position in the market is relative to its competition, so too is the value a buyer associates with a brand purchase. In most purchase situations, buyers have alternatives made up of brands in their consideration set. If a viable competitor exists, the alternative serves to establish a frame of reference. In negotiation, this is called the BATNA – best alternative to a negotiated agreement. Buyers consider best alternatives too. It might seem that buyers are rational in their assessment of value as the sum of consequences associated with a purchase. But it's worth remembering that people oftentimes behave irrationally. Behavioral economics and consumer psychology shed insight into the phenomenon of irrationality in buyer behavior. We first introduced this concept in Chapter 2. Here we'll review the most influential psychological patterns related to buyer perceptions of price.

For the most part, people really don't know how much things are worth. They want a fair price, but they have to use cues to guess what a fair price might be. William Poundstone, the author of *Priceless: The Myth of Fair Value* (2011), put it this way: "People tend to be clueless about prices. Contrary to economic theory, we don't really decide between A and B by consulting our invisible price tags and purchasing the one that yields the higher utility. We make do with guesstimates and a vague recollection of what things are 'supposed to cost'" (Poundstone, 2011: 28). Consumers use reference prices as a heuristic in these situations.

Reference prices are prices the buyer has knowledge of and uses as a point of comparison in evaluating the price of the product under consideration. There are two sources of reference prices: internal and external. Internal reference prices are prices held in memory or perceived by the buyer. Internal reference prices could be based on the last price the buyer paid for a similar product, a price cap the buyer has set for him- or herself (also known as a reservation price), recall of prices seen or advertising in the past, knowledge of what others paid for a similar product, and beliefs as to what a fair price might be. External reference prices are supplied by other sources including the marketer or store setting. For example, if you are shopping for a new pair of shoes, you can use the prices of the shoe assortment in the store as reference prices. Marketers can use advertising and in-store signage (or on-page copy for e-commerce) to provide external reference price cues (e.g., Was $90 – Now just $50!).

In this digital age, external reference prices are easily available. Our smartphones mean we can search for price comparisons at anytime, from anywhere – even while shopping in a store. There are also price comparison apps that will automatically alert us to retailers offering a product for less, even as we browse items in an online store. Apps like Keepa point to the lowest price vendors on Amazon and include a price fluctuation history. Users can see whether the price has been stable or tends to fluctuate and whether the price is likely to go down soon. The availability of price information is called price transparency. Neil Davidson, in *Don't Just Roll the Dice* (2009) put it this way: "People base their perceived values on reference points. If you're selling a to-do list application, then people will look around and find another to-do list application. If they search the Internet and discover that your competitors sell to-do list applications at $100 then this will set their perception of the right price for all to-do list applications" (Davidson, 2009: 19).

People may be prone to loss aversion or splurging depending upon the payment mode being used. Research suggests that people spend more when using debit and credit cards and less when using cash. Cash spenders will spend more if they have small bills and change than if they have large bills. They will hesitate to break a $100 bill but wouldn't hesitate to use a mix of smaller bills. It's thought that loss aversion is to blame. We may perceive more sense of loss when exchanging physical currency. Cryptocurrencies, like Bitcoin, are accepted as exchange currency in some markets. For example, online retailer Overstock accepts Bitcoin and other cryptocurrencies for payments in more than 100 countries, amounting to about $50,000 in Bitcoin transactions each week (Roberts, 2017). How the use of cryptocurrencies like Bitcoin and the use of digital wallet apps affect buyer behavior is yet unknown.

Buyers may fall prey to beliefs and perceptions that harm their ability to make optimized purchase decisions. For example, many consumers believe that Amazon offers at or near the lowest prices on a broad range of goods, even when that's not the case. In fact, Amazon strategically selects some products on which they will aggressively compete on price, but charge higher prices on others. In one study, products sold by Jet.com were 27% cheaper than the same items on Amazon (Heda, Mewborn and Caine, 2016). When Amazon shoppers search for products on the site, the search results include one featured option presented in the "buy box". Shoppers assume the preselected choice shown in the buy box is the best choice from the list of alternatives, especially on price. That's a faulty perception. Actually, Amazon's algorithm puts an Amazon-sold product (direct from Amazon, rather from a reseller using Amazon's platform) or an Amazon partner product in the buy box more than 75% of the time. It would just take a few moments for shoppers to scan the page of search results and spot the cheaper options, but 82% of Amazon shoppers simply buy the choice shown in the buy box. In a study of 250 products sold on Amazon, the average price difference between the product recommended in the buy box and the cheapest price shown in the product search results was $7.88. A customer who bought all 250 items studied from the buy box would have paid 20% more, about $1,400 extra, than if they had purchased the cheapest item shown (Angwin and Mattu, 2016).

You can see the puzzling behaviors. In some ways, consumers are empowered by price transparency, but also overlook opportunities to save money. Mental costs are a possible explanation. Mental costs are soft costs incurred in times of choice overload, friction, and anxiety, and whose debt we pay with intangible resources like time, effort, and worry. In contrast, product prices represent hard costs we pay with monetary resources. Flint McGlaughlin, CEO of MECLABS Institute, explained: "The marketer must remember cost is not just a mathematical calculation; it is especially a *psychological* calculation. A low material cost does not necessarily mean a low mental cost" (Burnstein, 2018). In the Amazon example, the company provided a heuristic that could overcome the buyer's sense of choice overload. It's effective because it reduces the mental costs required to purchase.

DIGITAL SOLUTIONS FOR OPTIMAL PRICING STRATEGIES

By this point, you might be thinking it's no wonder that marketers report struggling with pricing decisions! Fortunately, the digital technologies changing the face of commerce also benefit marketers when it comes to pricing. These tools and processes become part of the organization's price-management structure.

DYNAMIC PRICING

Among the most impactful applications affecting pricing are dynamic pricing algorithms. Algorithmic pricing generally refers to automated decision-making and price adjustments using machine learning and artificial intelligence (Katsov, 2018). Have you ever searched for a product online in the morning and gone back to look at it again later in the day only to find the price has changed? If so, you have seen a pricing algorithm in action.

Sellers use dynamic pricing algorithms to adjust prices in response to changes in the marketplace. Online sellers can change prices automatically and in real-time by setting algorithmic rules or using self-learning algorithms. The algorithms can consider several variables to set the best price for a specific product, customer, and time. Some of the variables used by dynamic pricing algorithms include product supply, competitor prices, demand indicators like recent views, customer data including demographics, current location, connected device, and past spending patterns.

Amazon and its many third-party sellers use algorithmic pricing. Amazon's dynamic pricing bot monitors competitors' price changes and automatically lowers Amazon's price to match or beat the competition's new price. Jeff Bezos, CEO of Amazon, explained why, saying "Your margin is my opportunity" (Lashinsky, 2012). A study of the algorithmic patterns of Amazon's third-party sellers found that algorithmic sellers change product prices tens or even hundreds of times per day (Chen, Mislove and Wilson, 2016). This is illustrated in Figure 7.2. Amazon is not the only beneficiary of the value of algorithmic pricing. A survey of more than 1,700 executives found that nearly half are using some dynamic pricing algorithms (Burns and Murphy, 2018). Dynamic pricing algorithms are not a pricing strategy in and of themselves. Rather they are tools that can help organizations streamline repetitive pricing tasks, such as monitoring and analyzing competitors' prices, and optimize profitability through better price management (Gruyaert and Meehan, 2018).

McKinsey identified five specific variations of dynamic pricing models that can be valuable to marketers in different situations (Benmark, Klapdor, Kullmann and Sundararajan, 2017). The long-tail model sets an introductory price for new or long-tail items through intelligent product matching. The elasticity model uses time-series methods and big data analytics to calculate how a product's price affects demand in situations of seasonality, cannibalization, and competitive moves. The KVI model estimates how much each product affects consumer price perception, using actual market data. The competitive-response model recommends price adjustments based on competitor prices updated in real-time. The omnichannel model coordinates prices among the retailer's offline and online channels.

PRICE-OPTIMIZATION MODELING

While dynamic pricing makes it possible to dynamically alter product prices when certain conditions are met, price-optimization models analyze "what-if" scenarios that can inform pricing decisions. Table 7.4 describes some of the most common types of price optimization models (Dolzake, 2015). Price-optimization models are mathematical programs that calculate how demand varies at different price levels. They can be used to forecast demand and predict sales response to pricing strategies, use of price adjustments like discounts and deals, and promotions.

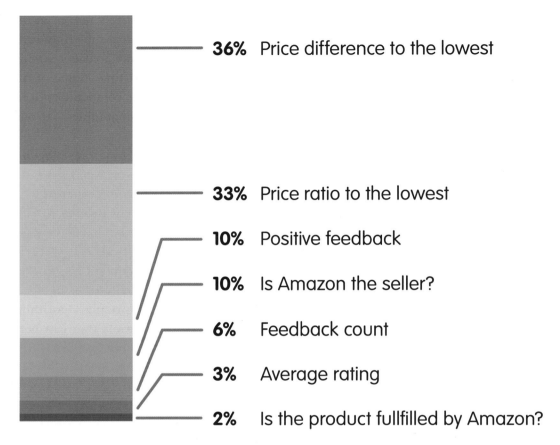

FIGURE 7.2   Visualizing the Effects of Algorithmic Pricing

Source: Katsov (2018)

TABLE 7.4   Types of Price-Optimization Models

Model	Description
Lift	Quantifies the effect of price discounts on sales.
Price threshold	Identifies price bands beyond which sales will decline significantly.
Price elasticity	Measures likely impact of price changes on demand.
Price gap	Determines optimal price difference to differentiate from competitor price.

These techniques make it possible to offer differentiated pricing, also known as price customization. Price customization offers different prices to customers who value the product differently. Imagine that you are shopping online for a juicy novel for your upcoming vacation. In the past, you had a high conversion rate, tending to purchase the novels you viewed descriptions of, but never paying more than $19.99. A friend of yours is price sensitive and prefers the $1.99 ebook deals that appear periodically. If you both view the same novel, you may see a higher price than your friend. The same databases we can use to customize real-time offers, retarget ads, and develop personas make it possible for firms to estimate what each individual buyer is willing to pay and set a price based on that estimate (Arnesen, Cohen and Obermiller, 2012). From a marketing perspective, customized pricing results in the highest level of profitability, highest purchase conversion rates, and highest customer satisfaction with the price charged (Arnesen et al., 2012). The price chosen maximizes the price a buyer is willing to pay without risking the loss of a sale.

PRICING SOFTWARE AS A SERVICE (SAAS)

Pricing software, typically sold as an SaaS subscription, can provide valuable support for an organization's price-management function, particularly when organizations have a large product portfolio. For example, using historical performance of price promotions, a software solution can assess the probability of success for future promotions. A study by Bain & Company found that pricing effectiveness for firms using pricing software was more than twice that of non-users (Burns and Kermisch, 2018).

McKinsey's Price Advisor software is an example. It offers a strong analytical tool capable of modeling market characteristics, analyzing "what-if" pricing scenarios, and using analytics, machine learning, and artificial intelligence to make price recommendations down to the SKU-product level. **SKU** is an acronym for stock-keeping unit, a unique alphanumeric code assigned to a product to identify price and product description. The pricing software includes intelligence services to analyze historical data and monitor current conditions like competitor prices in real-time to support algorithmic pricing. Other pricing software brands include Vendavo and Price f(x) (Burns and Kermisch, 2018).

FAIR-PAY PRICING MODEL

Though yet to be widely adopted, the concept of **fair-pay pricing** has great potential for pricing digital goods. Fair-pay pricing is a digital, interdependent pricing method that integrates try before you buy, pay-what-you-want pricing, relationship pricing, and the influence of social capital (Bertini and Reisman, 2013). Buyers are able to try the product first and then pay what they want, within the constraints of any rules set by the seller, even if the amount is zero. They must justify the price they paid with specific reasons. Sellers rate the buyers on fairness, producing fairness rating scores. High fairness ratings unlock rewards, while low fairness ratings restrict the buyer's ability to pay what they want on future purchases. Richard Reisman, the creator, posits that this pricing method can optimize value for both buyers and sellers (Reisman, 2019).

PRICE SETTING FOR A PRIVATE-LABEL YOGURT BRAND

Danone controls about 17% of the $83 billion global yogurt market. That kind of market leadership can be intimidating for private-label brands, so it's no wonder that Carrefour was worried about setting the right price for its private-label yogurt. Historically, private-label brands (also known as store brands) competed as low-cost alternatives to name brands. If Carrefour followed tradition, its private-label yogurt would be priced lower than Danone's yogurt portfolio. Carrefour's cost of goods sold totaled €1.29 and the comparative Danone yogurt retailed at €2.99. These represented Carrefour's price floor and price ceiling. Next, the company needed to decide whether to stick with a cost-based approach to set price or embrace the benefits of customer value-based pricing.

The pricing team knew that consumer impressions of private-label brands were changing. Nielsen carried out a survey of 30,000 consumers in 60 countries to study consumer perceptions of private-label brands (Nielsen, 2014). The findings are good news for Carrefour and other private-label brands. According to the survey results, price is still the most important factor driving consumer purchases of private-label brands – 69% of the participants said it was important for them to get the best price on a product and 70% said they purchase private labels as a way to save money. They also said that, based on their personal experiences, private-label brands were of high quality, providing the benefits they associate with name brands but at a great price. In addition, 62% said they feel like smart shoppers when they buy private-label brands, suggesting that there are psychological benefits as well as financial and functional benefits for these shoppers.

Other research shows that European consumers have high expectations for dairy products and have a high willingness to pay to get high-quality products (Ngoulma, 2015). This would usually suggest a bias toward name brands, but private-label brands are delivering quality and other premium attributes along with better prices. Private-label brands own 39% of the market share of grocery products in the EU, and in many European countries they outperform the leading name brand product. With consumer adoption, private-label brands have been increasing prices, narrowing the price differential compared to name brands. These industry trends are promising, but Carrefour is also cognizant of the depressed demand associated with brand price wars in France and Greece (IRI, n.d.). This price decision isn't one to be made lightly.

Initially, the company was leaning toward a product launch priced at €1.99, which compares favorably to Danone priced at €2.99. Customer research revealed that the Carrefour brand outperformed Danone on a key attribute: moms viewed Carrefour's yogurt as healthier and less damaging to their children's teeth than Danone because it contains a lower sugar content. Optimization models estimated the benefit's value to be about €0.30. Carrefour set a launch price of €2.29 – still great value compared to Danone, but with a higher margin than the cost-based price. Marketing communications promoting the launch emphasized the health benefits of yogurt and the value of reduced sugar diets (and not the price advantage). Over time, this may position

Carrefour to raise prices by framing purchase choices as the best nutritional choice rather than as the best choice for saving money. The decision was a success. Sales volume surpassed the targets.

Other evidence of the success of the pricing strategy is the competitor response. Danone announced it may cut prices up to 30% in European markets to better compete against the private-label yogurt brands (Astley, 2012). Danone's price drop will place its list price very close to Carrefour's price point. The question is, if the price is about the same, will people prefer the name brand? Or will the value of the health benefit protect Carrefour's market share?

Danone will also introduce a non-milk-based yogurt to its product portfolio, a niche market with little competition. Danone hopes adding a milk-alternative yogurt will appeal to the small but fast-growing number of people identifying as vegan (*The Star*, 2018). Carrefour is watching. If sales of non-dairy yogurts grow, it would be another opportunity for a private-label entry that undercuts Danone's prices (*The Star*, 2018).

PRME

TWININGS' COMMITMENT TO KENYAN TEA FARMERS LOWERS THE TRUE PRICE OF TEA

Tea is the most-consumed non-alcoholic beverage after water in the world. For some, enjoying a cup of tea is a treasured ritual and it's been called the world's most affordable luxury. The average retail price of a cup of tea is roughly 7 cents! That price, though, obscures the costs associated with the sustainability infringements that take place to bring that cup of tea to the retail market.

Kenya is the third-largest tea-producing country in the world and the source of about 16% of Twinings' tea. Tea exports make up 25% of Kenya's total agricultural export income, making tea a major determinant of livelihood among Kenyans. In some areas of the world, tea is grown on large plantations, but in Kenya, tea is cultivated on small farms. Income farmers earn from selling tea leaf to processing companies pays wages to farm hands and covers the costs of crop cultivation. This income can be unstable though, with crops varying with weather and other factors. The price paid for tea leaf is kept low because of the buying power of corporations like Twinings and Tata tea farther down the supply chain.

Hired workers earn an average annual wage of $1,000, just 62% of the living wage needed to support the essential needs of a family in rural Kenya. Many of the workers are women and children. Without a proper income, people are unable to provide for themselves and their family, including health, education, nutrition, and proper housing,

(Continued)

and are trapped in poverty. This also affects the economic growth of a given country. The poverty exacerbates other problems including hunger, poor health, dirty water and inadequate sanitation, gender inequality, unemployment and lack of economic growth, and social inequalities. Many of the tea farms can't provide sufficient clean water and adequate sanitation facilities. The problems create a vicious cycle. Poor sanitation leads to illnesses, causing farm workers to miss work, thereby lowering their earned income.

What does this mean for you? The retail price you pay for a cup of tea is determined by the costs of cultivating tea leaves on tea farms, fermenting and drying tea leaf, and finally blending and packaging (Bergman, de Groot Ruiz and Fobelets, 2016). Add on a margin and you have the retail price – averaging 7 cents per cup. But what is the true price? That's the question True Price, a social enterprise based in the Netherlands, wants you to ask. You see, the retail price of tea doesn't include the social and environmental costs incurred as tea is produced. The farmers working for unlivable wages in unsanitary conditions are paying the social costs. True Price calculates the true prices of many of the most commonly purchased products in the world – tea, coffee, bread, among others. It envisions a world in which all products are sustainably produced and sold for a true price. For a cup of tea, the true price is 10 cents. If customers agreed to a 3 cent price increase per bag of tea, the revenues generated could provide a living wage for farm workers in Kenya.

Fortunately, in the meantime, Twinings is making a difference for Kenyan tea farmers. As part of its sustainability initiatives, the company has targeted impact efforts related to SDG 1 (no poverty) as well as a health initiative for women farmers (Twinings, 2018). Twinings created Farmer Field Schools (FFS) to provide training for farmers on improving agricultural output, minimizing costs, and managing their farms. FFS farms earn on average 24% more in profits than conventional farms. Already FFS farms have increased worker wages, paying significantly more than non-FFS farms. As farm management improves, farms are producing more sellable tea leaf per hectare and selling tea leaf at market at higher prices. Last year, revenues for small Kenyan farms increased more than 30% over the previous year, due to increased prices and a strong-quality crop.

Twinings also launched a program for the girls and women working on Kenyan tea farms. Kenya is ranked 126th out of 155 countries on the UN's Gender Inequality Index. HERhealth provides access to farm-based health clinics for basic services and health education. More than 5,000 people have been helped so far and the benefits go beyond good health and more equality. Women in the program have been able to increase their income by reducing absences due to illness, bringing them closer to providing food and essentials for their family.

  Visit **https://study.sagepub.com/tuten** for free additional resources related to this chapter.

CHAPTER SUMMARY

Price is the only P in the marketing mix that is directly related to generating revenue. This means that pricing decisions need to be thoroughly researched, analyzed, and adjusted during the life of a product. Despite that, many companies and marketers do not devote adequate resources to continuous pricing strategy; pricing strategy like promotions is ongoing with cycles of adaptation and adjustment throughout the life of the product, not a set-it-and-forget-it decision. Price goes beyond the cost of production and must take into account external factors like perceived consumer value, market demand, and competitor pricing – all of which are fluid in the changing market environment.

The first step in pricing decision-making is determining what the price objective of the company is, ranging from maximizing profit to being a low-cost leader among competitors. Price setting also means factoring in down-stream price adjustments including discounts. Emerging technologies, like algorithms, models, and software, have made it easier than ever to offer the most profitable form of pricing – customized pricing for individual consumers. These technologies, especially in e-commerce, can help companies with price realization in real-time. This managing of the price gap, or the difference between the price a company wants to charge and the price consumers are willing to pay, is critical, considering price is one of the most effective ways to increase profit. Managing that gap means having an understanding of how consumers are looking beyond the price of a product when they consider costs and when they assign value.

REVIEW QUESTIONS

1. What is meant by customer value-based pricing? How is it different from value pricing?

2. What is cost-based pricing?

3. Why is price elasticity of demand an important consideration when using cost-based pricing?

4. What pricing objectives might marketers choose?

5. What situations favor the use of competitive-based pricing?

6. How does psychology influence the way people respond to prices?

7. How is technology changing the work of pricing strategists?

KEY TERMS

1. **Algorithmic pricing** – automated decision-making to manage prices and make price adjustments using optimizing algorithms that use machine learning and artificial intelligence.

2. **Break-even pricing** – determines the price at which total costs would be recovered at the forecasted sales volume.

3. **Competitive-response model** – recommends price adjustments based on competitor prices updated in real-time.

4. **Comprehensive value management (CVM) program** – encompasses other organizational functions whose role affects price management.

5. **Cost-plus pricing** – the desired unit profit is added to the unit cost to determine the price.

6. **Dynamic pricing algorithms** – used by sellers to adjust prices in response to changes in the marketplace.

7. **Elasticity model** – uses time-series methods and big data analytics to calculate how a product's price affects demand in situations of seasonality, cannibalization, and competitive moves.

8. **External reference prices** – prices supplied by other sources including the marketer or store setting.

9. **Fair-pay pricing** – a digital, interdependent pricing method that integrates try before you buy, pay-what-you-want pricing, relationship pricing, and the influence of social capital.

10. **Internal reference prices** – prices held in memory or perceived by the buyer.

11. **KVI model** – estimates how much each product affects consumer price perception, using actual market data.

12. **Long-tail model** – sets an introductory price for new or long-tail items through intelligent product matching.

13. **Omnichannel model** – coordinates prices among the retailer's offline and online channels.

14. **Optimal pricing strategies** – the sustainable price point that delivers the highest level of profitability, as measured by free cash flow.

15. **Pocket price waterfall** – the decline in price with each discount visually illustrated.

16. **Pocket prices** – the price realized from a B2B sale.

17. **Price ceiling** – the highest price the market is willing to pay.

18. **Price customization** – offers different prices to customers who value the product differently.

19. **Price elasticity of demand** – how sensitive the market is to price fluctuations equal to the percentage of change in unit volume demanded divided by the percentage change in price.

20. **Price floor** – break-even price at which total costs are covered.

21. **Price getting** (also called **price realization**) – the process of managing the gap between the price the company wants to charge and the price it can actually get.

22. **Price leakage** – the amount lost when list prices are adjusted using discounts and allowances and pocket price is less.

23. **Price management** – the organizational function responsible for supporting pricing-related processes, structuring roles and responsibilities, and putting necessary tools and systems in place to select price strategy, set prices, make price adjustments, measure performance, and adapt pricing as needed.

24. **Price-optimization models** – analyze "what-if" scenarios that can inform pricing decisions.

25. **Price strategy** – a chosen and purposeful policy for price setting designed to achieve objectives while supporting market perceptions of value consistent with the product's positioning and value proposition.

26. **Price transparency** – the availability of price information.

27. Pricing capability grid – captures the relationship between a firm's price-management capabilities and price effectiveness.

28. Pricing infrastructure – dictates the roles and responsibilities, the processes, and the systems and tools put in place to support effective price management.

29. Pricing orientation – the organization's strategic view of pricing in its marketing strategy as well as the methods used to reach pricing decisions that support a competitive advantage.

30. Reference prices – prices the buyer has knowledge of and uses as a point of comparison in evaluating the price of the product under consideration.

31. SKU – an acronym for stock-keeping unit, a unique alphanumeric code assigned to a product to identify price and product description.

32. Target return pricing – determines the price that would produce the target rate of return given unit costs, capital investments, and forecasted sales volume.

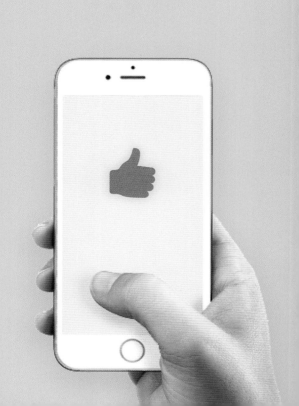

Chapter 8

DISTRIBUTING VALUE: PLACE

In this chapter, we'll learn the answers to the following questions:

1. What are marketing channels and why are they important?

2. What are the types of channel intermediaries and what work do they perform?

3. What elements are included in a channel strategy?

4. How are channel functions affected by Industry 4.0 technology?

INTRODUCTION

Part of our value equation is distributing value. In other words, marketing must bring the product to the target market for an exchange to take place. Without bringing the product to the right place at the right time, marketing will not succeed. There must be a channel through which the exchange can take place. The distribution channel decisions made to reach a target market make up the place component of the marketing mix. Peter Drucker emphasized the importance of distribution channels, stating "the market and the distributive channel are often more crucial than the product" (Drucker, 1964/2016: 20). In this chapter, our focus is on the process of designing an effective channel strategy.

Historically, most organizations stuck with the tried and true, choosing established channels consistent with traditional industry practices. This is no longer the case. Technology is the driver for major changes in buyer expectations that affect channels of distribution: 1) buyers expect to interact with brands across channels, from web to retail to mobile app, depending on their needs at any given moment, and (2) they expect channels to be fully integrated and capable of providing a seamless experience. Channels have become dynamic webs, comprising many direct and indirect ways to reach and serve customers. Fortunately, the underlying digital developments also create opportunities for restructuring the distribution process and channel relationships. The most important of these is the potential for a truly integrated, end-to-end planning and execution platform that enables channel partners throughout the entire value chain to collaborate, communicate, and adjust dynamically (Dutzler et al., 2016).

OPENING VIGNETTE

ZARA'S DIGITAL SUPPLY CHAIN IS KEY TO FAST FASHION

Zara is a fashion brand based in Spain with more than 2,200 physical retail stores in 96 markets and e-commerce access to many more. Because of Zara's ability to deliver affordable, fashionable clothes in a much shorter cycle than typical in the fashion world, the brand has become synonymous with fast fashion (Nash, 2016). The company is even known for delivering new styles to stores worldwide in just 25 days! This challenging feat is illustrated in Figure 8.2.

How does Zara do it? Zara's founder says the key to success is "to have five fingers touching the factory and five touching the customer" (Nash, 2016). Analysis of Zara's channel strategy aligns with this philosophy. Throughout the Zara supply chain, the company is committed to making great products, managing costs, and delivering a superior customer experience. Zara is a model for how an organization can leverage Zara is a fashion brand based in Spain with more than 2,200 physical retail stores in 96 markets and e-commerce access to many more. Because of Zara's ability to deliver affordable, fashionable clothes in a much shorter cycle than typical in the fashion

FIGURE 8.1   Zara's Speed to Market

Source: Image courtesy of WiNG, 2007. Accessed via wikicommons.

world, the brand has become synonymous with fast fashion (Nash, 2016). The company is even known for delivering new styles to stores worldwide in just 25 days!Zara's founder says the key to success is "to have five fingers touching the factory and five touching the customer" (Nash, 2016). Analysis of Zara's channel strategy aligns with this philosophy. Throughout the Zara supply chain, the company is committed to making great products, managing costs, and delivering a superior customer experience. Zara is a model for how an organization can leverage Industry 4.0 technologies to fully integrate its supply chain in order to create a formidable competitive advantage (Ruiz, 2017). To succeed, it must accurately and quickly forecast fashion trends and demand, design products, source the materials from its more than 2,000 suppliers, make the apparel, transport the finished supply to markets in five continents, and merchandise its stores, all the while managing time, costs, inventory, data, and processes. The result is that Zara averages realized prices of 85% of suggested retail while the industry average is just 60% (Ferdows, Lewis and Machuca, 2004). Some of its practices run counter to industry standards. It owns many of its supply sources, manufacturing plants, and retail stores, while other fashion brands outsource many of these functions to channel partners. In fact, it manages all stages of its supply chain – product design, sourcing, manufacturing, warehousing, transportation, and retail sales. Customers can shop online and offline, get same-day delivery, pay with mobile apps,

(Continued)

make returns and exchanges, benefit from styling advice, and contribute fashion ideas (Aftab, Yuanjian, Kabir and Barua, 2018). Zara's basic distribution channel is visualized in Figure 8.2.

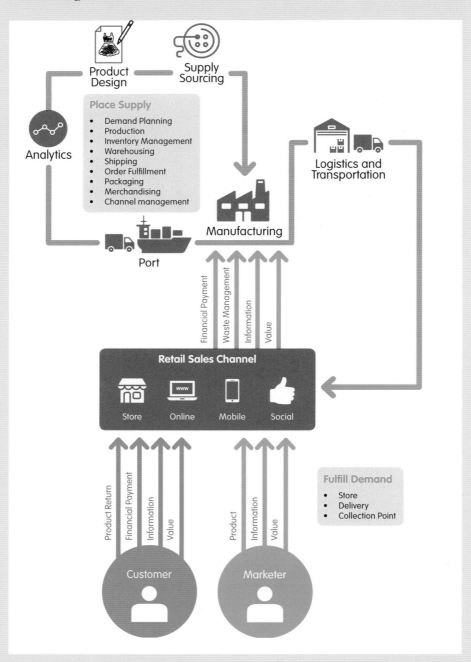

FIGURE 8.2   Zara's Channel of Distribution

The arrows in Figure 8.2 demonstrate the interdependent relationships between those involved in the channel of distribution. Store managers place orders for stock twice weekly. Central warehouses prepare store shipments by tagging, pre-pricing, and loading them on trucks or airplanes for routing to store locations. Shipments reach most stores in Europe within 24 hours, US stores in 48 hours, and stores in Asia in 72 hours.

Zara has invested heavily in technology designed to create an exceptional customer experience and deliver the product customers want, when and where they want it (Evans, 2018). Zara reaches customers in many markets via online stores and it promises online access to anyone anywhere in the world within two years. It has also invested heavily in high-tech, physical stores. For example, at its flagship store in London, customers can use a hologram-enabled mirror to visualize outfits without bothering to try them on, work with tech-equipped personal shoppers, or use self-service checkout kiosks. Those who wish to order online but pick up in the store will have their purchases retrieved by a robot.

Industry 4.0 technologies are integrated throughout Zara's distribution channel! (Research Briefs, 2019). For example, data (some captured using IoT sensors, even embedded in wearables) and analytics drive the forecasting of trends. Artificial intelligence is used to speed the product design process. AI analyzes real-time fashion trends like online responses to fashion bloggers and streaming runway shows to identify patterns, silhouettes, colors, and styles driving interest among fashionistas. Then algorithms compare those styles and colors to Zara's existing style catalog and generate new designs where gaps are identified. A human designer eventually takes over, but the automation and analytics are key to Zara's speed to market and success in picking the hottest new fashions. Digital twin technologies are part of Zara's material sourcing and agile production process. IoT sensors and blockchain ledgers track raw materials and finished garments, cutting down on theft, counterfeiting, and unethical suppliers. Robots make warehousing tasks more efficient, and connected trucks ensure the final deliveries are seamless. Of course, all of the channel functions and partners have real-time access to data and reports via cloud computing.

THE ROLE OF CHANNELS IN THE MARKETING MIX

In marketing, a channel of distribution is the path an organization's product takes (including any necessary activities such as transforming and transporting inputs and the organizations involved) to reach the target market. Simply, a distribution channel is a "route to market", the market being "where" the target market may buy the product. For this reason, we conceptualize distribution as place in the marketing mix.

By distributing the product (what the buyer needs) to the target market (who will buy) in the right place (where the buyer wishes to purchase), the buyer and seller have the opportunity to engage in an exchange of value. Without distribution, value capture eludes us (Kelly, 2015). Any connection between buyers and sellers that allows or contributes to the occurrence of an exchange can be thought of as a marketing channel. Channels play roles throughout the customer journey – providing information, selecting and ordering, paying, receiving delivery, and using post-purchase services. Likewise, channels play roles through the journey the product makes on its route to market – manufacturing, packaging and assortment, transportation, and presentation.

Historically, this route to market has been depicted as a linear chain, as a progressive sequence of steps necessary to supply the market, called a supply chain. A **supply chain** is a system of organizations, people, activities, information, and resources involved in moving a product or service from supplier to customer. Supply chain activities involve the transformation of natural resources, raw materials, and components into a finished product that is delivered to the end customer (Nagurney, 2006). Some of the primary supply activities are materials procurement, manufacturing and production, warehousing, inventory management, transportation and logistics, and distribution, as depicted in Figure 8.3.

FIGURE 8.3   A Simple View of Distribution Through the Supply Chain

Though the term supply chain is still commonly used, the metaphor of a chain is limited in its capacity to express the value created by convergence in the marketing channel. Just as we discussed in Chapter 1, the living organizations involved in the chain, the digital connectivity, data, and processes, and the physical interfaces can converge to produce added value. Convergence means it is possible to create *distribution ecosystems* that are interdependent, interconnected, customizable, decentralized, automated, collaborative, optimizable, and far more valuable compared to traditional supply chains (Kelly and Marchese, 2015). A better image for connected supply chains in this era of marketing convergence is that of a *value web*.

PARTNERS IN THE SUPPLY CHAIN

Channel partners are intermediaries (meaning they mediate exchange utility) specializing in the distribution functions required to deliver value to the market. The channel partnerships, sometimes called supply partnerships, are contractual and ongoing relationships between the supplier and intermediaries specifying the objectives, policies, and procedures for facilitating the effective distribution of the supplier's products (Buzzell and Ortmeyer, 1995). For instance, agreements could specify activities such as ordering procedures, packing, price marking, new product development and testing, sales promotion activities, stocking, and more.

The primary categories of intermediaries include manufacturer (supplier), distributor (also called wholesaler), and retailer. There may also be additional roles depending upon the industry such, as jobbers, agents, vendors, and so on. The manufacturer supplies the channel system. Wholesalers are intermediaries who service other intermediaries in the channel. Retailers are final-tier intermediaries who sell products to the end customer. In other words, wholesalers are customers of the manufacturer as well as suppliers (sellers) to the next intermediary in the channel. Retailers are customers of wholesalers or manufacturers who supply them.

FUNCTIONS AND VALUE IN THE CHANNEL

The functions channel partners may perform can be categorized as demand generation and supply fulfillment. Remember in Chapter 1, we discussed that exchange provides different types of utility. The same concept applies to the value that intermediaries bring to the channel. This is because intermediaries mediate the exchange relationship to align form, place, time, and ownership in order to generate demand for the supplier products and fulfill the demand for the customer.

Distribution channels create efficiencies because they reduce the number of transactions necessary for goods to flow from many different manufacturers to large numbers of customers. Breaking bulk is an example of how efficiency is created. Wholesalers and retailers purchase large quantities (usually cases) of goods from manufacturers but sell only one or a few at a time to many different customers. Second, channel intermediaries reduce the number of transactions when they create assortments – they provide a variety of products in one location – so that customers can conveniently buy many different items from one seller at one time. Independent intermediaries do business with many different manufacturers and many different customers.

Intermediaries also provide facilitating services for other channel members. Some examples include extending credit for financing purchases, logistics, transportation and delivery, providing technical support, providing channel intelligence, managing warranties, providing sales support, managing inventory, forecasting demand, and stocking. For example, retailers typically do not have the infrastructure, systems or resources to perform all of the necessary supply chain activities.

CHANNEL STRATEGY

The channel strategy will be developed using the channel design process to identify and select among the many channel alternatives. The strategy will specify channel type, partners, and structure. An effective channel strategy serves end consumers in terms of how and when they prefer to purchase – not just what they want to purchase – through an infrastructure that provides the necessary functions and benefits at the lowest cost to the company. It is through the chosen strategy that the brand will deliver its value proposition to customers. Planners must be sure the channel strategy is consistent with the overall marketing strategy. Ultimately, a channel strategy is a series of trade-offs and compromises that align the company's resources with what it should do to satisfy its target customers and stay ahead of competitors. The channel strategy architecture must consider the desired relationships with channel partners to achieve the necessary distribution functions efficiently, the desired control in managing end customer relationships and customer experiences, and the target market characteristics and desires for variables like ease of order accessibility, sales platforms, speed, and payment modes. Major decisions included in the channel strategy are channel format and length, distribution intensity, channel modes and sales platforms.

CHANNEL FORMAT AND LENGTH

Channel designs may be direct and/or indirect. A direct distribution channel is organized and managed by the firm itself. Direct channels require that the organization has the necessary skills and resources to perform the necessary functions. When companies lack those capabilities, they choose an indirect distribution channel which relies on channel partners to perform designated distribution functions. Some companies choose to run direct and indirect channels concurrently. For example, Dell sells products direct to individuals and small businesses through its e-commerce site, www.dell.com. It also partners with retailers like Best Buy.

The number of intermediaries in the channel determines the length of the channel, called channel level. Generally, B2B channels parallel consumer channels in that they may be direct or indirect. Direct channels are more common to business-to-business markets. The simplest indirect channel in industrial markets occurs when the single intermediary – a merchant wholesaler referred to as an industrial distributor rather than a retailer – buys products from a manufacturer and sells them to business customers. Figure 8.4 illustrates several typical channel lengths.

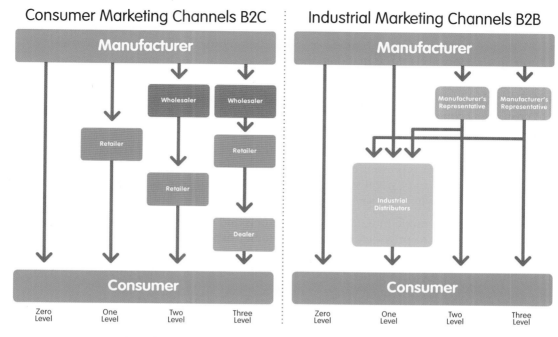

FIGURE 8.4   Channel Formats and Length

SALES CHANNELS AND MODES

Whether the channel design is direct or indirect, the number of channel modes and sales platforms can vary to meet buyer preferences. There are four types of sales channel, which vary in terms of the number of sales channels and the integration of those channels.

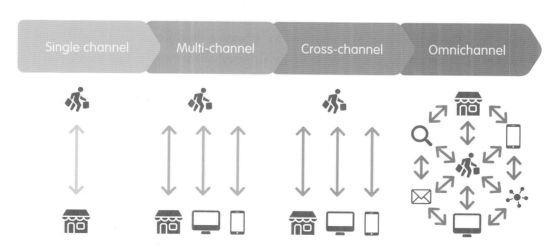

FIGURE 8.5   Types of Sales Channels

Source: Adapted from Identic (2017)

Figure 8.5 depicts the channel modes that can be chosen.

- A single channel offers one mode of sales channel for buyers, such as physical retail store locations. Note that this doesn't mean there is only one store location, but rather only a single type of distributor is available to customers.

- A multi-channel mode offers more than one type of sales channel. For example, customers could shop at physical retail stores, at the brand's own e-commerce website, and at manufacturer outlet locations.

- A cross-channel mode offers more than one type of sales channel for each retailer or channel partner representing the offer. For example, customers could shop with multiple retailers in physical stores and on the retailer's e-commerce website. Each distributor integrates services across all of the sales channel modes.

- An omnichannel mode integrates sales channels and sales modes across an entire channel strategy to provide a seamless customer experience.

Technology has definitely influenced the shift from traditional, single channels to the focus on omnichannel distribution, as depicted in Figure 8.6.

CHANNEL DISTRIBUTION INTENSITY

As organizations develop their marketing channel strategies, an important question arises regarding distribution intensity. There is some freedom in most industries for a firm to determine which channels they will use, and how much volume each channel will receive. Weighing the pros and cons of various channels, both in terms of the number of channels and the volume within each channel, can have a significant strategic impact on a firm's position in a market.

Generally speaking, there are three ways to frame the distribution intensity decision: 1) intensive, 2) selective, and 3) exclusive. An intensive distribution attempts to saturate the market with access to the offer at many different distribution outlets. It will take advantage of as many sales outlets, distributors, and direct selling opportunities as the organization can justify. This is common for convenience goods like beverages, snacks, household items, and other common low-cost goods. In short, intensive distribution uses many channels to reach potential customers and seeks to achieve a high volume of sales. Selective distribution focuses on fewer channels, chosen to accomplish goals like geographic reach, retailer specializations, sales service needs, and/or lower volume situations. This approach provides more control of how products are sold, at what price, and in which regions than does intensive distribution. The third level is exclusive distribution. It uses very few channels to present a strong brand presence and a sense of scarcity combined with meaningful customer experiences. If every store carrying watches sold the Cartier

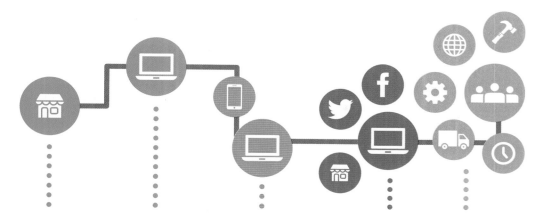

HISTORICAL

PHYSICAL STORE

"If you build it, they will come."

- Location, variety and price-based business model
- Focus on supply chain efficiency

PAST

E-COMMERCE

"We need an online store."

- Attention and resources aimed at building an online presence for the business
- Separate organizational structure, and responsibility for new channel

RECENT PAST

MULTI-CHANNEL

"It's a multi-channel, multi-screen world now."

- Interdependent influences between online and physical stores become apparent
- Customer expectations outpace retail model delivery capabilities
- Must align retail execution and customer preferences with channel-specific processes, metrics and user traditions

PRESENT

OMNICHANNEL

"Relevant products and services anywhere, anytime."

- Connected consumers interact both physically and digitally at the same time
- Profitability by channel proves elusive while distinctions between channels fade
- Digital innovation is driven by customers' desire to interact whenever and wherever they want

FUTURE

ECOSYSTEM

"Utilize ecosystem of products and services."

- Retailers use the networks of their partners and vendors to deliver what customers want, where they want it, and when they want it, seamlessly

FIGURE 8.6   The Evolution from Traditional Marketing Channels to Omnichannel

brand, Cartier's brand could be harmed. Plus efficiency would be lost because the retail locations would not fit the target market well. This form is best for firms with low-volume, high-margin sales.

DIGITAL IMPLICATIONS FOR CHANNELS OF DISTRIBUTION

E-commerce as a sales channel has long been an option for marketing channels of distribution. Increases in Internet penetration around the world and the adoption of smartphones have helped to drive ongoing growth for online sales. As we learned in earlier chapters, buyers embrace the Internet to search for information, seek out opinions and reviews on possible choices, check prices and sales, make purchases, and receive customer service. These functions are enhanced by big data, algorithms, and other technologies. Mobile devices support these functions giving way to the focus on omnichannel capabilities. Market demand for truly integrated shopping experiences has largely driven the growth of omnichannel distribution.

For the channel partners, Industry 4.0 technology can facilitate management of the supply chain in many ways. An overview of the relationships between the various technologies and supply chain applications are reflected in Figure 8.7.

Remember, traditionally, supply chain functions operated as a set of discrete steps as various channel partners took responsibility for functions along the brand's value chain. Lack of integrated back-end systems limits the efficiencies possible for each partner as well as those related to interrelated decisions of the partners. For instance, if a retailer is low on stock of chocolate bars, but can't relay that information in reverse through the supply chain partners, it may not be able to meet demand. Likewise, the manufacturer may not produce sufficient chocolate bars without sales information from the retailer. We will discuss chocolate bars in more detail in the case studies at the end of this chapter.

Digitization makes it possible for the chain to act as a fully integrated ecosystem with transparent information for all of the channel partners – from the suppliers of raw materials, to the transporters of those supplies, to the manufacturers who create finished goods, on to wholesalers and retailers, and finally to the customers (Berttram and Schrauf, 2016). To make this work as envisioned, the channel network must leverage the technologies we've discussed. For example, the Internet of Everything and blockchain enable tracking of materials through the logistics system. Cognitive technologies make it possible for ordering of supplies and materials to be automated and even autonomously deployed through the system. Robotics enhance warehousing functions, including storage, cataloging, and picking for deliveries.

In a product's journey from warehouse shelf to customer doorstep, the "last mile" of delivery is the final step of the process – the point at which the package finally arrives at the buyer's door. In addition to being a key to customer satisfaction, last-mile delivery is the most expensive, hassle-intensive, and time-consuming part of the shipping process.

If you've ever tracked a package online and seen that it was "out for delivery" for what felt like forever, you already understand that the last-mile problem is inefficiency. That's because the final leg of shipment typically involves multiple stops with low drop sizes. In rural areas, delivery points along a particular route could be several miles apart, with only one or two packages getting dropped off at each one. In cities, the outlook isn't much better;

Industry 4.0 Technology	Supply Chain Applications
Big Data and Analytics	Real-time data on logistics, inventory optimizes movement and reduces costs; Demand sensing; Real-time decision-making; Shared information across system
Cognitive Technologies	Autonomous industrial robots and transportation; Dynamic inventory management; Integrate data for automated processes like driverless trucks; Predictive maintenance and routing
Internet of Everything	Network machines, systems, and partners in supply chain; data capture; Asset tracking; Provide visibility throughout supply chain
Additive Manufacturing	3D printing of spare parts and prototypes; Reduce spare part inventories and transportation costs for supplies; Production line simulations for optimization and planning
Digital Reality	Provides instruction for maintenance and repair needs; Planning for logistics; Display supporting information; Aftermarket self-services using augmented reality support and demonstrations
Blockchain	Documentation; Tracking materials throughout manufacturing and distribution; End-to-end transparency; Quality-control and risk mitigation

FIGURE 8.7   Industry 4.0 Across the Supply Chain

Source: Adapted from Deloitte (2017c)

what urban areas make up for in stop proximity is quickly negated by the near constant delays of traffic congestion and difficulty parking. It can also be difficult to find delivery addresses. According to Forbes, more than 75% of the world's 7.4 billion people do not have a reliable mailing address. All of these issues result in high delivery costs. Worldwide, the cost of global parcel delivery exceeds $70 billion annually, with Germany, China, and the US accounting for 40% of the market. As a percentage of total shipping costs, last-mile delivery costs account for the largest portion at 53% overall (Dolan, 2018). At the same time, Amazon's fast and free shipping has set a high bar for customer expectations, making it difficult for other marketers to satisfy consumers.

The market is also growing rapidly, particularly in developing areas like India, where parcel delivery volume increased 300% last year. Demand for delivery including items purchased P2P has even inspired a replacement acronym for B2C. X2C stands for "anything to customer". What's behind this growth in delivery demand? Not surprisingly, e-commerce. Figure 8.8 depicts channels of distribution and the last-mile challenge.

If buyers were willing to pay for the increased delivery costs, the challenge would not be as critical, but most people remain price sensitive when it comes to shipping fees. McKinsey conducted a survey of nearly 5,000 consumers in China, Germany, and the US. Almost a quarter of participants were willing to pay a premium, even upwards of 35% for same-day delivery, regardless of product category. For groceries and small electronics, 45% were willing to pay a shipping premium for fast delivery. But for other product categories, 75% of respondents remained price sensitive and 70% preferred the cheapest available option for home delivery.

As such, last-mile delivery is a top priority for applying technology to process improvements. In an Industry 4.0 environment, companies must invest resources in developing adaptable distribution networks that make products available to consumers when and where they want them, but also control costs. There are several innovative ideas companies ranging from start-ups to market leaders are testing to solve the last-mile challenge.

The use of crowdsourced distribution networks is frequently mentioned as a possible solution. Just as private individuals offer alternatives to taxis, they can take over last-mile deliveries by picking up orders at a designated service point and delivering them to the customer addresses. However, McKinsey estimates that crowdsourced delivery will capture only a small portion of the delivery market, in part due to the reliability issues of working with a large fleet of independent contractors and government regulations for contract labor around the world.

Instead, autonomous guided vehicles (AGV), sometimes combined with the use of parcel lockers and/or drones, are expected to capture up to 80% of the demand for parcel delivery. Cost estimates suggest AGV with drone delivery will produce costs savings of up to 40% over current delivery methods as long as labor costs exceed $10 per hour, resulting in a 15 to 20% increase in profit margins or a decrease in price to customers (Joerss, Schröder,

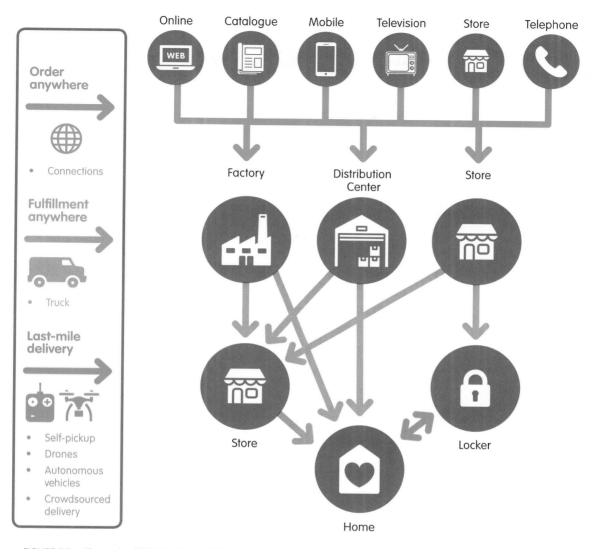

FIGURE 8.8   Channels of Distribution and the Last Mile

Neuhaus, Klink and Mann, 2016). Some companies are already testing AGVs for last-mile delivery. DoorDash and Postmates have been testing delivery bots developed by Starship Technologies, founder of the highly successful communication product, Skype. Consumers use a mobile app to request delivery, which triggers a six-wheeled autonomous delivery robot to collect and deliver the purchases. Volvo has developed an in-car app for new models that enable the car's trunk to serve as a parcel locker to accept drone-delivered packages. Grocery store chain Kroger is testing the use of AGVs to deliver groceries. Traditional delivery as we know it will remain for businesses with high delivery volumes, particularly for B2B deliveries. But the vast majority of short-term deliveries will be automated.

FIGURE 8.9   Implications of Digitalization on Channel Partners in the Supply Chain

Source: Schmidt, Rutkowsky, Petersen, Klötzke, Wallenburg and Einmahl (2015)

Delivery solutions like AGVs will require substantial investments, but start-ups are also contributing to last-mile delivery solutions. For example, the mobile app nuDeliverIt optimizes routes for faster delivery while providing customers real-time visibility of the package along the delivery route. A London-based start-up called what3words developed an alternative to the traditional street address system that could eliminate many inaccurate addresses. The system divides the planet into 57 trillion 3 × 3 meter squares, each of which is assigned a unique combination of three words (NuVizz, 2016).

This is just one application of Industry 4.0 for channels of distribution. Other advances include real-time and in-store inventory management capabilities made possible by IoT sensors, data capture and management, and algorithmic modeling. These systems can enable all the partners in the supply chain to see availability of materials, parts, and final inventory, making it possible to reduce costs of extra stock and enable advanced planning for procurement. Blockchain and IoT sensors will make it possible to track and validate quality and origin standards on materials, enhancing transparency from end to end. These are a few examples, but Industry 4.0 technologies will affect the process and value of every task throughout the supply chain (Dutzler et al., 2016).

Forecasting has always been a challenge, but advanced analytics may finally minimize the gap between what customers want and what the channel partners bring to market. Data and analytics enable predictions of demand to facilitate smart procurement and warehousing, management of spare materials, and shifts in trends that may influence sales. When used effectively, analytics can enable the creation of "what-if" scenarios for better planning throughout the channel of distribution. Figure 8.9 highlights examples of Industry 4.0 technology contributing to supply chain management and distribution.

A study by A.T. Kearney identified several benefits supply chain executives anticipate from the digitization of supply chains, including improved decision-making, better product and service quality partner to partner, and lower costs for inventory warehousing, transportation, and administrative expenses (Schmidt et al., 2015).

CASE STUDY

TONY'S CHANNEL OF DISTRIBUTION

Tony's Chocolonely is a Dutch-based, certified B-corp company that manufacturers and distributes chocolate bars. In a few short years, the company has earned more than $55 million in annual revenues and has become the leading chocolate brand in the Netherlands (Bliss, n.d.).

(Continued)

Certainly its product components – bright packaging, limited edition variations, commitment to sustainability, and quality – have contributed to the brand's success. The brand embraces experiences to help drive publicity. One of its retail stores is on a tour of Amsterdam! (Trip Advisor, n.d.). In the US, the brand launched an experiential "Chocotruck" at South by Southwest (SXSW) in Austin as the first stop on a mobile tour of festivals, concerts, university campuses, and other locations (Modern Slavery News, 2019). But the company eschews any advertising and it charges a price premium for its products. Fans pay as much as 30% more for a Tony's Chocolonely bar compared to another brand's bar of similar quality (Banks-Louie, 2018). The company has achieved 50% annual growth rate since 2005. This is especially impressive when considering the $175 premium (above "fair trade" prices) for every metric ton of cocoa beans it purchases. Is the success tied solely to Tony's commitment to the SDGs? That's surely part of it, but Tony's has also leveraged its channel strategy to reach the most profitable chocolate markets in the world.

First, let's take a look at Tony's supply chain from sourcing raw materials to reaching the end consumer. This is an indirect channel, with many channel partners providing channel functions, resulting in selective distribution. Figure 8.10 illustrates the basic stages.

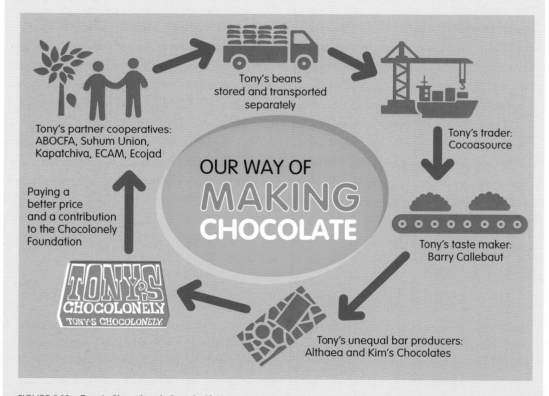

FIGURE 8.10   Tony's Chocolonely Supply Chain

© Accenture. How we used blockchain to make supply chain transparent and traceable. Used with permission.

1. Sourcing raw materials: Tony's Chocolonely does not source cocoa beans from mass commodity markets. Instead it partners with several cooperatives representing thousands of farmers around the world (Chain Point, n.d.).

2. Transporting to wholesale trader: once the beans are harvested, they are transported to a central trader, Cocoasource. This stage acts as a hub to centralize the beans from thousands of farmers in hundreds of locations.

3. Transporting to manufacturer: Cocoasource transports the beans in bulk to Barry Callebaut, a chocolate maker in Belgium.

4. Manufacturing: Barry Callebaut processes the cocoa beans into chocolate. It then sends the chocolate to a chocolatier company that provides pouring, molding, and packaging operations (PYMNTS, 2017).

5. Transporting to wholesalers and retail market: at this point, there is a finished product that can be transported via ship, rail, and/or truck to wholesalers and retailers in the chosen markets to be sold to consumers. Wholesalers are essential to help stock Tony's in high-end independent confectionary shops and coffee cafés that need smaller volumes of products to sell than do larger retailers.

6. Retailing: the bars are sold to consumers at retailers in Scandinavia, Europe, the UK, and the US. Tony's Chocolonely can be found in supermarkets and specialty chocolate stores as well as its own eponymous stores in Scandinavia (Amsterdam Wonderland, n.d.). In the US, Tony's is stocked at several grocery chains including Whole Foods, Fresh Market, Kings, and Safeway (Nieburg, 2017).

Tony's also uses blockchain, artificial intelligence, and predictive modeling technologies to manage its long and complex channel. First, the company worked with consulting firm, Accenture, to examine how blockchain could support its goal of 100% slave-free cocoa. The result allowed the company to track the point of origin for specific shipments of cocoa beans by logging every batch in the system and following the beans through the channel from farm to trader to manufacturer and on to exporter. Not only does the system support Tony's SDG mission, it is also valuable for quality control. Should there be any problem with a shipment of chocolate bars such as defects or food safety concerns, the issues can be traced back through the chain to manufacturing batches and even specific shipments of raw materials. The tracking can also confirm sales volume on the blockchain, which allows the company to make any needed adjustments in production to meet demand as well as verify retail performance (Alberda and Janssen, 2018).

The company partnered with MarTech provider ChainPoint to build a custom platform for its blockchain protocol, which it calls the BeanTracker. The result is a fully transparent "bean to bar" supply chain, recording the origin and flow of the

(Continued)

cocoa beans and ultimately the chocolate bars. The system also collects data, which can be used for reporting, analytics, and predictive modeling. Next in the MarTech stack is Descartes Global Logistics Network™ (Descartes GLN). This partner provides an SaaS that utilizes the blockchain protocol along with cognitive technologies to support exports from shipment through to retail placement, order, and sales transaction (Silvera, 2017).

Tony's Chocolonely partnered with Oracle Planning and Budgeting Cloud Service for artificial intelligence and predictive modeling services to analyze order and inventory levels, assess trends, forecast need for raw materials, and estimate sales trends (Banks-Louie, 2018). Because Tony's Chocolonely doesn't buy beans from commodity bean markets, it has few alternatives if it underestimates its need for beans and its partner farms can't supply enough beans. Tony's has built its brand – and its bar – intentionally to highlight its commitment to sustainability while embracing channel strategy and digital advances that make its mission feasible (MacEachern, 2018).

PRME

TONY'S CHOCOLONELY AND SDGS IN THE SUPPLY CHAIN FOR CHOCOLATE

Who doesn't love chocolate? Whether it's a special treat, the consolation prize for a rough day, or just a part of daily life, chocolate is a staple for many. We've already learned that consumers are increasingly seeking out brands that contribute to the SDG goals. But what could that have to do with chocolate and channels of distribution? Tony's Chocolonely chocolate bars are chocolate bars manufactured by a Dutch company with a mission of ending child slavery. Now, you might not buy them if they weren't delicious. Fortunately, they are. The result is a brand that was not only chosen as the 2018 Sustainable Brand Index winner in The Netherlands, but is also loved by chocoholics in Scandinavia, Europe, the UK, and the US! Consumers awarded Tony's Chocolonely the highest score in environmental and social sustainability compared to all other brands in the study (Seignette, 2018).

The brand was born when Teun van de Keuken, a Dutch investigative television reporter, learned that millions of children work in African cocoa farms. The farms produce the majority of the world's cocoa but rely heavily on child labor. According to Tony's annual report, the children use dangerous tools, carry heavy loads, and work long hours that make a traditional education impossible. Teun first tried to change the industry. When that failed, he began his own company, using the English version of his Dutch name, Teun. Why chocolonely? Teun explained, "The chocolate industry was a lonely place for 100% slave free crusaders" (MacEachern, 2018). It's slogan states "crazy about chocolate, serious about people" (https://tonyschocolonely.com/us/en/our-story).

Even the molds for the chocolate bars are an important part of Tony's message. Instead of typical squares one might associate with Hershey's or Cadbury's animal shapes, Tony's bars are divided into unequally shaped pieces. These are meant to represent the unfair and unequal cocoa industry. The industry is worth more than $100 billion worldwide (Leonetti, 2019). CEOs are paid millions. At the other end of the supply chain, children laboring in the cocoa farms may earn 78 cents a day (Balch, 2018).

Tony's is a certified B-corp company – a for-profit company that meets social sustainability and environmental standards. Tony's *Annual FAIR Report* (Tony's Chocolonely, 2018) shares current statistics on figures of child slavery in the cocoa industry, including those that occur at Tony's own partner farms (Rushe, 2019). According to Tony's SDG Charter, it focuses on three primary SDGs: 1) no poverty, 2) reduced inequalities, and 3) responsible production and consumption.

Tony's recognized that child slavery was largely tied to the inability for farming families to earn a living wage. "Most child labour happens on a local level, in small scale holdings. These children are often from the families of cocoa farmers who are very poor themselves. In order to prevent child labour, we need to address these kinds of vulnerabilities. One of the ways we can do this is by paying the living wage" (UNRIC, 2018). Paying fair trade prices for cocoa beans with its 7,000 farmers across six cooperatives, the company can increase the wages paid to adults and decrease the reliance on child labor (Nieburg, 2017).

In addition, the company instituted the use of monitoring systems to identify situations of child slavery. One of the primary tools is the use of blockchain tracking to ensure the providence of the beans used in manufacturing. The tracking is farm specific, enabling Tony's to ensure that its chocolate is made from 100% slavery-free cocoa beans (MacEachern, 2018). The company also worked with the Child Labor Monitoring and Remediation System (CLIMRS) to identify incidences of child labor, necessary in order to enable change initiatives with offending farms. It's not all good news all the time. The monitoring system has identified 268 cases of child labor at Tony's partner farms (Rushe, 2019).

Lastly, the company is committed to responsible production and promotes responsible consumption in several ways. The company donates part of its revenues to the Chocolonely Foundation. It funds projects designed to discourage slavery. Grants can be used as micro-loans, as school funds, and to produce educational programs in the West African communities where the farms are located (MacEachern, 2018). The company is also featured in a documentary about the chocolate industry called *The Chocolate Case*. The film documents the findings of three journalists as they uncover

(Continued)

child slavery in the cocoa production chain and their attempts to persuade large corporations in the chocolate industry to commit to ending the use of child labor. Spoiler
alert – when their efforts are for naught, the journalists commit to creating the first
"slave-free" chocolate bar – "Tony's Chocolonely" (UNRIC, 2018). It relies on its customers to pay a price premium for delicious chocolate that is responsibly produced.
Tony's had clearly targeted the components of the supply chain to meet the brand's
mission – beginning with farming the very ingredients necessary to manufacture the
chocolate and ending with delivery to the customer.

 Visit **https://study.sagepub.com/tuten**
for free additional resources related to this chapter.

CHAPTER SUMMARY

In marketing, a channel of distribution is the manner in which an organization delivers its product to the market. A supply chain is the system of organizations, people, activities, information, and resources involved in moving a product or service from supplier to customer. Some of the primary supply activities are materials procurement, manufacturing and production, warehousing, inventory management, transportation and logistics, and distribution. Today's advanced distribution ecosystems, though, might be more accurately thought of as value webs.

Channel partners are intermediaries (meaning they mediate exchange utility) specializing in distribution functions. The primary categories of intermediaries include manufacturer (supplier), distributor (also called wholesaler), and retailer. There may also be additional roles depending upon the industry, such as jobbers, agents, vendors, and so on. The manufacturer supplies the channel system. Wholesalers are intermediaries who service other intermediaries in the channel. Retailers are final-tier intermediaries who sell products to the end customer.

Channel strategy specifies channel type, partners, and structure. It is through the chosen strategy that the brand will deliver its value proposition to customers. Major decisions included in the channel strategy are channel format and length, distribution intensity, channel modes, and sales platforms. Channel designs may be direct and/or indirect. A direct distribution channel is organized and managed by the firm itself. Direct channels require that the organization has the necessary skills and resources to perform the necessary functions. When companies lack those capabilities, they choose an indirect channel which relies on channel partners to perform designated distribution functions. Channels can also vary in distribution intensity ranging from intensive, to selective, to exclusive.

Industry 4.0 technologies enable companies to track, measure, predict, and react to changes in the supply chain using blockchain and IoT and then modeling scenarios with data, predictive modeling, and algorithms. These technologies have also facilitated a new form of market, known as platforms.

REVIEW QUESTIONS

1. What is a channel of distribution? What is its relationship to supply chain management?

2. Why is place important in the marketing mix?

3. Why do channel partners work together? What functions do different channel partners provide?

4. What is the difference between a direct channel and an indirect one?

5. Why would a brand select different levels of distribution intensity?

6. What are the drivers of omnichannel distribution?

7. How are digital technologies solving challenges that existed in traditional channels of distribution?

KEY TERMS

1. **Channel of distribution** – the manner in which an organization moves its products into the marketplace.

2. **Channel partners** – intermediaries specializing in distribution functions.

3. **Channel strategy** – a series of trade-offs and compromises that align the company's resources with what it should do to satisfy its target customers and stay ahead of competitors.

4. **Channel strategy architecture** – must consider the desired relationships with channel partners to achieve the necessary distribution functions efficiently, the desired control in managing end customer relationships and customer experiences, and the target market characteristics and desires for variables like ease of order accessibility, sales platforms, speed, and payment modes.

5. **Demand generation** and **supply fulfillment** – functions that channel partners may perform.

6. **Direct distribution channel** – organized and managed by the firm itself.

7. **Exclusive distribution** – uses very few channels to present a strong brand presence and a sense of scarcity combined with meaningful customer experiences.

8. **Indirect distribution channel** – relies on channel partners to perform designated distribution functions.

9. **Intensive distribution** – attempts to saturate the market with access to the offer at many different distribution outlets.

10. **Manufacturer** – supplies the channel system.

11. **Retailers** – final-tier intermediaries who sell products to the end customer.

12. **Selective distribution** – focuses on fewer channels, chosen to accomplish goals like geographic reach, retailer specializations, sales service needs, and/or lower volume situations.

13. **Supply chain** – a system of organizations, people, activities, information, and resources involved in moving a product or service from supplier to customer.

14. **Wholesalers** – intermediaries who service other intermediaries in the channel.

Chapter 9

COMMUNICATING VALUE: PROMOTION

In this chapter, we study the design and use of integrated marketing communications campaigns. We'll learn the answers to the following questions:

1   What is the role of promotion in the marketing mix?

2   What communication modes may be used in integrated marketing communications?

3   How can we distinguish between paid, earned, and owned media?

4   By what process does communication occur?

5   What are the steps for creating an effective integrated marketing communications campaign?

INTRODUCTION

Pragmatically speaking, buyers can't choose what they don't know about – that's a major reason why promotion is part of the marketing mix. Promotion is communication designed to inform, persuade, and/or remind prospective buyers and customers in order to meet marketing objectives such as to influence an attitude or drive specific behaviors. The promotion P is frequently called marketing communications (or MARCOM), the collective term for all the various ways to meet a brand's communications objectives, whether to inform, persuade, and/or remind. Marketing communications may utilize many modes, including advertising, branded content, public relations, social media marketing, events, experiences, sponsorships, direct marketing, sales promotion, and personal selling, as well as media such as online, television, and mobile.

A brand's marketing communications should be integrated, meaning that they should "speak with one voice". Broadly speaking, integrated marketing communications (IMC) is the coordinated and consistent design of all promotional messages (regardless of communication mode) such that all touchpoints with stakeholders support the intended brand position. Why is integration important? Lisa Allocca, president of Red Javelin Communications, explains: "Integrated marketing enables a company to speak with a unified voice regardless of channel or device. It creates a surround-sound effect that amplifies your brand in an increasingly chaotic marketplace. The integration of marketing channels has never been more important or more challenging" (Allocca, 2018).

OPENING VIGNETTE

VISIT CALIFORNIA'S "DREAM BIG" INTEGRATED MARKETING COMMUNICATIONS CAMPAIGN

California's travel and tourism industry dreams big. The Golden State has been the No. 1 United States destination for years, but the state dreams of being the top destination in the world!

Tourism is important to California. Travelers spend more than $100 billion per year in the state. Tourism employs more than 1 million Californians (making it the state's fourth largest employer), and the industry generates several billion dollars in local and state tax revenues each year.

Visit California, a non-profit organization, is California's destination marketing organization (DMO). The organization promotes California to end consumers in the United States and abroad to grow inbound travel to the state and increase the average amount spent per visitor. It also services other organizations in the state, including city and regional DMOs, wine growers associations, hotels, restaurants, tour providers, and so on. Other trade industry members include people and organizations (travel agents, airlines, etc.) who influence trip decisions.

Though visitors from the United States make up the highest percentage of California visitors, the average amount spent per visitor is highest among guests from abroad. Consequently, Visit California targets tourists from around the world using targeted promotional mix elements for each one. Every country target has been profiled to provide target audience insights and these guide the specific marketing communications. In the United States, Australia, Brazil, Canada, China, Mexico, and the United Kingdom, Visit California focuses on digital display advertising, social media marketing, email marketing, search engine advertising, and advertising in traditional media like television. In France, Germany, Japan, and South Korea, the focus is on digital advertising. In India, Italy, Scandinavia, and the Middle East, the emphasis is on personal selling and public relations targeting trade organizations like travel agencies.

In addition to the extensive branded content available on the Visit California website, the DMO maintains another website just for the organizations and trade groups it services (see https://industry.visitcalifornia.com). This site provides a wealth of ready-to-use promotional assets including inspirational California photography, video stories, blog posts, event schedules, and more. In so doing, Visit California facilitates the spread of its marketing communications via publicity and the marketing communications of related organizations.

Visit California's campaign must effectively communicate to multiple target audiences that are diverse in many ways in order to ensure that its $100 million per year budget is well spent. Visit California's campaign theme is Dream Big and its campaign creative and messaging consistently reflect this theme (Visit California, 2017). Whether advertising, blog posts, photographs on Instagram, festival themes, or any other marketing communications approach, Visit California says "Dream big!".

THE ROLE OF PROMOTION IN THE MARKETING MIX

Organizations rely upon strategically developed marketing mixes to ensure a strong value proposition for customers, meaning that the organization can offer a product the customer wants, at a price the customer perceives as a reasonable value, delivered at the right place and the right time. The promotional arm of the marketing mix is tasked with ensuring customers understand the brand's value proposition, recall the brand at the point of purchase, prefer the brand to competing brands (due to a perceived advantage, likeability, image congruence, or a host of other persuasive factors), know why they should buy the brand and where they can buy it, and what they should expect to pay. Marketers may also seek to build brand equity, develop brand awareness, develop positive brand associations, position the brand, and differentiate the brand from the competition – aspects we will discuss further in Chapter 11 when we focus on branding.

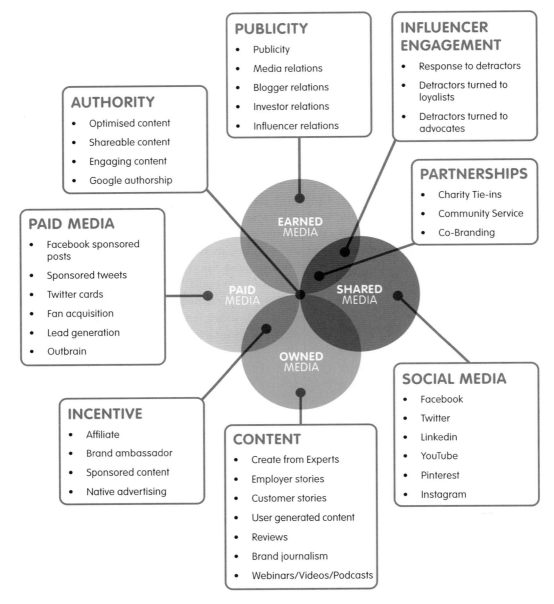

FIGURE 9.1   The PESO Model

Source: PESO Model created by Gini Dietrich. Accessed via LMMC (2016)

MEDIA AND MODES IN THE PROMOTIONAL MIX

Marketers have many choices when it comes to planning how they will communicate with target markets. Media refers to the type or channel of communication. Generally, media content is categorized into four segments – paid, earned, shared, and owned – known as the PESO model and shown in Figure 9.1 (Macnamara, Lwin, Adi and Zerfass, 2016). Simply, paid media are communication channels that require payment, whether for space, impressions, or affiliation. For example, marketers can buy ad space in a magazine, pay for a specified number of ad views from website visitors, and sponsor organizations like the NFL. All of these are types of paid media. Earned media are unpaid channels of communication through which people, news organizations, and other third parties share information in the form of publicity and/or word-of-mouth communication. Shared media, sometimes identified as social media, are communication channels in which marketers, people, journalists, and other participants can share content (their own and that of others). Owned media are communication channels that are literally owned by the organization in question such as a brand's website, a company catalog, and a company newsletter. Marketers have complete control over their owned media. You can see in Figure 9.1 that there are overlaps across the four types of media. For example, when people talk about a brand in social media, that is also earned media. When people share a brand's how-to video from its website, owned media overlaps with shared media. As such, the PESO model demonstrates another example of the era of marketing convergence.

The promotional (or MARCOM) mix, shown in Figure 9.2, refers to the combination of communication elements (or modes) that can be used to deliver the brand's message to the market. Table 9.1 lists examples of each mode.

- Advertising: non-personal, paid media communications by an identifiable sponsor. It appears in media such as television, radio, magazines, newspapers, billboards, mobile, and online.

- Branded content: original content created for or by a brand or sponsored by the brand. It ensures attention to the brand message because the brand message is inextricably linked to the content. It can be published in the brand's owned media channels, in paid channels, or on shared, social channels. It may also inspire earned media.

- Public relations (PR): includes communication activities that help an organization to receive positive publicity, recover from negative publicity, and generate positive word-of-mouth communication. It is primarily earned media, though other media types may generate publicity.

- Social media marketing: refers to marketing communications developed for social media channels. As such, it may include advertising on social network sites (paid media), publishing branded content on social channels (shared media), engaging with other participants (shared media), and facilitating word-of-mouth recommendations via reviews and ratings (earned media).

- Events, experiences, and sponsorships: events and sponsorships provide brands with a way to gain publicity (earned media) and advertising space (paid media) associated with an event and/or celebrity. These events create experience opportunities, but brands may also plan their own interactive, immersive brand

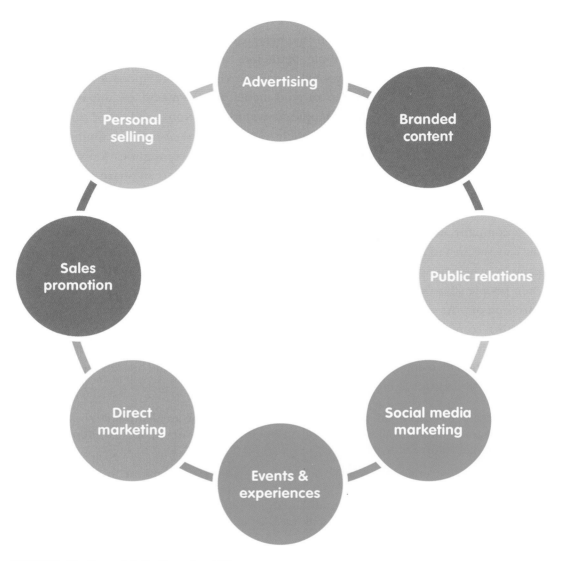

FIGURE 9.2   The Elements in the Promotional Mix

experiences. Participants may share the experience on social media (shared media) and journalists may cover the events (earned media).

- Direct marketing: direct marketing is sometimes called interactive marketing communications because it always includes a response device so that the target market can respond. When in the form of digital advertising, it is paid media. In other situations, direct marketing may be owned media (e.g., a catalog). Direct/interactive marketing can utilize any form that can elicit a direct response from the target audience – mail, telephone, fax, email, mobile, and online.

TABLE 9.1 Examples of Typical MARCOM Modes

Advertising	Direct Marketing	Public Relations	Social Media Marketing	Events, Experiences	Branded Communications	Sales Promotion	Personal Selling
Television ads	Email marketing	Press releases	Brand presence on popular channels	Sports (team, athlete, event)	Branded video programming	Coupons	Sales presentations
Magazine ads	Catalogs	Speeches	Video content	Festivals	Branded advergames	Sales	Relationship building
Newspaper ads	Direct mail	Seminars	Blogs	Movies	Branded mobile apps	Premium/gifts	Sales meetings
Online display ads	Telemarketing	Community relations	Shared photos	Music	Branded books	Sampling	Trade shows
Online video ads	Infomercials	Company reports (e.g., annual report, sustainability report)	Social conversations	Tours	Branded seminars/training	Trade shows	Samples
Billboard ads	Mobile offers	Lobbying	Social publications	Cause-related events (e.g., 5k runs)	Podcasts	Exhibits	Demonstrations
Search advertising	Direct selling	Interviews	Social entertainment	Flash mobs	Websites, microsites	Rebates	Incentive programs
Posters	Shopping-enabled interactive TV	Influencer outreach	Brand-related UGC	Seminars	eBooks	Allowances	Publications

- **Sales promotion**: a short-term, added-value offer designed to motivate a specific response. Sales promotions can be targeted to channel members (for instance, offering discounts to retailers from manufacturers) or to end consumers (for instance, sales and coupons). They may be communicated using any of the media types in the PESO model.

- **Personal selling**: interpersonal communication in which a brand representative uncovers and satisfies the needs of a customer to the mutual benefit of both. Representatives may include company salespeople, direct sellers, and/or brand ambassadors. It is typically categorized as paid media, but may overlap with other media types.

Now that we've reviewed the basics, we'll review some of the nuances of each mode, with a special focus on digital advertising.

ADVERTISING

Advertising has been affected by digital innovations more than any other promotional mix element. Though traditional media are still heavily used, digital advertising has been the fastest-growing category for ad media while traditional media including newspapers and magazines have declined. Most spending on digital advertising will be spent with Google, Facebook, and Alibaba (McNair, 2018).

DIGITAL ADVERTISING FORMATS

There are many forms of digital advertising. Some of the most common ones are defined in Table 9.2.

TABLE 9.2   Typical Forms of Digital Advertising

Digital Ad Type	Definition
Display ads	Banner advertising may include graphics and/or text. Display ads may be designed in a variety of formats and sizes and may be adapted for desktop, mobile, and tablet devices.
Expandable banners	Display ads with interactive capabilities such as expanding when the viewer interacts with the ad.
Rich media (video) ads	Display ads with extensive capabilities for interactivity, use of video and graphics, and data capture.
Search ads	Text ads delivered in response to specific search words or phrases entered by visitors to the search site.
Native ads	Ad design specific to vehicle and designed to blur the lines between ad and vehicle content.

DIGITAL AD TARGETING AND PROGRAMMATIC ADVERTISING

Digital advertising also offers targeting advantages that can enhance campaign effectiveness. The types of digital ad targeting are defined in Table 9.3.

TABLE 9.3   Types of Targeting Possible with Digital Advertising

Targeting Types	Definition
Category: Run of Media	Targeting parameters based on site characteristics.
Run of network	Ad placement may reach everyone who accesses any website in the network across the entire network.
Run of channel	Websites within an ad network are grouped by contextual relevance (i.e., ad network channels); ads are served across all the properties within the network channel.
Run of site	Publisher-specific targeting designed to reach everyone who accesses the publisher's website.
Run of section	Publisher-specific targeting with the added ability for marketers to limit ad display to specific content areas of the site.
Contextual targeting	Ad content is matched to the site content; algorithms crawl webpages, find designated keywords to understand the site's content, and then serve the marketer's banner ads if appropriate.
Category: Inferred Data	Data gleaned from cookies, surveys, and online behaviors used to identify visitors with best propensity to respond.
Behavioral targeting	Targeting is based on the audience's online behavior (e.g., clicks, frequency, time spent, and types of websites visited) and serve an ad when someone demonstrates the desired behaviors.
Retargeting	Individuals who have already expressed interest by being exposed to or interacting with the brand online are served ads as they browse the Internet.
Look-alike modeling	Individuals who "look like" the marketer's preferred audience are targeted; the ad network finds consumers who exhibit similar online patterns to those consumers who have already demonstrated a desired behavior (such as a purchase or completing a form or downloading content).
Audience targeting	Audience targeting combines all of the behavioral targeting tactics into one descriptor within a media buy, thereby allowing real-time targeting optimization.

Most digital advertising is purchased and delivered using programmatic advertising, defined as the automated process of buying, selling, and placing advertisements, without human interaction in the transaction process. We've all seen ads for items we previously searched for online. These are served through programmatic advertising. While people set the rules used by the algorithms, the process and outcomes are primarily controlled by artificial intelligence (Grece, 2017). How does programmatic advertising work? Ads are targeted based on individual consumer profiles, which are built from data collected as people use the Internet. This means that programmatic advertisements make it possible to target people on an individual level. Ad delivery to the targeting consumer is managed by an ad network using an ad server. The buying and selling of the ad space (i.e., advertising inventories) occurs on an ad exchange virtually in real-time. An ad network is an aggregator or broker of advertising inventory for many publishers.

The level of automation these ad networks make possible provides effective targeting and high levels of efficiency, even when dealing with a huge volume of ad placements, but also creates challenges. Some risks include placing ads next to undesirable content, distributing ads that are inappropriate for some target audiences, distributing ads to non-humans (i.e., bots), delivering ads at less desirable times and locations, and a general lack of control and transparency in the process, pricing, and outcomes.

CHALLENGES FACING DIGITAL ADVERTISERS

In addition to the challenges associated with programmatic advertising, marketers also struggle to address 1) attribution and accountability, 2) audience accessibility and attention, and 3) ad fraud.

Attribution models, discussed further in Chapter 12, are used to measure which marketing communications contributed to meeting marketing objectives, such as driving website traffic and sales. Attribution makes it possible to assess accountability, the relative effectiveness of advertising units. Without accurate attribution, marketers are left in the dark as to what marketing communications were effective and accountable for contributing to the achievement of marketing objectives. Historically, last-click attribution was the standard – the digital ad that was clicked last received all the credit for the conversion. This view is flawed because consumers may have been influenced over time by many ads, across multiple devices, as well as other sources of information (Fanelli, 2018).

Accessibility to the targeted audience is also a major concern due in part to viewability limitations, the prevalence of ad blockers, and scrolling/viewing patterns that limit ad exposure. These issues harm campaign effectiveness and also cost advertisers money. The Interactive Advertising Bureau estimates that last year about 2 trillion display ads were paid for but not seen by the intended audience! A viewable display impression is defined as an ad that loads at 50% or more and remains present for at least one second. Online publishers often charge a premium for "above-the-fold" (ATF) impressions (ads shown on a webpage without scrolling), but ATF does not guarantee viewability. A study by Quantcast found that only 44% of above-the-fold ad impressions were actually viewable (Duggal, 2016).

Accessibility is also limited as Internet users adopt ad blockers. An ad blocker is a software that filters content and blocks advertisements on a webpage. They work as either stand-alone programs such as Ghostery, or web browser extensions such as the one offered for Google Chrome. The software targets ads like pop-ups, banner ads, sticky ads, interstitial ads, or auto-playing videos to allow users to surf the web without distractions or interruptions in their browsing experience. Estimates suggest that as much as 30% of Internet users have ad blockers and about 15% use ad blockers on their smartphones (Page Fair, 2015). People use ad blockers for many reasons, but reason #1 – digital ads are annoying! (Patel, n.d.). Advertisers have turned to other formats like native advertising to thwart ad blockers. Native advertising is paid media that presents the ad as a seamless part of the user experience respective to the platform, and Google now analyzes digital advertising "experiences" and censors ads that don't rise to its "ad experience guidelines" (Google, n.d.).

Accessibility is also affected by audience attention. If you want to watch video programming, you have an enormous number of options. That's media fragmentation. Media fragmentation is the breaking up of large audiences into smaller audience fragments due to the increase of media choices available. Every medium has experienced fragmentation within its own field, with hundreds of television channels, satellite radio, and magazines available for every interest group imaginable. When you study for class, do you also listen to music or keep apps open at the same time? If so, you are media multi-tasking. When media multi-tasking is accomplished with more than one device, it is called simultaneous screen usage. Some of the top activities for media multi-tasking and simultaneous screen usage are emailing, Internet browsing and searching, playing digital games, social networking, and watching online videos (Sterling, 2012). The average consumer owns between three and four connected devices and regularly switches between them to view content. These challenges make it difficult for marketers to design effective MARCOM plans.

Lastly, ad fraud, the deliberate manipulation to prevent the delivery of ad content to its targeted audience, is a major concern for digital advertisers. The cost of ad fraud reaches into the billions of dollars (Sternberg, 2018).

BRANDED CONTENT

According to the Content Marketing Institute, content marketing is a strategic marketing approach focused on creating and distributing valuable, relevant, and consistent content to attract and retain a clearly defined audience – and, ultimately, to drive profitable customer action (Content Marketing Institute, n.d.). The philosophy of content marketing emphasizes that brands should publish high-value content that pulls the audience in whether the content is published on owned, paid, or shared media.

The types and topics of branded content may cover an enormous range of material. Some examples include research, instructions, fact sheets, opinions, essays, poetry, fiction, information, fashion photos, advice, art, white papers, and more. It may be curated, sponsored, or original. If we revisit the Visit California opening vignette, it's clear to see how broad a concept branded content is. Visit California maintains a detailed website filled with valuable information about California and its many tourism experiences and options, including suggested road trips, planning guides, itineraries, festivals by hobbies and interests, and much much more.

Some branded content may include mandatory guidelines, warnings, and labels. But it also provides a venue for one of the most influential marketing communications trends of our time – story-telling. Josh Stinchcomb, Chief Experience Officer at Condé Nast, explained why branded stories are so vital, saying: "Consumers are increasingly less interested in traditional, disruptive advertising (and have the ability to skip it entirely!) so reaching them through opt-in story-telling is becoming more and more important" (Stinchcomb, 2017). Ultimately, branded content may include anything from the descriptions of apparel sold in a clothes catalog to podcasts to interactive games, and so on.

PUBLIC RELATIONS

Public relations (PR) uses communications to promote publicity in press media, word-of-mouth communication, and buzz (both online and off). These outcomes are earned media; the organization cannot ensure the media coverage by paying for media space. Rather the brand impressions must be earned through the organization's public relations efforts, community participation, sponsorships, charitable donations, success (e.g., notable product innovation), and social responsibility efforts. Earned media are valuable, not only because there is no direct media cost, but also because they have a high level of credibility with those exposed to the messages. Ideally, organizations will approach public relations proactively – relying on the tools to build a positive brand image. However, in crisis situations, organizations rely on reactive public relations to respond to the situation and protect the organization's brand equity. Crisis management is the use of public relations tools to manage, protect, and recover an organization's reputation when victim to negative publicity.

PR messages can be communicated using a variety of tools and channels, including press releases, speeches, interviews, announcements, donations and coordinated volunteer efforts, and relationship building with journalists, industry influencers, legislators, employees, community residents, and so on. Public relations activities are commonly used to meet marketing communications objectives such as building brand awareness, enhancing brand image, and building goodwill.

PR is a major element of the Visit California's IMC campaign. As a non-profit organization tasked with developing and protecting California's tourism industry, it manages relationships with the travel industry, government leaders, journalists and other media representatives, California residents, and partner organizations around the world (Visit California, 2017).

Visit California used several public relations tools as part of the Dream Big campaign: 1) press releases, 2) a website area devoted to providing journalistic support in the form of story ideas, facts and statistics, and publication-ready image assets, 3) messaging toolkits for journalists writing about state crises, such as the Butte and Valley fires, 4) pitch meetings with journalists to discuss story concepts, and 5) op-ed articles on tourism's impact on the state for publication in news outlets like the *Los Angeles Daily News*.

SOCIAL MEDIA MARKETING

Social media are the online means of communication, conveyance, collaboration, and cultivation among interconnected and interdependent networks of people, communities, and organizations enhanced by technological capabilities and mobility. **Social media marketing** is the use of social media to meet marketing objectives. Social media marketing campaign elements can leverage social community, social publishing, social entertainment, and social commerce.

Visit California uses social media extensively to share videos, articles, stories, photos, and links. When brands participate in social communities and people talk about the brand, share reviews and ratings, and share brand content with their network, earned media are created. For instance, many California tourist sites and support businesses are reviewed and rated on TripAdvisor.com. Visit California uses a specialist agency, ICOC, for the social media marketing work in its integrated marketing communications campaign (Nichols, 2015). Its social media activities target consumers in 11 countries using Facebook, Instagram, Sina Weibo, Twitter, and YouTube. The social media content and conversations are multi-lingual to ensure comprehension by each country's audience. Check out the brand's social presence by visiting these sites:

- YouTube Channel – www.youtube.com/user/VisitCA
- Facebook – www.facebook.com/VisitCalifornia
- Instagram – www.instagram.com/visitcalifornia/
- Twitter – https://twitter.com/VisitCA

The brand's social media content includes conversational posts, announcements and news, video stories and testimonials, photos and suggested travel itineraries optimized for social media participation (e.g., 10 Photo Ops for Instagram). Social publishing on YouTube has been an especially effective component in Visit California's social media efforts. The YouTube channel includes branded videos produced by Visit California (which overlap with the branded communications element) and curated travel videos from other YouTube channels. Some of the YouTube videos have earned more than 3 million views!

Though all social media marketing must remain consistent with the Dream Big campaign concept, some markets see customized content. For instance, in China, the social media campaign utilizes a celebrity endorser, Chinese film star Gao Yuanyuan. Explaining the choice, Visit California's CEO, Caroline Beteta, said, "Gao Yuanyuan embodies the California brand and spirit and will share her authentic passion for California with the Chinese public, inspiring their California dreams" (Schaal, 2014).

EVENTS, EXPERIENCES, AND SPONSORSHIPS

Events are themed activities and occasions to promote a product, cause, or organization. Planned events include festivals and other celebrations; entertainment, recreation, political and state, science, sport and arts events; and events within the domain of corporate and business affairs (such as meetings, conferences, conventions, fairs, seminars, and exhibitions). Events can occur online or offline, and can be participated in, sponsored, or hosted. Common types of online events include webinars, virtual events, and live streaming events. Events create experiences with the brand that can inspire word of mouth. Jonathan Edwards, the Strategy Director at Sledge, a UK experiential marketing agency, explained, "Advertising tries to persuade me – but a good experience also gives me a reason to persuade other people" (Edwards, 2013).

Sporting events like the UEFA European Championships are popular venues for brands using this promotional element. For instance, Nike and Adidas have endorsed athletes, bought advertising in and around the event, and offered fan experiences during the event and online (Barnett, 2016). Such event opportunities can also be co-activated in social media channels helping to spread the reach of the brand message beyond the actual event experience. When choosing events to include in a MARCOM plan, brands should consider several criteria: 1) category exclusivity (i.e., being the only brand in a product category associated with the event), 2) on-site signage, 3) broadcast ad opportunities, 4) proprietary area/branded zone at the event, 5) access to event spokespeople, 6) tickets and hospitality benefits, 7) access to the event prospect database, and 8) the right to promote products (IEG, 2014).

Results of a survey of consumers who experienced one or more branded events found that 1) 74% of attendees have a more positive opinion about a brand post-event, 2) 96% said that, assuming they had an interest in a product, they were more likely to purchase after the event, 3) 87% reported they had purchased a brand's product following an event, 4) of those who purchase at or after the event, 75% become repeat buyers, and 5) 96% said that they told a friend or family member about their experience and the brand running the event (Event Marketing Institute, 2015). According to the IEG Sponsorship Report, marketers spent more than $60 billion on events and experiences globally (IEG, 2014). The value can be well worth the investment, with organizations averaging a return on investment of five times the cost of the event (Event Marketing Institute, 2015).

Events are an experience, but marketers can also design more personalized, immersive brand experiences. When they do, it is known as experiential marketing. Experiential marketing creates a unique, real-time individual experience with a brand. The distinction can be summed up this way: event marketing is a *one-to-many* experience, while experiential marketing is a one-to-one experience (Korody, 2013). Ikea hosted a sleepover in its Essex store in the UK after noticing a Facebook fan group called "I wanna have a sleepover in Ikea" (Econsultancy, 2018). Participants were given manicures and massages, and had a bedtime story read to them by a reality TV star. A sleep expert was on hand to give advice on choosing a new mattress (see https://youtu.be/YMJD53fxihU). Vans created a branded space and experience in London, called House of Vans. In keeping with the brand's image of embracing art, music, skateboarding, BMX, street culture and fashion, the space featured an art gallery, a VansLab artist incubator space, live music venue, café and bar, gift store, and skater built and designed concrete bowl, mini ramp and street course (see https://youtu.be/-2p8ewZU4Ec).

DIRECT MARKETING

Direct, interactive marketing is interactive communications delivered directly to the target audience and used to stimulate a direct response from consumers. Other marketing communications can also be direct response, if there is a response device included in the message (e.g., a phone number or website). *Most digital advertising is direct response.* The difference here is that digital advertising can be direct, while not all direct marketing is digital. Direct marketing can utilize any form of media that can be delivered directly and in which a direct response device can be embedded. The most typical media for direct marketing are mail, telephone, email, and text. Email marketing has been the sweetheart of direct marketing for some time now, but cluttered inboxes have lessened its effect. Experts predict email marketing in the future will embrace some of the technological advances seen in digital advertising, such as interactive visual design, more personalization, and programmability. You can learn more about this area of promotions by visiting the Association of National Advertisers (ANA) at https://thedma.org.

SALES PROMOTIONS

Sales promotions are tools that offer the target audience (end consumer or channel member) an incentive to stimulate a behavior, such as a purchase or store visit. Sales promotions can be categorized by target: 1) consumer or 2) trade members. Consumer sales promotions include coupons, price deals, rebates, refunds, loyalty programs, bonus packs, premiums, contests and sweepstakes, and sampling. Trade sales promotions include allowances, discounts, and deals; cooperative advertising funding; trade show participation; promotional products; point-of-purchase displays (POP); and incentive programs like prizes or bonus money (typically tied to sales goals).

PERSONAL SELLING

Personal selling occurs when a company representative interacts directly with a customer or prospective customer to communicate about a good or service. The more complex, technical, and intangible the product, the more firms rely on personal selling to promote it. The selling processes vary depending upon the type of sales situation and type of salesperson, but generally they are similar. The steps include prospecting, planning and approaching, presenting, handling objectives, closing the sale, and following up after the sale.

Direct selling is a type of personal selling in which independent contractors market an affiliate firm's products in a personal context. Direct selling is sometimes thought of as part of place in the marketing mix, because representatives can take orders and payments and deliver products much like a retailer. However, in today's e-commerce environment, in which affiliate firms provide personalized e-commerce websites and ship direct to the customer, direct selling is more aligned with promotions. Consistent with a strategic view of direct selling (Peterson and Wotruba, 1996), direct sellers perform many communications functions including identifying prospects, explaining benefits in a way that is personalized for each prospect, developing relationships (possibly using social media events and/or in-person parties), and securing customers.

THE COMMUNICATIONS PROCESS

Brands that understand the communications process model are better able to successfully design, develop, and deploy effective marketing communications. The communications process model explains the nine elements involved and the process by which effective communication occurs. Figure 9.3 depicts the communications process.

ELEMENTS IN THE COMMUNICATIONS PROCESS

There are two primary players in the communications process: senders and receivers. As the originators of messages, senders develop messages and send the information to receivers using a communication channel, also known as a medium. Senders develop messages using encoding. Encoding is the conversion of the desired information into a message that can be delivered using a channel and understood by the intended receiver (through a process known as decoding). The message may include words, music, and/or signs and symbols. Decoding is the process by which a receiver interprets the meaning of the sender's message. In one-way communication, the process ends, but in two-way communication, the receiver can initiate a response (such as making a purchase) and/or feedback.

While the process may seem simple enough, effective communication is not that easy for marketers to achieve. Why?

- Senders must encode the message with words and symbols that mean the same thing to the receivers.

- The message must be delivered via a channel that can reach the intended receivers.

- The receivers must be able to decode the message.

- Noise, anything that interferes, distorts, or prevents the message transmission, may prevent receivers from receiving and/or decoding the message as the sender intended.

- The message must be designed to motivate the desired responses from the intended receivers.

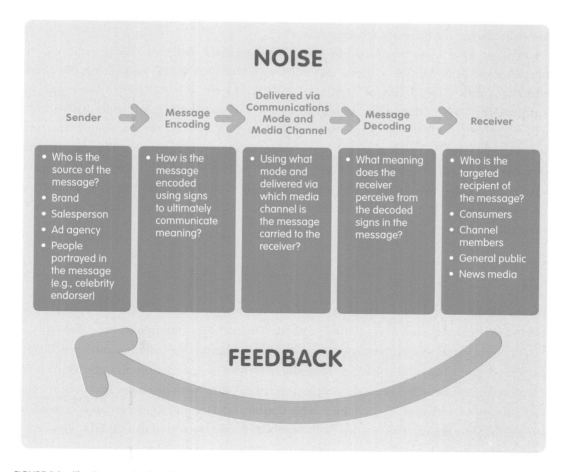

FIGURE 9.3   The Communications Process

IGNITING MESSAGE DECODING

Receivers can't decode a message unless they are exposed to it. The sender will choose a mode and medium that the receiver is known to consume. That alone will not guarantee exposure to the message. The receiver also has to pay attention in order for exposure and then decoding to take place.

The interruption-disruption model explains how marketers have historically addressed the issue of triggering receiver attention to messages. This model is associated with advertising more so than the other elements, but it applies generally to marketing communications as well. Advertising reaches its target audience by paying to place messages in media vehicles that are consumed by the target audience. The target audience chooses the content and media to consume and advertisers then interrupt the content with ads. Consumers accepted these interruptions, served in the form of advertising, because they accepted that it was a necessary price to pay for what was otherwise free content broadcast on television and radio, and printed in magazines. The programming was monetized by the advertiser paying the media owner for ad space (Guldimann, 2015).

Knowing that consumers don't like to be tricked and are easily irritated by interruptions, how can we achieve exposure and attention while respecting the target audience? Mark Guldimann of MediaPost advocates the use of "polite interruption" (Guldimann, 2015). Marketing communications that are politely interruptive have three characteristics: 1) they are interruptive, 2) they persist for an amount of time controlled by the receiver, and 3) they enable receiver engagement. The Advertising Research Foundation defines brand engagement as "turning on a prospect to a brand idea enhanced by the surrounding context" (Nail, 2006). For brands to benefit from this phenomenon, they must invite consumer participation and encourage consumers to engage with their brand.

DESIGNING EFFECTIVE IMC CAMPAIGNS

How do we apply the communications model to the design of IMC? There are several steps involved in the design and execution of integrated marketing communications campaigns. A campaign is a set/series of interrelated and coordinated marketing communications activities that deliver the same core message regardless of media. Campaigns may be short-term or long-term and brands may also supplement campaigns with seasonal promotions and other short-term activities. For instance, Visit California's Dream Big campaign is consistent and ongoing but it supplements this with seasonal promotions tied to holidays. Figure 9.4 illustrates the steps in developing a campaign and Table 9.4 explains the questions answered at each step in the process.

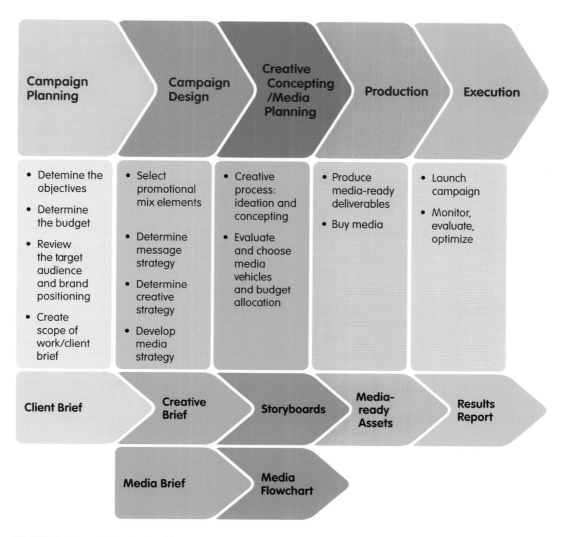

FIGURE 9.4   Steps in Developing Effective IMC Campaigns

TABLE 9.4   Answering Questions for an Effective Communications Campaign

Stage/Step	The Question You Must Answer	Key Points to Remember
Campaign Planning	What information should be included in the client brief?	There's a caveat in that the campaign is only as good as the brief.
Determine the objectives	What are you trying to accomplish?	A good campaign requires focus. If you try to do too much, you won't do anything well.

(Continued)

TABLE 9.4 (Continued)

Stage/Step	The Question You Must Answer	Key Points to Remember
Determine the budget	How much money do you have to make it happen?	If you don't have enough money to launch an effective campaign, you're better off not doing it. If you have a limited budget, look at slimming down your target audience, reducing paid placements, or increasing emphasis on earned media.
Review the target audience and brand positioning	Who are you trying to reach? What do you know about them? What do they believe about your brand?	"The general public" is not a target audience. If you try to reach everyone, you'll end up reaching no one.
Create scope of work/client brief	Who will perform the tasks required?	Agencies get paid big bucks for a reason. If the budget allows, agencies provide access to talented creatives and strategists. If an agency relationship isn't in place, this step may include a competitive pitch process.
Campaign Design	What information and insights should the creative brief and media brief feature?	The creative brief summarizes the most relevant information about the creative assignment to prepare the creative team, ensure their work is "on strategy", and inspire great ideas. The media brief summarizes the most relevant information for the media planner to ensure that media strategy reaches target audience.
Select promotional mix elements	Which communication modes can best reach the right audience while effectively delivering the brand message within the budget?	Using an integrated, multi-mode campaign increases the likelihood of reaching your audience with a consistent and memorable brand message.
Determine message strategy	What are you going to say to your audience so they'll take notice, listen, and take action?	What resonates for you may not work for your target audience. The difference between messaging that you like and messaging that is effective can be huge. Consumer insights are key.
Design creative strategy	What principle will guide the general nature and character of messages to be designed?	The strategy defines the means selected to achieve the campaign objectives. There are several choices; the challenge is choosing one that can be translated across multiple modes and media, effectively express the message, resonate with the target audience, all while being consistent with the brand's image and positioning.
Develop media strategy	Which media and vehicles are best, given the modes chosen, the creative strategy, the target audience, and the budget?	Choose the wrong media and vehicles and people won't be exposed to the campaign. The best creatives can't overcome bad media. Media planning is like a puzzle. The ideal choices you might make must be balanced against constraints like timing and budget.

Stage/Step	The Question You Must Answer	Key Points to Remember
Creative Concepting/Media Planning	How will the campaign design come to life in the form of art and copy (creative)?	Creative concepts and media plans shouldn't be designed to win awards, but to meaningfully communicate to the target market.
Creative process: ideation and concepting	What genre, story, images, and words will effectively deliver the message?	There are many appeals and executional styles. Creatives go through the creative process to ideate concepts that can gain attention, deliver the message, facilitate recall, and inspire action. Storyboards and other expressions of the chosen idea are developed for use by production.
Evaluate and choose media vehicles and budget allocation	Which vehicles will best meet the media strategy?	The media budget must be effectively allocated over the campaign's time period.
Production	What resources will be required over what timeline to produce the materials needed for the campaign?	Sometimes the managers of production are referred to as traffic, because there may be so many elements in production that it is necessary to anticipate and prevent traffic jams.
Produce media-ready deliverables and buy media	What campaign assets must be produced? To what specifications? On what timeline? What staffing needs are required to complete specialized tasks? How can media buys facilitate staying on budget and enhance campaign effectiveness?	Depending upon the modes and media chosen for the campaign, the production process may be performed in-house or outsourced to a production agency. The traffic department within the advertising agency or a project manager will ensure that the campaign assets (e.g., commercials) are ready on time and that the client and legal approvals have been granted.
Execution	How will deployment and ongoing campaign activity be managed?	Marketers don't have to wait until a campaign ends to assess effectiveness. Rather than asking how well a campaign met marketing objectives after it ends, marketers should assess the campaign at stages of execution throughout the campaign period. This allows for adjustments to be made.
Launch campaign	Where and when will the assets be distributed for deployment in the selected media and vehicles?	While campaigns may extend for long periods of time, a campaign schedule will guide the deployment of various campaign elements at strategic moments in the campaign calendar.
Monitor, evaluate, optimize	How will you know what worked and what didn't? Can underperforming campaign elements be corrected mid-campaign?	A campaign might garner attention and lead to positive attitudes but that doesn't mean that the messages influenced purchase behavior and generated sales revenues. You need a systematic way to assess the effectiveness of the campaign and each element and asset in the campaign. This assessment should be directly tied to the campaign's objectives.

CAMPAIGN PLANNING

Creating a campaign is a structured, disciplined process with specific deliverables, milestones, and participation from client and agency teams. Ultimately, the campaign must be consistent with the marketing plan which ties directly to corporate strategy. The first stage of the process begins in-house. It includes setting campaign objectives, budgeting, and reviewing target audience specifications and brand positioning.

SETTING OBJECTIVES

In this step, the brand is answering the question "What do we want to accomplish?". Objectives help to ensure consensus among the leadership team, guide decisions, and provide standards for measuring effectiveness later in the campaign process.

Another useful question when setting objectives is "What do we want the target audience to do (or think, or feel)?". This question is tied to our understanding of how people respond to communications and the stages that precede a behavior. Advertising communication models are theories about how advertising works. These theories explain and describe, at the individual buyer or consumer level, the process by which advertising communicates with and effectively persuades individuals to take action. Many of these models represent versions of the hierarchy of effects (HOE), varying in the number of stages identified from awareness to purchase intention. All HOE models follow a systematic process through which consumers move sequentially through the cognitive, affective, and conative stages. A common HOE model is the AIDA model, which depicts prospects moving from attention to interest to desire to action. The basic process is illustrated in Figure 9.5.

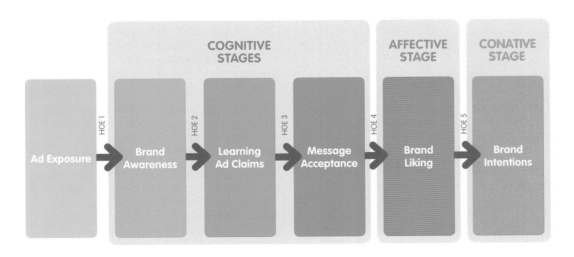

FIGURE 9.5   AIDA and Hierarchy of Effects

The process begins when the consumer is exposed to a marketing message. Exposure may be triggered by the marketing communications (based on the interruption-disruption model) or consumer-initiated. Ideally, the promotional message will guide the consumer through 1) cognition (e.g., attention, learning, and comprehension), 2) affect (e.g., feeling and attitude), and 3) intention (e.g., purchase) (Smith, Chen and Yang, 2008).

We can state our campaign objectives to reflect the next stage we want the target audience to move through. To understand how this process works, imagine how a brand would adjust its communication objectives if the campaign were introducing an innovative new product (build awareness) versus reinforcing its already strong brand image (reinforce liking and preference). This may sound easy enough – the campaign acts as a GPS system directing consumers through the stages to purchase. Unfortunately, understanding human behavior is a bit more challenging. These models assume that prospective buyers move through a general process of "think, feel, do", but that's not always the case. If you've ever made an impulse purchase, you probably followed a "do, feel, think" sequence, and in some situations people may follow a "feel, do, think" path.

BUDGETING

Budgeting is another important decision in this initial stage. Budgets determine, in particular, what media may be used in the campaign. It has to be decided, at least at a basic level, up front, in order to guide the strategic "ideation" (we'll talk more about ideation during the creative unit) for the message and the media. The best method is the objective and task method because it at least allows for one to assess the budget likely needed in order to accomplish what is desired from the campaign. It is a bottom-up budgeting technique, meaning the budget is built from the anticipated expenses of the campaign. That said, many brands will use some other method or a combination of methods. From a practical standpoint, an organization may set an annual limit on all promotional spending across divisions and brands (known as top-down budgeting). The most common top-down budgeting approaches are the percentage-of-sales method, in which the promotion budget is based on last year's sales or on estimates for the present year's sales, and the competitive parity method, which means the budget matches what the competitors will spend (Corfman and Lehmann, 1994).

TARGETING AND POSITIONING

To develop effective communications, the process must have a clear understanding of the target audience. The target audience has already been identified in the organization's marketing plan. In Chapter 3, we reviewed the segmentation bases and procedure for segmentation as well as the process for selecting which segments to target. You also learned how to create a buyer persona in that chapter. This step in the process of developing effective communications involves reviewing what we know about the target audience and using the target's persona to identify relevant information. Personas help us visualize, understand, and relate to the target audience. This deep understanding is critical to encoding effective messages with the right words and images, applying a creative approach that motivates, and identifying the media channels that will best reach them (Revella, 2015). Likewise, the brand position must be a consideration in any communications to ensure that the message is consistent with the position. As we discussed in Chapter 3, buyers have choices and a strong position will differentiate a brand from the competition.

PREPARING A CLIENT BRIEF

At this stage of the process, the organization must decide whether the campaign will be performed internally (if the organization has an in-house agency) or externally. When organizations hire multiple agencies, one is typically in a leadership position and is called the agency of record. Full-service agencies have capabilities across all aspects of campaign planning and execution, but some agencies (sometimes called boutiques) specialize in specific skills (such as creativity, media planning, research, and SEO) and/or in a communication element (i.e., advertising, PR, and so on). For instance, 360i specializes in digital media, while Sparks specializes in designing and executing branded experiences.

The brand manager will create a summary, known as a client brief (sometimes called a scope of work document), of the decisions made in the pre-planning stage and other project details. This document provides a description of the objectives, target audience, budget, brand positioning, expected deliverables, project scope, milestones and deadlines, and any mandatory guidelines that must be followed. Project scope can vary wildly – from single executions (known as one-offs) to fully integrated campaigns. The brief may be published as an RFP (request for proposal) to seek proposals from interested agencies. Agencies invest a lot of time and money to develop the content and concepts needed for a competitive proposal. In fact, research into pitching practices found the average agency cost for a large pitch to be upwards of $200,000 (IPA and ISBA, 2011).

CAMPAIGN DESIGN

Once the organization has chosen the agency and shared the client brief, concepting can begin. In this stage, the communication modes and the message, creative, and media strategies are determined. The decisions, along with information from the client brief, will be explained in the creative brief and the media brief. Table 9.5 explains the steps in writing a creative brief.

TABLE 9.5   Creative Brief Development

Step	Answers the Question	Can Be Stated As
1: Define the purpose	Why are creative materials and messages being crafted?	We want [this audience?] to [do what?] in order to [benefit how?].
2: Determine creative objectives	What should the audience think, feel, or do once exposed to the creative materials?	The audience believes that [what?], feels [how?], and plans to [do what?].
3: Describe the target audience	What do the audience personas tell us about the motivations, experiences, and attitudes that might be useful in choosing signs and symbols, colors, language, and other creative cues?	The audience needs [what?] and is motivated by [what?].
4: Identify barriers to the desired outcome	What current behaviors, conditions, and/or beliefs have prevented the target audience from adopting the desired belief, attitude, or behavior?	The audience shops [where? when? how?] and spends [how much?] on [what brands or substitutes?]. The audience believes [what?].
5: Highlight the key issue	What is the most important point to make?	
6: Determine the key promise	What benefits do we promise?	If the audience [does, believes, feels what?], then they will benefit [in what ways?]. The audience should [do, believe, feel what?], because [why?].
7: Identify support points	How can we make the key promise believable and persuasive? Should evidence of claims, testimonials, endorsements, or guarantees be included?	The audience will trust the message more if we include [what?]. The message will be more persuasive if it is [informational? transformational? transactional?].
8: Define the call to action	What specific action (e.g., call now, visit the website, talk to your doctor) should the audience take to receive the benefit of the promise?	The audience should [do what?].
9: Specify creative considerations	What creative strategies are aligned with the competitive situation, message, and objectives? What elements and media will be used? What creative appeals, executions, and tone are strategically aligned? What materials must be produced?	The [which?] creative strategies, [which?] creative appeals, and [which?] creative executions are most likely to be effective given the situation analysis and objectives. [What creative materials?] are needed for distribution via [which media?].
10: Note mandatories	What requirements must be adhered to? Are there legal regulations, brand identity rules, or other issues that will affect the creative materials?	Creative assets and materials must include [what?] and must not include [what?].

SELECT THE ELEMENTS OF THE PROMOTIONAL MIX

The first step in campaign design is to determine which elements of the promotional mix should be included given the objectives, target audience, and budget. We reviewed these elements earlier in the chapter. Here, the planner should consider the pros and cons of each element explained in Table 9.6.

TABLE 9.6   A Comparison of the MARCOM Mix Elements

Element	Pros	Cons
Advertising	<ul><li>Ability to place message in available paid media locations</li><li>Control over the message</li><li>Ability to use images, sound, movement, and story in the message</li><li>Ability to reach targeted audiences</li><li>Ability to use a variety of media</li><li>Low to moderate cost/contact</li></ul>	<ul><li>Depending upon media, high total cost</li><li>Low trust perceptions among consumers</li><li>May be perceived as irritating</li><li>Difficulty cutting through clutter</li></ul>
Direct marketing	<ul><li>Ability to target specific groups with tailored offers</li><li>Results are measurable</li><li>Multiple communication modes possible</li></ul>	<ul><li>Negative perception of some modes</li><li>Cost per contact can be high</li><li>Dependent upon contact list</li></ul>
Public relations	<ul><li>Costs primarily tied to human resources required to develop supporting materials (press releases, speeches, etc.)</li><li>High credibility when PR results in publicity</li><li>May result in word-of-mouth communication</li></ul>	<ul><li>Lack of control over outcome</li><li>Difficulty measuring reach and ROI</li><li>Potential for negative publicity</li></ul>
Social media marketing	<ul><li>Ability to build brand engagement</li><li>Ability to target by interests and channels</li><li>Multiple creative options in brand messages</li><li>Low relative paid media costs</li><li>Ability to repurpose content used in other media</li></ul>	<ul><li>Relatively low levels of automation possible</li><li>Limited measurement</li><li>Limited temporal impact (real-time)</li><li>Lack of control</li><li>Clutter</li><li>Channel fragmentation</li><li>Potential for mis-steps that then spread virally</li></ul>

Element	Pros	Cons
Events, experiences	• May result in strong memories and ability to recall brand messages • Potential to benefit from positive associations of partner brands • May build positive brand image • May inspire word-of-mouth communication and publicity • Potential to engage consumers	• Low reach relative to other options • Brand exposure limited to audience of event • Costs can vary • Most effective when exclusivity is an option
Branded communications	• High engagement potential • Message control • Invites audience rather than achieving exposure through interruption • Ability to promote brand viewpoints • May use paid and/or owned media outlets • May be relatively easy to execute (e.g., product placements)	• Requires brand to manage, direct, and produce content (or partner with those who can) • Relatively small reach • Difficulty in measuring ROI • May not be noticed • Cost and complexity depends on the execution chosen
Sales promotions	• Incentives drive behavior (sales, product trial, etc.) • Ability to build enthusiasm for brand • Aids in setting short-term objectives	• Provides positive reinforcement for behavior only when incentive is offered • Incentive may lower brand image and equity over time • Incentives may be abused
Personal selling	• Ability for salesperson to identify needs of prospect and tailor message • Ability to demonstrate benefits • Ability to build relationships	• High cost per contact • Difficult to ensure brand message is consistently delivered • Relationship strength may lie with salesperson rather than brand • Success may depend in part on motivation and drive of salesperson more so than brand offer • Potential limitations in reach, especially geographic

DETERMINE CREATIVE AND MESSAGE STRATEGY

The use of integrated marketing communications campaigns demands that the concept of creative and message strategy guide communications across all elements (Schumann, Artis and Rivera, 2001). Professor of Advertising Jef L. Richards is often quoted as saying "Creative without strategy is called 'art'. Creative with strategy is called 'advertising'". Creative strategy is defined as a policy or guiding principle that specifies the general nature and character of messages to be designed (Frazer, 1983). Table 9.7 summarizes the most common creative strategies used in marketing communications campaigns.

TABLE 9.7   Creative Strategies

Strategy	Definition
Generic	Explains the benefit (with no assertion of superiority); seeks to make the brand synonymous with the product category.
Preemptive	Asserts superiority along with a straight product or benefit claim.
Unique selling proposition	Emphasizes a unique physical feature that provides a superior benefit.
Brand image	Relays symbolic associations and meaning.
Positioning	Reinforces the desired mental niche relative to the competition (direct or indirect comparison, typically with a testable assertion).
Resonance	Attempts to evoke a memory and relate brand to memory's meaning and/or significance.
Emotional	Attempts to connect the brand to the target audience's emotions.

Message strategies have been conceptualized as 1) informational/rational/cognitive, 2) transformational/emotional/affective, and 3) transactional/action-oriented/conative. For simplicity, we will refer to the three types as 1) informational, 2) transformational, and 3) transactional. Informational messages focus on the consumer's practical, functional, or utilitarian need for the product or service and emphasize features of a product or service and/or the benefits or reasons for owning or using a particular brand. The objective is to persuade the target audience to buy the brand because it is the best available or does a better job of meeting consumers' needs by appealing rationally. Transformational messages relate to the customers' social and/or psychological needs for purchasing a product or service or their feelings about an experience. Many consumers' motives for their purchase decisions are emotional, and their feelings about a brand can be more important than knowledge of its features or attributes. Transactional messages are designed to lead directly to some type of consumer response. They may utilize an incentive like a coupon and/or other promotional efforts that might trigger a behavior such as a purchase, participation at an event, and registration in a loyalty program. Some of the most common campaign appeals are defined in Table 9.8.

TABLE 9.8   Common Campaign Appeals

Appeal	Description (Reason to buy is ...)
Fear	To protect one's self from physical or social harm.
Social approval	To belong, win friends, earn approval of others.
Vanity/egotism	To reinforce pride in one's appearance, qualities, abilities, achievements.
Comfort	To experience creature comforts.
Self-image	To feel better about one's self; to be a better person.
Excitement	To have more variety, fun experiences and avoid boredom.
Sex	To evoke desire.
Enjoyment	To experience pleasure; to enjoy things like food, wine, vacations.
Cause	To support a high-involvement cause such as breast cancer research, environmental sustainability, anti-smoking, education for at-risk children, etc.
Profit	To save money, make money, or keep from losing money.

The communications may follow one or more executional styles, the way the message is portrayed. Common executional styles are defined in Table 9.9.

TABLE 9.9   Campaign Executional Styles

Executional Style	Description
Slice of life	Depicts a scene based on common real-life situations.
Demonstration	Demonstrates the use of the product, benefit, or product characteristic.
Comparison	Names or implies one or more competitors and claims superiority.
Testimonial	One or more people recount experience with brand, satisfaction, and results of using product.
Endorsement	Celebrity or typical person authority recommend the brand.
Humor	Employs comedy, parody, or satire to be funny and amuse.
Lifestyle	Depicts the way a consumer group lives, possibly referencing interests and activities; implies that purchase of brand makes lifestyle attainable.
Announcement	Presented as a newscast or sales announcement.
Animation/cartoon	Visual elements are animated; may include use of an animated spokescharacter.
Problem and solution	Presents a problem and shows how product eliminates or reduces the problem.

(Continued)

TABLE 9.9 (Continued)

Executional Style	Description
Fantasy	Depicts a scene or story that is improbable or impossible but sparks imagination.
Scientific	Uses research or scientific facts to suggest brand superiority.
Musical	Conveys message through song; may include use of a jingle.

DEVELOP MEDIA STRATEGY

Media strategy ensures that the messages reach the target audience as effectively and efficiently as possible. Oftentimes, the creatives get the fame and fortune while people forget that without media the messages would never be consumed by the target audience. Choose the wrong media and vehicles and people won't be exposed to the campaign. The best creative can't overcome bad media. Media planning is like a puzzle. The ideal choices you might make must be balanced against constraints like timing and budget.

The media strategy explains how media objectives will be fulfilled within the budget constraints. It will outline how the campaign will get its message across. It will include all forms of relevant media – paid, earned, and owned. It will include strategic choices such as allocating media dollars where they can earn the greatest return, such as times when sales are highest, markets with the most sales potential, and target audiences with the greatest probability of purchase. Table 9.10 explains the typical media objectives.

TABLE 9.10 Media Objectives

Key Information	Example
Target audience	To deliver a target audience of affluent women age 35 and older, with children in the household, who take at least one vacation per year.
Geography	To provide a base of communication in key markets including the US, Australia, and China. Specific cities and regions with higher representation of target audience will be emphasized.
Promotional mix elements	To ensure all elements have coverage and elements requiring activation are supported.
Creative constraints	To use media that allow for the visual presentation of the offer, align with the tone of the creative, and encourage residual earned media through word-of-mouth communication, online reviews, and press coverage.
Timing	To deliver communications throughout the year with additional coverage during the summer.
Reach/frequency	To reach a minimum of 80% of the target audience an average of four times during each four-week period.

The media strategy will specify the media planner's decisions for 1) media mix and types (media mix), 2) geographic coverage (where), and 3) timing (when). Table 9.11 explains the advantages and disadvantages associated with each medium in the media mix. Table 9.12 lists the primary types of strategy statements included in media plans.

TABLE 9.11   Advantages and Disadvantages of Media Channels

Medium	Advantages	Disadvantages
Television	<ul><li>Visual impact</li><li>Ability to tell a story</li><li>Cost effective per contact</li><li>Targeting by interest and location possible through cable and satellite TV at a relatively low cost</li><li>Demonstration ability</li><li>Can relay excitement and entertainment value</li><li>Direct response feasible with iTV</li><li>Targeting by shopper data possible using programmatic and addressable TV</li><li>Online placements complement offline and provide access to streaming, on-demand audience</li></ul>	<ul><li>Audience fragmentation</li><li>Ad clutter</li><li>High absolute cost for network TV</li><li>High production costs for materials</li><li>Ensuring exposures challenging due to shift in viewer behaviors including viewing on-demand and streaming</li><li>Media multi-tasking inhibits message comprehension</li></ul>
Desktop Internet	<ul><li>Variety of ad formats possible</li><li>Many targeting options including contextual and behavioral</li><li>High coverage among Internet users globally (as much as 90% of users)</li><li>High reach possible</li><li>High frequency possible</li><li>Cost effective</li><li>Measurability</li><li>Adaptability in real-time</li><li>Ad variables easily tested to optimize effectiveness</li><li>Appropriate for demand-generation (direct response) and branding goals</li><li>Creative flexibility in use of copy, visuals, multi-media, and attention stimuli</li></ul>	<ul><li>Exposure limited by ad blockers</li><li>Subject to "banner blindness"</li><li>Perceived as irritating</li><li>Lack of control over ad placement as reputation management risk</li><li>Audience privacy concerns</li><li>Clutter</li><li>Brevity of exposure may inhibit comprehension and recall</li></ul>
	<ul><li>Creative flexibility to use detailed copy, color, and ad size</li><li>Perceived source credibility</li><li>Local, regional, and national targeting possible</li></ul>	<ul><li>Declining readership</li><li>Short life span</li><li>Low reproduction quality</li></ul>

(Continued)

TABLE 9.11   (Continued)

Medium	Advantages	Disadvantages
Newspapers	• Well-suited to announce local retail sales and distribute coupons • Short lead time • Congruent with informational message strategies • Complementary coverage offline and online	• Inefficient media buying for geographically dispersed targets • Unable to use attention-getting creative devices involving motion and sound
Mobile Internet	• Cost effective • Large reach possible • Geographic targeting possible • Access to audience 24/7 • Variety of formats available • Measurable • Capable of direct response	• Site functionality of m-sites less than traditional sites • Slow data transfer • Privacy concerns among audience • Variations in device standards – Android, Windows, Apple
Outdoor/place-based media/signage	• High reach • Relatively low cost • High frequency • Geographic targeting • Timing of exposures may occur just prior to point of purchase • Some locations achieve high attention due to minimal competition for attention (e.g., airports, subway trains)	• Limited use of copy • Primarily limited to static ads • Difficult to measure outcomes • Lack of targeting ability
Radio	• Use of sound • Ability to complement video ads • Targeting possible by geography and station genre • Short lead time • Useful for generating frequency • Low cost per contact and overall • Low production cost • Internet integration possible • Daypart flexibility	• Media buying inefficiencies for geographically dispersed audiences • Noise in the communications environment • Creative limitations (lack of visual images, motion)
Magazines	• Targeting by lifestyle and topic interest • High reproduction quality • Ability to use color, variations in ad size, detailed copy • Premium placements to align with content and utilize native advertising possible • Long life span • High pass-along rate • Integration with magazine website and tablet editions feasible	• High cost • Long lead times • Creative limitations for attracting attention (lack of motion, video) • Clutter

Medium	Advantages	Disadvantages
Branded content	• Control over message and message context • Perceived as high value, positive, and memorable • Creative flexibility in story-telling, format, audience, and channel	• Difficult to measure effectiveness • Limited reach • Potentially high production costs • Clutter
Direct marketing	• Precision targeting possible • Multiple distribution options (email, mail, phone, text) • Control over messaging and timing • Measurability	• Perceived as annoying, "junk", intrusive • Privacy concerns • High cost per contact • Low response rates

Note: MEDIA listed in order of percentage of global ad spend

TABLE 9.12   Strategic Media Decisions

Strategic Decision	Description	Key Considerations
Media mix	Which media should be used?	Consider the interplay between media objectives, media characteristics, and cost effectiveness. Media mix decisions should represent all promotional mix elements in the campaign (e.g., press, events, direct mail, sales promotions).
Geographic allocation	How will media coverage and spending be allocated by geography?	This decision is influenced by the uniformity of sales and presence of target audience members across geographic regions. The plan may propose equal coverage, spot coverage in high-value regions, or a combined approach.
Schedule	When should media coverage be present?	This decision asks whether media coverage should be equally spread (continuous) across the campaign timeline, or allocated using a variable (pulsing) or intermittent (flighting) pattern. The launch schedule for different campaign elements (e.g., events, publicity, advertising, website launch) will influence this decision along with the budget and seasonality of buyer behavior.

CREATIVE CONCEPTING AND MEDIA PLANNING
CREATIVE CONCEPTING

In this stage of the campaign development process, the agency's creative people will have the job of converting the creative and message strategy into an idea that can be effectively brought to life across the promotional mix elements chosen. A creative concept is an overarching "Big Idea" that can capture audience interest, influence their emotional response and inspire them to take action.

EVALUATE AND CHOOSE MEDIA VEHICLES AND BUDGET ALLOCATION

The media planner will select media tactics that can realize the media strategy. The tactics section of the media plan should include the following:

- List of media vehicles (the specific location within a media channel) recommended, categorized by promotional element and medium.

- Summary of the reach, frequency, and gross rating points the media tactics will accomplish by quarter and year.

- Summary of the dollars and percentage of budget allocated by campaign element and media, and by quarter and year.

- Flow chart representing everything included in the media plan for one full year as well as budget allocations, reach, and frequency.

PRODUCTION
CREATE CAMPAIGN ASSETS

Once the client has approved the campaign design, creative concept, and media plan, the production stage brings the campaign to life. The creative materials and assets needed for each campaign element and media placement are produced. The result is a set of campaign deliverables that meet specifications for distribution.

BUYING MEDIA SPOTS

During this stage, any media space specified in the media plan should be secured. A media buyer negotiates placement rates based on the expected advertising impressions. They use cost guidelines from past experience or cost projections provided by media forecasting companies. Once media are purchased, the media-ready materials are distributed.

EXECUTION
LAUNCH

Launch represents the official start of the campaign.

MONITOR, EVALUATE, OPTIMIZE

John Wanamaker, a department store owner and advertising pioneer, famously said, "Half my advertising is wasted, I just don't know which half" (AdAge, 1999a). The quote captures the importance of campaign evaluation. If possible, effectiveness measures should be monitored throughout the campaign so that changes can be made if needed. This is covered more in Chapter 12.

CASE STUDY

HATCHED'S CREATIVE WALLS APPROACH

Meet Hatched London, a marketing and advertising agency providing creative services in branding, design, content development, and advertising. Hatched seeks to provide "brand communication for independently minded brands". What does this mean? The company emphasizes that good brand communication shouldn't be reserved for big companies with big budgets. Rather, its ideal client is one with a point of view, strong values, and a purpose. Though Hatched describes itself as a creative agency, it is a full-service agency, planning and managing IMC projects from the initial brief through production and execution.

Hatched emphasizes that the brief isn't sufficient alone to support exceptional creative work. The Hatched team studies its client brands to "get under the skin of the brand". In so doing, campaign designs and creative work achieve consistency with the client's brand identity and positioning. Campaigns featured as case studies on the Hatched website (see www.hatchedlondon.com) utilize several MARCOM elements including branded content, advertising, sales promotions, events and experiences, and social media marketing. For example, a campaign for Best Places to Visit in Kent included digital advertising, web design (including mobile), deals for tickets, season passes and memberships, and asset production for use in social media communications. Importantly, the creative design work Hatched develops is executed across all possible touchpoints in a prospective customer journey – mobile, web (design and content), brochures, print ads, digital ads, social media assets, ticket imagery, and so on. Every single element that may be seen by a customer is designed with the same messages, color palette, typography, imagery, and so on. This is a key tenet of integrated marketing communications.

All stages of the campaign planning process are important, but Hatched's "Creative Walls" approach to determining creative strategy is unique. The approach seeks to ensure the client is included in the creative process. The Creative Walls approach has three phases: 1) Cool Wall, 2) Warm Wall, and 3) Hot Wall. The Cool Wall is a show and tell of all the initial research and creative concepts. These are ideas that serve as points of discussion to identify client preferences, learn more about what is needed from the campaign, and eliminate what won't work. The Warm Wall takes the "keepers" from the Cool Wall and illustrates those concepts. Further elimination will occur and preferred concepts will move forward. The remaining concepts will be fully finished and presented in the Hot Wall stage.

Importantly, Hatched establishes agreements with every client to specify its scope of work, responsibilities and timelines, and anticipated costs. The agreement includes details on the timing and participants for status meetings, project milestones, approval and feedback formats, among other specifications. Costs vary depending upon the scope of work, but might include services such as project management, creative design, copywriting, content production, artwork, website architecture design, programming, and creative asset delivery.

PROMOTING THE SUSTAINABLE DEVELOPMENT GOALS TO THE WORLD

The Sustainable Development Goals (SDGs) can't be accomplished by the United Nations alone. Governments, charities, businesses, and individuals must all be involved. This requires awareness of the SDGs – a task for promotions!

The first campaign – called the Global Goals campaign, which was led by Project Everyone to promote the SDGs – took place in 2015. The objective was to achieve awareness of the SDGs by reaching 7 billion people in 7 days (Magee, 2015). To prepare for the campaign, each goal was given a short, catchy name. For example, SDG 1 was rewritten from "End poverty in all its forms everywhere" to "No Poverty". "Conserve and sustainably use the oceans, seas and marine resources for sustainable development" became "Life Below Water". Rewording the goals helped to make them approachable and understandable for people around the world, regardless of their location or characteristics (Peters, 2015).

The campaign's central feature was a commercial, called #WeHaveAPlan, which aired in theaters around the world (United Nations Media Advisory, 2015). The advertisement, written and directed by ad legend, Sir John Hegarty of UK-based ad agency Bartle Bogle & Hegarty, showed the moment the United Nations ratified the Global Goals. The twist? The ad featured animated animals representing each country – the UK as a lion (Magee, 2015). It was touted as the first-ever global cinema ad with distribution in 30 countries. The commercial was produced in several languages and file formats to meet the media requirements of the theaters showing the video (Unique Digital, 2015).

Other components of the campaign included a crowdsourced song called "Tell Everybody", created from entries to a lyric-writing contest in Africa. Social media engagement was encouraged in several ways: 1) celebrities including John Legend and Kate Winslet posting selfies featuring their favorite goal, 2) soccer stars posting videos on YouTube of themselves taking the "dizzy goals challenge" and encouraging others to do so also, and 3) the band One Direction asking fans to submit photos and videos that describe the world they'd like to live in.

One Direction used the submissions to develop a film called "Dear World Leaders". Nearly 1 billion text messages about the SDGs were sent to billions of customers in more than 100 countries. Digital ads were displayed on the Google homepage, Yahoo, The Huffington Post, Twitter, YouTube, and other popular websites. A pop-up radio station streamed music and shows about the goals to 60 countries over seven days. Educators were encouraged to teach their students about the goals with "the world's largest lesson" (Gharib, 2015). A crowdsourced film called "We the People" featured celebrities (including Queen Rania of Jordan, Richard Branson, and Meryl Streep) and regular people who submitted videos of themselves reading their favorite goals (Stewart, 2015).

The campaign didn't make its goal of reaching 7 billion people, but it did achieve reach of more than 3 billion people overall, coverage in 170 media outlets, more than 4 million video views, engagement with 37 million people on social media, and 2.5 million impressions of the digital banner ads (Shorty Awards, 2016).

A second campaign featured a remake of the 1996 Spice Girls' Wannabe music video called #WhatIReallyReallyWant. Like the initial advertisement, it was shown in cinemas around the world. The song encouraged women with a "Girl Power" message to ask for what they really really want from the United Nations (West, 2016).

Since then, six global advertising agencies have formed a collaboration known as Common Ground to promote the SDGs. It launched with print ads highlighting specific sustainability issues running in *The Economist*, *The Wall Street Journal*, the *Daily Mail*, and *Le Figaro* (Vranica, 2016). Each company also adopted one goal to promote independently. For example, IPG promotes SDG 6 on access to water with videos, case studies, and educational materials (IPG, 2017).

A US-based advertising agency, Mekanism, launched a pro-bono campaign to promote the SDGs, entitled "One For All". It calls for unity in addressing problems like poverty, hunger, and gender equality. The campaign is built around a 30-second PSA, with a voiceover explaining that there are 7 billion people on earth and 193 UN member nations, but "the task of bettering our world is bigger than any one of us but it's smaller than all of us" (Oster, 2017).

To encourage more promotion, the Cannes Lions International Festival of Creativity introduced the SDG Lion. Awards like Cannes Lions are an essential part of the advertising industry. Advertising agencies use awards to bolster their reputations, attract employees, and win new business. Unfortunately, there is a dark side to the awards scene. Some agencies create work purely with the goal of winning awards, known as scam. Scam campaigns typically run with just enough media exposure to meet awards entry criteria. For example, a Singaporean agency, Grey, won a Cannes Lion for its 'I Sea' app, which claimed to be able to help find refugees stranded in the sea. It turned out that the app was only a prototype (Hicks, 2017). There's no doubt that the SDGs need to be promoted to the world, but it remains to be seen whether the SDG Lion inspires SDG washing.

online resources Visit **https://study.sagepub.com/tuten** for free additional resources related to this chapter.

CHAPTER SUMMARY

Promotion is communication designed to inform, persuade, and/or remind prospective buyers and customers in order to meet marketing objectives. The promotional arm of the marketing mix is tasked with ensuring customers understand the brand's value proposition, recall the brand at the point of purchase, prefer the brand to competing brands (due to a perceived advantage, likeability, image congruence, or a host of other persuasive factors), and know why they should buy the brand, where they can buy the brand, and what they should expect to pay. The promotional plan (sometimes called MARCOM) should produce integrated marketing communications (IMC), a term used to reflect the importance of unifying all aspects of communications between the brand and its stakeholders.

There are many media types and modes that can be used in the promotional mix. The media types are reflected in the PESO model, which identifies four media types: paid, earned, shared, and owned. Paid media are channels for which marketers must pay to share their messages. Earned media are publicity outcomes. Shared media are shared communications, whether from the brand or via word-of-mouth sharing from others. Owned media are channels literally owned and controlled by the brand.

The modes of promotion include advertising, branded content, public relations, social media marketing, events and experiences, direct marketing, sales promotion, and personal selling. Advertising is defined as non-personal, paid communications by an identifiable sponsor. Branded content is content that follows the content marketing approach of providing high-quality content for the target market. Direct and interactive marketing stimulate a direct response from consumers using any form of media, including mail, telephone, fax, email, and digital display ads. Public relations communications help an organization to bolster positive publicity, recover from negative publicity, or generate positive word-of-mouth communication. Social media marketing is the use of social media (interconnected and interdependent networks of people) to meet marketing objectives. Events and experiences, including sponsorship, provide brands with a way to gain publicity and advertising space with varying levels of participation or commitment. Sales promotions are short-term, added-value offers designed to motivate a specific response. Personal selling is interpersonal communication in which a salesperson uncovers and satisfies the needs of a customer to the mutual benefit of both, including direct selling.

Communications can be visualized as taking place between senders and receivers. Senders develop and encode messages and send the information to receivers using a communication channel, also known as a medium. Encoding is the conversion of the desired information into a message that can be delivered using a channel and understood by the intended receiver (through a process known as decoding). In one-way communication, the process ends, but in two-way communication, the receiver can initiate a response (such as making a purchase) and/or feedback.

There are five major steps in planning and executing an IMC campaign: 1) campaign planning, 2) campaign design, 3) creative concepting and media planning, 4) production and project management, and 5) execution. Campaign planning requires the marketer to determine the objectives of the campaign, determine the budget, review target audience and brand positioning, and create a scope of work and client brief. Campaign design consists of selecting the campaign's promotional mix elements, determining the message strategy and creative strategy, and developing a media strategy. Creative concepting and media planning is the stage at which the creative essence of the campaign is determined and media objectives are set. Production involves creating the necessary campaign assets according to required specifications. The execution stage includes the campaign launch, or official start of the campaign. It also includes the subsequent monitoring, evaluation, and optimization of its elements.

REVIEW QUESTIONS

1. What are the four components of the PESO model?
2. What are the modes of communications available for IMC campaigns?
3. What is advertising and what forms of digital advertising are available?
4. Why is branded content valuable?
5. What is public relations, what objectives can it meet, and what are the primary approaches?
6. How are brands using events and experiences to meet communications objectives?
7. How do sales promotions influence buyer behavior and what sales promotion devices can be used?
8. What are the steps in the campaign planning process?

KEY TERMS

1. **Accountability** – the relative effectiveness of advertising units.

2. **Ad blocker** – a software that filters content and blocks advertisements on a webpage.

3. **Ad network** – an aggregator or broker of advertising inventory for many publishers.

4. **Advertising** – non-personal, paid communications by an identifiable sponsor.

5. **Agency of record** – the agency designated to hold a leadership position among multiple firms hired by the client.

6. **Attribution models** – used to measure which marketing communications contributed to meeting marketing objectives.

7. **Banner blindness** – consumer's lack of attention paid to display ads online leading to the failure to cognitively process them.

8. **Bottom-up budgeting** – the budget is built from the anticipated expenses of the campaign.

9. **Brand engagement** – the process of building an emotional or rational attachment between a consumer and a brand.

10. **Branded content** – original content created or sponsored by the brand, and with which the brand is integrated into the content.

11. **Campaign** – a set of interrelated and coordinated marketing communications activities that deliver the same core message regardless of media.

12. **Campaign appeal** – the approach used to attract the attention of consumers and/or to influence their feelings toward the product, service, or cause.

13. **Client brief** – a clear and concise description of the objectives, target audience, budget, brand positioning, expected deliverables, project scope, milestones and deadlines, and any mandatory guidelines that must be followed.

14. **Communications process model** – the process by which effective communications is planned.

15. **Competitive parity method** – the budget matches what the competitors will spend.

16. **Content marketing** – strategic marketing approach focused on creating and distributing valuable, relevant, and consistent content to attract and retain a clearly defined audience.

17. **Creative brief** and **media brief** – concise, written documents that provide the most relevant information about and insights into the marketing situation, the objectives, the target audience, and the design decisions that will guide the creative team and the media planners, respectively.

18. **Creative strategy** – a policy or guiding principle that specifies the general nature and character of messages to be designed, a primary message theme.

19. **Crisis management** – the use of public relations tools to manage, protect, and recover an organization's reputation when victim to negative publicity.

20. **Decoding** – the process by which a receiver interprets the meaning of the sender's message.

21. **Direct (interactive) marketing** – interactive communications used to stimulate a direct response from consumers.

22. **Direct selling** – type of personal selling in which independent contractors market an affiliate firm's products in a personal context.

23. **Earned media** – messages that are distributed at no direct cost to the company and by methods beyond the control of the company.

24. **Encoding** – the conversion of the desired information into a message that can be delivered using a channel and understood by the intended receiver.

25. **Events, experiences, and sponsorships** – provide brands with a way to gain publicity (earned media) and advertising space (paid media) associated with an event and/or celebrity.

26. **Executional style** – the way a particular appeal is turned into an advertising message presented to the consumer.

27. **Informational messages** – focus on the consumer's practical, functional, or utilitarian need for the product or service and emphasize features of a product or service and/or the benefits or reasons for owning or using a particular brand based on the consumer's rationale.

28. **Integrated marketing communications (IMC)** – the coordinated and consistent design of all promotional messages such that all touchpoints with stakeholders support the brand's strategic position.

29. **Marketing communications** or **MARCOM** – the collective term for all the various types of planned messages used to build a brand and meet the brand's communications objectives.

30. **Media buyer** – negotiates placement rates based on the expected advertising impressions.

31. **Media fragmentation** – the breaking up of large audiences into smaller audience fragments due to the increase of media choices available.

32. **Media strategy** – ensures that the messages reach the target audience as effectively and efficiently as possible.

33. **Native advertising** – paid media that presents the ad as a seamless part of the user experience respective to the platform.

34. **Noise** – anything that interferes, distorts, or prevents the message transmission, which may prevent receivers from receiving and/or decoding the message as the sender intended.

35. **Objective and task method** – to assess the budget likely needed in order to accomplish what is desired from the campaign.

36. **Owned media** – channels the brand controls.

37. **Paid media** – purchased space to deliver brand messages.

38. **Percentage-of-sales method** – the promotion budget is based on last year's sales or on estimates for the present year's sales.

39. **Personal selling** – interpersonal communication in which a salesperson uncovers and satisfies the needs of a customer to the mutual benefit of both.

40. **Programmatic advertising** – the automated process of buying, selling, and placing advertisements, without human interaction in the transaction process.

41. Promotion – communication designed to inform, persuade, and/or remind prospective buyers and customers in order to meet marketing objectives such as to influence an attitude or drive specific behaviors.

42. Public relations (PR) – includes communication activities that help an organization to receive positive publicity, recover from negative publicity, and generate positive word-of-mouth communication.

43. Sales promotion – short-term, added-value offer designed to motivate a specific response.

44. SDG washing – organizational activities that positively contribute to one or more SDGs while creating or ignoring negative impact on others (Eccles and Karbassi, 2018).

45. Shared media (sometimes called social media) – communication channels in which marketers, public, journalists, and other participants can share content (their own and that of others).

46. Social media marketing – the online means of communication, conveyance, collaboration, and cultivation among interconnected and interdependent networks of people, communities, and organizations enhanced by technological capabilities and mobility.

47. Top-down budgeting – to set an annual limit on all promotional spending across divisions and brands.

48. Transactional messages – lead directly to some type of consumer response. They may utilize an incentive like a coupon and/or other promotional efforts that might trigger a behavior such as a purchase, participation at an event, or registration in a loyalty program.

49. Transformational messages – relate to the customers' social and/or psychological needs for purchasing a product or service or their feelings about an experience.

50. Viewable display impression – an ad that loads at 50% or more and remains present for at least one second.

PART IV

The Marketing Long Game

Chapter 10

EXTENDING VALUE: PEOPLE, PROCESS, AND PRESENCE IN THE CUSTOMER EXPERIENCE

In this chapter, we'll learn the answers to the following questions:

1 What is the nature of service? Why are services integral to marketing? How does service dominant logic acknowledge marketing's desire to create value for the customer?

2 How is technology affecting services marketing? What are the benefits to marketers?

3 What is the relationship between service design and customer experience? What factors influence customers' evaluations of customer experience?

4 What role do people, process, and presence play in the marketing mix for a service?

5 How do marketers use customer journey maps, service blueprints, and customer experience maps to redesign service episodes?

INTRODUCTION

In this chapter, we study the remaining components in the marketing mix – people, process, and presence. These three elements are instrumental for designing offers when the product being marketed is intangible. Services like banking, experiences such as attending a concert, and ideas (like contributing to research) are intangible. What's more, no matter the offer we are bringing to market, marketing relies on intangibles in order to succeed. Brands are intangible. The relationships marketing builds with customers are intangible. Intangible assets, including brand equity, relationship value, innovation, among others, make up 84% of shareholder value (Tableau, 2017). Service dominant (SD) logic, a theory positing that value creation occurs through exchange, declared service as the fundamental basis of exchange and defined service as the application of intangible assets for the benefit of oneself or others. In other words, services are an inseparable element of all products. SD logic sees service much as the jobs-to-be-done theory suggests that products are purchased to perform a job for the customer. The shift is apparent in the servitization of products as companies offer products-as-a-service, add service revenue streams, or augment products with services for added customer value (Rathmann, 2018). Perhaps it is no wonder then that services represent about 65% of global GDP and are the major driver of growth all over the world (D'Emidio, Dorton and Duncan, 2015).

In this chapter, you'll learn the role of people, process, and presence in the design and delivery of services. We'll discuss why the marketing mix was expanded from the original 4 Ps and how marketers identify opportunities to create winning service experiences.

First, let's see how Bank of Ireland applied services marketing design principles to improve customer experiences.

OPENING VIGNETTE

HOW BANK OF IRELAND IMPROVED CUSTOMER EXPERIENCE

Like many banks around the world, Bank of Ireland (BOI) faced a disruptive shift in what customers wanted from a bank. As a 234-year-old company, embracing digital finance was definitely beyond the company's comfort zone. Market research revealed many insights, all suggesting the need for BOI to redesign its service offerings. Connected banking customers want self-service options such as financial calculators and mobile apps for common tasks like making check deposits. Most banking customers want omnichannel options, including website and mobile banking. BOI may have felt fearful that the days of branch banking were past, but research also showed that customers still want human interaction in complex situations. For example, when completing a mortgage or personal loan application, 41% of respondents opt for the in-branch option. The company decided to begin with a service design program called "Bank of Ireland Experience Design". To effectively create new banking service channels for its customers, they needed to understand their customers' needs, the precise steps in the process of completing each type of banking service, and what characteristics the bank could control to make the experience satisfying.

Over the next eight months, teams worked to study customer needs and blueprint the service process for banking tasks. From the blueprints, the teams then looked for gaps that could serve as opportunities to delight the customer or solve frequent problems and sources of friction. The first challenge was in narrowing down the list of service episodes to blueprint. Episodes are "I need to" moments for the customers. Across the range of products offered by the bank (e.g., checking, savings, debit cards, credit cards, investments, etc.), there are many possible episodes (e.g., I need to make a deposit/withdrawal, check my balance, and so on). BOI prioritized these episodes by identifying those that were associated with the highest rate of customer complaints and those perceived by customers as most complex or sensitive in nature.

Fraud and bereavement services were among those targeted for service design. Customers felt fearful of fraud, and the bank's quick work at identifying possible fraud and resolving it could drive customer loyalty and advocacy. BOI manages the transition process for more than 15,000 deceased customers each year. The families are distressed and many times lack knowledge of the accounts in transition. These episodes were labor-intensive for the bank and difficult for the family members – a lose–lose situation. Considering the elements of service design within the bank's control, the team created a seamless process that eliminated redundant elements and developed an empathy-rich script for bank employees to use and personalize in interactions with the family. The redesign eliminated friction from the process and enhanced the people element of the customer experience. This solution enabled BOI make a better emotional connection with these vulnerable customers.

Digital applications for BOI's mobile and website channels focused on simple tasks with low variability, like opening a savings account or applying for a credit card. The digital application process was quick and easy, did not require a huge amount of information, and allowed for instant approval. BOI redesigned eight service episodes during the program and created a permanent design team led by a Chief Customer Officer. Establishing a permanent team made it possible for BOI to embrace continuous process improvement in its service design and delivery. As a result of the program, BOI achieved substantial improvements in the customer experiences associated with two high-risk service situations and lowered its operating costs for high-volume, standardized services.

SERVICES AND MARKETING'S PATH TO VALUE CREATION

Companies go to market with offers that promise a value proposition designed for target markets. We create value by creating and delivering a solution for a job the market needs done. The price the market is willing to pay will take into account the perceived value of the product's benefits and the perceived costs – including time, effort, and frustration. The better the customer experience, the higher the perceived value of benefits and the lower the perceived costs will be. It's smart business to deliver exceptional services. That's just the tip of the iceberg. Service excellence is associated with customer loyalty, higher customer lifetime value, and positive word-of-mouth communication. It can be a point of differentiation and source of competitive advantage.

SERVICE DEFINED

A **service** can be defined as a transaction in which service providers use resources such as skill and experience to benefit customers, but in which no physical goods are transferred from the seller to the buyer. It's also been defined as intangible acts provided by one for another that do not result in ownership. The SD logic definition highlights the use of intangible assets as resources used to create value, and that value is created by both the buyer and the seller. SD logic has largely been adopted as the dominant logic in services marketing.

A deep look at the research and principles of SD logic is beyond our scope and purpose, but there are a few key points to keep in mind as we study service design strategy. The relationship is interdependent in that buyers and sellers both benefit from the exchange (Lusch and Vargo, 2006). This principle is consistent with relationship marketing and customer relationship management (CRM) methods. While both buyers and sellers benefit from exchange, value is experiential and therefore unique to the person perceiving the experience. For this reason, marketers practice customer experience (CX) design principles and measure CX as well as other metrics like service delivery speed, customers served, and customer satisfaction. This is a simplified summary of SD logic, but it sets the foundation for our study of service design and the marketing mix.

SERVICE AND PRODUCT LEVELS

Services are products. They may be the core product or augmented elements of a product offer. A service is core when it is meets the customer's primary need or problem; the service is the basic reason for the business. Some examples of core services are telecommunications, banking, tourism, and dry cleaning. Augmented services add value to the core and help to differentiate a brand from the competition. When goods are exchanged as well, these are **hybrid offerings** on the good–service continuum. For instance, Dell markets computer technology equipment, but also provides consulting, maintenance to update equipment software over the life of the product, and trouble-shooting for performance issues.

Organizations may also offer facilitating services. These services facilitate the movement of the prospective customer through the customer journey. They provide benefits needed during the micro-moments (discussed in Chapter 2) customers typically experience. For example, facilitating services include providing information, recommending products, taking orders, billing, providing payment options, processing payments, and delivering orders. Consumers today have high expectations of facilitating services and consequently they are a major focus for marketers. An example is the challenge of speedy last-mile delivery to meet customer expectations for free shipping in two days or less. Among fast casual and fast food restaurants, digital ordering via mobile app is another popular example. A study among smartphone users in the US found that 58% of customers had ordered a meal via mobile app (Fast Casual, 2017).

SERVICE CHARACTERISTICS AND THE CUSTOMER JOURNEY

Services have unique characteristics that affect buyers' customer journeys and consequently marketing mix decisions. First, service is, by definition, intangible. Services do not have a physical presence. They cannot be touched, held, moved, or stored. The characteristic of intangibility makes it more difficult for prospective buyers to evaluate alternatives prior to purchase and to evaluate their satisfaction with the product post-purchase. Why? As intangibles, services are low in search qualities and high in experience and credence qualities – which are harder to evaluate! Search qualities are physical characteristics that can easily be evaluated. Tangible goods are high in search qualities. If you are shopping for a new dress, you can see the color and style and feel the fit and texture of the material. After the purchase, you have the dress in your closet to remind you of how stylish and flattering the color and fit are on you. As intangibles, services lack search qualities. Experience qualities are product attributes that customers encounter and observe as a participant in an event. These include how the buyer feels during the event, what he or she thinks and believes, and perceptions of pleasure or pain, good or bad. Experience qualities are difficult to evaluate before participating in the event itself. For example, we don't really know how enjoyable a cruise will be before we go. Credence qualities are product attributes we find difficult to evaluate even after experiencing them. Credence qualities are attributes related to trust, confidence, and credibility. How can a customer know whether a company is trustworthy? We may use cues like ratings, reviews, and recommendations to gauge whether we can confidently trust a brand to deliver on its promise to customers, but we may not ever know for sure – even after purchase. For example, if you hire an accountant to prepare your taxes, do you really know how much money you saved? Do you know whether you really got the lowest possible price on a hotel room or flight?

These product qualities aren't only relevant pre-purchase; they also affect evaluation post-purchase and consequently affect perceived customer satisfaction, product quality, and customer retention. Because customers have no physical product as evidence, like a reminder of the utility they gained from the purchase, they may not really consider whether the service was good or not! They need to be reminded to reinforce the customer relationship. Some services are not episodic, with a discrete beginning and end, but interminable (e.g., utilities like mobile phone service, Internet service, and electricity). Awareness of interminable services and their value to the buyer tend to drop below conscious awareness until a point of service disruption. The customers spend more time actively considering service failure and dissatisfaction.

Intangibility also means that there are cost implications for marketers to consider. Temporal assets used in providing the service are perishable. If we fail to use them, we've lost the opportunity. When the service requires a high degree of human participation, it exhibits the characteristics of inconsistency and inseparability. Inconsistency means that the service experience will vary each time the service is performed. To some extent, service variability is simply unavoidable because of the human element. To the extent possible, marketers strive for standardization and consistency because standardization creates cost efficiencies and manages customer expectations. Customer expectations directly impact perceptions of customer satisfaction post-purchase, because people feel satisfied when the value they experienced exceeds their expectation. For this reason, marketers are advised to manage expectations wisely!

GREAT SERVICE = A GREAT CUSTOMER EXPERIENCE

Marketers definitely want customers to feel satisfied with their customer experiences. Leonard Berry, one of the leading gurus in the field of services marketing, put it this way: "by definition, a good customer experience is good customer service, thus the customer experience is the service" (Berry, Wall and Carbone, 2006: 44).

It's been said that customers do not want products; they want experiences. Connected consumers are saying they want more than transactional engagements and gimmicks. In fact, a global study by Kantar Consulting (2018), reported in *Taking the Consumer Lifestyle Trends into 2018 and Beyond*, found engaging experiences to be the #1 lifestyle trend. Customers in transactional relationship states have a higher likelihood of switching brands than those in a stronger relationship state. We see this in action: 89% of customers say they have switched brands because of poor customer experiences. In contrast, an impressive 86% of customers have said that they are willing to pay up to 25% more for a superior experience. As we'll discuss, customers may value the experience in and of itself. But the broader implication is in the role experience plays in building relationship equity, the relational assets and liabilities associated with interactions with a brand's service providers, social benefits of the offering, or experience that adds to or subtracts from the perceived value of the offer (Palmatier, Dant, Grewal and Evans, 2006).

The concept of customer experience can be hard to define. It refers to participation in or observation of an event but also implies the participant engages in evaluation. How do they feel? What are they thinking? What behaviors are they engaging in? The Temkin Experience Ratings surveys thousands of consumers about their interactions with hundreds of companies across several industries to benchmark expectations for customer experience (Temkin, 2018). It describes customer experience using three dimensions: success, effort, and emotion. Specifically, people want their experiences to be successful (i.e., their needs were met; the job was done), they acknowledge the effort invested by the company and/or the company's employees, and they award value to how the brand made them feel.

To complicate matters, experience occurs moment by moment. An event could encompass several moments over a short or extended period of time. Kahneman explained that experiences are evaluated on the pleasure and/or pain the participant derives during an event (Kahneman, 2000). The experience utility includes the valence (good or bad) and the intensity (mild to extreme) of feeling. Events may include several real-time measures of pleasure and pain moment by moment (known as moment-based utility), which may all affect (some more than others) the overall evaluation. As marketers, this tells us that there are opportunities at several points in the customer journey, but some will matter more than others. It also suggests that there may be pleasurable moments and pain points, but experience utility can still be valuable if the good moments outweigh the bad.

EPISODES AS MOMENTS

Marketers use the concept of customer episode to practically define moments relevant to customer experience management. An episode includes all activities that customers and the brand perform to fulfill a specific set of customer needs, such as a job to be done. Episodes range from simple interactions (e.g., "I need to change my address on file") to more complex interactions (e.g., "I need to secure mortgage financing to buy a house"). Historically, marketers have focused on touchpoints as moments to manage, but episodes are more reflective of the service exchanges between brands and customers (Hawker, Melton, Wright, Burns and Engelhardt, 2018). For most companies, episodes can be grouped into three categories (Du Toit, Markey, Melton and Debruyne, 2017):

1. *Evaluation and purchase.* These are episodes related to the stages of decision-making.

2. *Usage.* These are episodes involving active engagement with the core value of the purchase (e.g., using driving directions on your smartphone, paying a bill with a digital wallet app on your phone, playing a video game).

3. *Post-purchase facilitating services.* These are episodes that are necessary for the customer to use the purchased benefit (e.g., shipping, billing, repairs).

SOURCES OF FRICTION

Eliminating friction has been mentioned earlier in the book, especially in Chapter 2, and the concept applies here as well. Friction occurs whenever a customer depreciates the value of the experience with the brand. In other words, friction is felt as pain. We even refer to pain points when studying buyer behavior. It can also harm the relationship between brand and buyer. So to maximize customer experience, we need to delight but also eliminate friction. Researchers studied sources of friction in several top brands including Nestlé S.A., ConAgra Foods, and Coca-Cola (Leach, 2017). There are five categories of friction: 1) process, 2) technology, 3) knowledge, 4) engagement, and 5) ecosystem.

1. **Process friction** occurs when customers are asked to complete more tasks than necessary to accomplish their goal. For example, if you are making an online purchase, process friction would occur if you are asked to enter a billing address and shipping address even though the addresses are the same.

2. **Technology friction** occurs when websites are confusing to navigate, search fails to produce useful results, webpages are slow to load, shopping carts fail to update, and other glitches.

3. **Knowledge friction** occurs when information is unclear, incomplete, inaccurate, or unavailable. Customers rely on brands for information when researching possible purchase options, developing product use knowledge, and trouble-shooting problems. Knowledge friction could be experienced by self-service customers, searching company sources of information as well as when dealing with an employee who lacks the knowledge the customer seeks.

4. **Engagement friction** occurs when customers are displeased with how the brand and its employees interact with the customer and the public at large. This is the most subjective form of friction in the study.

5. **Ecosystem friction** occurs due to a lack of integration within the organization's structure and/or with third-party partners. For example, many people like to move between customer service channels – social media to webchat to telephone as an example. This requires the organization to have omnichannel integration and shared data systems for customer care representatives.

Taking into account experience utility, services marketing episodes, and sources of friction, we can define customer experience as the value a customer derives from experience utility, either moment-based or overall, involving the positive or negative valence and level of intensity of emotions felt during the participation or observation of a service exchange. Companies recognize the importance of customer experience management: 89% say they compete primarily on the basis of customer experience. There's work to be done, though:

80% of companies said they believe they deliver superior experiences, but only 8% of customers agreed (Hyken, 2018).

PEOPLE, PROCESS, AND PRESENCE IN THE MARKETING MIX

People, process, and presence are elements of the marketing mix established to address the challenges of services marketing. We want to design offers that help buyers evaluate choices pre-purchase and minimize feelings of risk. We want to help customers remember how much value they received from services. We want to manage expectations and keep costs down. We want to optimize customer experience by providing pleasure moment by moment and reducing friction.

PEOPLE

The people dimension of the marketing mix refers to the human participants in the service encounter, namely employees and customers. As humans, beliefs, attitudes, biases, behaviors, and all matter of humanness may play a role in the service experience. In high-contact services, the employee (known as a boundary spanner or service provider) performing the service is inseparable from the production of the service and the customer's consumption of the service. Such services are higher in variability, but can also be valuable for building relational ties between customer and brand.

In traditional service settings, marketers influence the people dimension with the purposeful selection of employees with specific personality traits, uniforms, and training employees on topics like communication skills, empathy, product knowledge, and diffusing anger. Technology has radically transformed the people dimension of the marketing mix. It can replace or support human service providers, improve standardization and/or personalization of services, and exhibit thoughts and feelings. For example, service robots can replace human service providers for some services, improving standardization and lowering costs. Call centers staffed with hundreds of telephone service agents are being replaced by conversational chatbots. But in other fields, artificial intelligence, data modeling, and dynamic personalization deliver a more personalized and enhanced service to customers. Self-service empowers customers to complete service episodes on their own, without human interaction. Technology-enabled self-service, appropriate for transaction and standardized service episodes, is cost-efficient for brands and welcomed by customers: 75% of customers say self-service is convenient and 67% report they'd rather use self-service than speak with a company representative (CRMKID, 2015).

PROCESS

Process refers to the workflow by which the service is exchanged. These are any steps, procedures, or rituals performed by either the employee or the customer throughout a service.

Each and every service episode will have its own process. Some episodes will be prioritized over others by both customer and brand, depending upon their value potential and sensitivity.

Intelligent process automation (IPA) is an emerging set of new technologies that combines fundamental process redesign with robotic process automation and machine learning (Bughin, LaBerge and Mellbye, 2017). It can replace human effort in processes that involve aggregating data from multiple systems or taking information from one source for data entry in another. Smart workflows track the status of episodes from start to end and manage any transitions in the process. Machine learning can speed up service episodes by predicting what will be needed using recognized patterns.

Process is the most common cause of friction. For this reason, marketers analyze episodes using a technique called service blueprinting to identify friction, unnecessary steps, opportunities to incorporate pleasure, and ways to improve functional outcomes. The blueprints are then used to improve service process design. We'll cover service blueprinting in more depth later in the chapter.

PRESENCE

The final element in the marketing mix is presence. Traditionally, this element was called physical evidence because it referred to tangible cues in the customer's physical environment that influenced perceptions. To accommodate the use of such evidence, whether in physical or virtual environments, we use the term presence. Presence is valuable in the marketing mix because it can influence behavior and brand perceptions, particularly when the product is intangible (Bitner, 1992). A brand's name, logo, color choices, and other signs and symbols illustrate the power of presence indicators to relay meaning. Other presence cues customers might use include sensory elements in the purchase environment, known as the servicescape (Berry and Parasuraman, 1991). Servicescapes are built sets designed to incorporate artificial elements that relay the desired meaning (Bitner, 1992). Presence categories include ambience, layout of space, and signs, symbols, and artifacts. Ambience is an atmospheric variable. Artifacts are signs, symbols, or artistic objects that relay meaning (Marketing Wit, 2018). Artifacts typically represent culture and can be useful for setting expectations about norms and sharing a brand's values. For example, you may know that Nike's name is that of a goddess of victory, but the Nike campus also features a gallery of statues dedicated to iconic athletes. These are artifacts that communicate Nike's commitment to sport. Symbols can also be used to indicate status and positions of power. This includes clothing, office decor, and so on.

In a restaurant, a servicescape may be built with presence indicators such as dim overhead lighting, candlelight, leather chairs, classical music, exquisite fresh flower arrangements, in a spacious room providing for guest privacy. Brands pay special attention to the presence aspects of flagship stores because such elements not only affect buyer behavior, they also relay brand personality and image. In online environments, the goal is to give the customer a sense of being there. Some technologies like AR and VR create immersive presence.

When marketers use presence to design servicescapes, it's called evidence management, a purposeful design to present customers with the evidence they need to evaluate your value proposition and inform their beliefs about the brand. Think of it as impression management. Identify what you want customers to think and feel and then manage the evidence – the ambience, layout, and signs, symbols, and artifacts that match. No detail is too small!

SERVICE AND CUSTOMER EXPERIENCE DESIGN

Service design is the activity of analyzing, planning, and developing service episodes (people, process, and presence) to provide a more valuable customer experience and/or achieve brand benefits such as cost savings or branding. The approach builds on the culture of design, prominent among artists, creative designers, and architects, and brought to the forefront of marketing practices through the work of the highly lauded design consultancy IDEO (Zomerdijk and Voss, 2010).

Service design embraces four principles (Saco and Goncalves, 2008):

1. It aims to create services that are useful, useable, desirable, efficient, and effective.

2. It is human-centered, focusing on the customer experience.

3. It is a holistic approach that seeks to integrate strategy, systems, devices, data, and other aspects that are relevant to how customers interact during the service episode.

4. It is a systematic, iterative process, and interdisciplinary.

Service design uses visual mapping of customer journeys, service episode processes, and customer experiences. These are types of alignment diagrams, which are maps and diagrams used to visually represent business processes (Kalbach and Kahn, 2011). For customer experience goals, we will use all three maps to identify interactions and opportunities to create value (using people, process, or presence in the marketing mix); as such, it is a form of value-centered design. Figure 10.1 illustrates the relationship between the journey map, the service episode blueprint, and the customer experience map.

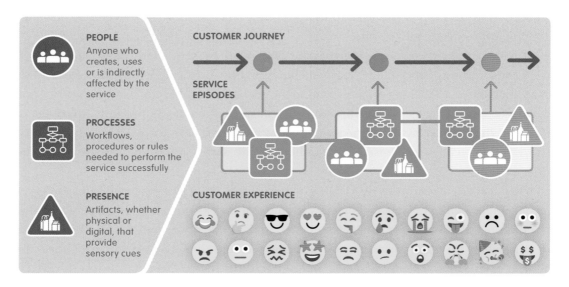

FIGURE 10.1   Customer Journey Map

Source: Inspired by Flaherty (2016)

CUSTOMER JOURNEY MAP

You learned about customer journey maps in Chapter 2. They illustrate the path a customer takes to accomplish a goal. In Chapter 2, we looked generally at a purchase decision. The goal in service design is to identify the job the customer needs done and map the typical journey for that job. An underlying goal of this step is to inventory and prioritize the customer's unmet needs and any activated value elements. The elements of value framework (covered in Chapter 6) is useful for this step.

SERVICE EPISODE BLUEPRINT

A **service blueprint** is a diagram depicting the process by which a service is provided, including employee and customer actions and any interactions as well as exposure to presence indicators. It includes swim lanes to represent multiple channels. In other words, the blueprint shows exactly what activities it takes for a company to provide a specific service and the actions and environment customers experience during the process (Gibbons, 2017). Each service episode, the job to be done for the customer, is depicted in a dedicated blueprint. Figure 10.2 illustrates several possible episodes customers of a telecommunications provider might experience.

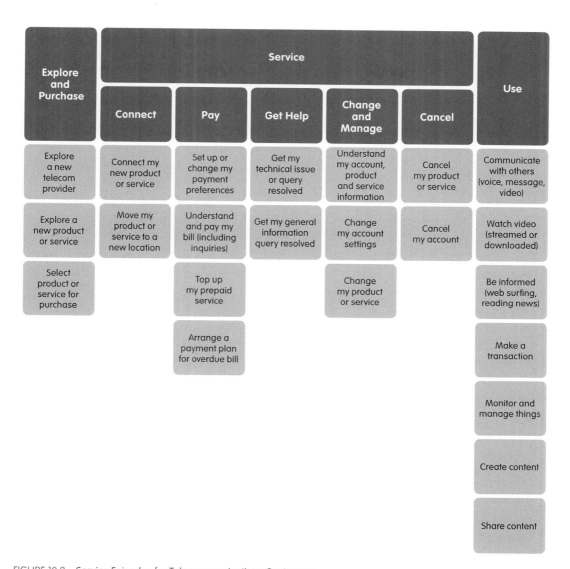

FIGURE 10.2   Service Episodes for Telecommunications Customers

Source: Copyright © Bain & Company, 2019. Reprinted with permission.

Lynn Shostack explained why service blueprints are so valuable for service design:

The root of most service problems is, in fact, lack of systematic design and control. The use of a blueprint can help a service developer not only to identify problems ahead of time but also to see the potential for new market opportunities … A blueprint encourages creativity, preemptive problem solving, and controlled implementation. It can reduce the potential for failure and enhance management's ability to think effectively about new services. The blueprint principle helps cut down the time and inefficiency of random service development and gives a higher level view of service management prerogatives.

(Shostack, 1984)

ELEMENTS OF SERVICE BLUEPRINTS

Service blueprints are more graphic than others, but every service blueprint comprises some key elements:

- *Customer actions*: steps, choices, activities, and interactions that the customer performs while interacting with a service to reach a particular goal. These customer actions are derived from the customer journey map.

- *Frontstage actions*: actions that occur directly in view of the customer whether human-to-human or human-to-computer.

- *Backstage actions*: steps and activities that occur behind the scenes, known as the line of visibility. These actions could be performed by a backstage employee (e.g., a coder) or by a frontstage employee who does something not visible to the customer (e.g., tech support entering complaint in the database).

- *Processes*: steps needed to deliver the service. This element includes anything that must occur for all of the above to take place. For example, it might include credit card verification, validating a shipping address, identity verification, and so on.

- *Lines*: the line of interaction depicts the direct interactions between the customer and the organization. The line of visibility separates all service activities that are visible to the customer from those that are not visible. The line of internal interaction separates contact employees from those who do not directly support interactions with customers/users.

- *Evidence*: any presence indicators the customer is exposed to during the process (Pruitt, 2017).

Figure 10.3 shows a sample of a service blueprint.

CUSTOMER EXPERIENCE MAP

In this step, the goal is to assess how the customer's experience is likely to vary moment by moment through the process depicted in the episode blueprint. Which points in the process should be prioritized? What moments are likely to be associated with the pain of friction? Where are pleasure moments? What is the underlying cause of friction? Mark the map in Figure 10.3 with emoticons to pinpoint these critical moments. For each of these, assess the episode frequency, quality, and economics associated with the experience (Du Toit et al., 2017). Episode frequency assesses the frequency with which the friction occurs on average. Episode quality captures value added, such as resolving a problem quickly.

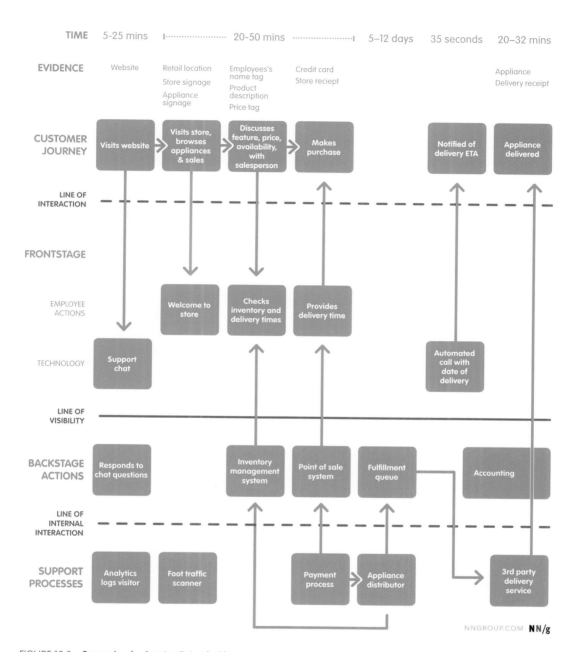

TIME   5-25 mins |·················→ 20-50 mins ·················| 5–12 days   35 seconds   20–32 mins

FIGURE 10.3   Example of a Service Episode Blueprint

Source: Service Blueprints: Definition by Sarah Gibbons on August 27, 2017 https://www.nngroup.com/articles/service-blueprints-definition/

Episode economics considers whether addressing points of friction could drive profitability through customer lifetime value or cost savings (Interaction Design Foundation, n.d.). This technique can also be useful for evaluating the value proposition for new service offerings like mobile apps (Shaw et al., 2018).

THE SOLUTION: REDESIGN THE EPISODE PROCESS TO DELIVER DESIRED CUSTOMER EXPERIENCE

The last step is to redesign the service to improve the customer experience. The redesign may be as simple as eliminating redundant steps in the process or as complex as integrating additional service channels (like the omnichannel options we covered in Chapter 8) or developing digital technologies in the MarTech stack. A new class of software has been developed known as Episode Analytics to facilitate the design analysis process.

FIGURE 10.4   Keys to a Positive Customer Experience

From the marketing perspective, the process portion of the service experience is likely to face the most revisions and improvements. Keep in mind that the people component is valuable for humanizing the brand, activating emotional benefits, building relationship quality, and encouraging empathy from customers – a characteristic that is especially useful in times of service failure. When customers feel empathy, they tend to assume any mistakes couldn't be helped and the service provider wasn't at fault. Likewise, consider how sensory elements could be built into the servicescape to set mood and expectations and communicate the brand's values and image. We'll go deeper into brand-building in Chapter 11.

Every brand will have a unique customer experience plan, but there are several characteristics likely to resonate with customers. KPMG, a consulting firm, evaluated customer experience characteristics for more than 100 brands across six B2B sectors. Figure 10.4 highlights the marketing actions to drive successful customer experiences. Brian Solis, a leading marketing consultant, recommends that brands treat service design as experience design, with explicit details in the design plan as to the senses stimulated, the emotions triggered, and the desired responses each and every interaction, touchpoint, moment, or exposure to presence cues will trigger (Solis, 2019).

CASE STUDY

HIGH UTILITY EPISODE – THE "FIRST NOTICE OF LOSS" JOURNEY IN INSURANCE (DIGITAL MCKINSEY, 2018)

In insurance, a key journey is when a customer files a claim, known in the industry as the first notice of loss (FNOL). FNOL is particularly challenging for insurers because they must balance multiple objectives at the same time: providing a user-friendly experience (for example, by offering web or mobile interfaces that enable self-service), managing expectations in real-time through alerts or updates, and creating an emotional connection with customers who are going through a potentially traumatic situation – all while collecting the most accurate information possible and keeping costs in line. One leading North American insurer discovered it could design advanced capabilities that would improve the customer experience and provide corporate value:

(Continued)

1. *Digitization.* This company improved response times by using digital technologies to access third-party data sources and connect with mobile devices. With these new tools, the insurer can now track claimant locations and automatically dispatch emergency services. Customers can also upload pictures of damages and both file and track claims online. The insurer also allows some customers to complete the entire claims process without a single interaction with a company representative.

2. *Advanced analytics.* Digitization of the FNOL journey provided the insurer with more and better data faster, which in turn allowed its analytics initiative to be more effective. The company is using advanced analytics to improve decision-making in the FNOL journey. For example, intelligent triage is used to close simple claims more quickly, and smart segmentation identifies claims likely to be total losses and those liable to require the special investigative unit (SIU) far earlier than before. Analytics are even being used to predict future staffing needs and inform scheduling and hiring, thereby allowing both complex and simple claims to be handled more efficiently.

3. *Intelligent process automation (IPA).* Once digital and analytics were in place, IPA was implemented. Automation tools were deployed to take over manual and time-consuming tasks formerly done by customer-service agents, such as looking up policy numbers or data from driving records. In addition to reducing costs, IPA sped up the process and reduced errors. This insurer drove a significant uplift in customer satisfaction while at the same time improving efficiency by 40%.

PRME

VISA'S COMMITMENT TO CASHLESS, DIGITAL PAYMENTS LEADS TO GREATER FINANCIAL INCLUSION

People want the purchase process to be fast, easy, and simple. People like to shop! They just don't like to pay (Krahe, 2018). Marketers have set out to improve the customer experience of paying using digital wallets, and other so-called "alternative payment methods (APMs)". While most purchases made using APMs are still mobile, in-app purchases, APMs are growing in popularity because they solve some of the typical pain points shoppers experience at the point of purchase (Bansal, Bruno, Denecker, Goparaju and Niederkorn, 2018). Consumers report that digital wallets are attractive because they like having more control when shopping, a more pleasant checkout experience, and a better understanding of their spending patterns (Ewing, Leberman, Rajgopal, Serrano and Steitz, 2014). As such, digital wallets result in an improved customer experience, but they may also facilitate progress toward accomplishing SDG 1: No Poverty.

APMs support financial inclusion, the process of ensuring affordable, effective, and safe access to financial services useful for basic consumer needs like paying bills, saving money, and acquiring credit (World Bank, n.d.). It may be hard to imagine, but about half the world's adults are "unbanked", dealing exclusively in cash transactions. At best, cash transactions may be inefficient, but they also carry greater risks and costs. Digital financial products and services – especially those delivered through mobile phones – make it efficient to serve low-income consumers, even those at the base of the pyramid (BOP) (World Economic Forum, 2018). People in the BOP have annual disposable incomes so low – under $2 a day – that they can barely afford anything other than food, non-alcoholic beverages, and housing (Gordon and Hodgson, 2016).

The countries with the largest share of adults at the BOP are India, Nigeria, China, Indonesia, Kenya, and South Africa (Gordon and Hodgson, 2017). From a marketing perspective, we shouldn't underestimate the value of the BOP segment. For instance, in Kenya, it accounts for 84% of annual expenditures on household needs. Kenya's top mobile wallet providers facilitate nearly half of the country's GDP, and the most popular one – M-Pesa – is responsible for 23% (Business Call to Action, 2017)! China is home to more than 200 million unbanked adults, but 80% have access to mobile phone-based payment options. In fact, 75% of digital commerce and 40% of in-person spending in China is transacted with APMs like Tencent and Alipay (Bansal et al., 2018).

Many believe that shifting to a cashless society can support economic growth and help to alleviate poverty, particularly for those who are living in subsistent conditions (Arnould and Mohr, 2005). In cash-dependent cities, the move to mobile, digital payments promotes financial inclusion by giving more individuals access to financial services (Visa, 2017a). Visa is contributing to the goal of greater financial inclusion, having opened first-time accounts for more than 100 million previously unbanked people with its mobile wallet platform (Ewing et al., 2014). The company is also identifying policy innovations and raising awareness and support for financial literacy (Visa, 2017b).

online resources Visit https://study.sagepub.com/tuten for free additional resources related to this chapter.

CHAPTER SUMMARY

For intangible goods like services, intangible assets are critical to value creation and to positioning those services in the minds of consumers. Whether a company is offering a service as a core product or as an element in a product offer, the customer experience surrounding that service affects a customer's perceived value and perceived cost. The elements of people, process, and presence – the last 3 Ps of the marketing mix – are instrumental in designing and delivering services to a company's customers. Considering the experiential nature of services and the uniqueness of customers, relationship management and shaping the customer experience to increase value become difficult tasks for marketers. The human element inherent to both sides of the service exchange means that marketers must plan for variability in the service experience.

The technology landscape is rapidly changing this human factor historically involved in services; marketers now have innovative technologies like AI at their disposal to replace human support and service providers, allowing for a greater standardization of services. However, technology can also play a role in the elements of process and presence. Using data via CRM systems to eliminate friction in organizational processes, marketers can manage and reduce the five types of friction, which minimizes the effect these occurrences within the process have on the customer's perceived value and therefore the overall brand. In addition, technology and the rise of online shopping and services mean that marketers often have to frame their presence, or servicescape, in a virtual environment; this is an important consideration when mapping out a service. Understanding how the final 3 Ps work together, marketers can use service design with a holistic aim to provide the best possible customer experience while using a service.

REVIEW QUESTIONS

1. Why does service dominant logic say all exchanges are service exchanges?

2. Why do services require additional elements in the marketing mix?

3. What is the role of people in the marketing mix?

4. How does process affect the customer experience in a service exchange?

5. What are some examples of presence cues? How are presence cues different online or in a physical store?

6. What are the differences between customer journey maps, service blueprints, and customer experience maps?

KEY TERMS

1. **Alignment diagrams** – maps and diagrams used to visually represent business processes.

2. **Credence qualities** – product attributes that are difficult to evaluate even after experiencing them.

3. **Customer episode** – includes all activities that customers and the brand perform to fulfill a specific set of customer needs.

4. **Customer experience** – the positive or negative valence and level of intensity of emotions felt during the participation or observation of a service exchange.

5. **Ecosystem friction** – occurs due to a lack of integration within the organization's structure and/or with third-party partners.

6. **Engagement friction** – occurs when customers are displeased with how the brand and its employees interact with the customer and the public at large.

7. **Episode economics** – considers whether addressing points of friction could drive profitability through customer lifetime value or cost savings.

8. **Episode frequency** – assesses the frequency with which the friction occurs on average.

9. **Episode quality** – captures value added such as resolving a problem quickly.

10. **Experience qualities** – product attributes that customers encounter and observe as a participant in an event.

11. **Facilitating services** – services that facilitate the movement of the prospective customer through the customer journey.

12. **Hybrid offerings** – when both services and goods are sold together.

13. **Intelligent process automation (IPA)** – an emerging set of new technologies that combines fundamental process redesign with robotic process automation and machine learning.

14. **Knowledge friction** – occurs when information is unclear, incomplete, inaccurate, or unavailable.

15. **Line of visibility** – steps and activities that occur behind the scenes.

16. **Moment-based utility** – several real-time measures of pleasure and pain moment by moment within an event.

17. **Presence** – tangible cues in the customer's physical environment that influence perceptions.

18. **Process friction** – occurs when customers are asked to complete more tasks than necessary to accomplish their goal.

19. **Relationship equity** – the relational assets and liabilities associated with interactions with a brand's service providers, social benefits of the offering, or experience that adds or subtracts from the perceived value of the offer.

20. **Search qualities** – physical characteristics that can easily be evaluated.

21. **Service** – the application of intangible assets for the benefit of oneself or others.

22. **Service blueprinting** – analyzing episodes to identify friction, unnecessary steps, opportunities to incorporate pleasure, and ways to improve functional outcomes.

23. **Service dominant (SD) logic** – a theory positing that value creation occurs through exchange.

24. **Servicescape** – a built set designed to incorporate artificial elements that relay the desired meaning.

25. **Technology friction** – occurs when websites are confusing to navigate, search fails to produce useful results, webpages are slow to load, shopping carts fail to update, and other glitches.

Chapter 11

MAINTAINING VALUE: BRANDING AND BRAND MANAGEMENT

In this chapter, we learn about how branding contributes to marketing success by supporting brand awareness and brand image marketing initiatives. We'll cover how brand identities can be expressed in art and copy, using words, stories, voice, tone, color, typography, and images. We'll learn the answers to the following questions:

1   What is the role of brands in marketing? What benefits do brands provide and how do they work?

2   What is brand equity? How does brand knowledge affect brand equity?

3   How do we develop and manage brands? What are the elements of brand management?

4   How do we use the brand identity planning framework to codify our brand and establish brand cues in the form of brand style guidelines?

5   How can marketers leverage brand value to establish brand portfolios? What is the relationship between brand portfolio management and brand architecture?

INTRODUCTION

The marketing mix describes the elements that make up offers; offers designed to provide value to target markets. Brands bring the offer to market. They represent the offer's source and, importantly, the brand serves as the entity with which customers choose to do business. As such, the value of relationships in marketing is clear. You probably don't like making deals with people you don't trust. If you know someone, you'll be much more comfortable doing business with that person. Brands work much the same way. The integrated elements of the marketing mix form a brand's foundation and brands employ the elements to establish identity and reputation.

Initially, brands were simply non-generic names that informed customers of a product's source (McLaughlin, 2011). Now a brand is more like the face a company presents to the world. The brand name can add value and utility for the buyer, drive interest and purchase intentions, and communicate accountability for the buyer's post-purchase experience. Brands differentiate their products from those of competitors, but more importantly, brands reveal the values embodied in an organization to consumers, shareholders, employees, and society at large.

There are many definitions of the word, brand. Here are a few that highlight the value and scope of the concept.

A brand is:

- "the intangible sum of a product's attributes: its name, packaging, and price, its history, its reputation, and the way it's advertised" (David Ogilvy, cited in Biel, 1999: 161)

- "the sum total of how someone perceives a particular organization, and branding is about shaping that perception" (Ashley Friedlein – Econsultancy, cited in Cohen, 2011).

- "a name, term, sign, symbol, or design or a combination of them, intended to identify the goods and services of one seller or group of sellers and to differentiate them from those of the competitor" (Phillip Kotler, 1997: 453)

- "a customer experience represented by a collection of images and ideas; often, it refers to a symbol such as a name, logo, slogan, and design scheme" (American Marketing Association, n.d.)

All of these definitions are accurate. The real magic, though, happens when people associate a brand with meaning. Brands then become the collective perceptions and impressions people believe. In this way, brand meaning is co-created and an example of the current era of marketing convergence. Brands have become one of the most valuable intangible assets a company can own. How valuable? The CEO of Quaker Oats once reflected: "If this business were to be split up, I would be glad to take the brands, trademarks, and goodwill and you could have all the bricks and mortar – and I would fare better than you" (Rivkin and Sutherland, 2004: 9). Where once the brand was nothing more than an identifier, brands now add value in their own right.

OPENING VIGNETTE

AIRBNB'S COMMITMENT TO EXPRESS BRAND ESSENCE

Think about the last time you went on holiday. Did you stay in a hotel? With a friend? Did you book accommodation through Airbnb? Airbnb is a web platform for listing and renting accommodation around the world. The listings offered on Airbnb's platform range from cheap options in iconic locations like a studio in Paris near the Eiffel Tower

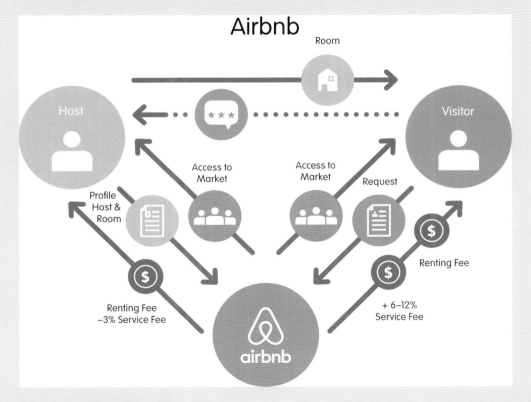

FIGURE 11.1 Airbnb's Business Model

Source: © 2019 Airbnb, Inc. Used with permission.

(Continued)

for under $50 per night to fantasy options like one of more than 3,000 castles! In fact, you can book lodging with Airbnb from its more than 5 million unique listings, in more than 81,000 cities across 191 countries. On average, more than 2 million people stay in a place they booked through Airbnb on any given night!

Though people use Airbnb to find lodging, Airbnb does not offer lodging as a product category (and doesn't compete directly against hotel brands). Rather, it connects and facilitates transactions between hosts and guests using the Airbnb platform, earning commissions from hosts and transaction fees from guests. The more peer-to-peer exchanges between hosts and guests via the Airbnb platform, the more revenue Airbnb earns. Consequently, Airbnb has two distinct target markets (hosts and guests).

Figure 11.1 illustrates the Airbnb business model and Table 11.1 summarizes its business model, value proposition, positioning, target markets, and marketing mix.

TABLE 11.1 Airbnb Marketing Plan Summary

Business model	Platform, sharing community.	Freemium; free for hosts to list and travelers to search but commissions assessed on successful bookings.
Vertical market	Lodging in private accommodations.	Expansion into travel, tourism, events and experiences markets.
Target markets	1. Hosts. 2. Travelers.	Demographics: varied. Geographics: thousands of cities across 191 countries globally. Psychographics: risk tolerant, traveler, cosmopolite, social, innovator. Benefits sought: financial and experiential value.
Value proposition	1. Hosts can earn extra money from an existing asset. 2. Travelers can stay at a place that feels like home, experience the culture of a local, and maybe even save some money.	Pain points addressed for hosts with "smart pricing" tool, webinars, and other educational materials to coach hosts to make the most of their listings. Pain points of trust addressed with reviews of hosts and other indicators of safety and quality. Add-ons for experiences on location.
Positioning	1. Hosts can monetize their spaces, passions, and talents to become hospitality entrepreneurs. 2. Travelers can experience the world as if they belong – like a local at home.	

Marketing mix elements of offer	Product: platform to facilitate exchanges P2P between hosts and travellers.	
	Promotion: advertising to promote tourism and travel to stimulate primary demand as well as secondary demand.	
	Price: range of prices offered by hosts that can meet any price range desired by peer guests; platform pricing is freemium model – free to list and search but exchanges generate commissions to Airbnb.	
	Place: online via any device with efforts to increase ease of booking via mobile app.	
	People: hosts are offered training to optimize the guest experience in order to improve their location brand experience and the Airbnb reputation.	
	Process: online journey for search, evaluation, booking, and review post-experience but future emphasis on reducing friction in the process.	
	Presence: imagery of locations, experiences, hosts, and guests in a variety of settings and stories.	

Where does branding fit into all of this? It must seem that Airbnb has it made! With a market valuation of more than $30 billion, it's the epitome of a unicorn, a word used to describe a private company with a valuation over $1 billion. Indeed, today, Airbnb has strong brand awareness, ensuring that it may be considered by travelers as an option for purchasing overnight accommodations.

While it might be hard to imagine, once upon a time, Airbnb did not enjoy the benefits of brand awareness. In fact, the company nearly failed. You see, when Airbnb launched in 2008, it was among the early entrants in the disruptive category of "brand platforms" within which the product facilitated collaboration P2P in the sharing economy. Even among people who would benefit from a solution like the one the company offered, how would they use it if they didn't even know it existed? This is

(Continued)

a basic but seminal role branding plays in marketing. Airbnb has evolved in just 10 years to truly embrace branding.

Brand names mark the source of the offer. Airbnb is a great brand name! Yes? Well, it wasn't the original name! The brand launched as AirBed&Breakfast. Ouch! Check out the summary in Table 11.2 of how Airbnb's brand as evolved in just 10 short years.

TABLE 11.2   The Evolution of the Airbnb Brand

Element	Then	Transitional	Now
Name	AirBed&Breakfast	Airbnb	Airbnb
Slogan	Forget hotels	Travel like a human	Belong anywhere
Call to action	Book rooms with locals	Welcome home	Live there
Logo	**AirBed&Breakfast**	*airbnb*	△ airbnb

Source: © 2019 Airbnb, Inc. Used with permission.

THE ROLE OF BRANDS

Brands identify themselves using names and symbols, as well as other design elements. These brand names and logos are trademarked assets used as tangible cues to relay meaning. When you see a product with a brand you recognize, you can draw references about the product's quality, efficacy, and desirability. Just as services use tangible elements as a source of search attributes, brands do as well. While the name, logo, and slogan are akin to a brand's signature, announcing the brand's presence, they are superficial without the depth of meaning provided by other brand elements including brand positioning, brand identity, and brand culture. Branding simply means marketing the brand to communicate and reinforce the relationships between the image associations and the brand elements. It is the process of developing a brand such that the tangible elements like name and logo stand for something. It is marketing's attempt to purposefully influence people's perceptions of a brand.

Here are some fast facts about the value of brands:

- About 84% of the value of all businesses is intangible value, of which brand value is the largest component.
- Strong brands out-perform average businesses on shareholder returns – BrandZ's portfolio of strong brands grew by 124.9% from 2006–2017 versus 34.9% for the MSCI World Index.

- Strong retail brands average three times the sales volume of weak brands and earn a 13% price premium.

- Brand-building activity drives stronger sales growth for periods of six months or longer compared to short-term sales promotions used to drive temporary sales lifts (Roach, 2018).

HOW BRANDS WORK

Brands communicate product features and benefits to prospective buyers, serve as a heuristic for purchase decisions, set expectations for product quality, and differentiate a brand from competitors. How? A simple explanation, based on the associative network memory model, goes like this. An associative network is simply a chain of associations one records and stores in memory and that can facilitate recall. The associative network memory model is a conceptual representation of the associations in memory depicted as a set of nodes and interconnecting links where nodes represent stored information or concepts and links represent the strength of association between this information or these concepts (Keller, 1987). As a person is exposed to brand assets, the tangible elements that represent a brand, they are stored in his or her mind as a mental network. They exist as a memory structure of the images, colors, sounds, symbols, stories, experiences, and our thoughts, feelings, and experiences. People use these mental brand networks as subconscious shortcuts (i.e., heuristics) to make brand choices (Shaw, 2015). When networks of brand associations are visually depicted, they are called brand concept maps (John, Loken, Kim and Monga, 2006). You might be acting upon a mental structure like this when you go with your gut reaction when making a decision. People often make decisions, seemingly on auto-pilot, by using mental shortcuts like these.

Brand awareness refers to a person's ability to identify a brand. When brand awareness is aided, it is called brand recognition; when unaided, it is brand recall. The strength, favorability, and uniqueness of brand attributes influence attitudes toward the brand and brand associations which form brand image. Brand image links to the brand name node. Basically, the brand name and other brand symbols act as an anchor that enables people to retrieve information about brand associations and their perceptions of the brand from memory.

STRATEGIC BRAND MANAGEMENT AND THE PURSUIT OF BRAND EQUITY

Strong brands don't happen overnight. It takes time for the market to learn to associate the brand name with the desired meaning, develop brand awareness, and build a brand image that is differentiated from competitors, positive, and strong. If all goes well, the brand grows in value – known as brand equity. Brand equity refers to the sum of brand assets and liabilities associated with a brand, brand name, and related symbols such as a logo, which add to or subtract from the value of a firm's offer (Aaker, 2013). It is associated with several desirable benefits including brand affinity, customer loyalty, positive word-of-mouth communication, decreased price sensitivity, and repeat purchases. Most of the time, marketers focus on brand assets, marveling at the billions of dollars in brand equity held by the world's most valuable brands. But it's worth noting that brand equity is a perception of value, and value (as we learned in Chapter 7) is always the sum of perceived consequences – the good and the bad. Marketers work hard to add value: branding, but if the market perceives a brand as undesirable, untrustworthy, unreliable, and so on, equity could be a liability.

Another way to understand brand equity is as the capitalized value of profits that are driven by the brand name association separate and distinct from those driven by the product offered (Stanford Business, 2006). At the level of a unit purchase, you could think of brand equity as the incremental value of a branded product over a generic one. Imagine you've stopped in a local pub for a drink after work. You'll likely pay quite a bit more for Smirnoff and tonic than you would for vodka tonic poured with the bar's house brand. The difference in prices is justified by the perceived value of Smirnoff's brand (and its related associations like Russian, royalty, pure, quality, versatile, rebel, independent, unconventional, perfect). The value of the high-ball poured from the well? It represents offer equity, the sum of benefits and costs of the offer and its attributes (excluding brand effects) (Palmatier and Sridhar, 2017).

Remember our discussion of reference prices in Chapter 7? The incremental value attributed to a branded product is drawn from comparisons to generic products or competitor brands used as reference points. Brand and offer equity, along with relationship equity (value derived from social aspects between buyer and seller), make up total value to the customer, known as customer equity (Palmatier and Sridhar, 2017). Customer equity links the financial value firms derive from customers to the values which drive customer purchase behavior.

How much brand equity does Airbnb have? Estimates suggest the intangible value of the Airbnb brand exceeds $5 billion (Pathiaki, 2018)! In fact, Airbnb's brand equity now exceeds that of every hotel brand with the exception of Hilton, which remains the most valuable lodging brand.

A FRAMEWORK FOR CUSTOMER-BASED BRAND EQUITY

The Customer-Based Brand Equity Framework illustrates the relationships among the variables that influence brand equity, as seen in Figure 11.2. Consistent with the associative network memory model, the framework highlights the roles of two primary variables on brand equity: 1) brand awareness and 2) brand image. Image associations and brand awareness result in brand knowledge, which facilitates the purchase journeys of prospective buyers, ultimately contributing to brand equity. Image can be influenced by attributes of the marketing mix such as price, product features, packaging, quality, advertising, and so on. For this reason, branding is indelibly linked to controllable variables in the marketing mix. Equity derived from marketing mix attributes is called attribute-based equity (Stanford Business, 2006). Image is also influenced by perceived benefits, which may be functional, symbolic, or experiential. These associations drive non-attribute-based equity (Stanford Business, 2006) by creating emotional and symbolic connections between a brand and its target market.

As marketers, we can influence image perceptions using product design, marketing communications, customer experience management, positioning, packaging, and brand characteristics. These are decisions marketers can control. However, brand image is *not entirely* within a brand manager's control. People are exposed to other sources of influence and brand information in the environment like word-of-mouth communication from friends, social media posts, news stories, online reviews, competitor comparisons, and so on. Essentially, any association the market has established with the brand could potentially influence how brand image is perceived.

To the extent that attributes, benefits, and other brand associations are *favorable, strong,* and *unique* (relative to the competition), brand image should be positive and contribute to brand equity. We'll spend much of our time in this chapter learning about branding decisions marketers make to achieve the desired brand image. That said, brand awareness – just getting to the point at which the brand name will pop into people's minds – contributes more to brand equity than brand image!

BRAND EQUITY IN THE DIGITAL AGE

Brand value is perhaps more important now than ever before. Why? People want less friction. They want purchases to be simple, fast, and easy. Airbnb's CEO, Brian Chesky, recognizes the role of friction on his business, saying "Friction is the biggest product thing we're working on. We have a new product called insta-book. About 1–2% of properties have it. It's like a hotel. You click, and it's reserved" (Thompson, 2013).

AI assistants and voice technology are already capable of serving as salespeople taking orders via smart devices. Voice-command-driven purchases could cause a major disruption in the distribution of market share by brand. We've already seen that most people who shop on Amazon buy the product recommended in the buy box, even when it is not the least expensive option displayed. Voice-command purchases will have a similar bias. The AI assistant will likely default to the brand preferred by the controlling platform, which may be a platform's own private-label brand or a brand partner. Futurists warn that frictionless shopping will lead to the commoditization of brands. Analysts predict that, in the next two years, 50% of all online product searches and one in three purchases will be made via voice (Deloitte, 2017a).

FIGURE 11.2   Customer-Based Brand Equity Framework

Source: Adapted from Keller, K. (1993) 'Conceptualizing, measuring, and managing customer-based brand equity', *Journal of Marketing*, 57 (January), 7.'

Amazon's Echo and Alexa assistants are positioned to capitalize on this by pushing more of Amazon's private label products into the market. This is happening already. Since 2017 Amazon has launched more than 80 new brands including the Amazon Basics product line and sales of its private label grew 90% (Howland, 2017). In this new world, consumers may not even be given a choice to buy a brand unless they ask for it by name. Brands could end up at the mercy of an algorithm controlled by the platform. That is, unless the brand's customers love it so much, they explicitly ask for it by name. This will be the new imperative for brands.

MANAGING BRAND STRATEGY

A **brand strategy** is a long-term plan for guiding a brand's development and growing brand equity. **Brand management** is the organizational function that oversees brand strategy.

Because brand equity can play a role in organizational performance like stock valuations and investor confidence, brand managers are tasked with monitoring environmental forces that may impact a brand's market power and making adjustments to protect and advance the brand's competitive position. They also facilitate the relationship between branding and marketing and guide decisions about how best to leverage brand equity while protecting against cannibalization and brand dilution. As the role of brand manager has evolved, so too has its functional definition. **Strategic brand management** encompasses the design and construction of brand identity, implementation of brand-oriented marketing programs, evaluation of brand performance and brand equity valuation, and the design and management of brand portfolios (Keller, 2013).

DESIGNING BRAND IDENTITY

We learned how brands work earlier in the chapter. To build brand equity, we must establish brand knowledge, including awareness and perceptions of brand image, in the minds of the target market. As we market the brand, the brand attributes, benefits, and other associations will be linked to tangible characteristics of the brand (e.g., brand name, brand logo) to establish and reinforce a memory network that can increase the likelihood that our brand will be remembered, included in a consideration set, positively evaluated, and purchased. In brief, we take the following steps:

1. Evaluate the 3Cs: consumer characteristics, competitive rivalry, and company context.

2. Identify a brand image that embodies favorable, strong, and unique brand associations.

3. Construct a brand identity system to portray the brand and associations consistent with the desired brand image.

4. Design tangible brand elements which can concretize the identity associations in a memory network.

What results from this process? The outcome will be a comprehensive brand identity system that will be used by brand managers to market the brand itself. This is commonly called branding.

It's worth noting that the promotions P in the marketing mix (i.e., marketing communications covered in Chapter 9) typically seeks to generate demand or to build the brand. A demand orientation means that the marketing communications are designed to sell products. A brand orientation means that the marketing communications are establishing and/or reinforcing the brand's memory network! The tension created as brand managers and sales managers vie for limited budgets is a key reason you may hear of arguments between those in marketing and those in sales. Which side is right? Well, according to Gary Vaynerchuk, branding should always be the first priority. He wrote,

> At the end of the day there is only one thing that constitutes 'brand.' It's how you feel in the moment you interact with the product, service or business. When I say 'Pepsi' and 'Coca-Cola' and 'IBM' and 'Sears' you have a very specific innate reaction to your feeling about that brand ... Why I focus so much on legacy, is I want you to have a positive reaction when you hear my name. I want you to feel good when you think about what I've done ... I want you to have a positive connotation. A good feeling when you think of me. *The reality is, the greatest companies in the world don't sell. They brand.*
>
> (Vaynerchuk, 2017, emphasis added)

BRAND IDENTITY AND BRAND IMAGE: WHAT'S THE RELATIONSHIP?

You've already heard about the role brand image plays in driving brand equity. But how can marketers build a specific, desired brand image when image is a perception in the minds of the target market? There lies the challenge for brand managers.

Image perceptions are influenced by attributes and associations, some of which we can control but some we cannot. The controllable elements are used to construct a brand identity that will represent the brand in the marketplace. Brand identity is how the brand identifies itself to the world, assigns character labels, and reflects its values. You see, brands express themselves to the outer world, just as you and I do. You want others to see you in a certain light – maybe as friendly, confident, laid-back, competent, honest, and so forth. You manage the impressions others have of you by portraying your desired identity with your actions, the way you dress, what you say and how you say it. If you've taken an organizational behavior class, you may have studied impression management. Brand identities are how brands manage the impression they make on those in the target market.

The identity we project to others is sometimes called a persona (much as we studied buyer personas in Chapter 2 to gain insight into target audiences). Carl Jung, a psychoanalyst who first conceptualized archetypes as a framework for understanding one's self, defined a persona as what we would like to be and how we wish to be seen by the world (Cherry, 2019). The word "persona" is derived from a Latin word that literally means "mask"! In other words, a brand persona – the brand identity – reflects how the brand wishes to be perceived. This relationship is illustrated in Figure 11.3. As people are exposed to the brand identity attributes, they develop brand associations that influence perceptions of brand image. In other words, *identity is created to impress the desired brand image.* Brand identity is how the brand would like to be perceived, while brand image is how it is perceived.

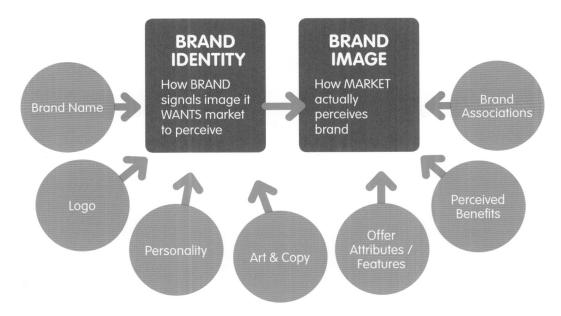

FIGURE 11.3   The Relationship Between Brand IMAGE and Brand Identity

CRAFTING BRAND IDENTITY

The brand identity planning model, illustrated in Figure 11.4, depicts the components that contribute to brand identity. Let's see how these components work together to make up the intangible asset known as a brand. We'll cover each layer in the model and return to our Airbnb example to illustrate:

- brand purpose
- brand identity system
- brand offers in the market
- brand identity imprint.

BRAND PURPOSE

Functional	Emotional	Symbolic/ Aspirational	Societal	Sustainable Legacy
Brand solution to market need	Brand-buyer relation bond, lovemark	Brand commitment to needs, values, and goals of socio-cultural communities	Purpose contributes societal benefits	Brand ideology, brand cultural steward, activist, and advocate

---- DESIRED BRAND SHARE TYPE ----

MIND SHARE	HEART SHARE	SELF SHARE	VALUE SHARE	LEGEND SHARE

BRAND IDENTITY SYSTEM

Brand as Offer	Brand as Person	Brand as Symbol	Brand as Organization	Brand as Platform
• Offer attributes/ benefits • Value proposition • Propositioning • Customer experience	• Brand personality • Brand archetypes	• Symbolic heritage • Metaphors, myths, and stories • Artifacts and language	• Mission and vision • Core values • Performance and behaviors	• Shared ownership • Ecosystem for influence, change, and activism • Authenticity, accountability, transparency, trust, shared governance

BRAND OFFERS IN THE MARKET

BRAND BENEFITS LADDER	VALUE PROPOSITION	POSITIONING	CUSTOMER EXPERIENCE MANAGEMENT

BRAND IDENTITY IMPRINT (BRAND STYLE GUIDELINES)

Visual Design Elements
- Imagery
- Logo
- Layout
- Color
- Typography

Brand Story and Copy Design Elements
- Story
- Characters
- Personality Traits
- Voice
- Tone

FIGURE 11.4   Brand Identity Planning Model

BRAND PURPOSE

Today brands are encouraged to embrace a purpose. Don't believe me?

"Brand purpose" was even selected as the Association of National Advertisers' 2018 *Marketing Word of the Year* (Duggan, 2018)! Accenture defines brand purpose as "The reason why something exists. For companies, it is the foundation of every experience. It is the underlying essence that makes a brand relevant and necessary" (Barton, Ishikawa, Quiring and Theofilou, 2018). A brand's purpose expresses the positive impact the brand wants to make in the world.

Simon Sinek, author of *Start With Why*, says brand purpose answers the why question. Most importantly, Sinek claims that brands that focus on why are typically far more successful than brands that focus on what (they sell) (Sinek, 2011). Allen Adamson, a brand consulting expert, said it this way: "Every brand makes a promise. But in a marketplace in which consumer confidence is low and budgetary vigilance is high, it's not just making a promise that separates one brand from another, but having a defining purpose" (Adamson, 2009). BrandZ's most recent ranking of the world's most valuable brands identified the five characteristics found in the top 100 brands. A compelling brand purpose was first on the list (BrandZ, 2018).

Figure 11.4 illustrates that there is a brand purpose spectrum such that a brand purpose may range from a superficial purpose of meeting a functional need at one end of the spectrum to a substantive contribution by establishing a sustainable legacy at the other end (Sable and Jones, 2018).

- A functional brand purpose seeks to provide a solution to a problem.
- An emotional brand purpose seeks to develop a relationship with customers.
- A symbolic/aspirational brand purpose represents a community and their beliefs.
- A societal brand purpose contributes to a social issue through corporate social responsibility (CSR) programs.
- A brand purpose at the sustainable legacy end of the spectrum seeks to contribute to the world.

Each level of brand purpose aligns to a desired market response: mind share, heart share, self share, value share, and legend share (BBDO, 2001). Mind share occurs when people are aware of a brand and its functional utility. Heart share occurs when people feel emotional attachment to the brand. Self share occurs when people use the brand to symbolize their own self-identity. Value share occurs when brands contribute to societal needs and provide a bridge through which its customers also contribute. Brands that contribute to an existential search for meaning as a sustainable legacy may earn legend share (BBDO, 2001).

A recent study highlighted that consumers wouldn't care if three out of four brands they use every day disappeared. Does this mean brands are not making a meaningful impact on consumers' lives? Probably. Brands tend to define purpose by the problems they solve for customers or the emotions customers feel. Today's consumer is more likely to be motivated intrinsically by their core values and beliefs. Traditional drivers such as price, taste, and convenience remain important in their buying decisions, but social impact, health and wellness, safety, and experience have emerged as value drivers. More than half of consumers reported that they weight intrinsic value drivers more heavily than traditional ones when making purchase decisions (Walker Smith and Curry, 2017).

Do buyers really care about purpose? It wasn't so long ago that marketers viewed corporate social responsibility as a necessary, but unrewarded trait. Brand purpose proposes brands do even more, ideally embedding purpose in their strategies and operations. Is it worth it? Recent research suggests that it is. A third of consumers report actively choosing to buy from brands they believe are doing social or environmental good (Walker Smith and Curry, 2017). Accenture Strategy's report *From Me to We: The Rise of the Purpose-led Brand* revealed survey results of nearly 30,000 people across 35 countries. More than 60% of respondents said they wanted to do business with brands willing to take a stand on important issues (Barton et al., 2018). Accenture's survey results are consistent with the Edelman Earned Brand study, which found that 64% of consumers worldwide will make a purchasing decision based on a brand's social or political position (Edelman, 2018). The Edelman report also revealed a major shift in how people think about responsibility and accountability when it comes to addressing societal challenges: the majority of the 8,000 people interviewed believed brands have more power to solve social issues than do governments and non-government organizations (NGOs). Will a commitment to purpose lead to enhanced brand equity? A study by Cone suggests it will. The research findings revealed three benefits purpose-driven brands enjoy: deeper loyalty among consumers, growth in customer acquisition, and a willingness among customers to amplify the brand message by playing the role of brand ambassador (Dailey, 2018).

Igniting Purpose-Led Growth, a report on the findings of a global survey of more than 20,000 consumers and in-depth interviews with more than 500 marketing executives by Kantar Consulting, describes brand purpose as a journey. While the report advocates brands embrace purpose beyond the traditional stakeholder view, it also warns brands against misusing purpose as propaganda. The study identified five characteristics of effective purpose-led branding (Sable and Jones, 2018):

1. *Meaningful* in its intent to resolve a societal problem.
2. *True* to the brand's mission, vision, and identity.

3. *Unique* among those embraced by the brand's competitive set.

4. *Coherent* in its integration with the brand's marketing strategies.

5. *Business-proof* in that contributions to purpose also contribute to the organization's bottom-line objectives.

Table 11.3 features several brand purpose statements.

TABLE 11.3   Brand Purpose Statements

Brand	Brand Purpose Statement
Virgin Money	Everyone is better off
IKEA	Create a better everyday life for the many people
Google	Organize the world's information making it universally accessible and useful
Nike	Bring inspiration and motivation to every athlete in the world
LinkedIn	Connect the world's professionals making them more productive, successful
Facebook	Give people power to build community and bring the world closer together
BT Group	Use the power of communication to make a better world
Unilever	Make sustainable living commonplace
Lloyds Group	Helping Britain prosper

Despite the value of a clear brand purpose for guiding brand identity, not all brands have embraced the concept of purpose. A study of executives and their use of purpose-led branding classified companies into one of three segments:

1. Prioritizers (39%) are companies with a clearly articulated purpose.

2. Developers (48%) are companies that do not yet have a clearly articulated purpose but are working on it.

3. Laggards (13%) are companies that have not yet begun to even think about purpose (Sable and Jones, 2018).

Brands also need to be careful about how they use the buzz word "purpose". The concept is prone to criticism because it is frequently misunderstood, incorrectly executed, or outright abused. For example, simply supporting charities is a positive corporate contribution to the public but it does not connect to a brand's greater why.

CASE STUDY

AIRBNB'S BRAND PURPOSE

Airbnb is an example of a brand striving to attain the sustainable legacy end of the brand purpose spectrum. Its purpose is "To make people around the world feel like they can 'belong anywhere'". A service that was once known for couch-surfing, air mattresses (hence the "air" in Airbnb), and cheap lodging, the company wanted to better articulate its purpose. After extensive research, the brand realized it's about being at home anywhere we are. The brand's end game was to make people around the world feel like they could belong anywhere, as shown in Figure 11.5. In Airbnb's view, its purpose reaches far *beyond* travel. If fully actualized, the brand purpose could contribute to the human experience. The purpose relates to the needs and values of all people: individual needs for safety, security, affiliation, and belonging. Do these sound familiar? They should – these are the need levels expressed in Maslow's Hierarchy of Needs and present in the value schemes we've covered throughout the book. Since Airbnb expressed its purpose, its brand equity has increased nearly three times in value!

FIGURE 11.5   Airbnb Communicates its Purpose, Belong Anywhere

Source: © 2019 Airbnb, Inc. Used with permission.

BRAND IDENTITY SYSTEM

The second level of the model codifies the brand's identity from a variety of perspectives. The result is brand essence, the "heart and soul" of the brand. It is sometimes called a brand mantra and should capture the gestalt of the brand's identity. For example, Walmart's brand essence is described like this: "The Walmart brand identity is like a great pair of jeans: a perfect fit, comfortable for our customers, associates and suppliers. It projects a relaxed and friendly image. We love wearing it every day. And it's very, very strong" (Walmart, 2010). For Airbnb, it might go something like this: "We believe travel is better when you experience it as an insider" (Pankraz, 2018).

Brand identity models approach identity from five perspectives, as shown in Figure 11.4 earlier: 1) brand as offer, 2) brand as person, 3) brand as symbol, 4) brand as organization, and 5) brand as platform (Aaker, 1996). Each perspective sheds insight into the brand's identity by addressing what the brand is, who the brand is, how the brand and customer relate, and why the brand exists.

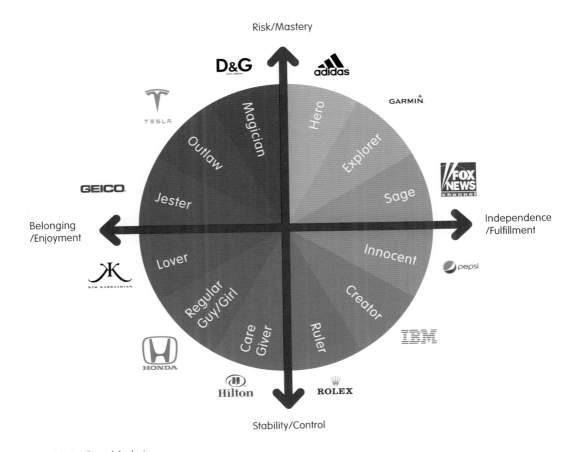

FIGURE 11.6   Brand Archetypes

Brand Personality

Of the extended brand identity perspectives, brand personality (or brand as person) receives much of the focus in branding design. Just as people have personality characteristics, brand research has demonstrated that brands can be personified and their personality traits clearly expressed. Examples include trustworthy, innovative, reliable, friendly, rugged, and wholesome (Aaker, 1997). The BrandZ study of brand equity includes a brand personality assessment because personality strength is closely linked to brand equity. Brand personalities increase perceptions of consumer–brand relationships and also improve brand likeability (Millward Brown, 2013). For example, Walmart identified five traits that characterize its brand personality: 1) caring, 2) real, 3) innovative, 4) straightforward, and 5) positive (Walmart, 2010).

Another approach to identifying brands using human traits is the use of brand archetypes. Brand archetypes, listed in Figure 11.6, portray stereotypical character traits. The underlying archetype is thought to explain the driving force or motivation behind the brand. Some examples include the explorer, the outlaw, the ruler, the sage, and the creator.

CASE STUDY

AIRBNB'S BRAND PERSONALITY AND ARCHETYPE

Airbnb's brand personality can be characterized as inclusive, safe, adventuresome, open-minded, active, diverse, supportive, and inspirational. When marketers talk about brand personality, the underlying assumption is that the brand will be seen as a person with all the nuances of personality. While Airbnb embraces its personality traits, it also strives to be seen from its broader brand purpose of belonging. For example, the illustrations used on the Airbnb website and in other marketing communications represent a broad array of people from all walks of life (Hom, n.d.). That wasn't always the case.

In a blog post called "Your face here: Creating illustration guidelines for a more inclusive visual identity", Jennifer Hom, an illustrator at Airbnb, explained that illustration serves as a major reflection of the Airbnb community. Early illustrations followed a model many organizations use to dehumanize illustrations of humans – cartoon people outlined in blue or grey. The goal is to eliminate elements of diversity while focusing on humanness. As people responded with the phrase "It doesn't represent me", Hom recognized that the generic approach to illustrating humans was failing (Hom, n.d.). Even more importantly, it didn't represent Airbnb's brand identity. Hom went on to create illustrations that reflect everyone – because with Airbnb, everyone belongs anywhere!

Can you guess the Airbnb brand archetype? It aligns best with the explorer archetype, which embraces discovery, freedom, adventure, joy, and purpose. As Airbnb has refined its brand purpose to emphasize belonging, it has also incorporated elements of the care giver archetype.

In addition to brand as person, other categories of brand identity associations include brand as offer, brand as organization, brand as symbol, and brand as platform. Brand as organization includes organizational attributes such as core values, organizational mission statements, and other organizational characteristics. Brand as offer acknowledges the associations of brand image that arise from the design of the offer (across the marketing mix) brought to market, such as product features, benefits associated with the offer, the value proposition, and brand positioning. Brand as symbol includes symbolic and cultural elements that may be associated with the brand, such as metaphors, stories, myths, artifacts, rituals, and language. Brand as platform is a new addition to the brand identity system which acknowledges the brand identity implications tied to brand ecosystems. Brand platforms can be thought of as a digitized environment built to support a two-sided market. A two-sided market is an environment in which multiple groups such as consumers as suppliers and consumers as buyers can execute exchanges using a platform, which is typically provided by a third party. The platform hosts multiple stakeholders in a digital environment, facilitating value exchanges and channel flows (tied to the types of channel flow explained in Chapter 8) such as communications, product information, and ordering and payment between participants (Kim, 2016). Junic Kim, a researcher at Konkuk University, describes platforms as "ecosystems of coexistence". Brand as platform represents the identity associations that arise from multiple stakeholders who converge in a branded digital environment to co-create brand-related experiences. Platforms are digital, automated, interactive, and functional with the ability to capture, store, curate, and interpret data from all the relevant participants in the ecosystem (Kim, 2016). In so doing, brand platforms can result in new and potentially unexpected brand associations. While not all brands follow a platform business model, the concept of brand as platform acknowledges the role brands can play as a conduit for shared values and contributions to a purpose.

CASE STUDY

AIRBNB'S BRAND IDENTITY SYSTEM REFLECTED IN TYPE

Airbnb created its own typeface to use in its communications, called Cereal. Why the name? It relates to the founders' story of survival. Before Airbnb, Joe Gebbia and Brian Chesky were just two young professionals – much like you! They were struggling to pay rent but had a brainstorm! There was a big conference in their hometown of San Francisco and all the hotel rooms were sold out. They could let travelers sleep on air

(Continued)

mattresses in their apartment for a nightly fee! It worked, and the next day they created airbedandbreakfast.com. That's where it all started.

Even though marketing likes to say "build a better mousetrap and the world will beat a path to your door", the co-founders were still struggling to make ends meet. Desperate, they decided to make special-edition Cheerios boxes for the 2008 presidential candidates: "Obama O's" and "Cap'n McCains". They literally made the boxes with hot glue guns and cardboard! Though they spent several subsequent months eating the Cap'n McCains, they made enough on the Obama O's to stay afloat (Gallagher, 2017). And that is why today Airbnb uses a proprietary font known as Cereal (Airbnb design, n.d.). Figure 11.7 shows the font. It is part of the brand's identity imprint, but the story behind the name is part of the brand's mythology – part of its "brand as symbol" identity. Both play important roles in building iconic brand identity.

FIGURE 11.7   Airbnb's Proprietary Cereal Typefont

Source: © 2019 Airbnb, Inc. Used with permission.

BRAND OFFERS IN THE MARKET: BRAND BENEFITS LADDER, VALUE PROPOSITION, POSITIONING, AND CUSTOMER EXPERIENCE

The third level of the framework revisits key elements of the offer and its impact on the brand identity. Carol Phillips of Brand Amplitude called the three elements – benefits, value proposition, and positioning – the trinity of brand strategy (Phillips, 2012). Why? At this level of the model, brand identity associations are identified based on the go-to-market planning and execution used to segment, target, and position an offer with a value proposition tied to the features and benefits of the marketing mix. In other words, this level of the brand identity system acknowledges that brand knowledge is influenced by the benefits of product, place, promotion, people, process, presence, and price reflected in the offers brought to market and reflected in the value proposition and positioning statement.

Brand positioning is how the brand wants to be perceived in the context of competitive alternatives. Positioning differentiates a brand offer from competing offers by pointing out sources of relative advantage and unique attributes. Here, positioning should still distinguish the brand from competitors, but it takes a higher level view than positioning of a specific product offer (which we covered in Chapter 3). For example, Walmart's positioning statement is: "For price-sensitive shoppers, Walmart is the retailer that helps them feel 'smart' and live better because only Walmart delivers unbeatable prices on the brands they trust, in an easy, fast, one-stop shopping experience". Airbnb's positioning statement might go something like this: Airbnb is the travel partner who believes people belong and connects people to opportunities for healthy travel that is local, authentic, diverse, inclusive, and sustainable.

The value proposition is the basis for positioning and the brand promise made to the target market. It expresses the value the brand promises to deliver and the reasons the market can believe in the promise. The brand promise though can typically be expressed in a word or phrase as the most salient benefit the brand offers. Walmart expresses its brand promise with three key phrases: 1) unbeatable prices, 2) quality products, and 3) easy shopping. Airbnb emphasizes the word "belonging". Brand identity and offer design have an interdependent relationship. Any brand knowledge the target market has will color its perception of the value and desirability of an offer. Likewise, the offer design is made up of features and benefits that will be associated with the brand.

BRAND IDENTITY IMPRINT: STYLE AND ICONOGRAPHY GUIDELINES

The final phase of brand identity formation is determining how the brand identity will be communicated to the world. Brand identity is intangible, so we rely on visual imagery and verbal cues as tangible design elements, known as brand assets. Brand assets are distinctive images, icons, messages, stylized words, stories, and other elements that can identify and characterize a brand. They express the brand identity with art and copy. Figure 11.4 lists the key design elements.

AIRBNB'S BRAND ASSOCIATIONS AT THE OFFER LEVEL

When the company first launched, it was called Air Bed & Breakfast. CEO, Brian Chesky, said "It was literally supposed to be all about air beds. Today we have 123 people staying in castles" (Thompson, 2013). The value proposition was tied to offering the lowest price for lodging to travelers and a way to generate an additional stream of income for hosts. Chesky justified the initial value proposition, saying "At first, we thought, surely you would never stay in a home because you wanted to, you would only stay there because it was cheaper. But that was such a wrong assumption. People love homes. That's why they live in them. If we wanted to live in hotels, more homes would be designed like hotels" (Thompson, 2013). This insight is reflected in the tagline that followed those early days: "Forget hotels: stay with a local while traveling". Airbnb realized it competed against hotels but travelers could have a more authentic experience by staying in a private home. More recent taglines include "Belong Anywhere", "Live There", and "Welcome Home". All of these relate back to the ethos of community and belonging the brand established as its core purpose (Johnson, 2014).

Selecting the symbols that will represent a brand's purpose and values, personality, and promises is a responsibility with long-term consequences for the brand. Companies invest time and money developing linkages between the chosen symbols, the intended meaning, and the brand. It takes time and repetition to establish memory networks in a market. Once established, the brand assets will serve as brand triggers, a mnemonic device. A brand trigger refers to anything that is associated with the brand that causes people to think about the brand. Think McDonald's golden arches, Nike's swoosh, Apple's line-drawn apple, Android's droid. As a market, we learned that the symbols represented the brands over time. Now recognizing a brand with an iconic symbol is second nature. Can you think of other examples? Even colors can serve as brand triggers. Verizon red, John Deere green, Chanel's simple yet sophisticated black, Hermes orange. As the myth goes, Hermes chose orange out of necessity as it was the only color of paperboard available during World War II. Now Hermes is an iconic luxury brand. Google's logo colors might seem more appropriate for Crayola at first glance, but now signal Google's brand effectively around the world. The design elements *concretize* the brand identity, using secondary associations to express meaning quickly and effectively. Collectively, they make up the brand imprint, the tangible marks that designate the brand, which is codified in a brand style guide.

The brand style guide is a document that codifies how the brand presents itself to the world. Put another way, it's a reference tool that helps employees throughout the organization maintain consistency as to how the brand looks, feels, speaks, behaves, and sounds. Consistency is consistently among the list of must-dos to achieve strong brand equity. You've heard the phrase "sending mixed messages"? The same principle applies here. Inconsistency in imagery and/or messaging confuses the audience, making memory associations fuzzy or even dissonant. Think of all the possible employees who invoke the brand in their daily jobs! Salespeople, customer service reps, department heads, graphic designers, copywriters, recruiters, franchise owners, retailers … The point is that brands are a community asset. Their control can't really be centralized and limited to the creatives who brought the brand to life. Brand assets are used on webpages, brochures, business cards, emails, ads, promotional materials like coffee mugs and t-shirts, social media, business listings, stationery, invoices, uniforms, and on and on. Many brands will even establish guidelines for employee email signatures! And rightly so. Any outward-facing communication is a touchpoint between the brand and the market. The role of a brand style guide is so relevant to a brand's ability to build and reinforce associative memory networks necessary to earn brand equity that the guides are sometimes called brand bibles.

CASE STUDY

AIRBNB'S BRAND IDENTITY IMPRINT AND BRAND STYLE GUIDELINES

Airbnb designers collaborated with brand design agency DesignStudio to create the brand identity assets, the style guidelines, and a brand assets management system. In addition to Cereal, the original typography font Airbnb designed, and the illustrations developed to reflect the inclusiveness and diversity of hosts, guests, places, and experiences introduced earlier, Airbnb's imprint also included a new logo, a different color palette, and a variety of interactive, digital design components. Let's look at each of these in turn:

Logo: the major change in Airbnb's transformation is a new symbol the company named the "Bélo". The Bélo takes the form of an upside-down heart or a paper clip symbol, which also looks like the letter "A". It was designed to represent four things: people, place, love, and the "a" of Airbnb, as shown in Figure 11.8. "Belonging has always been a fundamental driver of humankind. So to represent that feeling, we've created a symbol for us as a community", Airbnb CEO Brian Chesky wrote in a blog post. "It's an iconic mark for our windows, our doors, and our shared values. It's a symbol that, like us, can belong wherever it happens to be" (Chesky, 2014). The company wants the symbol "to stand for something much bigger than travel" (Johnson, 2014).

(Continued)

Color: Airbnb's new style includes new colors too. The dreamy blue and white colors were switched to a reddish color. The color choice is meant to reflect emotions and love, but without appearing aggressive. A secondary color palette is shown in Figure 11.8.

Digital assets: Airbnb is also investing in code as a design tool. Digital brand assets don't only include layout and design, but also logic and data. For example, Airbnb created interactive, animated pictograms and an open-source animation tool called Lottie (Abdul-Karim, n.d.). Some of the pictograms are included in Figure 11.8.

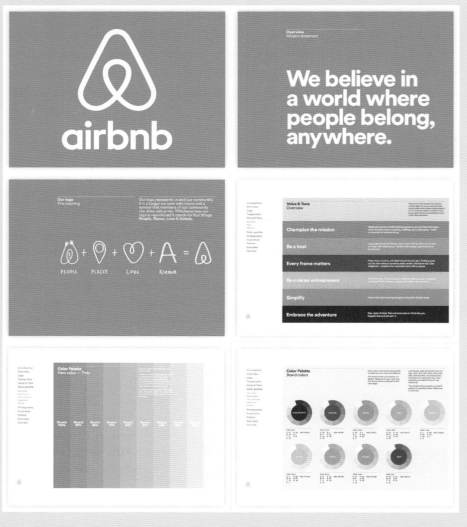

FIGURE 11.8   Airbnb's Brand Identity Imprint

Source: © 2019 Airbnb, Inc. Used with permission.

EVALUATING POTENTIAL BRAND ASSETS

You can see how these simple design choices serve to express brand identity in the marketplace. But once established, triggers are difficult to erase – as what was learned would then need to be unlearned. In some ways, this stage of brand identity formation seems the most frivolous and superficial. After all, this is the brand's style, its persona. In other ways, it comes with the most risk because it is at this stage that the brand decides what to show the world.

There are four questions to consider when choosing brand assets:

1. Brand linkage – does the asset intuitively trigger thoughts of the brand?

2. Brand uniqueness – is the brand association with the asset distinctive?

3. Sentiment – are any negative emotions associated with the asset?

4. Brand alignment – does the asset fit with the brand's values and identity?

The BrandZ study of the most valuable brands found that brands using brand assets effectively is a trait of high-equity brands. The three characteristics of effective brand asset usage included 1) clarity, 2) consistency, and 3) communication (Guerrieria, 2018).

- *Clarity* refers to simple, clean, uncomplicated, connected use of color, design, and phrasing. A distinctive color palette is used to connect, amplify, and build a unique and instantly recognizable identity.

- *Consistency* means to deploy brand assets over time, across channels and products – drawing on heritage where relevant. Think exposure, exposure, exposure at all touch points and opportunities to embed assets and reinforce recognition.

- *Communication* means the brand reinforces relevant brand purpose, principles, and messaging. Assets are used as opportunities to invoke reminders of key messages to maximize influence at points of decision-making.

BUILDING BRAND PORTFOLIOS

In addition to establishing and building a brand's identity, brand managers also design brand architecture, which depicts how brands are structured across the company's product portfolio (Aaker, 2016). It depicts how brands within a company's portfolio are related to, and differentiated from, one another. You can think of it as a kind of brand family tree. Figure 11.9 illustrates the types of brand architecture. The master brand or branded house strategy uses the master brand with a descriptor on a new offering. The branded house option leverages an established master brand, requires a minimum investment in each new offering, and enhances the clarity and synergy of the portfolio.

FIGURE 11.9   Brand Architecture

Source: Figure courtesy of Inesentrena, 2011. Accessed via wikicommons.

The second option is the endorsed brand strategy, in which the offering is endorsed by an existing master brand. The role of the endorser brand is to provide credibility and reassurance that the endorsed brand will live up to its claims (Christensen et al., 2005). An endorsed brand is not completely independent of the endorser but it has the autonomy to develop its own brand identity.

The most autonomous option is to create an entirely new brand, unconstrained by any associations with a master brand. When a collection of independent brands is assembled, it is called a house of brands. P&G is an example. It owns 80 brands with little identifying relationship to P&G or to each other.

HAVAIANAS' BRAND EMBRACES THE CULTURAL FABRIC OF BRAZIL

Havaianas is to Brazil what Apple is to the United States. More than a pair of flip-flops, they are part of the country's self-image, a product that embodies the idea of Brazil as a carefree country of surf, samba, and soccer. The brand embodies the essence of democracy, as a brand for poor and wealthy alike. Havaianas was born in 1962 as a basic flip-flop sold in Brazilian street markets. The name, Havaianas, translates as Hawaiian in Portuguese. Some say the flip-flop design was inspired by the traditional footwear worn by Japanese geishas. Others claim that this style of footwear can be traced to around the same time period as the invention of the wheel. The flip-flops were a staple for the poor, largely regarded as a necessity, alongside essentials such as beans and rice. The brand became so closely associated with the poor working classes that they became a symbol of poverty (Interbrand, 2013).

Wealthier people in Brazil also owned Havaianas, because the flip-flops were so durable and comfortable. But they were only wearing them at home, because they were embarrassed to be seen wearing a poor person's footwear. The brand reposi-tioned on the basis of its functional attributes in the 1990s. The functional benefits were the reason why people – whether poor or wealthy – wore them. They are simple, comfortable, and durable. The repositioning strategy worked. People were no longer embarrassed to be seen in Havaianas and that made it possible for people of all social classes to wear them. Havaianas' brand manager explained: "The beauty of this is that the wealthy people wear them and are proud of wearing them as much as the poor people today". This is the heart of why the brand is a symbol of democracy.

Today, Havaianas is a global success. It has a cult-like following and celebrities like Jennifer Aniston have raved about their dedication to the brand. Millions of pairs are exported each year to more than 80 markets around the world (Interbrand, 2010; Silverstein, 2013). They are seen everywhere – on the beach, along the street, and sometimes even at red carpet events. Havaianas is focused on creating brand experi-ences to engage its fan base and maintain its global fashion status.

Among the benefits of a valuable brand is the ability to weather a crisis. Time will tell whether loyalty to the Havaianas brand will help it recover from negative press coverage. The owners, part of the Batista family, confessed to bribing nearly 1,900 politicians to secure cheap government loans for their businesses (Wood, 2017). Needing cash to pay the fine once the scandal broke, they sold Havaianas for more than $1 billion. Fans of the brand are relieved Havaianas was sold to another Brazilian company. One said, "Havaia-nas truly embodies the ideals of Brazil. Therefore, it was good that the company was sold to another Brazilian company" (Kurczy, n.d.). The company has since suffered a 7.3% sales decline in Brazil and a 1.4% decline internationally. The brand is ranked among the top 20 most valuable brands in Brazil. According to Interbrand, the Havaianas' brand equity is estimated to be worth $184,564,187 (Interbrand, 2017). Does this mean the brand will be strong enough to weather negative press in the short term?

PRME BOX

DESIGNING THE BRAND IDENTITY AND STYLE GUIDELINES FOR THE UN'S SUSTAINABLE DEVELOPMENT GOALS

Throughout the book, we've explored brands that are contributing to the UN's 2030 Agenda for Sustainable Development by addressing the Sustainable Development Goals

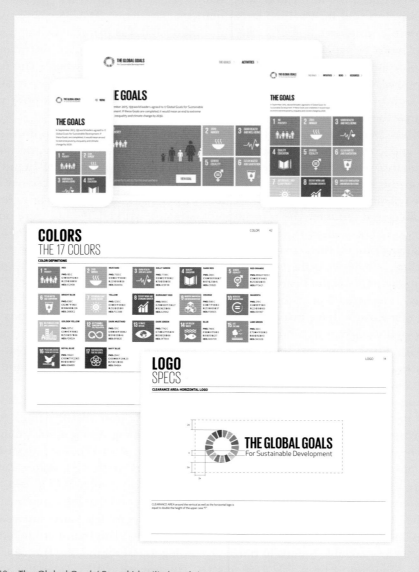

FIGURE 11.10   The Global Goals' Brand Identity Imprint

Sources: The New Division (2018); The Global Goals for Sustainable Development (n.d., 2015). Used with permission.

(SDGs). Establishing a brand identity and style guide for the UN's Global Goals was an absolute imperative early in the initiative. Doing so would help drive awareness of the SDGs around the world and provide a shared language for organizations and people to use to discuss the problems and possible solutions.

As organizations around the world learned about the SDGs and committed to their success, press releases, publicity, performance reports, and more would follow. To effectively control the brand identity of the Global Goals as thousands of organizations collaborated with the initiative and developed marketing materials related to it, the UN needed a brand style guide that defined every element of the SDGs' brand identity imprint. To facilitate the effective and frequent use of the brand imprint, downloadable brand assets for a variety of uses, media, and situations were also created and made available on a dedicated website: www.globalgoals.org/resources.

The design task fell to the agency Trollback+Company, a branding and design studio with offices in New York and Sweden. After conducting discovery research, the team set about establishing the brand identity imprint that would serve as the consistent representation of the Global Goals brand around the world, in all applications whether digital, print, event, experience, and so on. You can view the entire guideline and the brand assets at www.globalgoals.org/resources. Some of the brand assets are shown in Figure 11.10.

The basic system includes short names for the 17 goals, colorful icons, a logotype, and bold typography. To make the goals easy to refer to, each one was given a short name that summarizes the primary nature of the goals. "SDGs" stands for Sustainable Development Goals – not the catchiest of phrases. The design team renamed the initiative as "The Global Goals". The team created the assets to reflect brand associations of hope, optimism, change, inspiration, culture, determinism, and action. Logos and icons were created for each of the 17 goals as well as the sub-goals. While different colors are used for each of the primary goals, the icons follow a standard pattern: a circle in the form of a wheel, with colored spokes, and the squares in different colors bearing symbols to represent each of the individual goals (The Global Goals for Sustainable Development, n.d.).

online resources Visit **https://study.sagepub.com/tuten** for free additional resources related to this chapter.

CHAPTER SUMMARY

Brands serve as the entity with which customers choose to do business, with brands bringing the offer to the market. Brand equity refers to the sum of brand assets and liabilities associated with a brand, brand name, and related symbols such as a logo, which add to or subtract from the value of a firm's offer. To build brand equity, we must establish brand knowledge, including awareness and perceptions of brand image, in the minds of the target market. Because brand equity can play a role in organizational performance like stock valuations and investor confidence, brand managers are tasked with monitoring environmental forces that may impact a brand's market power and making adjustments to protect and advance the brand's competitive position. To be able to codify our brand and establish brand cues, the brand identity planning model looks at the brand purpose, brand identity system, brand offers in the market, and brand identity imprint. In addition to establishing and building a brand's identity, brand managers also design brand architecture, which depicts how brands are structured across the company's product portfolio.

REVIEW QUESTIONS

1. How does branding support marketing strategy?

2. How do brands work to create brand knowledge and influence purchase decisions?

3. What is brand equity?

4. What are the components that are involved in establishing brand identity?

5. What are the identity perspectives that categorize the types of brand associations that can be represented in a brand's identity?

6. Why are specific attributes and benefits of product offers relevant for brand identity?

7. What kinds of design elements are included in brand style guides?

8. What is brand architecture?

KEY TERMS

1. **Associative network memory model** – a conceptual representation that views memory as consisting of a set of nodes and interconnecting links where nodes represent stored information or concepts and links represent the strength of association between this information or these concepts.

2. **Attribute-based equity** – equity derived from marketing mix attributes.

3. **Brand archetypes** – stereotypical brand character traits.

4. **Brand architecture** – how brands are structured across the company's product portfolio.

5. **Brand as offer** – acknowledges the associations of brand image that arise from the design of the offer (across the marketing mix) brought to market such as product features, benefits associated with the offer, the value proposition, and brand positioning.

6. **Brand as organization** – includes organizational attributes such as core values, organizational mission statements, and other organizational characteristics.

7. **Brand as platform** – a new addition to the brand identity system which acknowledges the brand identity implications tied to brand ecosystems.

8. **Brand assets** – the tangible elements that represent a brand.

9. **Brand assets management system** – a database that organizes a brand's library of assets for use in its branding and marketing communications.

10. **Brand as symbol** – includes symbolic and cultural elements that may be associated with the brand such as metaphors, stories, myths, artifacts, rituals, and language.

11. **Brand awareness** – a person's ability to identify a brand.

12. **Brand concept map** – a visual map of the nodes and links in an associative network reflecting brand associations.

13. **Brand equity** – the sum of brand assets and liabilities associated with a brand, brand name, and related symbols such as a logo that add to or subtract from the value of a firm's offer.

14. **Brand essence** – the "heart and soul" of the brand. It is sometimes called a brand mantra and should capture the gestalt of the brand's identity.

15. **Brand identity** – how the brand identifies itself to the world, assigns character labels, and reflects its values.

16. **Brand identity planning model** – the components that contribute to brand identity.

17. **Brand image** – the strength, favorability, and uniqueness of brand attributes and associations.

18. **Brand imprint** – the tangible marks that designate the brand, which is codified in a brand style guide.

19. **Brand knowledge** – made up by brand awareness and brand image.

20. **Brand management** – the organizational function that oversees brand strategy.

21. **Brand personality** (or **brand as person**) – the brands are personified and their personality traits clearly expressed.

22. **Brand purpose spectrum** – a continuum reflecting the degree of brand contribution relative to purpose.

23. **Brand recall** – when brand awareness is unaided.

24. **Brand recognition** – when brand awareness is aided.

25. **Brand strategy** – a long-term plan for guiding a brand's development and growing brand equity.

26. **Brand style guide** – document that codifies how the brand presents itself to the world.

27. **Brand trigger** – any sensory cue such as a color, symbol, and sounds that is associated with the brand that causes people to think about the brand.

28. **Branded house strategy** – a strategy that uses a master brand across the company's product portfolio.

29. **Branding** – marketing the brand to communicate and reinforce the relationships between the image associations and the brand elements.

30. **Customer-Based Brand Equity Framework** – illustrates the relationships among the variables that influence brand equity.

31. Customer equity – total value to the customer.

32. Emotional brand purpose – seeks to develop a relationship with customers.

33. Endorsed brand strategy – the offering is endorsed by an existing master brand.

34. Functional brand purpose – seeks to provide a solution to a problem.

35. Heart share – occurs when people feel emotional attachment to the brand.

36. House of brands – collection of assembled independent brands in a company's product portfolio.

37. Legend share – earned by brands that contribute to an existential search for meaning as a sustainable legacy.

38. Master brand – a brand that represents the company as a whole and is used alongside other product specific brands (e.g., Hyundai Sonata, Hyundai Kona, etc.).

39. Mind share – occurs when people are aware of a brand and its functional utility.

40. Non-attribute-based equity – equity derived from image associations to intangible characteristics.

41. Offer equity – the sum of benefits and costs of the offer and its attributes (excluding brand effects).

42. Persona – the identity we project to others.

43. Relationship equity – the relational assets and liabilities associated with interactions with a brand's service providers, social benefits of the offering, or experience that adds or subtracts from the perceived value of the offer.

44. Self share – occurs when people use the brand to symbolize their own self-identity.

45. Societal brand purpose – contributes to a social issue through corporate social responsibility (CSR) programs.

46. Strategic brand management – encompasses the design and construction of brand identity, implementation of brand-oriented marketing programs, evaluation of

brand performance and brand equity valuation, and the design and management of brand portfolios.

47. Sustainable legacy – seeks to contribute to the world.

48. Symbolic/aspirational brand purpose – represents a community and their beliefs.

49. Two-sided market (also called platform or exchange ecosystem) – an environment in which multiple groups such as consumers as suppliers and consumers as buyers can execute exchanges using a platform, which is typically provided by a third party.

50. Unicorn – a private company with a valuation over $1 billion.

51. Value share – occurs when brands contribute to societal needs and provide a bridge through which its customers also contribute.

Chapter 12

MANAGING VALUE: ANALYTICS AND MARKETING VALUE MANAGEMENT SYSTEMS

In this chapter, we'll learn the answers to the following questions:

1 Why should marketing analytics be a top priority for marketers? What challenges have limited marketing's use of analytics in the past?

2 How does analytics help marketers to manage value? What role does analytics play in marketing planning?

3 When using an MVMS for marketing analytics, what are the steps in the process?

4 How do Industry 4.0 technologies contribute to MVMSs and marketing analytics?

INTRODUCTION

We've learned that marketing strives to meet objectives for the firm for growth, competitive advantage, and financial success. Chapter by chapter, we've covered the information and procedures marketers use to accomplish those objectives: buyer behavior; segmentation and targeting; positioning; planning marketing strategy; designing offers that meet buyer needs, aligning with the brand's positioning, and establishing a competitive advantage using the 7 Ps; and branding to build brand equity.

But how do we assess whether our marketing activities performed well? How do we acquire information that could improve performance in future marketing programs? How do we know whether they were productive, given resource constraints we may have faced? How can we assess the value the activities contributed to objectives like market share, revenues, customer lifetime value, or brand equity? Did the target markets respond to our marketing activities as predicted? Which product features drove purchases? To what extent was pricing strategy optimized given demand? How did our channel strategy perform? What can we learn to improve the reach of the advertising media buy? Did process improvements along the customer journeys result in more positive customer experiences? Whew … marketers need to answer many questions and this list is just the tip of the iceberg.

Here lies the power of marketing analytics. Simply, marketing analytics is the analysis of data to derive reliable, relevant, and useful information of value in performing the marketing function. Data and marketing analytics are used to answer questions like these, providing marketing managers with high-level insights or granular analyses of individual marketing mix variables. For example, in Chapter 7, we warned against decreasing prices in the hopes of increasing demand because, in most situations, the marginal increase in demand is insufficient to offset the drop in revenues caused by the price decrease. It should be possible to compare the projected market demand for a set of potential price points and determine which price point generated higher demand and/or marginal revenue. Armed with this information, the marketing manager is able to set the most optimal price to achieve the marketing objectives.

The questions and the need for actionable answers capable of improving marketing decision-making must always be the foundation for marketing analytics. It is the need specifications of the marketing manager upon which the parameters for analysis are established – including the required variables and their measures, data sources, valuable metrics, and the selected statistical techniques. Figure 12.1 captures the questions marketing managers pose and their relationship to different types of statistical analysis.

In the era of Industry 4.0 and marketing convergence, we see a shift from ad hoc marketing analytics systems to more powerful, yet specialized SaaS platforms, and now to comprehensive platforms capable of managing the volume, complexity, and interdependence demands typical for marketing analytics. These are known as marketing value management systems (MVMSs).

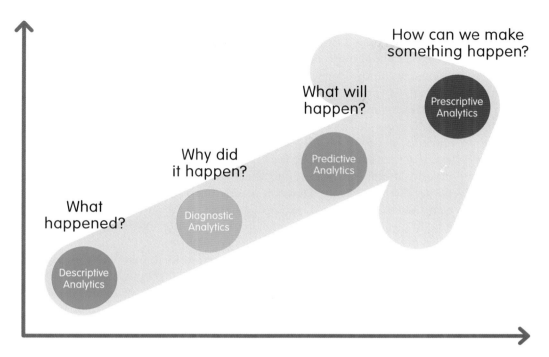

FIGURE 12.1   How Marketers Use Information Gleaned from Marketing Analytics

Source: Based on Benabderrahmane (2017)

With an MVMS, a company can construct a comprehensive performance assessment that measures the value it has created, its productivity in value creation, and the potential and probability for creating value in the future, both short- and long-term. They can also support advanced analytics like predictive modeling to gauge probable outcomes for a variety of marketing situations. The opening vignette shows how the British multinational alcoholic beverage giant, Diageo, benefits from its MVMS.

OPENING VIGNETTE

DIAGEO – MANAGING VALUE AND DRIVING MARKETING PERFORMANCE WORLDWIDE

There are 200 brands in Diageo's brand portfolio. Some are established, legacy brands like Guinness and Johnny Walker, while others are newer like Deleon tequila. Some are market share juggernauts while others are niche brands. Some are sold globally

(Continued)

across the 180 countries where Diageo has a market presence, while others are local brands. In fact, Diageo's brand portfolio addresses consumer demand in every category of alcoholic beverage at almost every price point.

With such diversity in products, brands, and target markets, it's no wonder that Diageo follows different marketing strategies depending upon the situation. In developed markets, it promotes its premium, high-priced, legacy and prestige brands. In emerging markets, it offers brands at affordable prices with the objective of developing primary demand for alcoholic beverages. All in all, the company manages thousands of unique offers. Because of the sheer number of strategic and tactical marketing decisions this represents, Diageo's leadership worried that its marketing budget wasn't as productive as it could be. Enter Catalyst, an MVMS created by Boston Consulting Group (BCG) and customized for Diageo's marketing analytics needs across its geographic markets and brand portfolio (Tesseras, 2018).

BCG explains that Catalyst is a cloud-based software platform that uses the power of data and analytics to help "marketing leaders derive meaningful insights, optimize marketing decisions, and drive winning results from a robust set of business data" (BCG, n.d.). With an easy-to-use interface, Catalyst enables the average marketing professional to take complex data and identify how to optimize brand performance, budget allocations, marketing mix designs, and campaign effectiveness – all without the help of a data scientist!

Some companies invest in building a proprietary MVMS, but platforms like Catalyst are based on a core platform that is customizable. The result is a faster and less expensive route to implementing an MVMS with state-of-the-art features, including automated data management, data connectors to pull data from multiple data sources, analytics and modeling capabilities, visualization engine, communications pipeline to push insights to the relevant teams, and project management features. Perhaps best of all, the interface is fast, intuitive, and easy to use, encouraging utilization across the marketing function. At Diageo, Catalyst is being used by 1,200 marketers across 55 countries to make strategic and planning decisions like the right budget for each brand based on potential profitability (Parsons, 2017b). Diageo's goal is to enable any marketing employee who is involved in allocating budget in marketing investments to deliver the best possible result. The marketing managers can demonstrate return on investment, justify expenditures on activities that drive growth, and eliminate spending that doesn't drive the desired impact.

Diageo says the investment it made in Catalyst is paying off. It's already seen improvements in the rate of return on its marketing investments (Tesseras, 2018). Since launching the MVMS, across Diageo's brand portfolio, net sales are up nearly 2%. That may not sound like much, but it equates to an increase of more than $140 million in net sales! Operating profits increased 6.1%, a net gain of nearly $175 million. Johnnie Walker's net sales are up by 7%; Baileys by 6%; Tanqueray by 16%; and Guinness by 4% (Tesseras, 2018).

Andrew Geoghegan, Diageo's Global Consumer Planning Director, also credits Catalyst for the company's recognition at the 2018 IPA Effectiveness Awards, a prestigious award competition to recognize exceptional marketing effectiveness. Diageo landed three IPAs in 2018: one recognizing the company for best dedication to marketing excellence and two recognizing exceptional brand campaign effectiveness (one for Guinness' *Made of More* campaign and the other for Baileys' *Don't Mind If I Baileys* campaign). Commenting on his excitement with the IPA recognition, Geoghegan said, "At Diageo we are obsessed with making every dollar, pound and rupee we spend count, and believe that data and analytics can work in tandem with great creativity to drive world class advertising. We're proud that the work we have done with our marketing effectiveness tool Catalyst makes marketing effectiveness part of the day jobs of all 1200 of our marketers around the world" (Diageo, 2018).

MAKING ANALYTICS A TOP PRIORITY FOR MARKETERS

Historically, marketing has been one of the least measured functions in business. It accounts for substantial expenses for the organization because of the investments necessary to drive innovation, cover the cost of marketing communications, and other related expenses. While other functions were expected to be accountable for expenditures and their return on investment, marketing was not. Why? For one, marketing has long been viewed as part art, part science. The creativity that brings marketing to life lends itself to qualitative assessments or even simple heuristics! The other excuse has been the difficulty in tying specific marketing activities with quantifiable outcomes to assess marketing performance. Marketing performance is the effectiveness and efficiency with which an organization's marketing activities achieve marketing objectives (Gao, 2010). Efficiency can be thought of as doing things right, while effectiveness refers to doing the right things (Drucker, 1963).

Fortunately, marketers are increasingly turning to marketing analytics and MVMSs to measure marketing performance, inform marketing planning, determine how budgets and other resources are best allocated to meet objectives, and anticipate trends that could impact marketing success in the long term. A measure is a number derived from taking a measurement. A metric is a calculation using measures. Both are data inputs used in marketing analytics. Insights derived from data and analytics inform marketing actions that influence the management of marketing's sources of value. This is the logic behind addressing marketing analytics from the perspective of *managing value*.

The results of the 2019 CMO Survey, a study of more than 2,000 Chief Marketing Officers representing a cross-section of industry sectors and firm size, suggest that the measurement imperative is driving an increase in the use of marketing analytics (Moorman, 2019). Participants reported using marketing analytics to guide their decisions in 43% of marketing projects on average. Given the power of analytical tools, the use of analytics to optimize marketing in less than half of marketing decisions may seem disappointing. But five years ago, only 29% of marketing project decisions were driven by marketing analytics.

Why the shift among marketers? We can sum it up in one word: necessity. Though marketing is still viewed as a mix of art and science, and establishing marketing attribution can still be difficult, today's CEOs, CFOs, and investors are demanding marketing accountability. Marketing attribution refers to the assessment of the relative value or return on investment of the marketing tactics, media, and touchpoints in achieving marketing objectives such as converting prospects to customers.

Necessity also stems from the impact of Industry 4.0 technologies on marketing functions and the organization's need to manage it. PwC's report *Industry 4.0: Building the Digital Enterprise* presents the findings of their Industry 4.0 survey of more than 2,000 executives across 26 countries, representing nine major industrial sectors (Geissbauer, Vedso and Schrauf, 2016). Participants anticipate that these technologies will create new revenue sources, cost savings, and efficiencies as they enable 1) digitization of

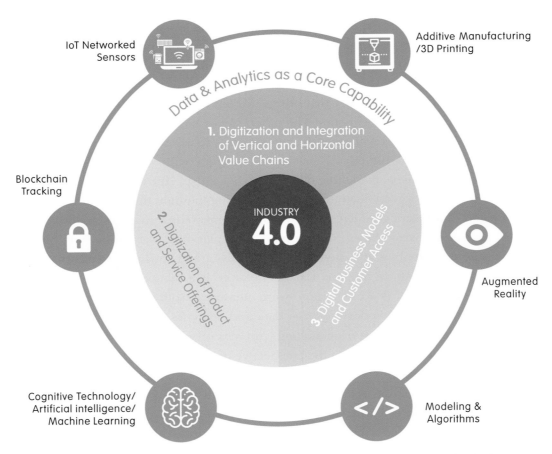

FIGURE 12.2   Data Analytics as Must-Have Organizational Capability to Achieve Digitization Benefits of Industry 4.0

Source: Geissbauer, Vedso and Schrauf (2016)

functions throughout the value chain, 2) digitization of products and other elements of the marketing mix, and 3) spurn new business models. But importantly, because data acts as both fuel and by-product of Industry 4.0, data science as an organizational competence will be an essential prerequisite for achieving the benefits of digitization. The implication: only those organizations with mastery of data science and analytics will be able to fully transform the capabilities, benefits, and outputs of Industry 4.0 technologies into smart operations, smart marketing, and disruptive business models (Geissbauer et al., 2016). Figure 12.2 illustrates the central role of data analytics mediating the relationship between Industry 4.0 data and the benefits of digitization made possible by Industry 4.0.

CHALLENGES REMAIN

Despite the progress, marketers still face substantial challenges when it comes to measuring marketing performance and implementing MVMSs. According to the 2019 CMO Survey results, only 36.4% of the participants said they have defined quantitative measures to assess relevant variables and marketing outcomes (Moorman, 2019). More than half the CMOs said they use qualitative heuristics like their gut intuition or impressions of sentiment from influencers such as salespeople, colleagues, and customers, and 12.9% admitted they don't assess marketing outcomes at all. A higher percentage of B2B firms used qualitative heuristics while a higher percentage of B2C firms had defined quantitative measures. The lack of defined measures for marketing metrics may be in part tied to the CMOs' perception of the relative contribution of marketing analytics to marketing performance outcomes. On average, the CMOs attributed just 4% of marketing performance outcomes to the application of marketing analytics. Nearly 19% of B2B CMOs and 15% of B2C CMOs said they had not been able to show the impact of marketing analytics on performance outcomes. According to McKinsey's DataMatics study (Bauer, Fiedler, Jacobs and Spillecke, 2016), this belief is unfounded. The study showed that organizations in the top quartile of analytics performance were 20 times better at attracting new customers and more than five times better at retaining existing ones than firms in the bottom quartile. A possible explanation is failure to connect analytics insights to the decision-makers who need them. Data scientists create impressive models but may not effectively translate the results into actionable findings that are easily understood by marketing managers.

MANAGING VALUE WITH MARKETING ANALYTICS

Marketers need answers to a seemingly endless set of questions, many of which may seem downright puzzling or impossible to answer. At a systemic level, we need to know:

1. What is happening in the market environment that might inform our understanding of buyer behavior, competitive threats, or potential opportunities for future strategies?

2. How are our current marketing activities performing relative to marketing strategy and objectives?

3. Are we innovating, building relationships, investing in brand equity, and other activities that will contribute to future success?

The answers become assets used for a variety of purposes, such as 1) assessing and reporting performance to stakeholder groups, including employees, investors, customers, publicists, the general public, regulators, and partners; 2) contributing to strategic anticipation; 3) optimizing the design of the marketing mix given parameters like target market characteristics; and 4) improving internal processes used in delivering the customer value proposition and electing trade-offs when resources are limited.

Marketers may report on findings in a range of publications such as annual reports, press releases, white papers, and sales presentations. Depending upon the stakeholder group and objective, publishing performance data could serve to influence brand reputation, encourage publicity in news organizations, or fulfill accountability requirements to investors and regulators.

Strategic anticipation is the ability of an organizations to recognize, understand and interpret, and then respond to future trends and uncertainties (Reilly, 2016). Brands are at a competitive advantage when they have strategic anticipation. As we learned in Chapter 5, responding to or avoiding threats and identifying opportunities to leverage, such as being the first to seize a new market, contribute to success in marketing strategy. Consider this quote: "Today's business landscape is characterized by an unprecedented, accelerating and complex mix of risks and opportunities. Your entire market can be disrupted in a short time by innumerable factors, be it a new technology or a sudden lack of natural resources. New markets are emerging rapidly due to megatrends such as population growth, resource scarcity or global health risks. Meanwhile, consumers and investors are better informed than ever before" (Deloitte, 2017a).

Marketing mix optimization (MMO) is another marketing analytics application. Basically, MMO is a statistical approach (sometimes called marketing mix modeling or MMM) to marketing attribution – identifying which elements of the marketing mix are working more or less effectively, estimating the value of investments in those elements, and then adjusting how marketing budgets are spent to optimize the results. It helps answer the questions: 1) What variables are driving performance? 2) What is their relative impact? 3) How does the return on investment compare for different line items in the marketing budget (for instance, advertising vs. sales promotions)? 4) What is the optimal allocation of budget funds? It also helps marketing managers consider "what-if" scenarios and the likely consequences of various decisions, rather than relying on intuition.

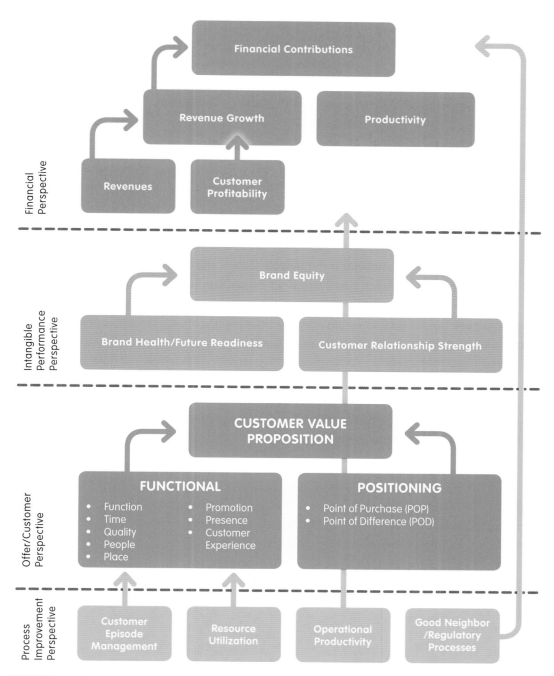

FIGURE 12.3   Value Management Strategy Map

Source: Inspired by the Balanced Scorecard Strategy Map, Exhibit 2, in Kaplan and Norton (2001)

Process improvements can be identified using analytics, enabling marketers to reduce costs, improve customer experience across various episodes, and better deliver value across the activities underlying the marketing mix. When processes are targeted for improvement, the focus is on measuring costs, opportunities to reduce waste and increase revenues, and operational performance (Du Toit, Engelhardt, Sager and Fruechtl, 2018).

IMPACT OF MARKETING ANALYTICS ON PERFORMANCE

A study of how brands use marketing metrics found that the top performing organizations measured several key performance indicators (KPIs), defined as "the quantifiable measures an organization uses to determine how well it meets its declared operational and strategic goals" (Schrage and Kiron, 2018), including customer satisfaction, share of wallet, and margin, among others. These KPIs informed decisions on targeting, brand positioning, price strategy, and budget allocation (Strategy&, 2005). Research on the impact marketing analytics contributes to profitability related an organization's use metric, a measure of the number of applications an organization uses marketing analytics to inform, to its profitability. The average use metric was 2.9 applications from a list, including customer acquisition and retention, segmentation, marketing mix optimization, promotion strategy, branding strategy, pricing strategy, multichannel strategy, product strategy, and new product development (Ariker, Diaz, Moorman and Westover, 2015). The results found that applying marketing analytics approaches to one additional application yielded a .39% increase in profits and a .61% improvement in ROI. Despite the value, less than 40% of organizations studied used analytics to improve these marketing activities.

MAPPING THE VALUE PERSPECTIVES

A strategy map operationalizes the various marketing value perspectives so that measures and metrics can be identified and defined for use in the organization's marketing analytics approach. An example is shown in Figure 12.3.

Adapted from Kaplan and Norton's Balanced Scorecard Strategy Map (Kaplan and Norton, 1992), the value management strategy map identifies the value perspectives of marketing strategy: financial performance (revenues and costs), intangible performance, customer value proposition and the marketing mix, and internal processes for delivering the value proposition. For each perspective, relevant measures and metrics can then be identified for use in a balanced scorecard. A balanced scorecard clearly defines the financial and non-financial measures of success and the long-term growth and short-term productivity targets for performance (Kaplan and Norton, 1992).

Table 12.1 demonstrates measures and metrics that relate to each value perspective in Figure 12.3.

TABLE 12.1   Mapping Value Perspectives to Marketing Measures and Metrics

Perspective	Question Addressed	Measures/Metrics
Financial	Are the marketing strategies producing financial gains?	Sales growth Revenue growth Profitability
Intangible performance	Are marketing activities supporting sustainable success through brand-building, customer relationship management, and strategic anticipation to support future innovation?	Brand equity Customer lifetime value Customer loyalty Innovation readiness Brand awareness Brand image Organizational health
Customer/marketing mix	Are marketing strategies and tactics meeting the needs of the target market, differentiating the brand from competition, and driving market share, sales, and margin?	Customer satisfaction Customer retention Conversion rate Competitive position Perceived value contribution Segment performance
Process improvement	Is the company improving processes to improve service quality, achieve cost efficiencies, and better utilize resources in its delivery of the value proposition?	Time to complete process Error rate/service failure rate Service recovery rate Cost per episode Efficiencies gained through design-to-cost Inventory management

PERSPECTIVES AFFECTING THE SELECTION OF METRICS TO MEASURE

Several perspectives should be considered when selecting the set of metrics to be measured to evaluate performance and its parameters in order to produce a comprehensive evaluation. These are time orientation, duration of the measurement period, and financial versus non-financial assessments.

TIME ORIENTATION

This perspective refers to the lessons marketers can learn by embracing past thinking, present thinking, and forward thinking. The past-thinking perspective looks backward at the outcomes of previously implemented marketing activities (i.e., ex-post analysis).

These metrics are known as lag indicators because they measure the current situation but do not influence it. Market share and return on marketing investment (ROMI) are examples. The present-thinking perspective requires metrics that can guide marketing decisions necessary to create value in the current market setting, meeting customer needs and doing so better than the competition (i.e., ex-durante analysis). We may use a variety of data and analytics to plan and correct marketing strategies, whether to segment and target markets, position relative to competitors, optimize the value customers perceive in the offer, measure brand associations affecting brand equity, or identify variables with the most potential to drive a lift in sales, revenue, and profitability. The forward-thinking perspective is concerned with measuring the ability to perform successfully in the future (i.e., ex-ante analysis). For instance, measures of strategic anticipation, innovativeness, and resources could indicate the likelihood of future success. Sometimes, these are called health metrics. This quote sums up their purpose: "There's nothing wrong with good accounting results and rising share prices, but they don't necessarily indicate whether a company is fundamentally healthy, in the sense of being able to sustain its current performance and to build profitable businesses in the future" (Dobbs and Koller, 2015). Essentially, health metrics supplement those for historical performance by providing a glimpse into the future (Dobbs and Koller, 2015).

MEASUREMENT DURATION

The relative time frame within which a variable is measured can be short-term (<1 year), medium-term (1–5 years), or long-term (>5 years) (Dobbs and Koller, 2015). Short-term metrics are especially useful for gauging responsiveness to changes in marketing decisions and activities such as sales promotions and price adjustments. Medium-term metrics are particularly valuable for assessing strategic marketing activities such as brand-building, establishing a pipeline for new product launches, and developing the strength of customer relationships. Long-term metrics assess such items as the sustainability of a brand's competitive advantage and success, identifying and exploiting new areas of growth through market development or product innovations (Dobbs and Koller, 2015). Environmental changes in the economy, population characteristics, cultural and social patterns, and so on can also be viewed by relative duration.

FINANCIAL AND NON-FINANCIAL

Best practices encourage the use of both financial and non-financial performance measures to ensure the performance assessment captures all the primary areas of value the marketing team seeks to manage. Financial metrics like growth in revenues, profitability, and return on marketing investment are standard lag indicators of marketing performance. But they can't tell the whole story. For instance, a brand may have strong financial performance following a tactical series of sales featuring discounted prices that incentivized short-term demand.

But what if the deep discounts created brand associations that the brand quality was in decline such that future sales volumes might suffer? What if inventory is so depleted that the brand is unable to meet demand until new stock arrives, encouraging former customers to switch to a competitor? Using only financial measures limits the ability to understand what causes underlie performance measures.

A FRAMEWORK FOR MANAGING VALUE WITH AN MVMS

Thus far, we've primarily focused on the advantage of managing value with marketing metrics and analytics and examples of the types of metrics available. Big data brings with it the ability to automate analytics and make marketing adjustments based on real-time results, allowing for data transparency and for data and analytic insights to be shared by marketing partners. Marketing organizations therefore benefit from the functional scope and scale of enterprise analytics platforms. As introduced earlier in the chapter, we call these marketing value management systems. It's important to note that in MarTech stacks, organizations will frequently partner with several vendors who are involved in some way with the organization's marketing analytics. For example, analytics may be generated to demonstrate the performance specific to various marketing software solutions in the MarTech stack such as Google Analytics, Salesforce CRM analytics, Facebook analytics, and so on. These are valuable but limited to informing decisions relative to the performance of marketing activities in that specific MarTech software service. A fully developed MVMS is capable of pulling data from a variety of sources (called data ingestion), cleaning data to ensure quality and compatibility, transforming data to create new variables (called data wrangling), displaying an easy-to-use graphical interface with which a comprehensive menu of analytical options are presented, calculating complex measures quickly even with millions of data points, providing visualization to enhance the readability, usability, and interpretation of reports, and managing workflow tasks across the marketing team.

Figure 12.4 illustrates the 6D MVMS Process Model, identifying each step in the process.

STEP 1: SPECIFY DATA NEEDS AND DEFINITIONS

In "The art of performance management", BCG recommends taking a strategic and holistic approach (Ghesquieres et al., 2017). The measures and metrics need to be defined using what BCG refers to as a "single source of truth" (Ghesquieres et al., 2017). In other words, the meaning of each variable to be measured and the process for calculating each metric will be standardized across the organization. The result is sometimes called a universal data taxonomy or data dictionary. Standardization helps to ensure accuracy in how results are interpreted and applied over time, across marketing roles, and regardless of the stakeholder group.

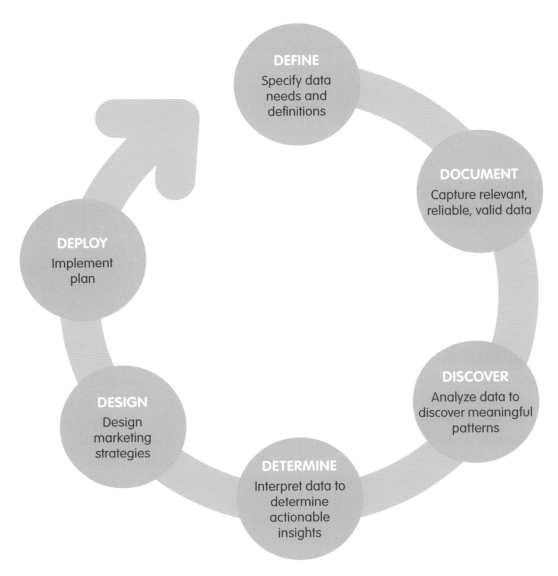

FIGURE 12.4   The 6D MVMS Process Model

Source: Inspired by Ghesquieres, Kotzen, Nolan, Rodt, Roos and Tucker (2017)

STEP 2: CAPTURE RELEVANT, RELIABLE, VALID DATA

Data must be collected for the required variables and refined for use in the MVMS. Data may be purchased from third-party sources and/or generated internally. For example, organizations can buy census data from companies like Experian, panel data on shopping patterns and media usage from companies like Nielsen, and digital footprint data captured from cookies as people use the Internet.

STEP 3: ANALYZE DATA TO DISCOVER RELIABLE PATTERNS

Measuring and analyzing data simply because it's available and feasible won't facilitate useful and actionable marketing insights. In fact, it could even be detrimental, resulting in mounds of information that overwhelm marketing decision-makers – a dreaded condition known as analysis paralysis. The analysis should be driven by the questions posed by marketing managers for specific applications (Bauer et al., 2016). The system and its metrics should stem from the need for specific information, how marketing will act upon or use the information, the appropriate metrics given what information is needed, and how it will be used (Ghesquieres et al., 2017). Figure 12.5 summarizes the relationship between questions and analytics. Table 12.2 defines some of the most common analytical techniques (Waite, 2009).

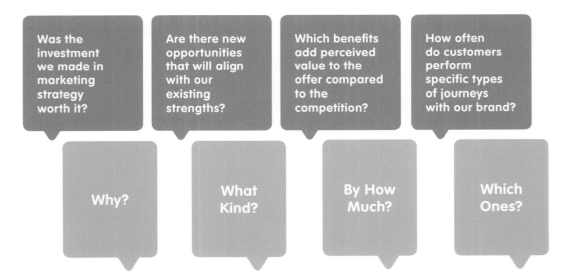

FIGURE 12.5   Questions Driving Marketing Analytics

TABLE 12.2   Analytical Techniques

Technique	Questions Answered
Optimization models	How do we do things better? What is the best decision given a complex situation?
Predictive modeling	What will happen next? How will the market respond?
Forecasting	What if these trends continue? How much is needed? When will it be needed?
Statistical analyses (e.g., cluster analysis, discriminant analysis, regression analysis)	What is the relationship between variables? How can we classify data in meaningful ways? How can we explain what has happened? What is the value of a customer segment?
Reporting	Where do we stand on KPIs?

STEP 4: INTERPRET DATA TO DETERMINE ACTIONABLE INSIGHTS

The goal of a MVMS is to generate marketing intelligence. In so doing, the system itself becomes an asset for creating value. The implications are reported to the relevant decision-makers for use in designing or changing marketing activities.

STEP 5: DESIGN MARKETING STRATEGIES

The findings should be applied to the relevant marketing decisions. Thomas Edison explained, "The value of an idea lies in the using of it".[1] Jennifer Belissent, a principal analyst at Forrester, sums it up like this: "Your data is worth nothing unless you – or someone you do business with – use the data to derive value. The formula remains simple: Data + Use = Value" (Belissent, 2018).

STEP 6: IMPLEMENT PLAN

The impact of marketing analytics is experienced after the marketing activities are implemented. Some of the value gained in terms of performance gains and cost reductions is exemplified in Table 12.3.

TABLE 12.3   Impact of Marketing Analytics on Marketing Applications

Application	Increase on Sales Impact – %	Application	Cost Reduction Impact
Product assortment optimization	2%	Predictive maintenance	20–50% of service costs
Cross-sell/up-sell	2%	Marketing spend effectiveness	5–10% cost reduction
Price optimization	2%	Demand planning	20–30% of warehousing costs
Ad optimization	1.5%	Supply chain optimization	10–30% of logistics costs
Retail shelf space optimization	1.5%	Workforce planning	10–20% of service costs

Exhibit from 'The consumer decision journey', June 2009, *McKinsey Quarterly*: www.mckinsey.com. Copyright © 2019 McKinsey & Company. All rights reserved. Reprinted with permission.

Does analytics sound exciting to you? Read the Marketing Analyst Job Description provided at the end of the chapter to learn more about the responsibilities of analysts.

---

[1]Retrieved from www.brainyquote.com/quotes/thomas_a_edison_136633 (accessed 2 April 2019).

INDUSTRY 4.0 CONTRIBUTIONS TO MARKETING ANALYTICS AND MVMS

The Industry 4.0 technologies have several implications for marketing analytics and MVMSs. Figure 12.6 illustrates the value associated with advanced analytics applications.

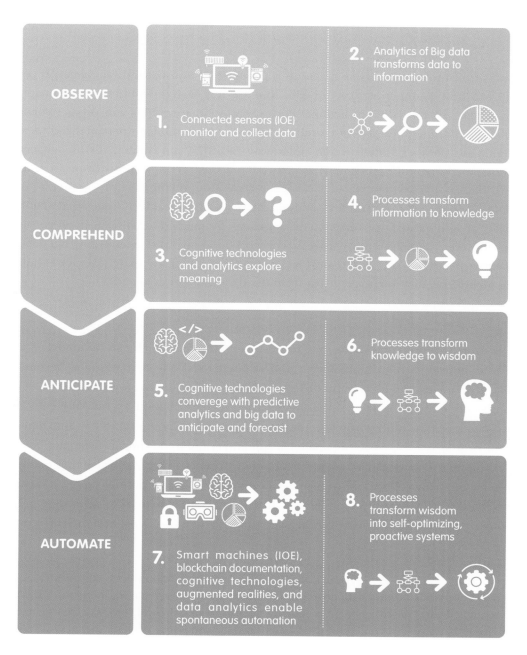

OBSERVE

1. Connected sensors (IOE) monitor and collect data
2. Analytics of Big data transforms data to information

COMPREHEND

3. Cognitive technologies and analytics explore meaning
4. Processes transform information to knowledge

ANTICIPATE

5. Cognitive technologies converege with predictive analytics and big data to anticipate and forecast
6. Processes transform knowledge to wisdom

AUTOMATE

7. Smart machines (IOE), blockchain documentation, cognitive technologies, augmented realities, and data analytics enable spontaneous automation
8. Processes transform wisdom into self-optimizing, proactive systems

FIGURE 12.6   Based on Industry 4.0 Roadmap for Effective MVMSs

Let's take a brief look at how technology can impact marketing analytics.

BIG DATA AND ANALYTICS

Access to data and analytics capabilities are at the heart of MVMSs. However, data sets with millions of variables and data points can present a challenge. Marketing analysts must identify the relevant variables and reliable data sets to ensure valuable results.

COGNITIVE TECHNOLOGIES

Cognitive technologies such as machine learning (ML) and natural language processing (NLP) can find complex patterns in data that are not easily identifiable by humans and use the patterns to make predictions. For example, organizations can predict consumer purchases, recognize fraudulent credit card activity, and automate personalized targeting of digital ads (Renner, Cotteleer and Holdowsky, 2018). When combined with sensors and cameras, tracking and reporting of structured and unstructured information in real-time is possible. Cognitive-language technologies include natural language processing, semantic computing, and sentiment and text analysis. They are statistical techniques that enable the analysis of written and spoken human languages by machine. Artificial intelligence and automation can automate entire processes or workflows involved in analyzing big data sets. Machine learning is a set of statistical techniques that automate analytical model-building using algorithms that iteratively learn from the data (Renner et al., 2018).

INTERNET OF EVERYTHING (IOE)

IoE[2] sensors capture continuous, real-time streams of data which can be analyzed at the sensor point using artificial intelligence and/or piped to an off-site platform to become part of a larger data set and used in predictive analytics and modeling. IoE means having more touch points to acquire data, gathering a variety of information by tracking customers, which facilitates the ability of marketing analytics to identify the types of campaigns that customers are most responsive to, and what conditions and trends impact customer behavior. For example, IoE sensors can collect data about product usage. Consider that connected coffee makers can collect and transmit data about how many pots of coffee a customer brews per day. That data can then be used in a segmentation analysis to determine persona characteristics among users that can be used to identify similar prospects the coffee maker

---

[2]Recall that IoT is defined as "a suite of technologies and applications that equip devices and locations to generate all kinds of information – and to connect those devices and locations for instant data analysis and, ideally, 'smart' action. Conceptually, the IoT implies physical objects being able to utilize the Internet backbone to communicate data about their condition, position, or other attributes", according to Deloitte (2018b).

manufacturer can target for acquisition, identify high-value segments for a partner coffee brand to target, or compare the time of day when customers are brewing coffee and identify possible media buys for advertising in similar time slots. For a brand like Keurig that sells both coffee makers and coffee pods, it can even see whether variations in the amount of coffee brewed corresponds to Keurig's sales volume. This could alert Keurig to competitive threats, customer switching behaviors, and estimates of customer loyalty.

AUGMENTED REALITY

Augmented reality can contribute to marketing analytics as a data source and as a user interface to improve how employees who rely on marketing metrics benefit from analytics. Much like IoE, augmented reality devices and applications can capture data on user behaviors which can be integrated to complement data on other relevant variables for analysis. For example, AR applications could be used to simulate customer experiences, capturing data for use in other analyses. Perhaps a more exciting contribution is the use of augmented reality apps to relay metrics in real-time to marketing employees at the moment they are needed to guide interactions with customers, suppliers, salespeople, and so on. For example, Avon wanted to find a more efficient and faster way to deliver product performance metrics to salespeople working the floor in its retail stores in Brazil. Avon's MDSS was time-consuming, clunky, only accessible from computers behind the sales floor, and limited in the value of its reports. MicroStrategy, a provider of custom mobile marketing software solutions and an enterprise analytics platform, created a custom AR application that Avon's staff can use with a tablet on the sales floor. When they point the tablet (called the Avon Beauty Display) at a product, the app's augmented reality dashboard instantly shows product details, inventory, and sales metrics in real-time (Frederick, 2018).

While Industry 4.0 technologies are incredibly exciting for the realm of marketing analytics, the sheer amount of data involved requires an MVMS platform to manage the collection, integration, housing, analysis, visualization, and reporting (Grover, 2018).

WHEN MVMSs DON'T PRODUCE ACTIONABLE ANSWERS

There are several reasons behind ineffective MVMSs, but three of the major reasons are 1) failure to map the metrics to the information's purpose, 2) ill-defined data definitions, and 3) satisficing on system functionality to retrofit existing systems. Let's take a brief look at these problems. It's tempting to cull a list of popular marketing metrics and plow forward. But the chosen metrics should map to the information needed to meet objectives. Without mapping metrics by needs and objectives, marketers may end up with a mass of metrics and statistics, all useless, irrelevant, or disconnected from marketing activities. Everyone must know what the data means and adopt one definition of the variables. One executive put it this way: "our leadership team spends so much time trying to make sense of the data and debating whether it is right that we never get around to exploring what it really means for the business!" (Ghesquieres et al., 2017). Lastly, many organizations develop measurement platforms and databases for different divisions or purposes, resulting in a hodgepodge of legacy systems. The frustration can be heard in this quote: "We've stitched together our performance management system on blood, sweat, and Excel. It's a nightmare" (Ghesquieres et al., 2017). In today's data-driven environment, the systems can be dysfunctional, suffering from challenges that include, but are not limited to, a lack of shared and standardized definitions of variables, an inability to merge and analyze data across systems, and difficulties in accessing reports for decision-makers across marketing functions (Ghesquieres et al., 2017).

CASE STUDY

MARKETING ANALYST JOB DESCRIPTION SAMPLE (OCULUS, N.D.)

Curious about what the role of marketing analyst might look like? This is how a company described the job of a marketing analyst in a recent job posting.

> The AR/VR organization includes products, AR and VR software and content, and research and development labs. We are looking to form a new team called AR/VR Market Analytics to create a customer strategy across these product groups. This team will help us to scale our AE/VR technology for the next billion people and beyond, by developing and creating essential insights. You will use your understanding of customer segments and work closely with product and marketing leadership to influence key strategic decisions. You will need to have the ability to identify and prioritize strategic opportunities and collaborate well with others in order to design and execute ambiguous and complex projects, compare data from various sources and provide recommendations that influence our long-term product roadmaps.

CASE STUDY

MCKINSEY'S ASSESSMENT OF CUSTOMER LOYALTY (COURT, ELZINGA, FINNEMAN AND PERREY, 2017)

The ease of searching and comparing product information online has reduced the customer loyalty brands previously enjoyed. To understand the impact of declining loyalty, McKinsey analysts studied loyalty patterns of 125,000 consumers for 30 product categories and 350 brands. The findings were startling. Of the 30 categories in the study, only three product categories were driven by brand loyalty – mobile phone carrier, auto insurance provider, and investment services. In the other product categories (including computing devices, cosmetics, consumer-packaged goods, apparel, and automobiles), consumers compared competing offers to get the best value and were prone to switch among brands (Court et al., 2017).

The study also identified three segments of consumers: 1) loyalists, 2) vulnerable repurchasers, and 3) switchers. Loyalists are faithful to the last brand they purchased without considering other choices, but only 13% of the consumers were loyalists. Vulnerable repurchasers (29% of consumers) shop around and consider other brands, but typically return to a favorite brand. Switchers purchase from other brands, driven by the offer, and made up 58% of consumers.

A result with clear implications for marketing strategy is that brands in a consumer's initial consideration set were more than twice as likely to be purchased as brands considered later in the purchase journey. Overall, 69% of the brands purchased by consumers who switched brands were part of their initial consideration set when they started shopping. The researchers created a metric called the customer growth indicator (CGI), which assesses the consideration a brand is able to command. A regression analysis demonstrated that CGI explains 60% to 80% of the variation in sales growth from one purchase to the next. This means that marketing efforts to drive brand recall and image will improve sales growth. The metric will be a useful brand health indicator as well (Court et al., 2017).

PRME

ASSESSING PERFORMANCE AND IMPACT FOR THE SDGS

When the United Nations launched the 17 Sustainable Development Goals (SDGs; also known as the Global Goals) in 2015, the targets for each goal seemed more aspirational than attainable. How well are the SDGs being met overall? The Bill and Melinda Gates Foundation studies this question annually and publishes a report, *The Stories Behind the Data*, of SDG goal targets and key performance indicators on its Goalkeepers website (see https://datareport.goalkeepers.org/). For example, for SDG 1: No Poverty, the most recent report demonstrates a decline in the percentage of the world's population living in extreme poverty, from 35% in 1990 to 9% in 2016 (Gates and Gates, 2017).

There's no doubt that brand commitments to the Global Goals are a critical component of success. The UN worked with partners to develop a guide to facilitate business involvement and commitments (*SDG Compass* – United Nations, 2015) and report on

(Continued)

progress annually (*UN Global Compact Progress Report* – United Nations, 2018). More companies are using the Global Goals to drive marketing strategy. Achieving the SDGs requires support from the business community to close the funding gap of $2.5 trillion per year, or about an expected 50% of the total $115 trillion cost of funding the goals (Eccles and Karbassi, 2018).

The *UN Global Compact Progress Report* surveyed 1,130 companies from 100 countries across six continents about their sustainability initiatives and their impact on achieving the Global Goals. Table 12.4 highlights the percentage of companies prioritizing each SDG, the percentage of companies reporting they make a positive impact toward the goal, and the percentage of companies reporting that they market products that facilitate goal achievement (United Nations, 2018). Exemplar measures and metrics for assessing impact are also included.

TABLE 12.4   Company Contributions to the Global Goals

Goal	% Prioritizing Goal	% + Impact	% Marketing-Related Products	Examples of Indicator Measures
01 No Poverty	28	45	33	• # of quality jobs increased for marginalized groups • Average annual income of target population • Average cost savings resulting from access to affordable goods and services • Ratios of standard entry level wage compared to local minimum wage
02 Zero Hunger	23	53	28	• Agricultural yield improvements • Proportion of rural farming households with land access • % of population unable to consume minimum caloric intake
03 Good Health	62	83	64	• Proportion of workers with access to health services made available or paid for by company • Type of injuries and injury rates, occupational diseases, lost work days, absenteeism
04 Quality Education	48	71	44	• Average investment for childcare provisions per working family • Training and educational programs offered by company, # of participants

Goal	% Prioritizing Goal	% + Impact	% Marketing-Related Products	Examples of Indicator Measures
05 Gender Equality	64	83	55	• Increased access to information and technology for women • Increased female participation in programs to enhance skills • Percentage of new suppliers screened using labor practices criteria • Ratio of basic salary and remuneration of women to men by employee category, by significant locations of operation
06 Clean Water	36	60	39	• # of employees receiving hygiene training • Percentage of facilities adhering to relevant water quality standard(s) • Percentage and total volume of water recycled and reused • Quality level of drinking water
07 Clean Energy	43	63	50	• Organization's energy consumption • Reduction of energy consumption • Amount of energy consumption from renewable energy sources
08 Decent Work and Economic Growth	69	89	65	• Proportion of workers working overtime on a regular basis • Frequency of fatigue-related incidents in the workplace • Return to work and retention rates after parental leave, by gender • Total number and rates of new employee hires and employee turnover by age group, gender, and region
09 Industry Innovation & Infrastructure	53	79	62	• $s invested in significant infrastructure and services • Increased Internet access • Investment in transport with private participation

(Continued)

TABLE 12.4 (Continued)

Goal	% Prioritizing Goal	% + Impact	% Marketing-Related Products	Examples of Indicator Measures
10 Reduced Inequalities	43	72	42	• Ratio of basic salary and remuneration of women to men by employee category, by significant locations of operation • Percentage of total employees by gender and by employee category who received a performance development review • Revenues and growth targets from inclusive business strategies
11 Sustainable Cities and Communities	37	61	49	• # of affordable housing units constructed as a result of initiative • Usage rates of public transport • $s invested in water and sanitation
12 Responsible Consumption/ Production	53	78	61	• Direct greenhouse gas (GHG) emissions • Organization's energy consumption within the organization • Rate of responsible disposal of old products • Materials used by weight or volume
13 Climate Action	48	64	52	• Extent of impact mitigation of environmental damage due to products marketed • Reductions in energy requirements of products and services • Company's renewable energy consumption and production targets • Use of recycled materials
14 Life Below Water	13	31	16	• Total environmental protection expenditures and investments by type • Total # and volume of significant spills • Size and location of all habitat areas protected or restored

Goal	% Prioritizing Goal	% + Impact	% Marketing-Related Products	Examples of Indicator Measures
15 Life on Land	21	42	26	• Total environmental protection expenditures and investments by type • # and type of threatened bird, fish, mammal, and plant species
16 Peace & Justice	28	53	28	• Monetary value of significant fines • # of non-monetary sanctions for non-compliance with environmental laws and regulations • # of grievances about human rights impacts filed, addressed, and resolved • Percentage of new suppliers screened using labor practices criteria • # of discrimination incidents and corrective actions taken
17 Partnerships for the Goals	40	66	40	• Total environmental protection expenditures and investments by type

The *UN Global Compact Progress Report* found that most companies report on their sustainability initiatives in a corporate sustainability report. However, most have not integrated sustainability metrics into their annual financial reports (United Nations, 2018). The report concluded that companies need to make improvements in monitoring and evaluating the results of their sustainability initiatives, including assessing overall impact for society and the organization (United Nations, 2018).

Demonstrating impact is a prerequisite for brands to benefit from consumer affinity for purpose-led brands and also facilitates engagement with other stakeholder groups like investors and employees. It also demonstrates brand commitment by minimizing accusations of "SDG washing". SDG washing refers to organizational activities that positively contribute to one or more SDGs while creating or ignoring negative impact on others (Eccles and Karbassi, 2018).

BENEFITS FOR BRANDS PURSUING GLOBAL GOALS

By improving the evaluation and assessment of activities and outcomes for SDG initiatives, brands can also benefit directly. One study distinguished between

(Continued)

organizational sustainability investments that were material versus immaterial and their relationship to the organization's financial performance. Materiality is the extent to which investments, activities, and strategies are important or relevant to the organization's business model and ability to deliver its value proposition (EY, 2016). In other words, materiality captures alignment between the brand's sustainability activities and its strategies and performance objectives. The researchers created a materiality performance score metric to examine the financial implications of the two types of sustainability investments (Khan, Serafeim and Yoon, 2015). Organizations that focused investments in sustainability activities that were material significantly outperformed those that did not and those that invested in immaterial activities.

ESTABLISHING AN ANALYTICS PLAN FOR ASSESSING SUSTAINABILITY IMPACT

Following the 6D MVMS Process Model can guide organizations through the steps necessary in mapping activities to strategy, establishing targets, and identifying measures and metrics for use in sustainability analytics. The *SDG Compass Guide* is also a useful resource because it explains the 17 SDGs and the targets established for each one and includes an inventory of hundreds of measures and metrics related to each SDG. Examples of these indicators are included in Table 12.4 (United Nations, 2015).

MEASUREMENT FRAMEWORKS FOR ASSESSING SDG IMPACT

Defining which indicators are relevant and how current business metrics align to them, as well as potentially developing additional ones and working out how to measure success against them, can be complex. Marketing analysts may benefit from using existing frameworks as a guide.

One such model is PwC's Total Impact Measurement & Management (TIMM) framework. It assesses total impact as a sum of an organization's impact on society and the environment (as well as tax benefits and the economy). Clients also have access to PwC's Impact Explorer tool, which assesses organizational costs and societal benefits using consistent and comparable units (Beagent and Evison, n.d.). Another framework is EY's Total Value analysis which focuses on assessing the indirect societal impact and direct organizational benefits of material investments in sustainability (EY, 2016).

  Visit **https://study.sagepub.com/tuten** for free additional resources related to this chapter.

CHAPTER SUMMARY

As brands prioritize value management, marketing analytics and performance assessments have become a priority. Analytics also provide information to guide decisions throughout the marketing planning process. Some marketers report a disconnect between assessment measures and metrics and the activities that should follow, but logically planning assessment as it relates to the information needs of the marketing decision-maker closes the gap. It is the need specifications of the marketing manager upon which the parameters for analysis are established – including the required variables and their measures, data sources, valuable metrics, and the selected statistical techniques.

In Chapter 1, we learned that Industry 4.0 technologies are made up of three system spheres: 1) physical, 2) digital, and 3) biological. Machines are the physical sphere. Data and cloud computing are the digital sphere. Sensing, perceiving, and reasoning (activities that are innately human) simulated with artificial intelligence, algorithms, modeling, and machine learning denote the biological sphere. Industry 4.0 triggered a new era in marketing – the era of marketing convergence. In the study of marketing analytics, we can see a clear illustration of convergence as the physical, digital, and biological spheres converge to enable capabilities previously unimaginable. The convergence is the foundation for collecting and storing data via physical devices, cloud computing power for data processing and analysis, and the biological sensing, reasoning, and intuition necessary to build actionable knowledge from data. While Industry 4.0 technologies are incredibly exciting for the realm of marketing analytics, the sheer amount of data involved requires an MVMS to manage the collection, integration, housing, analysis, visualization, and reporting requirements.

REVIEW QUESTIONS

1. How can we distinguish between the meaning of the terms marketing measures, marketing metrics, marketing analytics, and marketing value management systems?

2. Why are marketers increasingly embracing marketing analytics?

3. What are the steps in the 6D MVMS Process Model?

4. How can marketers use a strategy map to tie measures and metrics to their marketing objectives and strategies? What are the perspectives reflected in the strategy map?

5. How do Industry 4.0 technologies contribute to marketing analytics and value management?

KEY TERMS

1. **Analysis paralysis** – a situation in which an analyst or decision-maker is overwhelmed by data, or over-analyzes an issue, resulting in no action being taken.

2. **Balanced scorecard** – the financial and non-financial measures of success and the long-term growth and short-term productivity targets for performance.

3. **Cognitive-language technologies** – statistical techniques that enable the analysis of written and spoken human languages by machine.

4. **Health metric** – metric used to measure the ability for the organization to perform successfully in the future (i.e., ex-ante analysis).

5. **Key performance indicators (KPIs)** – the quantifiable measures an organization uses to determine how well it meets its declared operational and strategic goals.

6. **Lag indicator** – metric or measurement that assesses results of previously implemented activities.

7. **Machine learning** – a set of statistical techniques that automate analytical model-building using algorithms that iteratively learn from the data.

8. **Marketing analytics** – the analysis of data to derive reliable, relevant, and useful information of value in performing the marketing function.

9. **Marketing attribution** – the assessment of the relative value or return on investment of the marketing tactics, media, and touchpoints in achieving marketing objectives such as converting prospects to customers.

10. **Marketing mix optimization (MMO)** – a statistical approach (sometimes called marketing mix modeling or MMM) to marketing attribution, identifying which elements of the marketing mix are working more or less effectively, estimating the value of investments in those elements, and then adjusting how marketing budgets are spent in order to optimize the results.

11. **Marketing performance** – the effectiveness and efficiency with which an organization's marketing activities achieve marketing objectives. Efficiency can be thought of as doing things right, while effectiveness refers to doing the right things.

12. **Marketing value management systems (MVMSs)** – a comprehensive performance assessment system that measures the value it has created, its productivity in value creation, and the potential and probability for creating value in the future, both short- and long-term.

13. **Materiality** – the extent to which investments, activities, and strategies are important or relevant to the organization's business model and ability to deliver its value proposition.

14. **Measure** – a number derived from taking a measurement.

15. **Metric** – a calculation using measures.

16. **SDG washing** – organizational activities that positively contribute to one or more SDGs while creating or ignoring negative impact on others.

17. **Strategic anticipation** – the ability of an organization to recognize, understand and interpret, and then respond to future trends and uncertainties.

18. **Strategy map** – graphic used to operationalize the various marketing value perspectives so that measures and metrics can be identified and defined for use in the organization's marketing analytics approach.

19. **Universal data taxonomy** (or **data dictionary**) – standardization of meaning and measurement of each variable used in marketing analytics.

20. **Use metric** – a measure of the number of applications an organization uses marketing analytics to inform.

References

Aaker, D. (1996). *Building Strong Brands*. London: Simon and Schuster.

Aaker, D. (2013). What is brand equity? *Prophet*, 4 September. Retrieved from www.prophet.com/2013/09/156-what-is-brand-equity-and-why-is-it-valuable/ (accessed 10 June 2019).

Aaker, D. (2014). Need to differentiate? Consider organizational values. *Prophet*, 15 July. Retrieved from www.prophet.com/2014/07/202-need-to-differentiate-consider-organizational-values/ (accessed 27 May 2019).

Aaker, D. (2016). Branding a new offering: The brand relationship spectrum. *Prophet*, 27 July. Retrieved from www.prophet.com/2016/07/270-branding-a-new-offering-the-brand-relationship-spectrum/ (accessed 10 June 2019).

Aaker, J. (1997). Dimensions of brand personality. *Journal of Marketing Research,* 34(3), 347–356.

Abdul-Karim, S. (n.d.). Modern pictograms for Lottie. *AIRBNB Design*. Retrieved from https://airbnb.design/modern-pictograms-for-lottie/ (accessed 10 June 2019).

Accenture (2017) *Dynamic Digital Consumers*. Retrieved from www.accenture.com/pl-pl/_acnmedia/PDF-39/Accenture-PoV-DynamicConsumers.pdf (accessed 27 May 2019).

Acito, F., Day, R.L. and Lee, H. (1987). Evaluation and use of marketing research by decision makers: A behavioral simulation. *Journal of Marketing Research*, 24(2), 187–196.

Active Marketing (n.d.). Market segmentation: You're doing it wrong. Retrieved from www.activemarketing.com/blog/strategy/market-segmentation-youre-doing-it-wrong/ (accessed 27 May 2019).

AdAge (1999a). John Wanamaker. 29 March. Retrieved from https://adage.com/article/special-report-the-advertising-century/john-wanamaker/140185/ (accessed 29 May 2019).

AdAge (1999b). Marion Harper Jr. 29 March. Retrieved from https://adage.com/article/special-report-the-advertising-century/marion-harper-jr/140181/ (accessed 27 May 2019).

AdAge (2017). Coming from Netflix: New toys, merchandise based on its hit TV shows. 8 February. Retrieved from https://adage.com/article/media/netflix-plans-toys-merchandise-based-hit-tv-shows/307906/ (accessed 27 May 2019).

Adamson, A. (2009). Define your brand's purpose, not just its promise. *Forbes*, 11 November. Retrieved from www.forbes.com/2009/11/11/brand-defining-marketing-cmo-network-allen-adamson.html#26d744305109 (accessed 10 June 2019).

Aftab, M., Yuanjian, Q., Kabir, N. and Barua, Z. (2018). Super responsive supply chain: The case of Spanish fast fashion retailer Inditex-Zara. *International Journal of Business and Management*, 13(5), 212.

Ahmed, S.F. (2016). The global cost of electronic waste. *The Atlantic*, 29 September. Retrieved from www.theatlantic.com/technology/archive/2016/09/the-global-cost-of-electronic-waste/502019/ (accessed 27 May 2019).

Airbnb Design (n.d.). Introducing Airbnb Cereal. Retrieved from https://airbnb.design/introducing-airbnb-cereal/ (accessed 10 June 2019).

Alberda, J. and Janssen, R. (2018). How we used blockchain to make supply chains transparent and traceable. *Accenture*, 3 August. Retrieved from www.accenture-insights.nl/en-us/articles/improving-physical-supply-chains-with-blockchain (accessed 29 May 2019).

Ali, S. and Yusuf, Z. (2018). Mapping the smart home market 2018. *Boston Consulting Globe*, 1 October. Retrieved from www.bcg.com/publications/2018/mapping-smart-home-market.aspx (accessed 27 May 2019).

Allocca, L. (2018). Why integrated marketing needs to be the foundation of your B2B strategy. *Forbes*, 16 January. Retrieved from www.forbes.com/sites/forbesagencycouncil/2018/01/16/why-integrated-marketing-needs-to-be-the-foundation-of-your-b2b-strategy/#63ec8da06eff (accessed 29 May 2019).

Almquist, E., Senior, J. and Bloch, N. (2016). The elements of value. *Harvard Business Review*, September. Retrieved from https://hbr.org/2016/09/the-elements-of-value (accessed 23 May 2019).

Alvarez, C. (2009). Is your pricing a dot or a triangle? 8 October. Retrieved from https://web.archive.org/web/20160113084335/http://www.cindyalvarez.com/profitability/is-your-pricing-a-dot-or-a-triangle (accessed 29 May 2019).

Al-Weshah, G.A. and Deacon, J.H. (2009). The role of Marketing Information Systems in responding to external environmental factors: An empirical study of the Jordanian banking industry. *9th Global Conference on Business & Economics*. Retrieved from www.google.com/url?sa=t&rct=j&q=&esrc=s&source=web&cd=5&cad=rja&uact=8&ved=0ahUKEwi-soSTwp3OAhXEwiYKHUz7AL4QFghiMAQ&url=http%3A%2F%2Fwww.gcbe.us%2F9th_GCBE%2Fdata%2FGhazi%2520A.%2520Al-Weshah%2C%2520Jonathan%2520H.%2520Deacon.doc&usg=AFQjCNG8EPP13KlZOjH6N7SJpZjBpGy2Vg&sig2=ktDMSb-vZ0uTBTq4en1Ps1w (accessed 27 May 2019).

American Marketing Association (2013). Definition of marketing. Retrieved from www.ama.org/the-definition-of-marketing/ (accessed 23 May 2019).

American Marketing Association (n.d). Brand, Dictionary. Retrieved from www.ama.org/Pages/Dictionary.aspx?dLetter=B (accessed 23 October 2018).

Amitt, R. and Zott, C. (2010). Business model design: An activity system perspective. *Long Range Planning*, 43(2–3), 216–226.

Amsterdam Wonderland (n.d.). Tony's Chocolonely. 16 June. Retrieved from https://amsterdamwonderland.com/tonys-chocolonely-store/ (accessed 29 May 2019).

Andrivet, M. (2014). Airbnb's consistent rebrand focuses on the sense of belonging to a community. *The Branding Journal*. Retrieved from www.thebrandingjournal.com/2014/07/airbnbs-consistent-rebrand-focuses-sense-belonging-community/ (accessed 3 June 2019).

Angwin, J. and Mattu, S. (2016). Amazon says it puts customers first. But its pricing algorithm doesn't. *Pro Publica*, 20 September. Retrieved from www.propublica.org/article/amazon-says-it-puts-customers-first-but-its-pricing-algorithm-doesn't (accessed 29 May 2019).

Archer, J. (2018). Facial recognition to be used in British supermarkets for the first time. *The Telegraph*, 17 October. Retrieved from www.telegraph.co.uk/technology/2018/10/17/facial-recognition-used-british-supermarkets-first-time/ (accessed 23 May 2019).

Ariker, M., Diaz, A., Moorman, C. and Westover, M. (2015). Quantifying the impact of marketing analytics. *Harvard Business Review*, 5 November. Retrieved from https://hbr.org/2015/11/quantifying-the-impact-of-marketing-analytics (accessed 3 June 2019).

Arnesen, D., Cohen, M. and Obermiller, C. (2012). Customized pricing: Win-win or end run? *Drake Management Review*, 1(2). Retrieved from http://faculty.cbpa.drake.edu/dmr/0102/DMR010204R.pdf (accessed 29 May 2019).

Arnould, E.J. and Mohr, J.J. (2005). Dynamic transformations for base-of-the-pyramid market clusters. *Journal of the Academy of Marketing Science*, 33, 254–274.

Astley, M. (2012). Danone must cut prices to compete with private label brands – analyst. *Dairy Reporter*, 18 October. Retrieved from www.dairyreporter.com/Article/2012/10/19/Danone-must-cut-prices-to-compete-with-private-label-brands-analyst# (accessed 29 May 2019).

Baker, W., Kiewell, D. and Winkler, G. (2014). Using big data to make better pricing decisions. *McKinsey Insights*, June. Retrieved from www.mckinsey.com/business-functions/marketing-and-sales/our-insights/using-big-data-to-make-better-pricing-decisions (accessed 29 May 2019).

Baker, W.L., Marn, M.V. and Zawada, C.C. (2010). Building a better pricing infrastructure. *McKinsey Insights*, August. Retrieved from www.mckinsey.com/business-functions/marketing-and-sales/our-insights/building-a-better-pricing-infrastructure (accessed 29 May 2019).

Balch, O. (2018). Child labour: The true cost of chocolate production. *Raconter*, 20 June. Retrieved from www.raconteur.net/business-innovation/child-labour-cocoa-production (accessed 29 May 2019).

Baldé, C.P., Forti, V., Gray, V., Kuehr, R. and Stegmann, P. (2017). *The Global E-Waste Monitor 2017*. United Nations University (UNU), International Telecommunication Union (ITU) & International Solid Waste Association (ISWA), Bonn/Geneva/Vienna. Retrieved from www.itu.int/en/ITU-D/Climate-Change/Documents/GEM%202017/Global-E-waste%20Monitor%202017%20.pdf (accessed 27 May 2019).

Balmer, J.M.T. and Greyser, S.A. (2006). Integrating corporate identity, corporate branding, corporate communications, corporate image and corporate reputation. *European Journal of Marketing*, 40(7/8), 730–741.

Banks-Louie, S. (2018). Tony's Chocolonely delivers fair-trade, high-growth virtues. *Forbes*, 5 June. Retrieved from www.forbes.com/sites/oracle/2018/06/05/tonys-chocolonely-delivers-on-fair-trade-high-growth-virtues/#6afd2f621223 (accessed 29 May 2019).

Bansal, S., Bruno, P., Denecker, O., Goparaju, M. and Niederkorn, M. (2018). *Global Payments 2018: A Dynamic Industry Continues to Break New Ground*. McKinsey & Company, October. Retrieved from www.mckinsey.com/~/media/McKinsey/Industries/Financial%20Services/Our%20Insights/Global%20payments%20Expansive%20growth%20targeted%20opportunities/Global-payments-map-2018.ashx (accessed 29 May 2019).

Barnett, M. (2016). Battle of the brands: Nike vs. Adidas. *Nielsen Sports*, 8 June. Retrieved from https://nielsensports.com/nike-vs-adidas/ (accessed 29 May 2019).

Barry, J. and Weinstein, A. (2009). Business psychographics revisited: From segmentation theory to successful marketing practice. *Journal of Marketing Management*, 25(3–4), 315–340.

Barton, R., Ishikawa, M., Quiring, K. and Theofilou, B. (2018). *To Affinity and Beyond: From Me to We, the Rise of the Purpose-led Brand*. Accenture. Retrieved from www.accenture.com/_acnmedia/Thought-Leadership-Assets/PDF/Accenture-CompetitiveAgility-GCPR-POV.pdf (accessed 10 June 2019).

Bashford, S. (2017). What the future holds for connected cars in 2017 and beyond. *Campaign*, 30 August. Retrieved from www.campaignlive.co.uk/article/future-holds-connected-cars-2017-beyond/1442835#P2KPDtYbfkU20tYh.99 (accessed 27 May 2019).

Bauer, T., Fiedler, L., Jacobs, J. and Spillecke, D. (2016). The secret to great marketing analytics? Connecting with decision makers. *Forbes*, 6 January. Retrieved from www.forbes.com/sites/mckinsey/2016/01/06/the-secret-to-great-marketing-analytics-connecting-with-decision-makers/#3682bbaa2e9a (accessed 3 June 2019).

BBDO (2001). *Brand Equity Excellence: Brand Equity Review*, Volume 1. Retrieved from http://guvenborca.com/dosyalar/files/Brand_Equity.pdf (accessed 5 November 2018).

BCG (n.d.). The marketing suite. Retrieved from www.bcg.com/en-us/capabilities/marketing-sales/catalyst/marketing.aspx (accessed 3 June 2019).

Beagent, T. and Evison, W. (n.d.). PwC's Impact Explorer: A new tool for measuring and valuing your global impacts. *PwC*. Retrieved from www.pwc.co.uk/services/sustainability-climate-change/total-impact/impact-explorer.html (accessed 3 June 2019).

Bearing Point (2019). *Digital Leaders in UK 2019*. Retrieved from www.bearingpoint.com/en-gb/our-success/digital-leaders/ (accessed 23 May 2019).

Belissent, J. (2018). Your data is worth nothing – unless you use it. *Forrester*, 25 April. Retrieved from https://go.forrester.com/blogs/your-data-is-worth-nothing-unless-you-use-it/ (accessed 3 June 2019).

Bell, K. (2016). What clients want: 3 key aspects of the research reports. *FlexMR*. Retrieved from https://blog.flexmr.net/best-research-reports (accessed 27 May 2019).

Belz, F. and Peattie, K. (2012). *Sustainability Marketing: A Global Perspective*. Chichester: John Wiley and Sons.

Benabderrahmane, S. (2017). What can the Big Data eco-system and data analytics do for e-health? A Smooth Review Study. In I. Rojas and F. Ortuño (eds), *Bioinformatics and Biomedical Engineering*. IWBBIO 2017. Lecture Notes in Computer Science, vol. 10208. Cham: Springer.

Bengtsen, P. and Paddison, L. (2016). Beauty companies and the struggle to source child labour-free mica. *The Guardian*, 28 July. Retrieved from www.theguardian.com/sustainable-business/2016/jul/28/cosmetics-companies-mica-child-labour-beauty-industry-india- (accessed 27 May 2019).

Benmark, G., Klapdor, S., Kullmann, M. and Sundararajan, R. (2017). How retailers can drive profitable growth through dynamic pricing. *McKinsey Insights*, March. Retrieved from www.mckinsey.com/industries/retail/our-insights/how-retailers-can-drive-profitable-growth-through-dynamic-pricing (accessed 29 May 2019).

Bergman, E., de Groot Ruiz, A. and Fobelets, V. (2016). *The True Price of Tea from Kenya*. Joint Report by IDH and True Price. Retrieved from https://trueprice.org/wp-content/uploads/2016/04/TP-Tea.pdf (accessed 29 May 2019).

Berman, J. (2017). Can nonalcoholic beer save big brewers? *The Huffington Post*, 6 December. Retrieved from www.huffingtonpost.com/2015/02/24/nonalcoholic-beer-growth_n_6735702.html (accessed 27 May 2019).

Berry, L. and Parasuraman, A. (1991). *Marketing Services: Competing Through Quality*. New York: Free Press.

Berry, L., Wall, E. and Carbone, L. (2006). Service clues and customer assessment of the service experience: Lessons from marketing. *Academy of Management Perspectives*, 20(2), 43–57.

Bertini, M. and Reisman, R. (2013). When selling digital content, let the customer set the price. *Harvard Business Review*, 18 November. Retrieved from https://hbr.org/2013/11/when-selling-digital-content-let-the-customer-set-the-price (accessed 29 May 2019).

Berttram, P. and Schrauf, S. (2016). *Industry 4.0: How Digitization Makes the Supply Chain More Efficient, Agile, and Customer-focused*. PWC Strategy&. Retrieved from www.strategyand.pwc.com/media/file/Industry4.0.pdf (accessed 27 May 2019).

Bettencourt, L. and Ulwick, A. (2008). The customer-centered innovation map. *Harvard Business Review*, May. https://hbr.org/2008/05/the-customer-centered-innovation-map (accessed 4 July 2019).

Bhasin, H. (2018). Marketing mix of Tesco – Tesco Marketing mix, *Marketing* 91, 12 January. Retrieved from www.marketing91.com/marketing-mix-tesco/ (accessed 22 May 2019).

Biel, A.L. (1999). Exploring brand magic. In J.P. Jones (ed.), *How to Use Advertising to Build Strong Brands*. Thousand Oaks, CA: Sage, 157–176.

Biscarini, L., Guerrini, A., Ferri, G., Jhunjhunwala, P. and McCaleb, T. (2017). A new blueprint for pricing and revenue management in travel and tourism. *Boston Consulting Group*, 1 November. Retrieved from www.bcg.com/en-us/industries/transportation-travel-tourism/a-new-blueprint-for-pricing-and-revenue-management-in-travel-and-tourism.aspx (accessed 22 May 2019).

Bishop, B. (2017). Netflix doesn't want to be a better streaming service – it wants to be Disney. *The Verge*, 9 August. Retrieved from www.theverge.com/2017/8/9/16116896/net-flix-disney-deal-streaming-future-original-content-reed-hastings (accessed 27 May 2019).

Bitner, M. (1992). Servicescapes: The impact of physical surroundings on customers and employees. *Journal of Marketing*, 56, 57–71.

Blackshaw, P. (2006). The third moment of truth. *Click Z*, 17 October. Retrieved from www.clickz.com/the-third-moment-of-truth/67161/ (accessed 27 May 2019).

Blankson, C. and Kalafatis, S.P. (2004). The development and validation of a scale measuring consumer/customer derived generic typology of positioning strategies. *Journal of Marketing Management*, 20, 5–43.

Bliss, J. (n.d.). How this Dutch company made €44.9m in sales without advertising. *Truly Deeply*. Retrieved from www.trulydeeply.com.au/2018/05/tonys-chocolonely-confectionery-branding/ (accessed 29 May 2019).

Bloomfield, J. (2018). Netflix, Amazon and Alibaba contribute to biggest ever rise in BrandZ™ top 100 most valuable global brands. *Kantar UK Insights*. Retrieved from https://uk.kantar.com/business/brands/2018/brandz%E2%84%A2-top-100-most-valuable-global-brands-2018/ (accessed 22 May 2019).

Boddy, C. (2005). Projective techniques in market research: Valueless subjectivity or insightful reality? *International Journal of Market Research*, 47(3), 239–254.

Boland, D., Hinterbuber, A., Liozu, S. and Perelli, S. (2015). Firm pricing orientation and pricing decisions in industrial markets. In L. Robinson Jr. (ed.), *Marketing Dynamism & Sustainability: Things Change, Things Stay the Same….* New York: Springer, pp. 402–411.

Bradley, J., Laucks, J., Macaulay, J. and Noronhan, A. (2013). *Internet of Everything Value Index*. Cisco White Paper. Retrieved from www.cisco.com/c/dam/en_us/about/business-insights/docs/ioe-value-index-whitepaper.pdf (accessed 10 June 2019).

BrandZ (2018). 2018 BrandZ top 100 global brands. Retrieved from www.millwardbrown. com/brandz/rankings-and-reports/top-global-brands/2018 (accessed 3 June 2019).

Brinker, S. (2017). 57 marketing stacks and 21 essays from the 2017 Stackies & Hackies. *Chiefmartec*, 9 May. Retrieved from https://chiefmartec.com/2017/05/57-marketing-stacks-21-essays-shared-2017-stackies-hackies/ (accessed 27 May 2019).

Brynjolfsson, E., Hitt, L.M. and Kim, H.H. (2011). Strength in numbers: How does data-driven decisionmaking affect firm performance? *SSRN*, 12 December. Retrieved from https://papers.ssrn.com/sol3/papers.cfm?abstract_id=1819486 (accessed 27 May 2019).

Bughin, J., LaBerge, L. and Mellbye, A. (2017). The case for digital reinvention. *McKinsey Insight*, February. Retrieved from www.mckinsey.com/business-functions/digital-mckinsey/our-insights/the-case-for-digital-reinvention (accessed 29 May 2019).

Bulygo, Z. (n.d.). How Netflix uses analytics to select movies, create content, and make multimillion dollar decisions. *Neil Patel*. Retrieved from https://neilpatel.com/blog/how-netflix-uses-analytics/ (accessed 27 May 2019).

Burns, D. and Kermisch, R. (2018). Is pricing killing your profits? *Bain & Company*, 13 June. Retrieved from www.bain.com/insights/is-pricing-killing-your-profits/ (accessed 29 May 2019).

Burns, D., McLinn, J. and Porter, M. (2016). Understanding value: How to capture the pricing opportunity in chemicals. *Bain & Company*, 18 May. Retrieved from www.bain.com/insights/how-to-capture-pricing-opportunity-in-chemicals (accessed 29 May 2019).

Burns, D. and Murphy, J. (2018). The secret to B2B pricing in a digital world. *Bain & Company*, 1 August. Retrieved from www.bain.com/insights/the-secret-to-b2b-pricing-in-a-digital-world/ (accessed 29 May 2019).

Burnstein, D. (2018). Mental cost: Your customers pay more than just money. *Marketing Experiments*, 4 April. Retrieved from https://marketingexperiments.com/conversion-marketing/mental-cost-more-than-money?utm_source=zest.is&utm_medium=referral&utm_term=zst.5ad66e9db0665 (accessed 29 May 2019).

Business Balls (n.d.). Advertising tips and secrets. Retrieved from www.businessballs.com/sales-and-marketing/advertising-tips-and-secrets-11/ (accessed 23 May 2019).

Business Call to Action (2017). *New Horizons: Accelerating Sustainable Development Through Inclusive Business in Kenya*. United Nations Development Programme. Retrieved from www.businesscalltoaction.org/sites/default/files/resources/BCtA_InclusiveBus_Kenya_FINAL.pdf (accessed 29 May 2019).

Business Model Toolbox (n.d.). Airbnb. Retrieved from https://bmtoolbox.net/stories/airbnb/ (accessed 3 June 2019).

Buzzell, R.D. and Ortmeyer, G. (1995). Channel partnerships streamline distribution. *MIT Sloan Management Review*, Spring. Retrieved from https://sloanreview.mit.edu/article/channel-partnerships-streamline-distribution/ (accessed 29 May 2019).

Campbell, S., Marshall, G. and Thoeni, A. (2016). A resource-advantage theory typology of strategic segmentation. *European Journal of Marketing*, 50(12), 2192–2215.

Chain Point (n.d.). Tony's Chocolonely. Retrieved from www.chainpoint.com/our-customers/tonys-chocolonely/ (accessed 29 May 2019).

Chamie, J. (2017). Student debt rising worldwide. *YaleGlobal Online*, 18 May. Retrieved from https://yaleglobal.yale.edu/content/student-debt-rising-worldwide (accessed 27 May 2019).

Charara, S. (2018). Smart home sales explored: Just how many devices have been sold? *The Ambient*, 19 March. Retrieved from www.the-ambient.com/features/smart-home-device-sales-estimates-442 (accessed 27 May 2019).

Charoensuksai, N. and Wolny, J. (2014). Mapping customer journeys in multichannel decision-making. *Journal of Direct, Data and Digital Marketing Practice*, 15(4), 317–326. Retrieved from https://link.springer.com/content/pdf/10.1057%2Fdddmp.2014.24.pdf (accessed 27 May 2019).

Chen, L., Mislove, A. and Wilson, C. (2016). An empirical analysis of algorithmic pricing on Amazon marketplace. In *Proceedings of the 25th International Conference on World Wide Web*, pp. 1339–1349. International World Wide Web Conferences Steering Committee. Retrieved from https://mislove.org/publications/Amazon-WWW.pdf (accessed 29 May 2019).

Cheng, A. (2018). The surprising trend in beauty? Skincare sales growing the fastest among men's grooming products. *Forbes*, 15 June. Retrieved from www.forbes.com/sites/andriacheng/2018/06/15/the-gift-your-dad-really-wants-this-fathers-day-anti-aging-cream/#77d2deaa33ba (accessed 27 May 2019).

Cherry, K. (2019). The four major Jungian archetypes. *VeryWellMind*, 2 April. Retrieved from www.verywellmind.com/what-are-jungs-4-major-archetypes-2795439 (accessed 10 June 2019).

Chesky, B. (2014). Belong anywhere. *Medium*, 16 July. Retrieved from https://medium.com/@bchesky/belong-anywhere-ccf42702d010 (accessed 10 June 2019).

Chiang, K. (2017). Why good pricing strategy starts with market segmentation. *Ibbaka*, 8 June. Retrieved from www.ibbaka.com/blog/2017/6/8/why-good-pricing-strategy-starts-with-market-segmentation (accessed 27 May 2019).

Christensen, C.M., Cook, S. and Hall, T. (2005). Marketing malpractice: The cause and the cure. *Harvard Business Review*, December. Retrieved from https://hbr.org/2005/12/marketing-malpractice-the-cause-and-the-cure (accessed 27 May 2019).

Christensen, C., Hall, T., Dillon, K. and Duncan, D. (2016). Know your customers' "jobs to be done". *Harvard Business Review*, September. Retrieved from https://hbr.org/2016/09/know-your-customers-jobs-to-be-done (accessed 10 June 2019).

Christensen, C.M., Raynor, M.E. and McDonald, R. (2015). What is disruptive innovation? *Harvard Business Review*, December. Retrieved from https://hbr.org/2015/12/what-is-disruptive-innovation

CIM (2015). *Marketing and the 7 Ps: A Brief Summary of Marketing and How it Works*, The Chartered Institute of Marketing. Retrieved from www.cim.co.uk/media/4772/7ps.pdf (accessed 23 May 2019).

Cisco (2013). The Internet of Everything: Global Public Sector Economic Analysis, Frequently Asked Questions. Retrieved from www.cisco.com/c/dam/en_us/about/business-insights/docs/ioe-value-at-stake-public-sector-analysis-faq.pdf (accessed 10 June 2019).

Claessens, M. (2017). Characteristics of the product life cycle stages and their marketing implications. *Marketing-Insider*, 3 July. Retrieved from https://marketing-insider.eu/characteristics-of-the-product-life-cycle-stages/ (accessed 3 June 2019).

Clark, K.B. and Henderson, R.M. (1990). Architectural innovation: The reconfiguration of existing product technologies and the failure of established firms. *Administrative Science Quarterly*, 35(1), 9–30.

Clark, T. (2018). New data shows Netflix's number of movies has gone down by thousands of titles since 2010 – but its TV catalog size has soared. *Business Insider*, 20 February. Retrieved from www.businessinsider.com/netflix-movie-catalog-size-has-gone-down-since-2010-2018-2 (accessed 27 May 2019).

Claveria, K. (2019). 4 examples of how technology is changing consumer behavior. *Vision Critical*, April. Retrieved from www.visioncritical.com/4-examples-how-technology-changing-consumer-behavior-1/ (accessed 27 May 2019).

Cocheo, S. (2018). Can financial marketers hit the millennial moving target? *The Financial Brand*, 31 October. Retrieved from https://thefinancialbrand.com/76160/millennials-marketing-banking-segmentation/ (accessed 27 May 2019).

Cohen, H. (2011). 30 branding definitions. *Heidi Cohen*. Retrieved from https://heidicohen.com/30-branding-definitions/ (accessed 10 June 2019).

Condliffe, J. (2013). Netflix: "The goal is to become HBO faster than HBO can become us". *Gizmodo*, 30 January. Retrieved from https://gizmodo.com/5980103/netflix-the-goal-is-to-become-hbo-faster-than-hbo-can-become-us (accessed 27 May 2019).

Conroy, P., Narula, A. and Finn, J. (2015). Backyard without fences: Carving out territory in the changing consumer products terrain. *Deloitte Review*, 16, 32–45. Retrieved from https://www2.deloitte.com/tr/en/pages/consumer-business/articles/consumer-products-industry-trends.html (accessed 27 May 2019).

Content Marketing Institute (n.d.). What is content marketing? Retrieved from https://contentmarketinginstitute.com/what-is-content-marketing/ (accessed 29 May 2019).

Cook, G., Lee, J., Tsai, T., Kong, A., Deans, J., Johnson, B. and Jardim, E. (2017). *Clicking Clean: Who Is Winning the Race to Build a Green Internet?*. Greenpeace, 10

January. Retrieved from www.greenpeace.org/international/publication/6826/clicking-clean-2017/ (accessed 27 May 2019).

Coresight Research (2017). Deep dive: Global male grooming market. 9 March. Retrieved from www.fungglobalretailtech.com/research/deep-dive-global-male-grooming-market/ (accessed 27 May 2019).

Corfman, K.P. and Lehmann, D.R. (1994). The prisoner's dilemma and the role of information in setting advertising budgets. *Journal of Advertising*, 23(2), 35–48.

Cotteleer, M. and Sniderman, B. (2017). Forces of change: Industry 4.0. *Deloitte Insights*, 18 December. Retrieved from https://www2.deloitte.com/insights/us/en/focus/industry-4-0/overview.html (accessed 23 May 2019).

Court, D., Elzinga, D., Finneman, B. and Perrey, J. (2017). The new battleground for marketing-led growth. *McKinsey Insights*, February. Retrieved from www.mckinsey.com/business-functions/marketing-and-sales/our-insights/the-new-battleground-for-marketing-led-growth (accessed 3 June 2019).

Court, D., Elzinga, D., Mulder, D. and Vetvik, O.J. (2009). The consumer decision journey. *McKinsey Insights*, June. Retrieved from www.mckinsey.com/business-functions/marketing-and-sales/our-insights/the-consumer-decision-journey (accessed 27 May 2019).

Courtney, H., Kirkland, J. and Viguerie, P. (1997). Strategy under uncertainty. *Harvard Business Review*, November–December. Retrieved from https://hbr.org/1997/11/strategy-under-uncertainty (accessed 27 May 2019).

Creswell, J. (2018). How Amazon steers shoppers to its own products. *The New York Times*, 23 June. Retrieved from www.nytimes.com/2018/06/23/business/amazon-the-brand-buster.html (accessed 27 May 2019).

CRMKID (2015). Human interaction in a self-service environment. 14 December. Retrieved from http://crmkid.com/2015/marketing/human-interaction-in-a-self-service-environment/ (accessed 29 May 2019).

Cross, R.G. and Dixit, A. (2005). Customer-centric pricing: The surprising secret for profitability. *Business Horizons*, 48(6), 483–491.

Crowley, E. (2004). Market intelligence versus marketing research. *Quirk's Media*, December. Retrieved from www.quirks.com/articles/market-intelligence-versus-marketing-research (accessed 27 May 2019).

Croxford, R. (2018). Millennials and the smartphone savings revolution. *Financial Times*, 24 May. Retrieved from www.ft.com/savingapps (accessed 27 May 2019).

Dailey, W. (2018). Leading with purpose: The new business norm? *Stanford Social Innovation Review*, 15 August. Retrieved from https://ssir.org/articles/entry/leading_with_purpose_the_new_business_norm# (accessed 10 June 2019).

D'Aveni, R.A. (2007). Mapping your competitive position. *Harvard Business Review*, November. Retrieved from https://hbr.org/2007/11/mapping-your-competitive-position (accessed 27 May 2019).

Davey, J. (2019). UK grocers warn of chaos in no-deal Brexit as Tesco supermarket sacks 9000. *Financial Review*, 29 January. Retrieved from www.afr.com/news/world/uk-grocers-warn-of-chaos-in-nodeal-brexit-as-tesco-supermarket-sacks-9000-20190129-h1al6z (accessed 22 May 2019).

Davidson, N. (2009). *Don't Just Roll the Dice*. Cambridge: Redgate Books.

Davis, G. (2018). Big four grocers under the microscope: Six ways Tesco is deploying retail technology. *Essential Retail*, 25 July. Retrieved from www.essentialretail.com/features/big-four-six-ways-tesco/ (accessed 23 May 2019).

De Brujin, M. (2018). The growing importance of chatbots in the customer journey. *Digitalist Magazine*, 13 March. Retrieved from www.digitalistmag.com/customer-experience/2018/03/13/growing-importance-of-chatbots-in-customer-journey-05963800 (accessed 27 May 2019).

De Jong, M., Hoofstede, A., Van Hoof, J. and Walenberg, N. (2007). Projective techniques for brand image research: Two personification-based methods explored. *Qualitative Market Research: An International Journal*, 10(3), 300–309.

Decision Analyst (2010). Segmentation re-analysis. Retrieved from www.decisionanalyst.com/casestudies/segmentationreanalysis/ (accessed 27 May 2019).

Deloitte (2016). *Blockchain: Enigma, Paradox, Opportunity*. Retrieved from https://www2.deloitte.com/uk/en/pages/innovation/articles/blockchain.html (accessed 27 May 2019).

Deloitte (2017a). *2030 Purpose: Good Business and a Better Future*. January. Retrieved from https://www2.deloitte.com/content/dam/Deloitte/global/Documents/About-Deloitte/gx-2030-purpose-report.pdf (accessed 27 May 2019).

Deloitte (2017b). *Live Thrives in an Online World*. Retrieved from https://www2.deloitte.com/content/dam/Deloitte/global/Images/infographics/technologymediatelecommunications/gx-deloitte-tmt-2018-online-world-report.pdf (accessed 27 May 2019).

Deloitte (2017c). *Building Your Omni-Channel Journey*. August. Retrieved from https://www2.deloitte.com/content/dam/Deloitte/be/Documents/strategy/Omni-channel_Sales_Collateral-ONLINE.pdf (accessed 25 June 2019).

Deloitte (2018a). Digital reality: A technical primer. *Deloitte Insights*, 8 February. Retrieved from https://www2.deloitte.com/content/dam/insights/us/articles/4426_Digital-reality-primer/DI_Digital%20Reality_Primer.pdf (accessed 23 May 2019).

Deloitte (2018b). The Internet of Things: A technical primer. *Deloitte Insights*, 8 February. Retrieved from https://www2.deloitte.com/content/dam/insights/us/articles/4420_IoT-primer/DI_IoT-Primer.pdf (accessed 23 May 2019).

D'Emidio, T., Dorton, D. and Duncan, E. (2015). Service innovation in a digital world. *McKinsey Insights*, February. Retrieved from www.mckinsey.com/business-functions/operations/our-insights/service-innovation-in-a-digital-world (accessed 29 May 2019).

DesignStudio (n.d.). Airbnb. Retrieved from https://design.studio/work/Airbnb (accessed 3 June 2019).

Desjardins, J. (2017). The most overhyped sectors in tech, according to entrepreneurs. *Visual Capitalist*, 15 December. Retrieved from www.visualcapitalist.com/overhyped-sectors-tech-entrepreneurs/ (accessed 27 May 2019).

Diageo (2018). Diageo scoops awards for commitment to marketing effectiveness. 10 October. Retrieved from www.diageo.com/en/news-and-media/features/diageo-scoops-awards-for-commitment-to-marketing-effectiveness/ (accessed 3 June 2019).

Diamond, S. (2011). Reference guide on survey research. *In Reference Manual on Scientific Evidence* (3rd edn). Washington, DC: Federal Judicial Center/National Academy of Science, pp. 359–423.

Digitalist Magazine (2016). Our digital planet: See it, click it, touch it, buy it. January. Retrieved from www.digitalistmag.com/executive-research/our-digital-planet-see-it-click-it-touch-it-buy-it (accessed 27 May 2019).

Digital McKinsey (2018). *Digital Reinvention: Unlocking the How*. Retrieved from www.mckinsey.com/~/media/McKinsey/Business%20Functions/McKinsey%20Digital/Our%20Insights/Digital%20Reinvention%20Unlocking%20the%20how/Digital-Reinvention_Unlocking-the-how.ashx (accessed 29 May 2019).

Dintrans, P., Fuloria, S., Craver, C. and Winitz, M. (2013). *Segment-based Strategies for Mobile Banking*. Cognizant, Report, June. Retrieved from www.cognizant.com/InsightsWhitepapers/Segment-Based-Strategies-for-Mobile-Banking.pdf (accessed 27 May 2019).

Dobbs, R. and Koller, T. (2015). Measuring long-term performance. *McKinsey Insights*, March. Retrieved from www.mckinsey.com/business-functions/strategy-and-corporate-finance/our-insights/measuring-long-term-performance (accessed 3 June 2019).

Dolan, P. (2016). Data segments & techniques: a new lexicon. *IAB*, 22 January. Retrieved from www.iab.com/news/data-segments-techniques-a-new-lexicon/ (accessed 23 May 2019).

Dolan, S. (2018). The challenges of last mile logistics & delivery technology solutions. *Business Insider*, 10 May. Retrieved from www.businessinsider.com/last-mile-delivery-shipping-explained (accessed 29 May 2019).

Dolzake, C. (2015). Unlocking the power or pricing analytics for higher marketing returns. *WNS*. Retrieved from www.wns.com/insights/articles/articledetail/314/unlocking-the-power-of-pricing-analytics-for-higher-marketing-returns (accessed 29 May 2019).

Dosdall, M. (2018). Case study: Red Wings Shoe Company makes giant steps with SIOP. *EP Thought Leader Series*, 28 September. Retrieved from https://epthoughtleaders.com/case-study-red-wing-shoe-company-makes-giant-steps-with-siop/ (accessed 27 May 2019).

Doz, Y.L. and Wilson, K. (2011). Agile innovation: A footprint balancing distance and immersion. *California Management Review*, 53(2), 6–26.

Drucker, P. (1954). *The Practice of Management*. New York: Harper & Row.

Drucker, P. (1963). Managing for business effectiveness. *Harvard Business Review*, May. Retrieved from https://hbr.org/1963/05/managing-for-business-effectiveness (accessed 26 June 2019).

Drucker, P. (1964/2016). *Managing for Results: Economic Tasks and Risk-taking Decisions*. Oxford: Butterworth-Heinemann.

Drucker, P. (1973/1993). *Management: Tasks, Responsibilities, and Practices*. New York: Harper & Row.

DSDG (Division for Sustainable Development Goals) (n.d.). Sustainable Development Goals Knowledge Platform. Retrieved from https://sustainabledevelopment.un.org/sdgs (accessed 27 May 2019).

Du Toit, G., Engelhardt, J., Sager, P. and Fruechtl, K. (2018). Experience is the new product: Here's how to manage it. *Bain & Company*, 13 June. Retrieved from www.bain.com/insights/experience-is-the-new-product-heres-how-to-manage-it/ (accessed 3 June 2019).

Du Toit, G., Markey, R., Melton, J. and Debruyne, F. (2017). Running the business through your customer's eyes. *Bain & Company*, 7 July. Retrieved from www.bain.com/insights/running-the-business-through-your-customers-eyes/ (accessed 29 May 2019).

Dubey, A., Moeller, L.H. and Turner, M.D. (2015). Comprehensive value management: How consumer packaged goods companies can tame volatility in commodity prices. *Strategy&*, 1 December. Retrieved from www.strategyand.pwc.com/reports/comprehensive-value-management (accessed 30 October 2018).

Duggal, J. (2016). *The Road to Viewability: It's a New Era of Accountability for Vendors, Publishers, and Advertisers*. Quantcast. Retrieved from www.quantcast.com/wp-content/uploads/2015/04/Quantcast-Advertise-The-Road-to-Viewability-WhitePaper.pdf (accessed 29 May 2019).

Duggan, B. (2018). Brand purpose: ANA 2018 marketing word of the year. *ANA*, 7 December. Retrieved from www.ana.net/blogs/show/id/mm-blog-2018-12-brand-purpose-marketing-word-of-the-year (accessed 10 June 2019).

Duhigg, C. (2012). How companies learn your secrets. *New York Times Magazine*, 16 February. Retrieved from www.nytimes.com/2012/02/19/magazine/shopping-habits.html (accessed 27 May 2019).

Dutzler, H., Hochrainer, P., Nitschke, A., Schmaus, B. and Schrauf, S. (2016). *Industry 4.0: Opportunities and Challenges for Consumer Product and Retail Companies*. PWC Strategy&. Retrieved from www.strategyand.pwc.com/media/file/Industry-4-0-RC.pdf (accessed 27 May 2019).

Eccles, R. and Karbassi, L. (2018). The right way to support the sustainable development goals. *MIT Sloan Management Review*, 2 April. Retrieved from https://sloanreview.mit.

edu/article/the-right-way-to-support-the-uns-sustainable-development-goals/ (accessed 3 June 2019).

The Economist (2017). Millions of things will soon have digital twins. 13 July. Retrieved from www.economist.com/business/2017/07/13/millions-of-things-will-soon-have-digital-twins (accessed 27 May 2019).

Econsultancy (2018). 10 very cool examples of experiential marketing. *Econsultancy Blog*, 12 November. Retrieved from https://econsultancy.com/10-examples-experiential-marketing/ (accessed 27 May 2019).

Edelman (2018). Two-thirds of consumers worldwide now buy beliefs. 2 October. Retrieved from www.edelman.com/news-awards/two-thirds-consumers-worldwide-now-buy-beliefs (accessed 10 June 2019).

Edelman, D.C. and Singer, M. (2015). Competing on customer journeys. *Harvard Business Review*, November. Retrieved from https://hbr.org/2015/11/competing-on-customer-journeys (accessed 27 May 2019).

Edwards, J. (2013). Experiential essays: The most powerful form of marketing. *Campaign*, 25 June. Retrieved from www.campaignlive.co.uk/article/experiential-essays-powerful-form-marketing/1187676 (accessed 26 June 2019).

Emprechtinger, F. (2018). How the sharing economy is changing business models and products. *Lead Innovation Blog*, 3 October. Retrieved from www.lead-innovation.com/English-blog/sharing-economy-is-changing-business-models (accessed 27 May 2019).

EOS (n.d.). Additive manufacturing, laser-sintering and industrial 3D printing: Benefits and functional principle. Retrieved from www.eos.info/additive_manufacturing/for_technology_interested (accessed 27 May 2019).

ESOMAR (2009). *Guide on Distinguishing Market Research from Other Data Collection Activities*. Retrieved from www.esomar.org/uploads/public/knowledge-and-standards/codes-and-guidelines/ESOMAR_Codes-and-Guidelines_Maintaining-Distinctions-MRDM.pdf (accessed 27 May 2019).

ESOMAR (2015). *Global Market Research 2015*. Retrieved from www.esomar.org/uploads/public/publications-store/reports/global-market-research-2015/ESOMAR-GMR2015_Preview.pdf (accessed 27 May 2019).

ESOMAR (2017). *Global Market Research 2017*. Retrieved from www.esomar.org/knowledge-center/library?publication=2892 (accessed 27 May 2019).

EuroMonitor (2019). Unilever acquisition of Graze shows hunger for more snacking. EuroMonitor International Market Research Blog, 8 February. Retrieved from https://blog.euromonitor.com/unilever-acquisition-of-graze-shows-hunger-for-more-snacking/ (accessed 27 May 2019).

Evans, K. (2018). Zara fashions a more global presence by selling in 106 new markets. *Digital Commerce* 360, 13 November. Retrieved from www.digitalcommerce360.

com/2018/11/13/zara-fashions-a-more-global-presence-by-selling-into-106-new-mar kets/ (accessed 29 May 2019).

Event Marketing Institute (2015). *Event Track 2015: Event & Experiential Marketing Industry Forecast & Best Practices Study*. Retrieved from http://cdn.eventmarketer.com/wp-content/uploads/2016/01/EventTrack2015_Executive.pdf?_ga=1.2089073.1166920123.14 64299493 (accessed 29 May 2019).

Ewing, D., Leberman, D., Rajgopal, K., Serrano, E. and Steitz, J. (2014). The keys to driving broad consumer adoption of digital wallets and mobile payments. *McKinsey Insights*, January. Retrieved from www.mckinsey.com/business-functions/marketing-and-sales/ our-insights/the-keys-to-driving-broad-consumer-adoption-of-digital-wallets-and-mobile-payments (accessed 29 May 2019).

EY (2014). *Delivering Agile Innovation*. June. Retrieved from www.ey.com/Publication/ vwLUAssets/EY-delivering-agile-innovation-presentation/$FILE/EY-innovation-through-collaboration-presentation.pdf (accessed 27 May 2019).

EY (2016). *Total Value: Impact Valuation to Support Decision-making*. Retrieved from www.ey.com/Publication/vwLUAssets/ey-total-value-impact-valuation-to-support-decision-making/$FILE/ey-total-value-impact-valuation-to-support-decision-making.pdf (accessed 3 June 2019).

Fanelli, M. (2018). Getting attribution right: Today's advertising imperative. *MarTech Advisor*, 19 June. Retrieved from www.martechadvisor.com/articles/performance-and-attribution/ getting-attribution-right-todays-advertising-imperative/ (accessed 29 May 2019).

Farley, P. (2018). Tesco Labs: The drive for new technology, *Retail Connections*, 18 July. Retrieved from www.retailconnections.co.uk/articles/tesco-labs-drive-new-technology-2/ (accessed 23 May 2019).

Fast Casual (2017). Study: Fast casual customers want more digital ordering opportuni-ties. 7 December. Retrieved from www.fastcasual.com/news/study-restaurant-custom ers-want-more-digital-ordering-opportunities/ (accessed 29 May 2019).

Federal Trade Commission (2016). *Big Data: A Tool for Inclusion or Exclusion. Understanding the Issues*. Retrieved from www.ftc.gov/system/files/documents/reports/big-data-tool-in clusion-or-exclusion-understanding-issues/160106big-data-rpt.pdf (accessed 27 May 2019).

Ferdows, K., Lewis, M. and Machuca, J. (2004). Rapid-fire fulfillment. *Harvard Business Review*, November. Retrieved from https://hbr.org/2004/11/rapid-fire-fulfillment (accessed 29 May 2019).

Fitter, F., Perez, G., Raftery, T., Thalbauer, H. and Wellers, D. (2018). The blockchain solu-tion. *Digitalist Magazine*, 21 February. Retrieved from www.digitalistmag.com/execu tive-research/the-blockchain-solution (accessed 27 May 2019).

Flaherty, K. (2016). How channels, devices, and touchpoints impact the customer journey. Nielsen Norman Group, 4 December. Retrieved from www.nngroup.com/articles/chan nels-devices-touchpoints/ (accessed 3 June 2019).

Fleming, G. (2017). *The State of Consumers and Technology, Benchmark 2017*, US. Forrester, 28 June. Retrieved from https://cdn2.hubspot.net/hubfs/197229/The-State-Of-Consumers-And-Technology_-Benchmark-2017_-US%20(1).pdf (accessed 27 May 2019).

FlexMR (n.d.). ITV Agile Research Framework, Case Study. Retrieved from https://resources.flexmr.net/case-studies/itv-player (accessed 27 May 2019).

Fluckinger, D. (2018). Retail AI predicts consumer behavior for targeted marketing. *TechTarget*. Retrieved from https://searchcrm.techtarget.com/feature/Retail-AI-predicts-consumer-behavior-for-targeted-marketing (accessed 27 May 2019).

Ford (2017). *The Freedom to Move Drives Human Progress*. Retrieved from https://corporate.ford.com/microsites/sustainability-report-2017-18/doc/sr17-summary.pdf (accessed 27 May 2019).

Forrester Consulting (2015). *Moments That Matter: Intent-rich Moments Are Critical To Winning Today's Consumer Journey*. Retrieved from www.thinkwithgoogle.com/_qs/documents/670/forrester-moments-that-matter-research-study.pdf (accessed 25 June 2019).

Forte Consultancy (2010). 'Occasional' customer segmentation – uncovering hidden truths about customers. 5 March. Retrieved from https://forteconsultancy.wordpress.com/2010/03/05/treating-the-same-customer-differently-in-different-occasions/ (accessed 27 May 2019).

Frazer, C. (1983). Creative strategy: A management perspective. *Journal of Advertising*, 12(4), 36–41

Frederick, M. (2018). Augmented reality for instant access to KPIs. *Perficient*, 6 September. Retrieved from https://blogs.perficient.com/2018/09/06/microstrategy-augmented-reality-analytics/ (accessed 3 June 2019).

Fuchs, C. and Diamantopoulos, A. (2010). Evaluating the effectiveness of brand-positioning strategies from a consumer perspective. *European Journal of Marketing*, 44, 1763–1786. http://dx.doi.org/10.1108/03090561011079873.

Gallagher, L. (2017). AIRBNB's surprising path to Y Combinator. *Wired*, 21 February. Retrieved from www.wired.com/2017/02/airbnbs-surprising-path-to-y-combinator/ (accessed 10 June 2019).

Gallo, A. (2015). A refresher on price elasticity. *Harvard Business Review*, 21 August. Retrieved from https://hbr.org/2015/08/a-refresher-on-price-elasticity (accessed 29 May 2019).

Gao, Y. (2010). Measuring marketing performance: A review and a framework. *The Marketing Review*, 10(1), 25–40.

Gard, J.-C. and Eyal, E. (2012). The six steps to pricing power. *BCG*, 16 October. Retrieved from www.bcg.com/en-us/publications/2012/six-steps-to-pricing-power-insurance.aspx (accessed 3 June 2019).

Gartner (n.d.). Gartner Hype Cycle. Retrieved from www.gartner.com/en/research/methodologies/gartner-hype-cycle (accessed 12 June 2019).

Gates, B. and Gates, M. (2017). *Goalkeepers: The Stories Behind the Data*. Retrieved from https://datareport.goalkeepers.org/assets/downloads/Stories_behind_the_data_2017. pdf (accessed 3 June 2019).

Gavett, G. (2014). What you need to know about segmentation. *Harvard Business Review*, July. Retrieved from https://hbr.org/2014/07/what-you-need-to-know-about-segmenta tion (accessed 27 May 2019).

Geissbauer, R., Vedso, J. and Schrauf, S. (2016). *Industry 4.0: Building the Digital Enterprise*. PWC. Retrieved from www.pwc.com/gx/en/industries/industries-4.0/land ing-page/industry-4.0-building-your-digital-enterprise-april-2016.pdf (accessed 3 June 2019).

Gevelber, L. (2017). Micro-moments now: Why expectations for "right now" are on the rise. *Think With Google*, August. Retrieved from www.thinkwithgoogle.com/consumer-insights/consumer-immediate-need-mobile-experiences/ (accessed 27 May 2019).

Gharib, M. (2015). The U.N. wants you to take a selfie, spin around, listen to a llama. *National Public Radio*, 20 September. Retrieved from www.npr.org/sections/goatsand-soda/2015/09/20/441131516/the-u-n-wants-you-to-take-a-selfie-spin-around-listen-to-a-llama (accessed 29 May 2019).

Ghesquieres, J., Kotzen, J., Nolan, T., Rodt, M., Roos, A. and Tucker, J. (2017). The art of performance management. *BCG*, 30 April. Retrieved from www.bcg.com/publications/2017/finance-function-excellence-corporate-development-art-performance-management.aspx (accessed 3 June 2019).

Giametta, T. and Krakovsky, I. (2018). Monetizing data from the digital customer journey. *TargetMarketing*, 7 March. Retrieved from www.targetmarketingmag.com/article/mone tizing-data-from-the-digital-customer-journey/all/ (accessed 27 May 2019).

Gibbons, S. (2017). Service blueprints: Definition. *Nielsen Norman Group*, 27 August. Retrieved from www.nngroup.com/articles/service-blueprints-definition/ (accessed 29 May 2019).

Gilliland, N. (2018). Four innovative examples of eye-tracking technology in marketing campaigns & products. *Econsultancy*, 25 April. Retrieved from https://econsultancy. com/four-innovative-examples-of-eye-tracking-technology-in-marketing-campaigns-products/?cmpid=ECON-DAILYPULSE-US-090418-150654&utm_medium=email&utm_source=newsletter&utm_campaign=ECON-DAILYPULSE-US-090418-150654 (accessed 27 May 2019).

Gilmore, D. (2002). Understanding and overcoming resistance to ethnographic design research. *Interactions*, 9(3), 29–35.

Ginsburg, V. (2014). Unstable organizations can't grow. *Women On Business*, 29 August. Retrieved from www.womenonbusiness.com/unstable-organizations-cant-grow/ (accessed 23 May 2019).

The Global Goals for Sustainable Development (n.d.). Resources. Retrieved from www.globalgoals.org/resources (accessed 3 June 2019).

The Global Goals for Sustainable Development (2015). *Style Guide V2.1*. Retrieved from http://cdn.globalgoals.org/2015/08/150916_TGG_StyleGuide_v2_1_UNBRANDED.pdf (accessed 3 June 2019).

Gong, L., Morikawa, T. and Yamamoto, T. (2016). Comparison of activity type identification from mobile phone GPS data using various machine learning methods. *Asian Transport Studies*, 4(1), 114–128. DOI: 10.11175/eastsats.4.114. Retrieved from www.researchgate.net/publication/303222908_Comparison_of_Activity_Type_Identification_from_Mobile_Phone_GPS_Data_Using_Various_Machine_Learning_Methods (accessed 27 May 2019).

Goodall, C. (2007). Consumer segmentation: Research from the Henley Centre and Marks and Spencer. *Carbon Commentary*, 1 October. Retrieved from www.carboncommentary.com/blog/2007/10/01/consumer-segmentation-research-from-the-henley-centre-and-marks-and-spencer (accessed 27 May 2019).

Google (n.d.). Introduction to the ad experience report. Retrieved from https://support.google.com/webtools/answer/7159932?hl=en (accessed 27 May 2019).

Gordon, L. and Hodgson, A. (2016). Doing business at the bottom of the pyramid: Addressing diversity for commercial success. EuroMonitor, 30 July. Retrieved from https://blog.euromonitor.com/business-bottom-pyramid-addressing-diversity-commercial-success/ (accessed 29 May 2019).

Gordon, L. and Hodgson, A. (2017). Top 5 bottom of the pyramid markets: Diverse spending patterns and future potential. EuroMonitor, 3 March. Retrieved from https://blog.euromonitor.com/top-5-bottom-pyramid-markets-diverse-spending-patterns-future-potential/ (accessed 29 May 2019).

Goyal, P., Kazmi, A.A., Kumar, V. and Rahman, Z. (2012). Evolution of sustainability as marketing strategy: Beginning of new era. *ScienceDirect. Procedia–Social and Behavioral Sciences*, 37, 482–489.

Grece, C. (2017). The EU online advertising market: Update 2017. *European Audiovisual Observatory*. Retrieved from https://rm.coe.int/the-eu-online-advertising-market-update-2017/168078f2b3 (accessed 27 May 2019).

Greenberg, J. (2015). Netflix says streaming is greener than reading (or breathing). *Wired*, 28 May. Retrieved from www.wired.com/2015/05/netflix-says-streaming-greener-reading-breathing/ (accessed 27 May 2019).

Greenbook (2016). *GRIT Report: Greenbook Research Industry Trends Report 2016*. Retrieved from www.greenbook.org/grit/grit-archive (accessed 27 May 2019).

Grover, V. (2018). 5 ways IoT is changing digital marketing. *MarTechAdvisor*, 8 August. Retrieved from www.martechadvisor.com/articles/iot/5-ways-iot-is-changing-digital-marketing/ (accessed 3 June 2019).

Gruyaert, E. and Meehan, J. (2018). Six disruptive trends in pricing. *Wall Street Journal*, 2 March. Retrieved from https://deloitte.wsj.com/cmo/2018/03/02/6-disruptive-trends-in-pricing/ (accessed 29 May 2019).

Guerrieria, M. (2018). New metric helps brands build equity and value. Retrieved from www.millwardbrown.com/mb-global/our-thinking/articles-opinion/articles/brandz/global/2018/new-metric-helps-brands-build-equity-and-value (accessed 10 June 2019).

Guldimann, M. (2015). Why the future of advertising is polite interruptions. *Media Post*, 16 July. Retrieved from www.mediapost.com/publications/article/254130/why-the-future-of-advertising-is-polite-interrupti.html (accessed 29 May 2019).

Halper, F. (2013). *TDWI Checklist Report: Seven Use Cases for Geospatial Analytics*. Retrieved from www.victa.nl/alteryx/wp-content/uploads/TDWI-Checklist-Webinar-on-Data-Discovery. PDF (accessed 27 May 2019).

Hamel, G. and Prahaland, C.K. (2005). Strategic intent. *Harvard Business Review*, July–August. Retrieved from https://hbr.org/2005/07/strategic-intent (accessed 27 May 2019).

Harmon, R. (2003). Marketing information systems. *Encyclopedia of Information Systems*, Vol. 3. New York: Elsevier Science, 137–151.

Hawker, R., Melton, J., Wright, J., Burns, M. and Engelhardt, J. (2018). Breakthrough design for a better customer experience and better economics. *Bain & Company*, 13 June. Retrieved from www.bain.com/insights/breakthrough-design-for-a-better-customer-experience-and-better-economics/ (accessed 29 May 2019).

Heda, S., Mewborn, S. and Caine, S. (2016). Perception beats reality in pricing. *Bain & Company*, 14 December. Retrieved from www.bain.com/insights/perception-beats-reality-in-pricing (accessed 29 May 2019).

Hegarty, J. (2015). What I really really want. Hall & Partners. Retrieved from www.halland-partners.com/what-i-really-really-want-sir-john-hegarty (accessed 29 May 2019).

Heineken (2016). Moderate alcohol consumption becoming the new cool among millennial consumers. 11 January. Retrieved from www.theheinekencompany.com/media/media-releases/press-releases/2016/01/1977927 (accessed 27 May 2019).

Henrich, J., Kothari, A. and Makarova, E. (2012). Design to value: A smart asset for smart products. *McKinsey & Company*, March. Retrieved from www.mckinsey.com/~/media/mckinsey/dotcom/client_service/consumer%20packaged%20goods/pdfs/20120301_dtv_in_cpg.ashx (accessed 27 May 2019).

Hicks, R. (2017). Advertising that promotes SDGs to be awarded at Oscars of adland. *Eco-Business*, 18 September. Retrieved from www.eco-business.com/news/advertising-that-promotes-sdgs-to-be-awarded-at-oscars-of-adland/ (accessed 29 May 2019).

Hill, D. (1986). Satisfaction and consumer services. *Advances in Consumer Research*, 13, ed. R. Lutz. Provo, UT: Association for Consumer Research, 311–315.

Hine, D.W., Phillips, W.J., Driver, J. and Morrison, M. (2017). Audience segmentation and climate change communication. *Oxford Research Encyclopedia of Climate Science*. Retrieved from http://climatescience.oxfordre.com/view/10.1093/acrefore/9780190228620.001.0001/acrefore-9780190228620-e-390 (accessed 27 May 2019).

Hines, E. (2017). 10 stats you should know about the B2B buyer's journey. *Fronetics*, 1 June. Retrieved from www.fronetics.com/10-stats-know-b2b-buyers-journey/ (accessed 23 May 2019).

Hinterhuber, A. and Liozu, S. (2012). Is it time to rethink your pricing strategy? *MIT Sloan Management Review*, Summer. Retrieved from https://sloanreview.mit.edu/article/is-it-time-to-rethink-your-pricing-strategy/ (accessed 29 May 2019).

Hobbs, T. (2016). M&S targets attitude not age to rebuild fashion business. *Marketing Week*, 4 November. Retrieved from www.marketingweek.com/2016/11/04/ms-dismisses-segmentation-saying-fashion-attitudes-are-ageless/ (accessed 27 May 2019).

Hobbs, T. (2017). The Body Shop on how its new owners are trying to revive its 'activist spirit'. *Marketing Week*, 20 September. Retrieved from www.marketingweek.com/2017/09/20/body-shop-on-relocating-its-activist-spirit/ (accessed 23 May 2019).

Holmes, R. (2017). Are we entering the era of millisecond marketing? *ADWEEK*, 13 October. Retrieved from www.adweek.com/digital/ryan-holmes-hootsuite-guest-post-millisecond-marketing/ (accessed 27 May 2019).

Hom, J. (n.d.). Your face here: Creating illustration guidelines for a more inclusive visual identity. *AIRBNB Design*. Retrieved from https://airbnb.design/your-face-here/ (accessed 3 June 2019).

Horn, B. and Huang, W. (2016). Comparison of segmentation approaches. *Decision Analyst*. Retrieved from www.decisionanalyst.com/whitepapers/comparesegmentation/ (accessed 27 May 2019).

Howland, D. (2017). Amazon private brands grew 90% over last year. *RetailDive*, 3 October. Retrieved from www.retaildive.com/news/amazon-private-brands-grew-90-over-last-year/506353/ (accessed 26 June 2019).

Huang, Y., Hui, S.K., Inman, J.J. and Suher, J. (2013). Deconstructing the "first moment of truth": Understanding unplanned consideration and purchase conversion using in-store video tracking. *Journal of Marketing Research*, 50(4), 445–462.

Hürtgen, H. and Mohr, N. (2018). Achieving business impact with data. *McKinsey Insights*, April. Retrieved from www.mckinsey.com/business-functions/mckinsey-analytics/our-insights/achieving-business-impact-with-data (accessed 3 June 2019).

Hyken, S. (2018). Customer experience is the new brand. *Forbes*, 15 July. Retrieved from www.forbes.com/sites/shephyken/2018/07/15/customer-experience-is-the-new-brand/#329d-33f67f52IBM (accessed 29 May 2019).

IBM Watson Advertising (2018). IBM Watson Advertising and Red Wing Shoes Win 2017 IAC Award. 10 April. Retrieved from www.ibm.com/watson-advertising/news/ibm-watson-advertising-and-red-wing-shoes-win-2017-iac-award (accessed 27 May 2019).

Identic (2017). Omni-channel marketing: What you need to know. 2 February. Retrieved from www.identic.be/en/omni-channel-marketing/ (accessed 3 June 2019).

IEG (2014). Survey finds sponsors looking for slightly different benefits and services from properties. *IEG Sponsorship Report*, 31 March. Retrieved from www.sponsorship.com/iegsr/2014/03/31/Survey-Finds-Sponsors-Looking-For-Slightly-Differe.aspx (accessed 29 May 2019).

Information Age (2013). Tesco saves millions with supply chain analytics. Retrieved from www.information-age.com/tesco-saves-millions-with-supply-chain-analytics-123456972/ (accessed 22 May 2019).

Ingledew, S. (2017). Digital Darwinism predicted as changes in consumer behavior transform marketing landscape. *MarTech Advisor*, 17 March. Retrieved from www.martechadvisor.com/articles/digital-transformation/digital-darwinism-predicted-as-changes-in-consumer-behavior-transform-marketing-landscape/ (accessed 27 May 2019).

Inkwood Research (2019). *Global Male Grooming Product Market Forecast 2019–2027*. Retrieved from www.inkwoodresearch.com/reports/male-grooming-product-market/ (accessed 10 June 2019).

Innovation Hub (n.d.). Object marketing using digital twins. Retrieved from https://innovationhub.innogy.com/news-event/5oBYOxmMo0im8W8qMKgK6W/object-marketing-using-digital-twins (accessed 27 May 2019).

Interaction Design Foundation (n.d.). Service blueprints – Communicating the design of services. Retrieved from www.interaction-design.org/literature/article/service-blueprints-communicating-the-design-of-services (accessed 29 May 2019).

Interbrand (2010). *What About Brazilian Brands?* Retrieved from www.rankingmarcas.com.br/downloads/2010/what_about_brazilian_brands_english.pdf (accessed 10 June 2019).

Interbrand (2013). *The Best Asian Brands Issue*. Retrieved from www.interbrand.com/wp-content/uploads/2015/08/Interbrand-Best-Asian-Brands-2013.pdf (accessed 10 June 2019).

Interbrand (2017). Interbrand releases 2017 Best Brazilian Brands. 30 November. Retrieved from www.interbrand.com/newsroom/interbrand-releases-2017-best-brazilian-brands/ (accessed 10 June 2019).

International Society for Presence Research (2000). The Concept of Presence: Explication Statement. Retrieved from https://ispr.info/about-presence-2/about-presence/ (accessed 23 May 2019).

Internet World Stats (2019). Internet users in the world by regions – 31 March 2019. Retrieved from www.internetworldstats.com/stats.htm (accessed 27 May 2019).

IPA and ISBA (2011). The Good Pitch: Best pitch practices and principles. Institute of Practitioners in Advertising and Incorporated Society of British Advertisers. Retrieved from www.thegoodpitch.com/ (accessed 29 May 2019).

IPG (2017). IPG continues support of UN sustainable development goals. *IPG News Release*, 10 January. Retrieved from https://interpublicgroup.gcs-web.com/news-releases/news-release-details/ipg-continues-support-un-sustainable-development-goals (accessed 29 May 2019).

IRI (n.d.). Private label outperforms FMCG brands in Europe, as retailers up product quality in a bid to drive differentiation and loyalty – new IRI report reveals. Retrieved from www.iriworldwide.com/it-IT/Insights-it/news/Private-label-outperforms-FMCG-brands-in-Europe,-as-retailers-up-product-quality-in-a-bid-to-drive-d (accessed 29 May 2019).

I-Scoop (n.d.). Industry 4.0: the fourth industrial revolution – guide to Industrie 4.0. Retrieved from www.i-scoop.eu/industry-4-0/ (accessed 3 June 2019).

Janiszewski, C. (2009). The consumer experience. Association for Consumer Research 2009 Presidential Address. Retrieved from www.acrwebsite.org/janiszewski_presidential_address.pdf (accessed 27 May 2019).

Jetlore (2017). *Predictive Layouts*. Retrieved from https://cdn2.hubspot.net/hubfs/610079/Predictive%20Layouts.pdf (accessed 25 June 2019).

Joerss, M., Schröder, J., Neuhaus, F., Klink, C. and Mann, F. (2016). Parcel delivery: The future of the last mile. *McKinsey & Company*, September. Retrieved from www.mckinsey.com/~/media/mckinsey/industries/travel%20transport%20and%20logistics/our%20insights/how%20customer%20demands%20are%20reshaping%20last%20mile%20delivery/parcel_delivery_the_future_of_last_mile.ashx (accessed 29 May 2019).

John, D.R., Loken, B., Kim, K. and Monga, A.B. (2006). Brand concept maps: A methodology for identifying brand association networks. *Journal of Marketing Research (JMR)*, 43(4), 549–563.

Johnson, B. (2014). Airbnb unveils new identity and positioning. *Marketing Week*, 17 July. Retrieved from www.marketingweek.com/2014/07/17/airbnb-unveils-new-identity-and-positioning/ (accessed 10 June 2019).

Johnson, M.W., Christensen, C.M. and Kagermann, H. (2008). Reinventing your business model. *Harvard Business Review*, December. Retrieved from https://hbr.org/2008/12/reinventing-your-business-model (accessed 27 May 2019).

Judl, J., Tilkanen, J., Riddlestone, S. and Rubbens, C. (2018). *Creating Sustainable Smartphones: Scaling Up Best Practice to Achieve SDG 12*. Transform Together, 16 May. Retrieved from http://storage.googleapis.com/www.bioregional.com/downloads/Creating-sustainable-smartphones-Scaling-up-best-practice-to-achieve-SDG-12_Transform-Together_2018.pdf (accessed 10 June 2019).

Kahneman, D. (2000). Experienced utility and objective happiness: A moment-based approach. In D. Kahneman and A. Tversky (eds), *Choices, Values and Frames*. New York: Cambridge University Press and the Russell Sage Foundation, pp. 673–692.

Kalbach, J. and Kahn, P. (2011). Locating value with alignment diagrams. *PJIM*, 3(2). Retrieved from www.piim.newschool.edu/journal/issues/2011/02/pdfs/ParsonsJournal ForInformationMapping_Kalbach-James+Kahn-Paul.pdf (accessed 29 May 2019).

Kantar Consulting (2018). *Taking the Consumer Lifestyle Trends into 2018 and Beyond.* Retrieved from www.ifsa.eu.com/uploads/1/2/0/2/120245019/global_consumer_lifestyle_trends_-_grace_binchy_bord_bia.pdf (accessed 26 June 2019).

Kaplan, R. and Norton, D. (2001). Building a strategy-focused organization. *Ivey Business Journal*, May–June. Retrieved from https://iveybusinessjournal.com/publication/build ing-a-strategy-focused-organization/(accessed 3 June 2019).

Kaplan, R.S. and Norton, D.P. (1992). The balanced scorecard – measures that drive performance. *Harvard Business Review*, January–February. Retrieved from https://hbr. org/1992/01/the-balanced-scorecard-measures-that-drive-performance-2/ (accessed 3 June 2019).

Karr, D. (2017). The top 5 customer service challenges (and how to correct them). *MarTech*, 22 September. Retrieved from https://martech.zone/customer-service-challenges/ (accessed 27 May 2019).

Katsov, I. (2018). Algorithmic pricing, part I: The risks and opportunities, *Grid Dynamics*, 11 December. Retrieved from https://blog.griddynamics.com/algorithmic-pricing-part-i-the-risks-and-opportunities/ (accessed 29 May 2019).

Keane, S. and Stamm, J. (2005). Customer satisfaction and "feature fatigue". *Marketing Science Institute*, 1 January. Retrieved from www.msi.org/articles/customer-satisfac tion-and-feature-fatigue/ (accessed 27 May 2019).

Keith, R. (1960). The marketing revolution. *Journal of Marketing*, 24(3), 35–38.

Keller, K. (1987). Memory factors in advertising: The effect of advertising retrieval cues on brand evaluations. *Journal of Consumer Research*, 14(3), 316–333.

Keller, K. (1993). Conceptualizing, measuring, and managing customer-based brand equity. *Journal of Marketing*, 57 (January), 7.

Keller, K. (2013). *Strategic Brand Management* (4th edn). Harlow: Pearson Education.

Kelly, E. (2015). Introduction: Business ecosystems come of age. *Deloitte Insights*, 15 April. Retrieved from https://www2.deloitte.com/insights/us/en/focus/business-trends/2015/business-ecosystems-come-of-age-business-trends.html (accessed 29 May 2019).

Kelly, E. and Marchese, K. (2015). Supply chains and value webs. *Deloitte Insights*, 15 April. Retrieved from https://www2.deloitte.com/insights/us/en/focus/business-trends/2015/supply-chains-to-value-webs-business-trends.html (accessed 29 May 2019).

Kevan, T. (2017). GE looks for a line of sight on 3D builds with digital twins. *Rapid Ready Technology*, 18 December. Retrieved from www.rapidreadytech.com/2017/12/ge-looks-for-a-line-of-sight-on-3d-builds-with-digital-twins/ (accessed 27 May 2019).

Khan, M., Serafeim, G. and Yoon, A. (2015). Corporate sustainability: First evidence on materiality. Harvard University. Working Paper 15-073. Retrieved from https://dash.harvard.edu/bitstream/handle/1/14369106/15-073.pdf?sequence=1 (accessed 3 June 2019).

Kim, J. (2016). The platform business model and business ecosystem: Quality management and revenue structures. *European Planning Studies*, 24(12), 2113–2132.

Korody, C. (2013). Defining the differences between event marketing and experiential marketing. *CK Writes*, 23 August. Retrieved from www.ckwrites.com/event-marketing-and-experiential-marketing/ (accessed 29 May 2019).

Kotler, P. (1977). From sales obsession to marketing effectiveness. *Harvard Business Review*, November. Retrieved from https://hbr.org/1977/11/from-sales-obsession-to-marketing-effectiveness (accessed 23 May 2019).

Kotler, P. (1994). *Principles of Marketing*. Harlow: Pearson.

Kotler, P. (1997). *Marketing Management* (7th edn). Englewood Cliffs, NJ: Prentice Hall.

Kotler, P. and Keller, K. (2015). *Marketing Management*. New York: Pearson Education.

Kotler, P. and Lee, N. (2005). Worth repeating. *Social Marketing Quarterly*, 11(3–4), 91–103.

KPMG (2016) *Consumer Adoption: How to Predict the Tipping Point*. November. Retrieved from https://assets.kpmg.com/content/dam/kpmg/be/pdf/Markets/open-minds-consumer-adoption-predicting-tipping-point.pdf (accessed 27 May 2019).

Krahe, S. (2018). Why payment is the new key to the customer. *Wirecard*, 24 May. Retrieved from https://blog.wirecard.com/why-payment-is-the-new-key-to-the-customer/ (accessed 29 May 2019).

Kuefler, J. (2017). A glimpse into the future at the Gartner Digital Marketing Conference. *Callahan*, 31 May. Retrieved from https://callahan.agency/a-glimpse-into-the-future-of-marketing-at-the-gartner-digital-marketing-conference/ (accessed 27 May 2019).

Kurczy, S. (n.d.). Brazil's economy, explained in a pair of flip-flops. *Americas Quarterly*. Retrieved from www.americasquarterly.org/content/brazils-economy-explained-pair-flip-flops (accessed 26 June 2019).

Lafley, A.G. (2002). Letter to Shareholders. *P&G 2002 Annual Report*. Retrieved from www.pginvestor.com/Cache/1001181140.PDF?O=PDF&T=&Y=&D=&FID=1001181140&iid=4004124 (accessed 27 May 2019).

Lai, A. (2016). *The Rise of the Empowered Customer*. Forrester, 12 July. Retrieved from www.forrester.com/report/The+Rise+Of+The+Empowered+Customer/-/E-RES133207 (accessed 27 May 2019).

Laja, P. (2018). Pricing experiments you might not know, but can learn from. *CXL*, 31 October. Retrieved from https://conversionxl.com/blog/pricing-experiments-you-might-not-know-but-can-learn-from/ (accessed 29 May 2019).

Lamb, C., Hair, J. and McDaniel, C. (2013). *MKTG* (6th edn). Boston, MA: Cengage Learning.

Lang, J. and Zhu A.X. (2017). Omni-channel is disrupting the beauty purchase journey. *Beauty Packaging*, 30 November. Retrieved from www.beautypackaging.com/contents/view_experts-opinion/2017-11-30/omni-channel-is-disrupting-the-beauty-purchase-journey (accessed 27 May 2019).

Lashinsky, A. (2012). Amazon's Jeff Bezos: The ultimate disrupter. *Fortune*, 16 November. Retrieved from http://fortune.com/2012/11/16/amazons-jeff-bezos-the-ultimate-disrupter/ (accessed 29 May 2019).

Lazaroff, L. (2017). Netflix is about to do to Hollywood what it did to television. *The Street*, 22 October. Retrieved from www.thestreet.com/story/14344453/1/netflix-movies-hollywood-television-future.html (accessed 27 May 2019).

Leach, M. (2017). Customer friction: What CPG marketers need to know. *Media Post*, 16 November. Retrieved from www.mediapost.com/publications/article/310334/customer-friction-what-cpg-marketers-need-to-know.html (accessed 27 May 2019).

Lecinski, J. (2011). *Winning the Zero Moment of Truth*. Think With Google, June. Retrieved from www.thinkwithgoogle.com/marketing-resources/micro-moments/2011-winning-zmot-ebook/ (accessed 27 May 2019).

Lellahom, M.B. (2017). Cause-related marketing: A win-win for brands, charities and the consumer. *Entrepreneur*, 18 July. Retrieved from www.entrepreneur.com/article/297333 (accessed 23 May 2019).

Leonetti, A. (2019). Global chocolate market will reach $ 161.56 bn by 2024. *The US Industry News*, 22 January. Retrieved from http://usindustrynews.com/7095/global-chocolate-market-will-reach-161-56-bn-by-2024/ (accessed 29 May 2019).

Leszinski, R. and Marn, M.V. (1997). Setting value, not price. *McKinsey Insights*, February. Retrieved from www.mckinsey.com/business-functions/marketing-and-sales/our-insights/setting-value-not-price (accessed 29 May 2019).

Levitt, T. (1981). Marketing intangible products and product intangibles. *Harvard Business Review*, May. Retrieved from https://hbr.org/1981/05/marketing-intangible-products-and-product-intangibles (accessed 23 May 2019).

LMMC (2016). A PESO for your thoughts. 12 September. Retrieved from www.lmmc.co.uk/a-peso-for-your-thoughts/ (accessed 3 June 2019).

Lusch, R.F. and Vargo, S.L. (2006). Service-dominant logic: Reactions, reflections and refinements. *Marketing Theory*, 6(3), 281–288.

Lush (n.d.). We believe. Retrieved from www.lushusa.com/story?cid=article_we-believe-statement (accessed 27 May 2019).

Luth Research (2016). *Know Your Customer's Journey* (ebook). Retrieved from https://luthresearch.com/ebook/know-customers-journey-e-book-2/ (accessed 25 June 2019).

MacEachern, D. (2018). Good life case studies series: Tony's Chocolonely raises the (chocolate) bar to make the cocoa supply chain more fair ... and sustainable. *Sustainable Brands*, 21 May. Retrieved from https://events.sustainablebrands.com/sb18vancouver/tonys-chocolonely-raises-the-chocolate-bar-to-make-the-cocoa-supply-chain-more-fair-and-sustainable/ (accessed 29 May 2019).

Macnamara, J., Lwin, M., Adi, A. and Zerfass, A. (2016). "PESO" media strategy shifts to "SOEP": Opportunities and ethical dilemmas. *Public Relations Review*, 42(3), 377–385.

Madrigal, A.C. (2014). How Netflix reverse engineered Hollywood. *The Atlantic*, 2 January. Retrieved from www.theatlantic.com/technology/archive/2014/01/how-netflix-reverse-engineered-hollywood/282679/ (accessed 27 May 2019).

Maechler, N., Poenaru, A., Rüdt von Collenberg, T. and Schulze, P. (2017). Finding the right digital balance in B2B customer experience. McKinsey, April. Retrieved from www.mckinsey.com/business-functions/marketing-and-sales/our-insights/finding-the-right-digital-balance-in-b2b-customer-experience (accessed 27 May 2019).

Magee, K. (2015). Inside Hegarty's first global cinema ad. *Campaign*, 24 September. Retrieved from www.campaignlive.com/article/inside-hegartys-first-global-cinema-ad/1365370 (accessed 29 May 2019).

Magids, S. and Leemon, D. (2017). Building an emotional connection creates value in financial services. *The Financial Brand*, 13 July. Retrieved from https://thefinancialbrand.com/66326/banking-customer-experience-growth-strategy/ (accessed 27 May 2019).

Maloney, C. (2010). The secret to accelerating diffusion of innovation: The 16% rule explained. *Innovate or Die*, 10 May. Retrieved from https://innovateordie.com.au/2010/05/10/the-secret-to-accelerating-diffusion-of-innovation-the-16-rule-explained/ (accessed 27 May 2019).

Maltzer, K., Veider, V. and Kathan, W. (2015). Adapting to the sharing economy. *MIT Sloan Management Review*, Winter. Retrieved from https://sloanreview.mit.edu/article/adapting-to-the-sharing-economy/ (accessed 27 May 2019).

M&S (n.d.). Climate change. Retrieved from https://corporate.marksandspencer.com/sustainability/business-wide/climate-change (accessed 27 May 2019).

Manifesto for Agile Software Development (2001). Principles behind the agile manifesto. Retrieved from http://agilemanifesto.org/principles.html (accessed 27 May 2019).

Mantena, R. and Sundaraarajan, A. (2002). Competing in markets with digital convergence: Product differentiation, platform scope, and equilibrium structure, NYU Working Paper No. 2451/14170. Retrieved from http://pages.stern.nyu.edu/~rmantena/papers/msdec02.pdf (accessed 23 May 2019).

Marketing Science Institute (2012). Marketing in the ecosystem. 8 October. Retrieved from www.msi.org/articles/marketing-in-the-ecosystem-1/ (accessed 27 May 2019).

Marketing Wit (2018). Paramount examples of physical evidence in marketing. 1 March. Retrieved from https://marketingwit.com/examples-of-physical-evidence-in-marketing (accessed 27 May 2019).

Markman, J. (2018). This is why you need to learn about edge computing. *Forbes*, 3 April. Retrieved from www.forbes.com/sites/jonmarkman/2018/04/03/this-is-why-you-need-to-learn-about-edge-computing/#4d30ac5e1a56 (accessed 23 May 2019).

Marn, M.V., Roegner, E.V. and Zawada, C.C. (2003a). The power of pricing. *McKinsey Insights*, February. Retrieved from www.mckinsey.com/business-functions/marketing-and-sales/our-insights/the-power-of-pricing (accessed 29 May 2019).

Marn, M.V., Roegner, E.V. and Zawada, C.C. (2003b). Pricing new products. *McKinsey Insights*, August. Retrieved from www.mckinsey.com/business-functions/marketing-and-sales/our-insights/pricing-new-products (accessed 25 June 2019).

Marn, M.V. and Rosiello, R.L. (1992). Managing price, gaining profit. *Harvard Business Review*, September–October. Retrieved from https://hbr.org/1992/09/managing-price-gaining-profit (accessed 29 May 2019).

Marous, J. (2015). Use buyer personas to define digital banking consumers. *The Financial Brand*, 8 June. Retrieved from https://thefinancialbrand.com/52234/banking-segmentation-digital-persona-report/ (accessed 27 May 2019).

Marous, J. (2018). The massive millennial shake up in traditional wealth management. *The Financial Brand*, 20 March. Retrieved from https://thefinancialbrand.com/71459/millennial-wealth-management-banking-digital-cx-trends/ (accessed 27 May 2019).

Marr, B. (2018). The Internet of Things (IOT) will be massive in 2018: Here are the 4 predictions from IBM. *Forbes*, 4 January. Retrieved from www.forbes.com/sites/bernardmarr/2018/01/04/the-internet-of-things-iot-will-be-massive-in-2018-here-are-the-4-predictions-from-ibm/#21856714edd3 (accessed 27 May 2019).

Martin, C. (2018). Smart home devices working together tops brand loyalty. *Media Post*, 5 June. Retrieved from www.mediapost.com/publications/article/320268/smart-home-devices-working-together-tops-brand-loy.html (accessed 27 May 2019).

Maslow, A. (1970). *Motivation and Personality*. New York: Harper & Row.

Masters, K. (2016). The Netflix backlash: Why Hollywood fears a content monopoly. *The Hollywood Reporter*, 14 September. Retrieved from www.hollywoodreporter.com/features/netflix-backlash-why-hollywood-fears-928428 (accessed 27 May 2019).

Maxwell, M. (2015). Guest post: Lesson in leadership: Price – the neglected "P" – has Cinderella arrived at the ball? *Professional Pricing Society*, 25 September. Retrieved from http://professionalpricingsociety.blogspot.com/ (accessed 29 May 2019).

McAllister, C. (2017). TEI 106: Jobs to be done – with Tony Ulwick. *Product Innovation Educators*. Retrieved from https://productinnovationeducators.com/blog/tei-106-jobs-to-be-done-with-tony-ulwick/ (accessed 27 May 2019).

McKinsey (2014). *Product Excellence.* Retrieved from www.mckinsey.com/~/media/ McKinsey/Business%20Functions/Operations/Our%20Insights/Driving%20success%20 through%20true%20product%20excellence/Driving%20success%20through%20true%20 product%20excellence.ashx (accessed 3 June 2019).

McKinsey (2017). *Digital Reinvention.* January. Retrieved from www.mckinsey.com/~/ media/mckinsey/business%20functions/mckinsey%20digital/our%20insights/digital%20 reinvention/digital%20reinvention.ashx (accessed 27 May 2019).

McLaughlin, J. (2011). What is a brand, anyway? *Forbes,* 21 December. Retrieved from www. forbes.com/sites/jerrymclaughlin/2011/12/21/what-is-a-brand-anyway/#503b67652a1b (accessed 10 June 2019).

McNair, C. (2018). Global ad spending update. *eMarketer,* 20 November. Retrieved from www.emarketer.com/content/global-ad-spending-update (accessed 29 May 2019).

Mediatel Newsline (2018). MediaCom scoops Media Network of the Year at Cannes Lions. 22 June. Retrieved from https://mediatel.co.uk/newsline/2018/06/22/mediacom-scoops-media-network-of-the-year-at-cannes-lions/ (accessed 27 May 2019).

Medium (2016). Branded House vs House of Brands vs Hybrid. 15 January. Retrieved from https://medium.com/@JenBonhomme/branded-house-vs-house-of-brands-vs-hybrid-d3717e8db63f (accessed 3 June 2019).

Mills, J. (2015). Trends and innovations in male grooming. *Datamonitor Consumer,* April. Retrieved from www.vietbeautyshow.com/Portals/6/Trends%20and%20innovations%20 in%20male%20grooming.pdf (accessed 27 May 2019).

Millward Brown (2013). *Why Brand Personality Matters.* Millward Brown Perspectives, Volume 6. Retrieved from www.millwardbrown.com/docs/default-source/insight-docu ments/published-books/MillwardBrown_Perspectives_v6.pdf (accessed 10 June 2019).

Mintzberg, H. (1994). The rise and fall of strategic planning. *Harvard Business Review,* January–February. Retrieved from https://hbr.org/1994/01/the-fall-and-rise-of-strategic-planning (accessed 27 May 2019).

Mobile Payments Today (2017). Personal finance app Yolt sees success in the U.K. 1 December. Retrieved from www.mobilepaymentstoday.com/news/personal-finance-app-yolt-sees-success-in-the-uk/ (accessed 27 May 2019).

Modern Slavery News (2019). Chocotruck coming through: Tony's Chocolonely debuts interactive chocolate experience at SXSW. *ESC International,* 7 March. Retrieved from www.escinternational.org/feed-items/chocotruck-coming-through-tonys-chocolonely-debuts-interactive-chocolate-experience-at-sxsw-prnewswire/ (accessed 29 May 2019).

Moebius, R. and Staack, V. (2015). Strategic product value management: How companies can improve innovation, reduce costs and mitigate risk. *Strategy&,* 29 July. Retrieved from www.strategyand.pwc.com/reports/strategic-product-value-management (accessed 27 May 2019).

Mohieldin, M. and Vandycke, N. (2017). Sustainable mobility for the 21st century. *The World Bank*, 10 July. Retrieved from www.worldbank.org/en/news/feature/2017/07/10/sustainable-mobility-for-the-21st-century (accessed 27 May 2019).

Monllos, K. (2018). Budweiser highlights disaster relief efforts, real employees in 60-second Super Bowl spot. *Adweek*, 26 January. Retrieved from www.adweek.com/brand-marketing/budweiser-highlights-disaster-relief-efforts-real-employees-in-60-second-super-bowl-spot/ (accessed 27 May 2019).

Moon, Y. (2005). Break free from the product life cycle. *Harvard Business Review*, May. Retrieved from https://hbr.org/2005/05/break-free-from-the-product-life-cycle (accessed 27 May 2019).

Moore, C. (2018). Amazon ups its smart home game with a new Echo Show, microwave, and clock. *Digital Trends*, 20 September. Retrieved from www.digitaltrends.com/home/amazon-event-smart-home-2018/ (accessed 27 May 2019).

Moore, G.A. (1991). *Crossing the Chasm: Marketing and Selling High-tech Goods to Mainstream Customers*. New York: HarperBusiness.

Moorman, C. (2018). *The CMO Survey: Topline Results*. August. Retrieved from https://cmo-survey.org/wp-content/uploads/sites/15/2018/09/The_CMO_Survey-Topline_Report-Aug-2018.pdf (accessed 27 May 2019).

Moorman, C. (2019). *The CMO Survey: Highlights and Insights Report*. February. Retrieved from https://cmosurvey.org/wp-content/uploads/sites/15/2019/02/The_CMO_Survey-Highlights-and_Insights_Report-Feb-2019.pdf (accessed 3 June 2019).

Moran, J. (2016). Marketing to the segment of one. *Digitalist Magazine*, 5 January. Retrieved from www.digitalistmag.com/customer-experience/2016/01/05/marketing-segment-one-03919877 (accessed 27 May 2019).

Moreno, D., Rodríguez, R. and Zambrana, R. (2014). The relevance of portfolio management core competencies in outsourcing decisions. *SSRN*, 15 October. Retrieved from https://papers.ssrn.com/sol3/papers.cfm?abstract_id=2332655 (accessed 27 May 2019).

Morgan, N.A. and Piercy N.F. (1993). Strategic and operational market segmentation: A managerial analysis. *Journal of Strategic Marketing*, 1(2), 123–140. Retrieved from www.tandfonline.com/doi/abs/10.1080/09652549300000008 (accessed 27 May 2019).

Morris, D.Z. (2016). Netflix says geography, age, and gender are "garbage" for predicting taste. *Fortune*, 27 March. Retrieved from http://fortune.com/2016/03/27/netflix-predicts-taste/ (accessed 27 May 2019).

Morrison, M.A., Haley, E., Sheehan, K.B. and Taylor, R.E. (2011). *Using Qualitative Research in Advertising: Strategies, Techniques, and Applications*. Thousand Oaks, CA: Sage Publications.

Muijs, W. (2016). Why ING excels in customer experience and digital transformation. Business Architecture & Consultancy, 19 November. Retrieved from www.digitalsocial

strategy.org/bac/2016/11/19/why-ing-excels-in-customer-experience-and-digital-trans
formation/ (accessed 27 May 2019).

Mull, C. (2013). *B2B's Digital Evolution*. Think With Google, February. Retrieved from www.
thinkwithgoogle.com/marketing-resources/b2b-digital-evolution/ (accessed 27 May 2019).

Muller, E., Peres, R. and Mahajan, V. (2009). *Innovation Diffusion and New Product
Growth*. Marketing Science Institute. Retrieved from www.msi.org/uploads/summaries/
Exec_Summ_MSI_RKS_09-601.pdf (accessed 27 May 2019).

Müller, Z., Veér, B., Janurik, A., Radnói, L. and Bérdi, T. (2018). *The Anchor Moment: Customer
Experience Excellence Report*. KPMG. Retrieved from https://assets.kpmg/content/dam/
kpmg/hu/pdf/KPMG%20-%20The%20Anchor%20Moment.pdf (accessed 29 May 2019).

Nagurney, A. (2006). *Supply Chain Network Economics: Dynamics of Prices, Flows, and
Profits*. Cheltenham: Edward Elgar.

Nail, J. (2006). The 4 types of engagement. *iMedia Connection*, 15 October. Retrieved from
www.imediaconnection.com/articles/ported-articles/red-dot-articles/2006/oct/the-4-
types-of-engagement/ (accessed 29 May 2019).

Namaky, K. (2016). 4 reasons why Aveeno's brand positioning statement is great. *Gurulocity*,
28 October. Retrieved from https://gurulocity.com/aveeno-brand-positioning-statement-
examples-great/ (accessed 27 May 2019).

Nash, J. (2016). Manufacturing vs. IT: Mind the gap. *Information Week*, 4 January. Retrieved
from www.informationweek.com/iot/manufacturing-vs-it-mind-the-gap/d/d-id/1323744
(accessed 29 May 2019).

Nerkar, A. (2003). Old is gold? The value of temporal exploration in the creation of new
knowledge. *Management Science*, 49(2), 211–229.

Netflix (n.d.). Where is Netflix available? Retrieved from https://help.netflix.com/en/
node/14164 (accessed 27 May 2019).

Netflix (2017a). Netflix acquires Millarworld. 7 August. Retrieved from https://media.netflix.
com/en/press-releases/netflix-acquires-millarworld-1 (accessed 27 May 2019).

Netflix (2017b). Renewable energy at Netflix: An update. 14 June. Retrieved from https://media.
netflix.com/en/company-blog/renewable-energy-at-netflix-an-update (accessed 17 September
2019)

Netflix Investors (2018). Netflix's view: Internet entertainment is replacing linear TV. 22
January. Retrieved from www.netflixinvestor.com/ir-overview/long-term-view/default.
aspx (accessed 27 May 2019).

The New Division (2018). The Global Goals design. Retrieved from www.thenewdivision.
world/the-global-goals (accessed 3 June 2019).

Ngoulma, J. (2015). Consumers' willingness to pay for dairy products: What the studies
say? A meta-analysis. *MPRA*, 25 June. Retrieved from https://mpra.ub.uni-muenchen.
de/65250/1/MPRA_paper_65250.pdf (accessed 29 May 2019).

Nichols, L. (2015). Visit California seeks digitally savvy global agency partner. *PRWeek*, 26 May. Retrieved from www.prweek.com/article/1348756/visit-california-seeks-digitally-savvy-global-agency-partner#fBETdIeIx7ZVCceU.99 (accessed 29 May 2019).

Nieburg, O. (2017). Tony's Chocolonely eyes mainstream retail to show 'slave-free chocolate' works in the US. *Confectionery News*, 30 August. Retrieved from www.confectionerynews.com/Article/2017/08/31/Tony-s-Chocolonely-targets-US-mainstream-retail-after-going-national (accessed 29 May 2019).

Nield, D. (2017). All the sensors in your smartphone, and how they work. *Gizmodo*, 23 July. Retrieved from https://gizmodo.com/all-the-sensors-in-your-smartphone-and-how-they-work-1797121002\ (accessed 23 May 2019).

Nielsen (2014). The state of private label around the world. November. Retrieved from www.nielsen.com/content/dam/nielsenglobal/kr/docs/global-report/2014/Nielsen%20Global%20Private%20Label%20Report%20November%202014.pdf (accessed 29 May 2019).

Nielsen (2017). The changing face of beauty. 21 December. Retrieved from www.nielsen.com/in/en/insights/reports/2017/the-changing-face-of-beauty.html/.html?sortbyScore=false&tag=Category%3AFMCG+and+Retail (accessed 27 May 2019).

Nobel, C. (2013). Neuromarketing: Tapping into the "pleasure center" of consumers. *Forbes*, 1 February. Retrieved from www.forbes.com/sites/hbsworkingknowledge/2013/02/01/neuromarketing-tapping-into-the-pleasure-center-of-consumers/#ced0ed02745c (accessed 27 May 2019).

Normann, R. (1991). *Service Management: Strategy and Leadership in Businesses* (2nd edn). New York: John Wiley & Sons.

NuVizz (2016). What does UberRush mean to enterprises and the last mile? 20 June. Retrieved from https://nuvizz.com/uberrush-mean-enterprises-last-mile/ (accessed 29 May 2019).

Oculus (n.d.). Marketing analytics manager, AR/VR. Retrieved from www.oculus.com/careers/a1K6A000001qPpbUAE/ (accessed 3 June 2019).

O'Rourke, D. and Ringer, A. (2015). The impact of sustainability information on consumer decision making. *Journal of Industrial Ecology*, 20(4), 882–892. http://dx.doi.org/10.1111/jiec.12310.

Oster, E. (2017). Mekanism launches "One For All" effort for the United Nations. *AdWeek*, 30 January. Retrieved from www.adweek.com/agencyspy/mekanism-launches-one-for-all-effort-for-the-united-nations/124879/ (accessed 29 May 2019).

Osterwalder, A. (2013). A better way to think about your business model. *Harvard Business Review*, 6 May. Retrieved from https://hbr.org/2013/05/a-better-way-to-think-about-yo (accessed 27 May 2019).

Page Fair (2015). The 2015 ad blocking report. 10 August. Retrieved from https://pagefair.com/blog/2015/ad-blocking-report/ (accessed 29 May 2019).

Palmatier, R., Dant, R., Grewal, D. and Evans, K. (2006). Factors influencing the effectiveness of relationship marketing: A meta-analysis. *Journal of Marketing*, 70(4), 136–153.

Palmatier, R.W. and Sridhar, S. (2017). *Marketing Strategy: Based on First Principles and Data Analytics*. Basingstoke: Palgrave.

Pankraz, D. (2018). Obsess over your brand conviction, not brand purpose. *Mumbrella*, 14 May. Retrieved from https://mumbrella.com.au/obsess-over-your-brand-conviction-not-brand-purpose-517471 (accessed 10 June 2019).

Parsons, M. (2017a). The futurist: Individualisation is the future of marketing. *Marketing*, 3 February. Retrieved from www.marketing-interactive.com/features/the-futurist-individualisation-is-the-future-of-marketing/ (accessed 27 May 2019).

Parsons, R. (2017b). How Diageo is proving marketing effectiveness. *Marketing Week*, 11 October. Retrieved from www.marketingweek.com/2017/10/11/diageo-and-catalyst/ (accessed 3 June 2019).

Patchett, L. and Gwynn, S. (2018). Tesco goes big on Britishness with discounter brand Jack's. *Campaign Live*, 19 September. Retrieved from www.campaignlive.co.uk/article/tesco-goes-big-britishness-discounter-brand-jacks/1493351 (accessed 22 May 2019).

Patel, N. (n.d.). How marketers are getting their message across in an ad-blocking world. *Neil Patel*. Retrieved from https://neilpatel.com/blog/ad-blocking-world/ (accessed 29 May 2019).

Pathiaki, K. (2018). Airbnb brand value exceeds all but one hotel brand for the first time. *The Caterer*, 8 February. Retrieved from www.thecaterer.com/articles/520366/airbnb-brand-value-exceeds-all-but-one-hotel-brand-for-the-first-time (accessed 10 June 2019).

Pekala, N. (2010). Marketing segmentation in the digital age. *Marketing Researchers*. Retrieved from www.nancypekala.com/wp-content/uploads/2012/06/marketing-segmentation-digital-age.pdf (accessed 27 May 2019).

Peppers, D. and Rogers, M. (1993). *The One to One Future: Building Relationships One Customer at a Time*. New York: Doubleday.

Peters, A. (2015). The UN's Global Goals get a rebrand to spur people to action. *Fast Company*, 18 September. Retrieved from www.fastcompany.com/3051101/the-uns-global-goals-get-a-rebrand-to-spur-people-to-action (accessed 29 May 2019).

Peterson, R. and Wotruba, T. (1996). What is direct selling? Definition, perspectives, and research agenda. *The Journal of Personal Selling and Sales Management*, 16(4), 1–16.

Petro, G. (2014). Why pricing power is the real secret to value investing. *Forbes*, 6 August. Retrieved from www.forbes.com/sites/gregpetro/2014/08/06/why-pricing-power-is-the-real-secret-to-value-investing/#3d2ec06d2565 (accessed 29 May 2019).

Philips (2016). Brighter warehouse, lower energy bills. Retrieved from www.lighting.philips.com/main/cases/cases/industry-and-logistics/staci (accessed 27 May 2019).

Phillips, C. (2012). The trinity of brand strategy. *Branding Strategy Insider*, 28 December. Retrieved from www.brandingstrategyinsider.com/2012/12/the-trinity-of-brand-strategy.html#.W6OxIfZOlPa (accessed 27 May 2019).

Polman, P. (2017). Reaping the rewards of the Sustainable Development Goals. *LinkedIn*, 16 January. Retrieved from www.linkedin.com/pulse/reaping-rewards-sustainable-development-goals-paul-polman (accessed 17 May 2019).

Poundstone, W. (2011). *Priceless: The Myth of Fair Value*. New York: Hill & Wang Publishers.

Prasad, A.R. and Manimala, M.J. (2018). Circular social innovation in India. *SSIR*, 31 January. Retrieved from https://ssir.org/articles/entry/circular_social_innovation_in_india (accessed 27 May 2019).

Press, G. (2014). 12 big data definitions: What's yours? *Forbes*, 3 September. Retrieved from www.forbes.com/sites/gilpress/2014/09/03/12-big-data-definitions-whats-yours/#15668b-ca13ae (accessed 27 May 2019).

PRME (n.d.). Overview. Retrieved from www.unprme.org/about-prme/index.php (accessed 27 May 2019).

Project Breakthrough (2017). Autonomous road vehicles. 11 July. Retrieved from http://breakthrough.unglobalcompact.org/disruptive-technologies/autonomous-road-vehicles/ (accessed 27 May 2019).

Pruitt, J. (2017). How to create a blueprint for operational success. *Inc*, 24 August. Retrieved from www.inc.com/jeff-pruitt/how-a-service-blueprint-can-turn-your-business-aro.html (accessed 29 May 2019).

Pryhodko, G. (2017). Marketplaces by types of participants: C2C, B2C and B2B. *Marketplace Wiki*. Retrieved from http://wiki.rademade.com/marketplace-c2c-b2c-b2b (accessed 23 May 2019).

PYMNTS (2017). Making a "nicer" world with a smarter supply chain. 16 October. Retrieved from www.pymnts.com/news/retail/2017/tonys-chocolonelys-ethical-chocolate-industry-supply-chain/ (accessed 29 May 2019).

Ramaswamy, S. (2015). How micro-moments are changing the rules. *Think With Google*, April. Retrieved from www.thinkwithgoogle.com/marketing-resources/micro-moments/how-micromoments-are-changing-rules/ (accessed 27 May 2019).

Rao, A. (2017). Digital twins beyond the industrials. *PWC*, 13 February. Retrieved from http://usblogs.pwc.com/emerging-technology/digital-twins/ (accessed 27 May 2019).

Rathmann, C. (2018). Impact of servitization on profitability. *Industry Today*, 24 July. Retrieved from https://industrytoday.com/article/impact-of-servitization-on-profitability/ (accessed 29 May 2019).

Ray, B. (2017). IoT vs. Industry 4.0 vs. Industrie 4.0 – What's the Difference? *IOT for All*, 27 April. Retrieved from www.iotforall.com/iot-vs-industry-4-0-vs-industrie-4-0/ (accessed 23 May 2019).

Reilly, D. (2016). Why cultivating strategic anticipation is vital for future business success. *CMO*, 10 February. Retrieved from www.cmo.com/features/articles/2016/2/9/why-cultivating-strategic-anticipation-is-vital-for-future-business-success.html#gs.0vye0j (accessed 3 June 2019).

Reisman, R. (2019). Resource Guide to Pricing – Finding Fair Value Exchange. *The Fair Pay Zone*, 15 January. Retrieved from www.fairpayzone.com/p/pricing.html (accessed 29 May 2019).

Renner, R., Cotteleer, M. and Holdowsky, J. (2018). Cognitive technologies: A technical primer. *Deloitte Insights*, 6 February. Retrieved from https://www2.deloitte.com/insights/us/en/focus/cognitive-technologies/technical-primer.html (accessed 3 June 2019).

Research Briefs (2018). Zara's speedy apparel supply chain visualized. *CB Insights*, 26 October. Retrieved from www.cbinsights.com/research/zara-apparel-supply-chain/ (accessed 3 June 2019).

Research Briefs (2019). The future of fashion: From design to merchandising, how tech is reshaping the industry. *CB Insights*, 21 May. Retrieved from www.cbinsights.com/research/fashion-tech-future-trends/ (accessed 29 May 2019).

Retail Supply Chain Insights (2018). Red Wing Shoe Company is live with Red Wing for business. 4 January. Retrieved from www.retailsupplychaininsights.com/doc/red-wing-shoe-company-is-live-with-red-wing-for-business-0001 (accessed 27 May 2019).

Revella, A. (2015). *Buyer Personas: How to Gain Insight into Your Customer's Expectations, Align Your Marketing Strategies, and Win More Business*. Hoboken, NJ: Wiley.

RFi Group (2017). UK: ING launches smart money app Yolt. 14 July. Retrieved from www.rfigroup.com/rfi-group/news/uk-ing-launches-smart-money-app-yolt (accessed 27 May 2019).

Riemersma, F. (2018). What are the most popular MarTech tools according to 110 stackies? *MartechTribe*. Retrieved from https://martechtribe.com/blog/what-are-the-most-popular-martech-tools-according-to-110-stackies/ (accessed 27 May 2019).

Rigby, D.K., Sutherland, J. and Takeuchi, H. (2016a). The secret history of agile innovation. *Harvard Business Review*, 20 April. Retrieved from https://hbr.org/2016/04/the-secret-history-of-agile-innovation (accessed 27 May 2019).

Rigby, D.K., Sutherland, J. and Takeuchi, H. (2016b). Embracing agile. *Harvard Business Review*, May. Retrieved from https://hbr.org/2016/05/embracing-agile (accessed 27 May 2019).

Ritson, M. (2017). Mark Ritson: Facebook's segmentation abilities are depressingly impressive. *Marketing Week*, 9 November. Retrieved from www.marketingweek.com/2017/11/09/mark-ritson-facebook-segmentation/ (accessed 27 May 2019).

Rivkin, S. and Sutherland, F. (2004). *The Making of a Name: The Inside Story of the Brands We Buy*. Oxford: Oxford University Press.

Roach, T. (2018). Fwd to CEO: The most valuable business tool ever invented. *BBH Labs*, 22 March. Retrieved from http://bbh-labs.com/fwd-to-ceo-the-most-valuable-business-tool-ever-invented/ (accessed 10 June 2019).

Roberts, J.J. (2017). Beyond Bitcoin: Overstock lets customers pay with more than 40 alt coins. *Fortune*, 8 August. Retrieved from http://fortune.com/2017/08/08/overstock-digital-currency/ (accessed 27 May 2019).

Rogers, K. and Cosgrove, A. (2018). Eight forces that will shape the future consumer. *EY*, 24 May. Retrieved from www.ey.com/en_gl/growth/eight-forces-that-will-shape-the-future-consumer (accessed 27 May 2019).

Ross, A. and Srinivas, V. (2018). *Accelerating Digital Transformation in Banking: Findings from the Global Consumer Survey on Digital Banking*. Deloitte Insights. Retrieved from https://www2.deloitte.com/content/dam/Deloitte/us/Documents/financial-services/us-accelerating-digital-transformation-in-banking.pdf (accessed 27 May 2017).

Rossi, B. (2017). How Tesco is using AI to gain customer insight, Information Age, 17 May. Retrieved from www.information-age.com/tesco-using-ai-gain-customer-insight-123466328/ (accessed 22 May 2019).

Rouse, M. (2018). Omnichannel. *TechTarget*. Retrieved from https://searchcio.techtarget.com/definition/omnichannel (accessed 27 May 2019).

Ruiz, I. (2017). The Zara phenomenon: Due to cloud computing. *Leading Trends In Information Technology Blog*, 13 July. Retrieved from https://mse238blog.stanford.edu/2017/07/imunizr/the-zara-phenomenon-due-to-cloud-computing/ (accessed 29 May 2019).

Rushe, E. (2019). Tony's Chocolonely brings slave free chocolate mission to UK supermarkets Sainsbury's, Whole Foods. *Forbes*, 19 January. Retrieved from www.forbes.com/sites/elizabethrushe/2019/01/19/tonys-chocolonely-brings-slave-free-chocolate-mission-to-uk-supermarkets-sainsburys-whole-foods/#59f60a574096 (accessed 29 May 2019).

Sable, D. and Jones, L. (2018). *Purpose 2020: Igniting Purpose-led Growth*. Kantar Consulting. Retrieved from https://consulting.kantar.com/wp-content/uploads/2019/06/Purpose-2020-PDF-Presentation.pdf (accessed 27 May 2019).

Saco, R.M. and Goncalves, A.P. (2008). Service design: An appraisal. *Design Management Review*, 19(1), 10–19.

Salsify (2017). New research finds consumers use mobile devices for product information Whether shopping in-store or at home. *Cision*, 5 April. Retrieved from www.prnewswire.com/news-releases/new-research-finds-consumers-use-mobile-devices-for-product-information-whether-shopping-in-store-or-at-home-300434981.html (accessed 27 May 2019).

Samsung (2017). *Samsung Electronics Sustainability Report 2017*. Retrieved from https://images.samsung.com/is/content/samsung/p5/global/ir/docs/Samsung_Electronics_Sustainability_Report_2017.pdf (accessed 27 May 2019).

Saxena, A. (2018). *Making Online Shopping Smarter with Advanced Analytics*. Cognizant, June. Retrieved from www.cognizant.com/InsightsWhitepapers/Making-Online-Shopping-Smarter-with-Advanced-Analytics.pdf (accessed 27 May 2019).

Schaal, D. (2014). Visit California launches celebrity China social media campaign. *Skift*, 15 April. Retrieved from https://skift.com/2013/04/15/visit-california-targets-chinese-visitors-with-first-direct-campaign/ (accessed 29 May 2019).

Schmidt, B., Rutkowsky, S., Petersen, I., Klötzke, F., Wallenburg, C.M. and Einmahl, L. (2015). *Digital Supply Chains: Increasingly Critical for Competitive Edge.* European A.T. Kearney/WHU Logistics Study 2015. Retrieved from www.atkearney.com/operations-performance-transformation/article?/a/digital-supply-chains-increasingly-critical-for-competitive-edge (accessed 29 May 2019).

Schmitt, D. (n.d.). Optimizing pricing strategy: Knowing the 5 W's will help get your pricing right. *Canadian Marketing Association.* Retrieved from www.the-cma.org/disciplines/analytics/archive/optimizing-pricing-strategy (accessed 29 May 2019).

Schrage, M. and Kiron, D. (2018). Leading with next-generation key performance indicators. *MIT Sloan Management Review*, 16 June. Retrieved from https://sloanreview.mit.edu/projects/leading-with-next-generation-key-performance-indicators/ (accessed 3 June 2019).

Schumann, D., Artis, A. and Rivera, R. (2001). The future of interactive advertising viewed through an IMC lens. *Journal of Interactive Advertising*, 1(2), 43–55.

Sciuto, A. (2017). How Nestlé Waters reclaimed the customer relationship. *Think With Google*, November. Retrieved from www.thinkwithgoogle.com/marketing-resources/omnichannel/nestle-personalized-customer-relationship/ (accessed 27 May 2019).

Seignette, E. (2018). How a chocolate brand is leading the way. *Sustainable Brand Index*, 14 May. Retrieved from www.sb-index.com/news/2018/6/15/chocolate (accessed 29 May 2019).

Selfish Giving (2015). A short history of cause marketing, 9 February. Retrieved from www.selfishgiving.com/blog/short-history-cause-marketing (accessed 23 May 2019).

Semans, D. (2010). *Brand Positioning: The Key to Brand Strength.* Polaris Marketing Research. Retrieved from http://cdn2.hubspot.net/hub/58820/docs/polarismr_brand_positioning.pdf (accessed 27 May 2019).

Shaw, J., Agarwal, P., Desveaux, L., Palma., D.C., Stamenova, V., Jamieson, T., ... Bhattacharyya, O. (2018). Beyond "implementation": Digital health innovation and service design. *NPJ Digital Medicine*, 1(48). Retrieved from www.nature.com/articles/s41746-018-0059-8#article-info (accessed 29 May 2019).

Shaw, P. (2015). *Brand Purpose – Why Brands Need to Be Superheroes.* Ipsos, February. Retrieved from www.ipsos.com/sites/default/files/publication/1970-01/asi-brand-purpose-feb2015.pdf (accessed 10 June 2019).

Shorty Awards (2016). Global Goals – Project Everyone. 8th Annual Shorty Awards. Retrieved from https://shortyawards.com/8th/global-goals-project-everyone (accessed 29 May 2019).

Shostack, G.L. (1982). How to design a service. *European Journal of Marketing*, 16(1), 49–63.

Shostack, G. L. (1984). Designing services that deliver. *Harvard Business Review*, January. Retrieved from https://hbr.org/1984/01/designing-services-that-deliver (accessed 29 May 2019).

Silvera, M. (2017). Tony's Chocolonely expands internationally with the Descartes Global Logistics Network. *Descartes*, 16 May. Retrieved from www.descartes.com/de/news-events/general-news/tonys-chocolonely-expands-internationally-descartes-global-logistic-network (accessed 29 May 2019).

Silverstein, B. (2013). Havaianas: From peasant footwear to global fashion powerhouse. *Brand Channel*, 24 April. Retrieved from www.brandchannel.com/2013/04/24/havaianas-from-peasant-footwear-to-global-fashion-powerhouse/ (accessed 26 June 2019).

Simon, C. and Sullivan, M. (1993). The measurement and determinants of brand equity: A financial approach, *Marketing Science*, 12 (1), 28-52.

Sims, D. (2018). What's at stake in Cannes's battle with Netflix. *The Atlantic*, 16 April. Retrieved from www.theatlantic.com/entertainment/archive/2018/04/cannes-netflix-battle/558026/ (accessed 27 May 2019).

Sinek, S. (2011). *Start With Why*. New York: Portfolio.

Smith, R.E., Chen, J. and Yang, X. (2008). The impact of advertising creativity on the hierarchy of effects. *Journal of Advertising*, 37(4), 47–62.

Solis, B. (2019). Altimeter's top digital trends for 2019. *Brian Solis*, 29 January. Retrieved from www.briansolis.com/2019/01/altimeters-top-digital-trends-for-2019/ (accessed 29 May 2019).

Solomon, M., Marshall, G. and Stuart, E. (2009). *Marketing: Real People, Real Choices*. Oamaru: Pearson Education.

Soundrarajan, R. and Veldhoen, S. (n.d.). 2017 consumer packaged goods trends. *Strategy&*. Retrieved from www.strategyand.pwc.com/trend/2017-Consumer-Packaged-Goods-Trends (accessed 27 May 2019).

Spann, M., Molitor, D. and Daurer, S. (2016). Tell me where you are and I'll tell you what you want: Using location data to improve marketing decisions. *GfK Marketing Intelligence Review*, 8(2), 30–37. Retrieved from www.gfk-verein.org/en/publications/gfk-marketing-intelligence-review/all-issues/marketing-and-data-science/tell-me-where-you-are-and-ill-tell-you-what-you-want-using-location-data-improve (accessed 27 May 2019).

Spenner, P. and Freeman, K. (2012). To keep your customers, keep it simple. *Harvard Business Review*, May. Retrieved from https://hbr.org/2012/05/to-keep-your-customers-keep-it-simple (accessed 27 May 2012).

Stanford Business (2006). Calculating the dollar value of brand equity. 1 February. Retrieved from www.gsb.stanford.edu/insights/calculating-dollar-value-brand-equity (accessed 10 June 2019).

Stanhope, J. (2018). *The Forrester Wave™: Enterprise Marketing Software Suites, Q1 2018*. Forrester, 13 February. Retrieved from www.adobe.com/content/dam/acom/en/modal-offers/pdfs/203484550.en.aec.The-Forrester-Wave-Enterprise-Marketing-Software-Suites-Q1-2018.pdf (accessed 27 May 2019).

The Star (2018). Danone may add milk-free ranges to flagship brands. 30 June. Retrieved from www.thestar.com.my/business/business-news/2018/06/30/danone-may-add-milk-free-ranges-to-flagship-brands/ (accessed 29 May 2019).

Statista (2019). E-commerce share of total global retail sales from 2015 to 2021. Retrieved from www.statista.com/statistics/534123/e-commerce-share-of-retail-sales-worldwide/ (accessed 27 May 2019).

Stephens, D. (2016). *Essentials of Consumer Behavior.* New York: Taylor & Francis

Sterling, G. (2012). Study: 90 percent use multiple screens during the same day. *Marketing Land*, 31 August. Retrieved from http://marketingland.com/study-90-percent-use-multiple-screens-throughout-the-same-day-20386 (accessed 29 May 2019).

Sterling, G. (2017). Report: Google beats Amazon for product-search reach, but rival sees greater loyalty. *Search Engine Land*, 14 September. Retrieved from https://searchengineland.com/report-google-beats-amazon-product-search-reach-rival-sees-greater-loyalty-282570 (accessed 27 May 2019).

Sternberg, J. (2018). What is ad fraud and how does it happen? *AdWeek*, 24 July. Retrieved from www.adweek.com/digital/what-is-ad-fraud-and-how-does-it-happen/ (accessed 29 May 2019).

Stewart, C. (2014). How to evaluate external secondary data. *Market Research Blog*, 5 June. Retrieved from http://blog.marketresearch.com/how-to-evaluate-external-secondary-data (accessed 27 May 2019).

Stewart, R. (2015). We the People: How Meryl Streep, Malala and Stephen Hawking pulled together with ordinary voices for UN Global Goals social push. *The Drum*, 30 September. Retrieved from www.thedrum.com/news/2015/09/30/we-people-how-meryl-streep-malala-and-stephen-hawking-pulled-together-ordinary (accessed 29 May 2019).

Stinchcomb, J. (2017). IAB Content Studio Showcase: 5 questions for Josh Stinchcomb of 23 Stories x Condé Nast. *IAB Blog*, 11 October. Retrieved from www.iab.com/news/iab-content-studio-showcase-5-questions-josh-stinchcomb-23-stories-x-conde-nast/ (accessed 29 May 2019).

Strategy& (2005). *Managing Brands for Value Creation.* 1 March. Retrieved from www.strategyand.pwc.com/media/file/Strategyand_Managing-brands-for-value-creation.pdf (accessed 1 March 2019).

Strategyn (n.d.). Outcome-Driven Innovation. Retrieved from https://strategyn.com/outcome-driven-innovation-process/ (accessed 25 June 2019).

Strategyn Pricing Strategy (n.d.). Price the product right. Retrieved from https://strategyn.com/pricingstrategy/ (accessed 29 May 2019).

Sustainable Brands (2017). Sustainable living products continue to drive Unilever's growth. 19 May. Retrieved from https://sustainablebrands.com/read/walking-the-talk-1/sustainable-living-products-continue-to-drive-unilever-s-growth (accessed 27 May 2019).

Svahn, F., Mathiassen, L., Lindgren, R. and Kane, G.C. (2017). Mastering the digital innovation challenge. *MIT Sloan Management Review*, Spring. Retrieved from http://ilp.mit.edu/media/news_articles/smr/2017/58315.pdf (accessed 27 May 2019).

Tableau (2017). Forbes CMO practice marketing accountability report. Retrieved from www.tableau.com/learn/whitepapers/forbes-cmo-practice-marketing-accountability-report?ref=lp&signin=a0147d68fc06ee84128db5c7bf4fdfb2&reg-delay=TRUE (accessed 29 May 2019).

Temkin, B. (2018). Report: 2018 Temkin Experience Ratings (U.S.). *Experience Matters*, 20 March. Retrieved from https://experiencematters.blog/2018/03/20/report-2018-temkin-experience-ratings-u-s/ (accessed 29 May 2019).

TescoLabs (2017). Arcohol – a collaboration from Tesco Labs and ribot. 24 April. Retrieved from www.tescolabs.com/arcohol-a-collaboration-from-tesco-labs-and-ribot/ (accessed 23 May 2019).

Tesseras, L. (2018). Diageo claims marketing effectiveness drive is making its "pounds work harder". *Marketing Week*, 25 January. Retrieved from www.marketingweek.com/2018/01/25/diageos-marketing-effectiveness-drive-is-making-its-pounds-work-harder/ (accessed 29 May 2019).

Think With Google (n.d.). Micro-Moments Now: New consumer behaviors you need to know. Retrieved from www.thinkwithgoogle.com/data-collections/micro-moments-consumer-behavior-immediate-expectations/ (accessed 27 May 2019).

Think With Google (2015). Connecting data and people with the Internet of Things. July. Retrieved from www.thinkwithgoogle.com/intl/en-gb/consumer-insights/connecting-data-and-people-with-the-internet-of-things/ (accessed 27 May 2019).

Think With Google (2017a). Consumer Barometer Study 2017 – The year of the mobile majority. December. Retrieved from www.thinkwithgoogle.com/intl/en-154/marketing-collections/mobile/consumer-barometer-study-2017-year-mobile-majority/ (accessed 27 May 2019).

Think With Google (2017b). No decision is too small for today's consumers. Retrieved from www.thinkwithgoogle.com/feature/mobile-search-behavior/#/ (accessed 27 May 2019).

Thoeni, A.T., Marshall, G.W. and Campbell, S.M. (2016). A resource-advantage theory typology of strategic segmentation. *European Journal of Marketing*, 50(12), 2192–2215. https://doi.org/10.1108/EJM-08-2015-0585

Thomas, J.W. (2017). *Market Segmentation*. Decision Analyst. Retrieved from www.decisionanalyst.com/media/downloads/MarketSegmentation.pdf (accessed 27 May 2019).

Thompson, D. (2013). Airbnb CEO Brian Chesky on building a company and starting a "sharing" revolution. *The Atlantic*, 13 August. Retrieved from www.theatlantic.com/business/archive/2013/08/airbnb-ceo-brian-chesky-on-building-a-company-and-starting-a-sharing-revolution/278635/ (accessed 10 June 2019).

Titcomb, J. (2018). Netflix codes: The secret numbers that unlock thousands of hidden films and TV shows. *The Telegraph*, 4 September. Retrieved from www.telegraph.co.uk/on-demand/0/netflix-codes-secret-numbers-unlock-1000s-hidden-films-tv-shows/ (accessed 27 May 2019).

Treadway, J. (2016). Using an IoT gateway to connect the "things" to the cloud. *TechTarget*. Retrieved from https://internetofthingsagenda.techtarget.com/feature/Using-an-IoT-gateway-to-connect-the-Things-to-the-cloud (accessed 23 May 2019).

Trefis Team and Great Speculations. (2016). Here's how Estee Lauder is strengthening its position in the anti-aging market. *Forbes*, 12 December. Retrieved from www.forbes.com/sites/greatspeculations/2016/12/12/heres-how-estee-lauder-is-strengthening-its-position-in-the-anti-aging-market/#c807e33f3740 (accessed 27 May 2019).

Trip Advisor (n.d.). Tony's Chocolonely Store. Retrieved from www.tripadvisor.com/Attraction_Review-g188590-d13630594-Reviews-Tony_s_Chocolonely_Store-Amsterdam_North_Holland_Province.html (accessed 29 May 2019).

Twinings (2018). *Sourced With Care, Progress Report 2018*. Retrieved from www.sourcedwithcare.com/media/1502/sourced-with-care_progress-report_2018.pdf (accessed 29 May 2019).

Tyson, L. (2016). Buyer personas: Why and how we use them for focus. *Geckboard*, 14 July. Retrieved from www.geckoboard.com/blog/buyer-personas/#.WLIpLPnyuUl (accessed 27 May 2019).

Ulwick, T. (2016a). How to map a customer job. *The Marketing Journal*, 18 March. Retrieved from www.marketingjournal.org/how-to-map-a-customer-job-anthony-ulwick/ (accessed 27 May 2019).

Ulwick, T. (2016b). The jobs-to-be-done growth strategy matrix. *The Marketing Journal*. Retrieved from www.marketingjournal.org/the-jobs-to-be-done-growth-strategy-matrix-by-anthony-ulwick/ (accessed 27 May 2019).

Ulwick, T. (2017a). Customer needs through a jobs-to-be-done lens. *Medium*, 24 April. Retrieved from https://jobs-to-be-done.com/customer-needs-through-a-jobs-to-be-done-lens-23332c1fe64c (accessed 27 May 2019).

Ulwick, T. (2017b). Define markets around the customer's job-to-be-done. *The Marketing Journal*, 16 March. Retrieved from www.marketingjournal.org/define-markets-around-the-customers-job-to-be-done/ (accessed 27 May 2019).

Ulwick, T. (2017c). The history of jobs-to-be-done and outcome-driven innovation. *Medium*, 5 January. Retrieved from https://jobs-to-be-done.com/the-history-of-jobs-to-be-done-and-outcome-driven-innovation-a2fdfd0c7a9a (accessed 27 May 2019).

Ulwick, T. (2017d). Market segmentation through a jobs-to-be-done lens. *Medium*, 18 November. Retrieved from https://jobs-to-be-done.com/market-segmentation-through-a-jobs-to-be-done-lens-5ef9242de65 (accessed 27 May 2019).

UN Global Compact and KPMG (2016). *SDG Industry Matrix: Transportation*. Retrieved from https://home.kpmg.com/content/dam/kpmg/xx/pdf/2017/05/sdg-transportation.pdf (accessed 27 May 2019).

Unilever (n.d.). Sustainable living: About our strategy. Retrieved from www.unilever.com/sustainable-living/our-strategy/about-our-strategy/ (accessed 27 May 2019).

Unilever (2017). Report shows a third of consumers prefer sustainable brands. 1 May. Retrieved from www.unilever.com/news/Press-releases/2017/report-shows-a-third-of-consumers-prefer-sustainable-brands.html (accessed 27 May 2019).

Unique Digital (2015). Unique Digital completes worldwide delivery of UN's global goals. 25 September. Retrieved from www.uniquedigitalcinema.com/unique-digital-completes-worldwide-delivery-of-uns-global-goals/ (accessed 29 May 2019).

United Nations (n.d.). Big data for sustainable development. Retrieved from www.un.org/en/sections/issues-depth/big-data-sustainable-development/index.html (accessed 27 May 2019).

United Nations (2015). *SDG Compass Guide*. Retrieved from https://sdgcompass.org/wp-content/uploads/2015/12/019104_SDG_Compass_Guide_2015.pdf (accessed 3 June 2019).

United Nations (2018). *UN Global Compact Progress Report 2018*. Retrieved from www.unglobalcompact.org/docs/publications/UN-Global-Compact-Progress-Report-2018.pdf (accessed 3 June 2019).

United Nations Media Advisory (2015). Richard Curtis, Jimmy Wales, Tanya Burr, and Arjun Kapoor join launch event for the Global Goals campaign. 24 September. Retrieved from https://sustainabledevelopment.un.org/content/documents/8341Media_Advisory_Briefing_24%20September.pdf (accessed 29 May 2019).

UNRIC (2018). Ciné-ONU: The chocolate case. United Nations Regional Information Centre for Western Europe, 16 November. Retrieved from www.unric.org/en/latest-un-buzz/31180-cine-onu-the-chocolate-case- (accessed 29 May 2019).

Uttley, H. (2018). Tesco's big brand cull to fight Aldi and Lidl: Well-known names and Everyday Value range replaced by new lines of own products. *This Is Money*, 28 June. Retrieved from www.thisismoney.co.uk/money/markets/article-5897733/Tescos-big-brand-cull-fight-Aldi-Lidl-known-names-Everyday-Value-range-replaced.html (accessed 22 May 2019).

Vale, S. (2013). Classification of types of big data. *United Nations Economic Commission for Europe (UNECE) Statistical Division*. Retrieved from http://www1.unece.org/stat/platform/display/bigdata/Classification+of+Types+of+Big+Data (accessed 27 May 2017).

Van Wyk, J., Brooke, P. and Bornstein, J. (2018). Selling Industry 4.0. *Deloitte Insights*. Retrieved from https://www2.deloitte.com/insights/us/en/focus/industry-4-0/product-transformation-sales-mind-set.html (accessed 27 May 2019).

Varadarajan, R. (2012). Strategic marketing and marketing strategy. In V. Shankar and G. Carpenter (eds), *Handbook of Marketing Strategy*. Cheltenham: Edward Elgar Publishing, pp. 9–27.

Vaynerchuk, G. (2017). Sales vs. branding. *Gary Vaynerchuk*. Retrieved from www.garyvaynerchuk.com/sales-vs-branding/ (accessed 10 June 2019).

Vena, D. (2017). Netflix is a joke – and the joke is on you. *The Motley Fool*, 12 September. Retrieved from www.fool.com/investing/2017/09/12/netflix-is-a-joke-and-the-joke-is-on-you.aspx (accessed 27 May 2017).

Visa (2017a). *Cashless Cities: Realizing the Benefits of Digital Payments*. Retrieved from https://usa.visa.com/dam/VCOM/global/visa-everywhere/documents/visa-cashless-cities-report.pdf (accessed 29 May 2017).

Visa (2017b). *2017 Corporate Responsibility & Sustainability Report*. Retrieved from https://usa.visa.com/dam/VCOM/download/corporate-responsibility/visa-2017-corporate-responsibility-report.pdf (accessed 29 May 2017).

Visit California (2017). *Annual Marketing Work Plan FY17/18*. Retrieved from https://industry.visitcalifornia.com/-/media/PDFs/Publications/truncated-16-18-work-plan.pdf (accessed 29 May 2019).

Visser, N. (2018). *Yolt: Own back your financial data, Consumer Value Creation*, 17 February. Retrieved from https://consumervaluecreation.com/2018/02/17/yolt-own-back-your-financial-data/ (accessed 27 May 2017).

Volvo Group (2018). 3D printing the future for lighter engines. 5 March. Retrieved from www.volvogroup.com/en-en/news/2018/mar/3d-printing-the-future-for-lighter-engines.html (accessed 27 May 2017).

Voorberg, W., Bekkers, V. and Tummers, L. (2014). Co-creation in social innovation: Comparative case-study on the influential factors and outcomes of co-creation. *Lipse*, April. Retrieved from http://hdl.handle.net/1765/51069 (accessed 27 May 2019).

Vranica, S. (2016). Ad chiefs unite to support U.N. Sustainable Development Program. *The Wall Street Journal*, 23 June. Retrieved from www.wsj.com/articles/ad-chiefs-unite-to-support-u-n-sustainable-development-program-1466726404 (accessed 29 May 2019).

Waite, J. (2009). *Analytic Enterprise: Identifying Barriers and Overcoming Challenges*. SAS Institute. Retrieved from www.sas.com/content/dam/SAS/en_ca/User%20Group%20Presentations/Vancouver-User-Group/JamesWaite-AnalyticEnterprise-2011.pdf (accessed 3 June 2019).

Walker, B. (2015). Every day big data statistics – 2.5 quintillion bytes of data created daily. *VCloud News*, 5 April. Retrieved from www.vcloudnews.com/every-day-big-data-statistics-2-5-quintillion-bytes-of-data-created-daily/ (accessed 27 May 2019).

Walker Smith, J. (2018). *Follow the Money: Finding Growth in Uncomfortable Places*. Kantar Consulting. Retrieved from https://consulting.kantar.com/wp-content/uploads/2018/06/Kantar_Consulting_Follow_The_Money_Finding_Growth_in_Uncomfortable_Places.pdf (accessed 27 May 2019).

Walker Smith, J. and Curry, A. (2017). *The Third Age of Consumption*. Kantar Consulting. Retrieved from https://consulting.kantar.com/wp-content/uploads/2018/07/KantarConsulting-TheThirdAgeofConsumption.pdf (accessed 10 June 2019).

Wallace, T. (2019). The 17 ecommerce trends + 96 online shopping stats fueling sales growth in 2019. *Big Commerce*. Retrieved from www.bigcommerce.com/blog/ecommerce-trends/ (accessed 27 May 2019).

Walmart (2010). *Walmart Brand Guidelines*. Walmart Brand Center. Retrieved from www.walmartbrandcenter.com/WorkArea/DownloadAsset.aspx?id=6442451051 (accessed 10 June 2019).

Waste 360 (2017). Samsung sets principles to recycle Galaxy Note7's in an environmentally friendly manner. 28 March. Retrieved from www.waste360.com/e-waste/samsung-sets-principles-recycle-galaxy-note7-s-environmentally-friendly-manner (accessed 27 May 2019).

Watkins, M.D. (2007). Demystifying strategy: The what, who, how, and why. *Harvard Business Review*, 10 September. Retrieved from https://hbr.org/2007/09/demystifying-strategy-the-what (accessed 27 May 2019).

Weed, K. (2015). Unilever's Keith Weed: It is a brand's role to help consumers be responsible citizens. *Marketing Week*, 1 October. Retrieved from www.marketing-week.com/2015/10/01/it-is-a-brands-role-to-help-consumers-be-responsible-citizens/ (accessed 27 May 2019).

Weinstein, A. (2014). Target market selection in B2B technology markets. *Journal of Marketing Analytics*, 2(1), 59–69. Retrieved from https://link.springer.com/article/10.1057/jma. 2014.6 (accessed 27 May 2019).

Welfens, M.J., Nordmann, J. and Seibt, A. (2016). *Drivers and Barriers to Return and Recycling of Mobile Phones*. Wuppertal Institut. Retrieved from https://epub.wupperinst.org/frontdoor/deliver/index/docId/6158/file/6158_Welfens.pdf (accessed 27 May 2019).

West, G. (2016). Anatomy of an ad: Relaunching girl power for UN's Global Goals with #WhatIReallyReallyWant. *The Drum*, 29 July. Retrieved from www.thedrum.com/news/2016/07/29/anatomy-ad-relaunching-girl-power-uns-global-goals-whatireallyreallywant (accessed 29 May 2019).

Whaley, F. (2013). Is corporate social responsibility profitable for companies? *Devex*, 20 February. Retrieved from www.devex.com/news/is-corporate-social-responsibility-profitable-for-companies-80354 (accessed 23 May 2019).

Whitehouse, S., Goslinga, R., Michna, F., Gawinecki, M. and Menier, P. (2016). *Cashing In on Cashless Commerce*. A.T. Kearney. Retrieved from www.atkearney.com/financial-services/article?/a/cashing-in-on-cashless-commerce (accessed 27 May 2019).

Wind, Y. ([1978] 2018). Issues and advances in segmentation research. *Journal of Marketing Research*, 15(3), 317–337.

Wind, Y. and Bell, D.R. (2008). Market segmentation. In M. Baker and S. Hart (eds), *The Marketing Book*. Oxford: Butterworth Heinemann, pp. 222–244. Retrieved from https://

faculty.wharton.upenn.edu/wp-content/uploads/2012/04/0702_Market_Segmentation. pdf (accessed 27 May 2019).

Wood, Z. (2017). Havaianas flip-flop brand sold for £850m as scandal-hit owners sell stake. *The Guardian*, 13 July. Retrieved from www.theguardian.com/business/2017/jul/13/ havaianas-flip-flop-brand-sold-scandal-hit-owners-sell-stake (accessed 10 June 2019).

Wood, Z. (2018). Tesco trials "shop and go" app in till-free store, *The Guardian*, 28 June. Retrieved from www.theguardian.com/business/2018/jun/28/tesco-shop-and-go-app-till-free-store (accessed 23 May 2019).

World Bank (n.d.). Financial inclusion. Retrieved from www.worldbank.org/en/topic/finan cialinclusion (accessed 29 May 2019).

World Economic Forum (2018). *Advancing Financial Inclusion Metrics: Shifting from Access to Economic Empowerment*. White Paper, January. Retrieved from http://www3. weforum.org/docs/WEF_White_Paper_Advancing_Financial_Inclusion_Metrics.pdf (accessed 29 May 2019).

Worrell, C. (2017). Brand encounters of the frictionless kind: I believe brands need to generate positive friction. *WARC*. Retrieved from www.warc.com/content/article/atti cus/brand_encounters_of_the_frictionless_kind_i_believe_brands_need_to_generate_ positive_friction/116790 (accessed 3 June 2019).

Yang, C.F. and Sung, T.J. (2016). Service design for social innovation through participatory action research. *International Journal of Design*, 10(1), 21–36.

Zomerdijk, L.G. and Voss, C.A. (2010). Service design for experience-centric services. *Journal of Service Research*, 13(1), 67–82.

Index